Transformational Learning in Social Work and Human Services Education

Helen Katherine Mudd
Campbellsville University, USA

Kimberly Nicole Mudd-Fegett
Campbellsville University, USA

A volume in the Advances in Educational Marketing, Administration, and Leadership (AEMAL) Book Series

Published in the United States of America by
    IGI Global
    Information Science Reference (an imprint of IGI Global)
    701 E. Chocolate Avenue
    Hershey PA, USA 17033
    Tel: 717-533-8845
    Fax: 717-533-8661
    E-mail: cust@igi-global.com
    Web site: http://www.igi-global.com

Copyright © 2024 by IGI Global. All rights reserved. No part of this publication may be reproduced, stored or distributed in any form or by any means, electronic or mechanical, including photocopying, without written permission from the publisher.
Product or company names used in this set are for identification purposes only. Inclusion of the names of the products or companies does not indicate a claim of ownership by IGI Global of the trademark or registered trademark.

                Library of Congress Cataloging-in-Publication Data

CIP Pending

Transformational Learning in Social Work and Human Services Education
Helen Mudd, Kimberly Mudd-Fegett
2024 Information Science Reference

ISBN: 979-8-3693-2407-3
eISBN: 979-8-3693-2408-0

British Cataloguing in Publication Data
A Cataloguing in Publication record for this book is available from the British Library.

All work contributed to this book is new, previously-unpublished material.
The views expressed in this book are those of the authors, but not necessarily of the publisher.

For electronic access to this publication, please contact: eresources@igi-global.com.

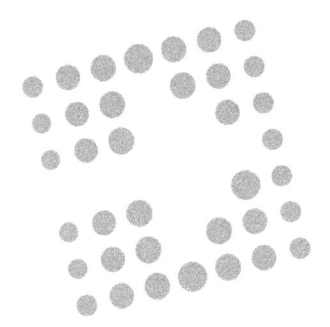

Advances in Educational Marketing, Administration, and Leadership (AEMAL) Book Series

Siran Mukerji
IGNOU, India
Purnendu Tripathi
IGNOU, India

ISSN:2326-9022
EISSN:2326-9030

MISSION

With more educational institutions entering into public, higher, and professional education, the educational environment has grown increasingly competitive. With this increase in competitiveness has come the need for a greater focus on leadership within the institutions, on administrative handling of educational matters, and on the marketing of the services offered.

The **Advances in Educational Marketing, Administration, & Leadership (AEMAL) Book Series** strives to provide publications that address all these areas and present trending, current research to assist professionals, administrators, and others involved in the education sector in making their decisions.

Coverage
- Academic Administration
- Educational Leadership
- Educational Marketing Campaigns
- Enrollment Management
- Faculty Administration and Management

IGI Global is currently accepting manuscripts for publication within this series. To submit a proposal for a volume in this series, please contact our Acquisition Editors at Acquisitions@igi-global.com or visit: http://www.igi-global.com/publish/.

The (ISSN) is published by IGI Global, 701 E. Chocolate Avenue, Hershey, PA 17033-1240, USA, www.igi-global.com. This series is composed of titles available for purchase individually; each title is edited to be contextually exclusive from any other title within the series. For pricing and ordering information please visit http://www.igi-global.com/book-series/advances-educational-marketing-administration-leadership/73677. Postmaster: Send all address changes to above address. Copyright © IGI Global. All rights, including translation in other languages reserved by the publisher. No part of this series may be reproduced or used in any form or by any means – graphics, electronic, or mechanical, including photocopying, recording, taping, or information and retrieval systems – without written permission from the publisher, except for non commercial, educational use, including classroom teaching purposes. The views expressed in this series are those of the authors, but not necessarily of IGI Global.

Titles in this Series

For a list of additional titles in this series, please visit: http://www.igi-global.com/book-series/advances-educational-marketing-administration-leadership/73677

Inclusive Educational Practices and Technologies for Promoting Sustainability
Santosh Kumar Behera (Kazi Nazrul University, India) Atyaf Hasan Ibrahim (University of Diyala, Iraq) and Faten Romdhani (Regional Board of Education, Bizerta, Tunisia)
Information Science Reference • copyright 2024 • 310pp • H/C (ISBN: 9798369369555)
• US $165.00 (our price)

Inclusivity and Indigeneity in Education for Sustainable Development
Santosh Kumar Behera (Kazi Nazrul University, India) Atyaf Hasan Ibrahim (University of Diyala, Iraq) and Faten Romdhani (Regional Board of Education, Bizerta, Tunisia)
Information Science Reference • copyright 2024 • 297pp • H/C (ISBN: 9798369328026)
• US $165.00 (our price)

Global Insights on Women Empowerment and Leadership
Malika Haoucha (University Hassan II of Casablanca, Morocco)
Information Science Reference • copyright 2024 • 315pp • H/C (ISBN: 9798369328064)
• US $245.00 (our price)

Exploring Educational Equity at the Intersection of Policy and Practice
José Sánchez-Santamaría (Universidad de Castilla-La Mancha, Spain) and Brenda Boroel Cervantes (Autonomous University of Baja California, Mexico)
Information Science Reference • copyright 2024 • 336pp • H/C (ISBN: 9798369316146)
• US $245.00 (our price)

Transformative Intercultural Global Education
Isabel María Gómez Barreto (Universidad de Castilla-La Mancha, Spain) and Gorka Roman Etxebarrieta (Universidad del Pais Vasco, Spain)
Information Science Reference • copyright 2024 • 457pp • H/C (ISBN: 9798369320570)
• US $245.00 (our price)

IGI Global
PUBLISHER of TIMELY KNOWLEDGE

701 East Chocolate Avenue, Hershey, PA 17033, USA
Tel: 717-533-8845 x100 • Fax: 717-533-8661
E-Mail: cust@igi-global.com • www.igi-global.com

Table of Contents

Preface xiii

Chapter 1
Transformative Social Work Education: The Hallmark of Empowerment 1
    Fred Moonga, University of Eswatini, Eswatini
    Sheila C. Kafula, Mulungushi University, Zambia

Chapter 2
A Conceptual Analysis on Transformational Learning Theory and Social Work Education 20
    Özge Kutlu, Burdur Mehmet Akif Ersoy University, Turkey

Chapter 3
Transformational Teaching: Learning That Extends Beyond the Walls of the Classroom 42
    Kimberly Mudd-Fegett, Campbellsville University, USA

Chapter 4
Transformational Leadership 63
    Kimberly Mudd-Fegett, Campbellsville University, USA
    Helen K. Mudd, Campbellsville University, USA

Chapter 5
International Field Education Through the Lens of Cultural Humility: Transformational Learning Abroad 84
    Lisa M. B. Tokpa, Uganda Christian University, Uganda

Chapter 6
Transformational Learning Abroad: Social Work Students and NGOs 116
    Jennifer Lanham, Campbellsville University, USA
    Elizabeth Ann Moore, Campbellsville University, USA

Chapter 7
Affectagogy: Learning With Heart - Nurturing Knowledge Through Emotional Bonds 141
    Ken Nee Chee, Faculty of Computing and Meta-Technology, Sultan Idris Education University, Malaysia

Chapter 8
Experiential Learning in the Digital Classroom to Improve Outcomes Related
to Diversity, Equity, and Inclusion 158
    Lauren Lunsford, Belmont University, USA
    Amanda Nelms, Belmont University, USA
    Sally Barton-Arwood, Belmont University, USA

Chapter 9
An Educationally-Beneficial Experience for Undergraduate Students: A
Service-Learning Mentoring Project With Native American Youth 169
    Crystal S. Aschenbrener, Campbellsville University, USA

Chapter 10
Nurse Educators Answering the Call to Missions 180
    Angie G. Atwood, Campbellsville University, USA

Chapter 11
Toward a Transformational Learning: Integrating Spiritual Diversity
Practices in Social Work Classrooms.. 193
    Pious Malliar Bellian, School of Social Work, Indiana University,
        Indianapolis, USA

Compilation of References 266

About the Contributors 319

Index 322

Detailed Table of Contents

Preface xiii

Chapter 1
Transformative Social Work Education: The Hallmark of Empowerment 1
    Fred Moonga, University of Eswatini, Eswatini
    Sheila C. Kafula, Mulungushi University, Zambia

Although the social work profession is inherently transformative, it is also going through transformation to meet local and global changes and challenges brought about by climate change and environmental degradation, social and health inequalities, poverty and sustainable development, among others. Experiential learning, social justice, inequalities, and empowerment are central to the transformation process. In this chapter, the authors discuss transformative social work education and how it fosters empowerment through experience. Transformative and experiential learning theories are examined, and it is shown how they contribute to transformation and empowerment. The authors argue that transformative social work education is the hallmark of empowerment because the profession (itself transformative), centralizes empowerment by enhancing capabilities of the people it serves. Field work education is perhaps the main transformation mechanism that social work uses. As such, social work education should nourish environments in which transformation would easily be fostered.

Chapter 2
A Conceptual Analysis on Transformational Learning Theory and Social Work Education 20
    Özge Kutlu, Burdur Mehmet Akif Ersoy University, Turkey

Transformational learning theory is a perspective that focuses on understanding the learning process from individuals' experiences. According to this theory, learning interacts not only with external influences, but also with the individual's inner thoughts, feelings, and experiences. In social work education, transformational learning theory is used as an important tool to support individuals' personal and professional development. Using this theory, social workers can help their clients discover their strengths and realize their potential. At the same time, this theory encourages social work students to recognize their own biases and approach social problems from a critical perspective. In this way, social work professionals can develop more effective strategies to ensure social justice and equality.

Chapter 3
Transformational Teaching: Learning That Extends Beyond the Walls of the
Classroom 42
Kimberly Mudd-Fegett, Campbellsville University, USA

Transformational teachers join students in a life-long learning process that involves commitment, passion, transparency, and a shared belief that students desire to learn to improve themselves. Transformational leaders motivate their followers by inspiring them to perform at their highest level. Likewise, transformational educators motivate their students to excel academically and always to be attuned to opportunities for personal growth. When educators take students outside the classroom walls, they present students with learning opportunities that far exceed what the words on the pages of a book can teach. One can lecture on the Coliseum's cobblestone streets or Dachau's gas chambers. However, it is vastly different to travel to Munich and stand before the furnaces of Dachau or to walk on the streets of Rome where Caesar once walked. When unique learning opportunities transform students, they become excited about learning. They develop newfound motivation, self-efficacy, and a larger vision of their education and goals.

Chapter 4
Transformational Leadership 63
Kimberly Mudd-Fegett, Campbellsville University, USA
Helen K. Mudd, Campbellsville University, USA

Transformational leadership is the process in which leaders play an idealized role model, stimulate and encourage innovative work behavior, provide inspirational motivation, engage in supporting and mentoring followers to achieve the organization's shared vision and goals, and create a connection that raises the level of motivation and morality in both the leader and the follower. This type of leader is attentive to the needs and motives of followers and supports each follower in reaching their fullest potential. The authors' experiences and success as transformational leaders and educators provide evidence of the truth of these findings. The authors will highlight personality characteristics, behaviors, and effects on practitioners, professors, and students of transformational leadership. The authors will show how transformational leaders and educators move followers from unquestioningly accepting provided information and directives to reflective, goal-oriented, critical thinkers.

Chapter 5
International Field Education Through the Lens of Cultural Humility:
Transformational Learning Abroad 84
    Lisa M. B. Tokpa, Uganda Christian University, Uganda

With the challenges facing our society today, it is critical that opportunities be provided for social work students to learn about difference, and how to work effectively with diverse populations. International field education is one important way to provide these opportunities to students in an immersive setting. The Uganda Studies Program provides experiential knowledge in this through a framework of cultural humility. Grounded in educational standards, the author presents considerations, challenges, and learning opportunities within cross-cultural exchanges. Power dynamics embedded in such exchanges are explored, and a challenge is presented to move towards active participation in redressing inequalities through mutually beneficial partnerships. A case is made, and a guide provided for American social work programs to adhere to its ethical mandate and responsibility to decolonize international field education in ways that support indigenous social work, local supervisors, and academicians, while simultaneously providing quality, competency-based student learning outcomes.

Chapter 6
Transformational Learning Abroad: Social Work Students and NGOs 116
    Jennifer Lanham, Campbellsville University, USA
    Elizabeth Ann Moore, Campbellsville University, USA

Partnering non-governmental organizations (NGOs) and social work students is effective in helping conflict-affected communities. It offers valuable knowledge, hands-on practice, and a fresh NGO perspective. However, it presents obstacles, such as personal biases and cultural barriers. To overcome these, social work students must prioritize mental wellness, keep unbiased views, and learn about local cultures. Transformative learning is an essential aspect of this partnership. NGOs assist folks facing significant life challenges, enabling students to understand difficulties beyond textbooks. Together, they positively impact communities by tackling complex issues, spreading awareness, and fostering inclusivity.

Chapter 7
Affectagogy: Learning With Heart - Nurturing Knowledge Through
Emotional Bonds... 141
*Ken Nee Chee, Faculty of Computing and Meta-Technology, Sultan Idris
Education University, Malaysia*

This chapter unveils Affectagogy, a transformative pedagogical approach that bridges the emotional and cognitive realms of learning. Recognizing the undeniable influence of emotions on knowledge acquisition, Affectagogy emphasizes the concept of learning with the heart to nurture knowledge through emotional bonds. It explores the synergistic relationship between affect (emotions and feelings) and pedagogy (teaching methods). The chapter introduces "human-touch learning," highlighting the significance of empathy, social interaction, and resilience-building in fostering deeper student engagement, motivation, and well-being. Practical guidelines are provided for implementing Affectagogy across educational levels, encompassing the thoughtful integration of educational technology. Ultimately, this chapter advocates for a holistic approach to education, emphasizing the cultivation of both emotional and intellectual intelligence. This balanced approach aims to prepare learners for success in an emotionally intelligent world, fostering resilience, empathy, and a lifelong love of learning.

Chapter 8
Experiential Learning in the Digital Classroom to Improve Outcomes Related
to Diversity, Equity, and Inclusion 158
*Lauren Lunsford, Belmont University, USA
Amanda Nelms, Belmont University, USA
Sally Barton-Arwood, Belmont University, USA*

The purpose of this chapter is to explore the utility and process for integrating an experiential service-learning experience that promotes diversity and inclusion into an online learning environment. Experiential education and service-learning opportunities have been found to be a successful means for students to interact with individuals from different backgrounds and improve their cultural awareness. Given the promise for experiential education to address and improve outcomes related to DEI, it is worthwhile to investigate ways to integrate these activities into online courses. This chapter aims to: (1) introduce the benefits of experiential education and rationale for its inclusion as a practice to improve outcomes related to diversity and inclusion, (2) provide an overview of the potential of e-service learning as a means to do this, (3) share an example e-service-learning project

Chapter 9
An Educationally-Beneficial Experience for Undergraduate Students: A
Service-Learning Mentoring Project With Native American Youth 169
 Crystal S. Aschenbrener, Campbellsville University, USA

Service-learning has been an increasingly used high impact approach to facilitate applied learning. Mentorship between undergraduate students and youth is commonly utilized as a tactic to support one of the goals of service-learning: addressing and fulfilling community needs. A consistently underserved and underrepresented population of youth are Native Americans who reside on rural reservations who often experience community-wide social problems. While often the impacts of mentorship on youth are researched, this study examines the impact on undergraduate students' perceptions after completing a mentoring intervention with Native American youth. A mixed method approach was designed, using pre- and post-surveys as well as a final reflective comprehensive paper to collect data. The results concluded that by completing the service-learning project in partnership with the Native American youth, it created positive impacts on the undergraduate students' educational perceptions, such as with an underrepresented culture, mentoring intervention, and applied research.

Chapter 10
Nurse Educators Answering the Call to Missions 180
 Angie G. Atwood, Campbellsville University, USA

Educators can personally impact college students' lives by leading medical mission trips. The purpose of this chapter is to discuss accepting the call to missions, the role of the nurse educator in mission work, challenges and opportunities, and cultural preparedness. Beyond didactic instruction and clinical training, engaging in mission work provides a transformative experiential way for instructors to develop holistic learning experiences. The word 'transformative' is an adjective that means causing or able to cause an important and lasting change in someone or something. A transformative experience like this helps students learn in a manner that will foster life-long learning. Assuming the role of a mission team leader involves guiding college students through experiences that extend beyond the traditional classrooms.

Chapter 11
Toward a Transformational Learning: Integrating Spiritual Diversity
Practices in Social Work Classrooms... 193
Pious Malliar Bellian, School of Social Work, Indiana University, Indianapolis, USA

There are inadequacies in the existing mode of instruction/pedagogical approaches in capturing sacred moments, diverse practices, and spiritual perspectives of multiple learners in social work classrooms. Diversification of social work discourse incorporating both secular and non-secular perspectives is a vital challenge that needs to be addressed. Recognizing this challenge, social work students and instructors needed a space to reach those 'sacred but transformative learning experiences,' producing new avenues and streams beyond acquiring new skills in the traditional sense of pedagogy. Therefore, this chapter proposes spiritual diversity practices and new strategies that can be applied in social work classroom settings for optimizing the transformational learning environment through non-traditional teaching methods. The chapter also proposes cultural humility as a spiritually-informed practice. Finally, potential recommendations are suggested.

Compilation of References 266

About the Contributors 319

Index 322

Preface

Transformational learning is a theory that delves into how individuals make sense of their life experiences, fostering profound changes in perspectives and understanding. Experiential learning, a proven and impactful approach to education, is grounded in one undeniable reality: people learn best through hands-on, immersive experiences. This approach is particularly vital in the fields of social work and human services, where practical engagement enhances educational value by promoting student reflection, critical thinking, service, engagement, and problem-solving.

A high-quality experiential or service-learning experience is not serendipitous; it requires meticulous planning and intention. This book aims to provide both the logistical and theoretical frameworks necessary for successful experiential learning. Included within these pages is an Experiential-Learning Guide complete with pre-planning logistics, resources, and evaluation tools essential for designing effective experiential-learning events.

This book is crafted for educators striving to deepen their understanding of transformational learning. We provide relevant theoretical frameworks for experiential learning, guiding professors and educational leaders in anchoring their projects on solid theoretical foundations. Practical ideas for applying transformational learning models are also offered, including tools, activities with templates, and resources ready to be integrated into the classroom.

For educational leaders, this book serves as a guide in developing and utilizing transformational leadership to boost the effectiveness and productivity of social work or human service programs. Transformational leadership principles can be harnessed to engage and train the next generation of non-profit leaders. Seasoned social work educators and administrators share their proven models of incorporating experiential and transformational leadership approaches.

This book is designed for educators and administrators with a keen interest in transformational, experiential, and service learning. Experiential learning can be seamlessly integrated into any discipline, creating a powerful educational experience. For those in social work, human services, and non-profit administration, the book offers comprehensive guidance on developing and utilizing transformational leadership to enhance program effectiveness and productivity.

We hope this book serves as a valuable resource for educators and administrators dedicated to enriching the educational landscape through transformational and experiential learning.

ORGANIZATION OF THE BOOK

Chapter 1: Transformative Social Work Education: The Hallmark of Empowerment

Fred Moonga, University of Eswatini, Swaziland
Sheila Kafula, Mulungushi University, Zambia

In this chapter, Fred Moonga and Sheila Kafula discuss how transformative social work education serves as a cornerstone for empowerment. They explore the profession's inherent transformative nature and its ongoing evolution in response to global challenges like climate change, social inequalities, and sustainable development. Central to this transformation is experiential learning, which fosters empowerment by enhancing individuals' capabilities. The chapter delves into transformative and experiential learning theories, illustrating how they contribute to empowerment. The authors highlight the pivotal role of fieldwork education in facilitating transformation and argue that social work education must cultivate environments conducive to such transformative experiences.

Chapter 2: A Conceptual Analysis on Transformational Learning Theory and Social Work Education: Transformational Learning & Social Work Education

Özge Kutlu, Burdur Mehmet Akif Ersoy University, Turkey

Özge Kutlu provides a conceptual analysis of transformational learning theory within social work education. This theory emphasizes the significance of personal experiences in the learning process, integrating external influences with internal thoughts and feelings. Kutlu discusses how transformational learning aids in personal and professional development, helping social workers and their clients discover strengths and potential. The chapter encourages social work students to recognize their biases and approach social problems critically, ultimately enabling them to devise effective strategies for promoting social justice and equality.

Preface

Chapter 3: Transformational Teaching - Learning that Extends Beyond the Walls of the Classroom

Kimberly Mudd-Fegett, Campbellsville University, United States

Kimberly Mudd-Fegett explores the dynamic nature of transformational teaching, where educators join students in a lifelong learning journey. This chapter emphasizes the role of transformational educators in inspiring students to excel academically and embrace personal growth opportunities. Mudd-Fegett underscores the importance of taking students outside the classroom for experiential learning, where firsthand experiences, such as visiting historical sites, significantly enhance learning. The chapter highlights how such unique opportunities foster student excitement, self-efficacy, and a broader vision for their education and goals.

Chapter 4: Transformational Leadership

Kimberly Mudd-Fegett, Campbellsville University, United States
Helen Mudd, Campbellsville University, United States

Kimberly Mudd-Fegett and Helen Mudd examine the concept of transformational leadership, where leaders serve as role models, inspire innovation, and mentor followers to achieve shared organizational goals. The chapter discusses the characteristics, behaviors, and impacts of transformational leaders, drawing from the authors' experiences. They illustrate how transformational leadership moves followers from passive acceptance to active, reflective, and goal-oriented critical thinking. This approach elevates both leaders and followers, fostering a deeper connection and heightened motivation and morality.

Chapter 5: International Field Education Through the Lens of Cultural Humility: Transformational Learning Abroad

Lisa Tokpa, Uganda Studies Program at Uganda Christian University, United States

Lisa Tokpa discusses the importance of international field education in social work, emphasizing cultural humility. The chapter presents the Uganda Studies Program as a model for providing experiential knowledge through cross-cultural exchanges. Tokpa addresses the power dynamics in such exchanges and advocates for mutually beneficial partnerships that support indigenous social work. The chapter challenges American social work programs to decolonize international field education, ensuring ethical responsibility and quality student learning outcomes.

Preface

Chapter 6: Transformational Learning Abroad
Social Work Students and NGOs

Jennifer Lanham, Campbellsville University/Carver School of Social Work- Full Professor, United States
Elizabeth Ann Moore, Campbellsville University, United States

Jennifer Lanham and Elizabeth Ann Moore explore the partnership between social work students and NGOs in addressing community conflicts. This chapter discusses the benefits of such partnerships, including hands-on practice and valuable insights into NGO operations. The authors emphasize the importance of mental wellness and cultural sensitivity for students in these settings. The chapter demonstrates how transformational learning through NGO partnerships helps students understand complex social issues and fosters community inclusivity.

Chapter 7: Affectalogy: Learning with Heart -
Nurturing Knowledge Through Emotional Bonds

Ken Nee Chee, Faculty of Computing and Meta-Technology, Sultan Idris Education University, Malaysia

Ken Nee Chee introduces Affectalogy, an innovative approach that integrates emotions into the learning process. This chapter explores how emotional connections enhance knowledge acquisition and retention, emphasizing the importance of "learning with heart." Chee examines the synergy between affect and pedagogy, illustrating how emotional bonds can profoundly impact the educational journey. The chapter provides insights into nurturing emotional connections to foster transformative learning experiences.

Chapter 8: Experiential Learning in the Digital Classroom to Improve Outcomes Related to Diversity, Equity, and Inclusion

Lauren Lunsford, Belmont University, USA, United States
Amanda Nelms, Belmont University, United States
Sally Barton-Arwood, Belmont University, United States

Lauren Lunsford, Amanda Nelms, and Sally Barton-Arwood explore the integration of experiential service-learning in online education to promote diversity, equity, and inclusion (DEI). This chapter outlines the benefits of experiential education in enhancing cultural awareness and interactions among students from diverse backgrounds. The authors provide a rationale for incorporating such practices in online courses and share an example of an e-service-learning project. The chapter aims to guide educators in creating inclusive and impactful online learning experiences.

Preface

Chapter 9: An Educationally-Beneficial Experience for Undergraduate Students: A Service-Learning Mentoring Project with Native American Youth

Crystal Aschenbrener, Campbellsville University, United States

Crystal Aschenbrener discusses a service-learning project where undergraduate students mentor Native American youth. This chapter examines the impact of the project on students' perceptions and educational experiences. Aschenbrener uses a mixed-method approach to analyze data from pre- and post-surveys and reflective papers. The results highlight positive changes in students' understanding of underrepresented cultures and the value of mentorship. The chapter underscores the educational benefits of service-learning in addressing community needs and fostering applied research.

Chapter 10: Nurse Educators Answering the Call to Missions

Angie Atwood, Campbellsville University, United States

Angie Atwood explores the role of nurse educators in leading medical mission trips, emphasizing the transformative impact of such experiences. This chapter discusses the challenges and opportunities of mission work, focusing on cultural preparedness and holistic learning. Atwood argues that mission trips provide a unique and transformative educational experience, fostering lifelong learning and personal growth. The chapter highlights the importance of nurse educators in guiding students through these impactful journeys.

Chapter 11: Toward a Transformational Learning: Integrating Spiritual Diversity Practices in Social Work Classrooms

Pious Malliar Bellian, Indiana University School of Social Work, United States

Pious Malliar Bellian addresses the need for integrating spiritual diversity practices in social work education. This chapter critiques traditional pedagogical approaches and proposes new strategies to capture diverse spiritual perspectives in the classroom. Bellian advocates for incorporating both secular and non-secular views to create transformative learning experiences. The chapter emphasizes cultural humility as a spiritually-informed practice and offers recommendations for optimizing the learning environment through non-traditional methods.

IN CONCLUSION

As we conclude this exploration of transformational learning in social work and human services education, we reflect on the collective insights presented by our esteemed contributors. This volume underscores the pivotal role of experiential learning in fostering personal and professional growth, enhancing capabilities, and promoting social justice and equity.

Each chapter has illuminated various facets of transformational learning, from its theoretical underpinnings to practical applications in diverse educational settings. We have seen how transformative social work education empowers individuals by deepening their understanding of life experiences and fostering critical reflection. We have delved into the significance of transformational leadership in motivating and mentoring future leaders, emphasizing the importance of emotional bonds and cultural humility in creating inclusive and impactful learning environments.

The contributions in this book highlight the necessity of integrating experiential learning beyond traditional classroom walls. Whether through international field education, service-learning projects, or study abroad programs, the chapters demonstrate the profound impact of hands-on, immersive experiences on students' personal and professional development.

As editors, we hope this book serves as a valuable resource for educators and administrators dedicated to enhancing the educational experiences of students in social work and human services. We believe that the practical tools, theoretical frameworks, and inspirational examples provided herein will guide and inspire educators to create transformative learning environments that not only educate but also empower.

In the face of global challenges and evolving societal needs, transformational learning stands as a beacon of hope and progress. By embracing these principles, we can cultivate a new generation of social workers and human service professionals equipped with the knowledge, empathy, and critical thinking skills necessary to effect meaningful change in the world.

We extend our deepest gratitude to all the contributors for their insightful chapters and to the readers for engaging with this work. Together, let us continue to strive for excellence in education, fostering environments where transformational learning can thrive and empower the next generation of changemakers.

Introduction

Welcome to *Transformational Learning in Social Work and Human Services Education*. This book comprehensively explores transformational learning theories and their application in social work and human services education. As editors, we have compiled a series of chapters from experienced educators and practitioners that collectively create a robust guide for those seeking to enhance their educational practices through experiential and transformational learning methodologies.

TRANSFORMATIONAL LEARNING: A FRAMEWORK FOR GROWTH

Transformational learning is a theory that emphasizes the profound ways in which individuals make sense of their life experiences. It is a holistic approach that involves the cognitive aspect of learning and encompasses the emotional and social dimensions. Experiential learning, which forms the book's bedrock, is a method that has proven its efficacy repeatedly by prioritizing hands-on experiences. This approach ensures that students are not merely passive recipients of information but active participants in their learning journey.

EXPERIENTIAL LEARNING: A CRITICAL COMPONENT

In the fields of social work and human services, experiential learning is indispensable. It facilitates reflection, critical thinking, service engagement, and problem-solving skills—essential components for any aspiring professional in these domains. High-quality experiential learning experiences are not coincidental; they require meticulous planning and intentional design. This book offers a logistical and theoretical framework to help educators craft meaningful experiential learning opportunities. An Experiential-Learning Guide includes pre-planning logistics, resources, and evaluation tools essential for designing successful experiential-learning events.

THEORETICAL FOUNDATIONS AND PRACTICAL APPLICATIONS

Understanding the theoretical underpinnings of experiential learning is crucial for educators. This book extensively overviews relevant theories to ground your experiential learning projects in solid academic concepts. Moreover, it presents practical tools, activities, and templates that can be seamlessly integrated into classroom settings. These resources are aimed at enhancing the educational experience by applying transformational learning models in practical, impactful ways.

TRANSFORMATIONAL LEADERSHIP IN EDUCATION

A significant portion of this book is dedicated to transformational leadership, a style of leadership that goes beyond traditional approaches. Transformational leaders inspire and motivate their followers to exceed their expectations and embrace continuous improvement. This type of leadership is crucial for educators and administrators in social work and human services. It helps cultivate an environment where students and staff are encouraged to grow, innovate, and achieve their fullest potential. This book delves into transformational leadership's characteristics, behaviors, and effects, providing a roadmap for leaders in these fields.

REAL-WORLD APPLICATIONS AND CASE STUDIES

The chapters in this book are rich with case studies and real-world applications. From international field education to integrating service learning in digital classrooms, the contributors share their insights and proven models for incorporating experiential and transformational learning in various contexts. Each chapter provides unique perspectives and practical advice on navigating the challenges and maximizing the benefits of these learning approaches.

FOR WHOM IS THIS BOOK?

This book is intended for educators and administrators committed to improving their understanding and application of transformational and experiential learning. Whether you are a professor, educational leader, or non-profit administrator, you will find valuable insights and actionable strategies to enhance your programs. The guidance provided here is applicable across disciplines, making it a versatile resource for creating powerful learning opportunities that transcend traditional classroom boundaries.

IN CONCLUSION

Transformational Learning in Social Work and Human Services Education is more than a reference book; it is a call to action for educators to embrace and implement transformational learning principles. Through thoughtful planning, intentional design, and a commitment to experiential learning, we can empower the next generation of social workers and human service professionals to impact the communities they serve profoundly. We invite you to delve into the following chapters, each a testament to the transformative power of education.

Chapter 1
Transformative Social Work Education:
The Hallmark of Empowerment

Fred Moonga
https://orcid.org/0000-0001-6401-7643
University of Eswatini, Eswatini

Sheila C. Kafula
Mulungushi University, Zambia

ABSTRACT

Although the social work profession is inherently transformative, it is also going through transformation to meet local and global changes and challenges brought about by climate change and environmental degradation, social and health inequalities, poverty and sustainable development, among others. Experiential learning, social justice, inequalities, and empowerment are central to the transformation process. In this chapter, the authors discuss transformative social work education and how it fosters empowerment through experience. Transformative and experiential learning theories are examined, and it is shown how they contribute to transformation and empowerment. The authors argue that transformative social work education is the hallmark of empowerment because the profession (itself transformative), centralizes empowerment by enhancing capabilities of the people it serves. Field work education is perhaps the main transformation mechanism that social work uses. As such, social work education should nourish environments in which transformation would easily be fostered.

DOI: 10.4018/979-8-3693-2407-3.ch001

INTRODUCTION

The social work profession has an enduring and endearing commitment to transform the lives of the vulnerable and oppressed groups (Moonga, 2018) regardless of the context. As rightly put by the International Federation of Social Workers (IFSW, 2012), social work is a transformative profession that centralises human rights and social justice. However, the promotion of human rights and social justice and the commitment to transformation are also enduring challenges. This is partly because the profession itself is in the process of transformation, and seeking an appropriate identity especially in Africa (Gray and Lombard, 2008; Twikirize and Spitzer, 2019). Thus, it cannot adequately achieve its transformative goal for the learners and service users. Nonetheless, the same challenges are creating impetus for transforming lives, communities and societies.

Over the past decades, globalisation, changes in economic systems, climate change-induced disasters, pandemics, and indigenisation efforts among other factors have combined to cause risk and vulnerability among many social work service users. They have also in the process influenced the transformation of social work education and practice globally. For instance, many schools of social work are streamlining disaster preparedness and management, environmental social work as well as issues of mental health in their curricula. The combined effects of these factors entail even more transformation. For example, because of climate induced disasters such as droughts and floods, people are adopting some climate change related adaptation mechanisms such as cultivating drought resistant crops and climate adaptive and resilient homesteads. Thus, despite changes, the purpose of social work remains steadfast, to transform lives, enhance problem-solving and empower people to take charge of their lives. We argue in this chapter that social work is inherently transformational and that the ultimate goal is empowerment.

According to Adams (2003), empowerment is a critical and reflexive activity in which experience of a situation is used to understand oneself and inform behaviour. This concept is discussed in detail later in this chapter and an attempt is also made to show how it relates to transformation. Transformative education can foster critical thinking and reflexivity and enhance empowerment. Lorenzetti et al (2017) note that social work learners require transformative learning to engage in critical thinking. According to Ellias, (1997), this would 'expand their consciousness through transformation of basic world view and specific capacities of the self' (Lorenzetti et al. 2017, p.). Criticality is important to social workers because sometimes they have to deal with oppressive systems to emancipate their service users. It also helps learners to question the status quo and take action to change the situation. From the structuralists point of view, what may be causing sufferings among social work service users could be structural systems that need to be confronted or lobbied as the case may be.

Cutting across three themes: transformational theory, transformational leadership and transformational learning, this chapter analyses transformational theory and how it can foster empowerment with the right leadership. Within this context, we attempt to advocate for and strengthen the empowering of social work learners and service users. This, we believe can change, develop, and sustain the welfare of vulnerable people served by the profession. The chapter argues that social work is fundamentally transformational and empowering to both professional social workers during training and the people they serve. The chapter is organised as follows: The next section is a discussion of global changes and how these are influencing the training and practice of social work. What follows is the discussion of the nature of learning followed by discussions of transformative learning theory (TLT) and experiential learning theory (ELT). Next is the discussion of empowerment and its importance in social work. Finally, an analysis of the transformative and empowering nature of Social work and then conclusion.

Social Work as a Response to Changing Needs

Social work was first introduced in colonial territories as remedial measures (Noyoo, 2021). However, in the last few decades, there has been a shift towards developmental social welfare which is considered more relevant to the needs and challenges of vulnerable people in these territories. For instance poverty and diseases which are the most critical challenges need to be tackled alongside development by having modern education systems and modern health care facilities, and improved water and sanitation measures among other developmental imperatives. Moreover, as Midgley (1995) argues, the social developmental approach includes the whole population while linking social and economic development aspects. But it is also transformative. As Dirkx (1998) notes, the developmental perspective is implicit in Mezirow's view of transformative learning as it makes learners construct new meanings of their situations as the world around them changes. Although Robert Boyd's transformative perspective (individuation) also has a developmental element. However, it has more focus on an individual.

Transformative learning as discussed in details later, helps to change the perspectives of the learners and/or service users. It requires transformative teachers and transformative leadership. To enhance food security for example, modern farming methods are required to increase food production while tackling issues of family planning to keep the population in check. These are examples of transformative approaches. Similarly, to increase access to social services, social workers need transformative approaches to influence government policy. Thus, although traditional methods of helping the needy exist to date, they fall short on transformation which is the essence of professional social work. Social workers are transformers, and they are change agents. But as discussed later in the chapter, for them to foster that change, they must be changed first through transformative learning which instils critical thinking and a broad knowledge base. Contemporary social work promotes social change for improved human rights and social justice outcomes and a broad knowledge base is required to do so (Bell, 2012). Before discussing transformative learning theory, we first discuss the nature of learning in general in the next section.

The Nature of Learning

All animals, humans included, learn on a daily basis in different ways. Three theories stand out in explaining the learning process and all are useful and are used in social work education and practice. These are cognitive, behaviourism, and social constructionism. There could be more. Space is limited to discuss these theories in detail. Therefore in brief, while cognitive theory focuses on the thought processes that define human behaviour, behaviourism focuses on observable actions from which behaviour and learning can be inferred. Social constructionism on the other hand relates to meaning-making derived from one's experience. It suggests that individuals mentally construct what they experience through cognitive processes.

Mezirow views knowledge as something an individual constructs (Dirkx, 1998). In emphasising the importance of constructionism in learning, and drawing from experiential learning theory, Kolb and Kolb (2011) propose a constructivist theory in which social knowledge is created and recreated in the perspective of the learner. All the three theories have important implications for, and application to learning in general and transformative learning in social work in particular and will be used in this chapter.

Kolb and Kolb, (2011) note that learning is an everyday process of human adaptation. Drawing from experiential learning theory, they assert that learning involves the creation of knowledge through grasping and transforming experience. Experience is at the centre of the learning process. It is experience that is transformed into knowledge. According to Lee and Greene (2004), human experience falls in three main domains, that is, cognitive, affective and behavioural. These domains determine the grasping of experience and ultimately knowledge. Kolb and Kolb (2011) assert that experience is grasped either as concrete experience or abstract conceptualisation. They argue that transformation of experience can be either through reflective observation or active experimentation. Generally, people learn in four main different styles, which are, *diverging, assimilating, converging and accommodating* (Kolb et al. 2014). They assert that someone endowed with a diverging style of learning has concrete experience and reflexive observation.

Kolb et al. (2014) characterised the diverging learning style as involving working in groups, active listening, preference for concrete experience and reflective observations. The last two are important in both grasping and transforming experience into action which is important to social workers as change agents. Learning also requires motivation. The learner should feel the need to acquire the presented knowledge. Else, they will feel like wasting time and energy. Thus, social work educators should motivate learners, they should make the learners appreciate the relevance of what is taught (Lee and Greene, 2008) in addition to exposing them to experience. For instance if someone feels that they are affected by the environment, they are likely to feel the need to learn about conservation because environmental degradation affects their wellbeing. That would make it easier to foster transformative learning because concrete experience of the consequences of environmental degradation would lead them to reflect on what course of action to take.

According to Mezirow (1991), transformative learners have a more inclusive world view, discerning its various aspects, are open to different points of view and can integrate their experiences into meaningful and holistic relationships (Dirkx, 1998). This perhaps explains why social work learners are exposed to a wide range of theories in various disciplines to widen their knowledge base, their self-awareness and broaden their world views. Dirkx (1998) argues that to Mezirow, transformative learning is the essence of adult development.

Learning involves experiencing or interacting with, and sometimes manipulating phenomenon and problem-solving. According to Kolb (1984), learning is the process whereby knowledge is created through the *transformation of experience* (cited in Kolb et al. 2014). Transformation is moderated by environment factors which influence what we learn and how we choose what to learn and sometimes how to learn it. As discussed later in the chapter, social workers learn both in the classroom and outside of it. Experience from either environment has a bearing on the learner's epistemologies.

Learning also occurs both in the formal and informal settings of human endeavours. It is holistic, and occurs at every level of humanity from an individual to society as a whole (Kolb and Kolb, 2011). That is, just as individuals learn, societies also learn. For instance, from time immemorial, humans and societies have learned to care for and preserve nature for their common good. The learning came from their experiencing their environment over the years. They therefore learn how destroying nature such as cutting-down trees can lead to climate change with adverse effects on their livelihoods through droughts, cyclones and floods for instance. As such overcoming such threats to human existence requires transformative change (Gray and Coates, 2015). It requires learning how not to live the way humans currently live (characterised with deforestation), having experienced some of the consequences of human activities on nature.

Learning also brings about self-awareness and awareness of experience. However, Mezirow (1991) notes that 'transformative education helps learners to move from a simple awareness of their experiencing to an awareness of the conditions of their experiencing and beyond this, to an awareness of the reasons why they experience as they do and to action based on these insights' (Lee and Greene, 2008:22). Thus, being aware of one's experience is not enough. It requires that a learner uses that awareness and the reasons thereof to change their situation, their environment and that of the people they serve in the case of social workers. That is empowerment and social work has been involved in this transformation but maybe more needs to be done. Although a lot has been done for many years especially in our relation to and advocacy for eco-social action, more still needs to be done. Obviously, this is different in other parts of the world.

Learning can also occur in groups or teams (Lewin, 1940 cited in Kolb and Kolb, 2011). In this context, group or team members interact and influence one another to achieve group goals. According to Argote et al. (2001), group learning is 'the activities through which individuals acquire, share and combine knowledge through experience with one another' (cited in Wilson, et al. 2007, p.1042). This is the essence of group work in social work in which group members perform learning tasks individually while striving at achieving the overall group goal as a team.

Group experience is not always cooperative and serene. There can be conflicts, differences, indifference and limited motivation among group members due to dynamics relating to divergent backgrounds. However, such conflicts and indifferences almost always wane with the passage of time either because group members come to understand one another, and therefore become tolerant, compromise or their values slowly converge because of the common group activities that bring them together in the first place as group norms reign. They will have learned from the conflicts and other aspects of group dynamics. As Kolb and Kolb (2011) note, it is the conflicts, differences and disagreements that drive the learning process in a group.

Although conflicts may be necessary for group development and understanding among group members, they not always drive the group learning process. The opposite can also happen. Conflicts can affect group cohesion and ultimately group learning experience and functioning. Some people may not reveal their true selves in the formative stage of the group or team. But since true personalities cannot be hidden forever, with time, they will manifest as the opposite of some members of the group. Thus, with such realities, group learning should be focused on resolving conflicts that may emerge among group members. This is important in preventing conflicts from distracting the group learning experience. Overall however, there is transformation that goes on in the individual as a member of the group and transformation of the whole group as members experience and perform different individual and collective tasks.

Sharing, group dynamics, communication, conflict resolution, and group leadership are some of the important aspects of the group or team learning process. As Kolb and Kolb (2011) note, 'to learn from their experience, teams must create a conversational space where members can reflect on and talk about their experience together' (p.52). Thus, group learning is characterised by interaction and sharing. Participation in group or team activities varies among group members. Some members are passive while others are always active and want to influence others. It thus requires transformative group leadership that can influence transformation of group experiences in positive group outcomes. In the next section we discuss transformative learning theory and how it explains the learning process.

Transformative Learning Theory

Transformative learning theory derives from the pioneering works of Mezirow (1978) in which a person engages in reflexive and affective adaptation and problem-solving. This results in efforts at making meaningful, and effective adjustment to their environment. It thus approximates the person-in-environment (PIE) (Minahan, 1981) perspective which has been hailed as the long-standing central approach to social work practice (Weiss-Gal, 2008). In the PIE or the ecological perspective, the individual and the environment are viewed as mutually influencing and mutually reinforcing in positive and negative ways. For instance, a student's home environment (such as inadequate food, poor nutrition, financial challenges, and violence between parents among other factors) has an effect on that student's performance at school. Similarly, a student's learning is affected by the school environment under which they learn. The school environment may include teachers, peers, infrastructure, bullying from other students, inadequate learning materials, and unreasonable workloads, recreation facilities and feedback mechanisms among others. According to Kolb and Kolb (2011), learning results from a synergy between the learner and their environment. This explains why social work has historically embraced the PIE in both learning and practice.

The purpose of learning is to transform an individual from one state of cognitive behaviour (ontological) to another. This means there should be an existing state of cognitive behaviour or frame of reference against which learning would be measured or evaluated. According to Mezirow (2000), frames of reference refer to 'broad, generalised, orienting predispositions that act as filter for interpreting the meaning of experience' (Lee and Greene, 2004, p.4). These are in a way, the learner's habits, meaning perspectives before learning has taken place. The learner should (ideally) perceive their ways of knowing (epistemology) and the world around them differently after learning has taken place. That is, learning should change their perspective. It should change their ways or methods of doing things. Critical in this process is experience and how the learner interprets what they learn from experience. Experience in this context includes the individual's interactions with their environment which includes one's family, peers, school, religion and other socialisation agents.

Carrying out learning activities under these environmental factors influence how and what a person learns. Transformative learning draws from cognitive and developmental psychology (Dirkx, 1998). Although it relates more to adult education, it has wider application to social work whose approach is mostly transformative and empowering. According to Frenk et al (2010), learning has three successive levels thus: informative, formative and transformative learning respectively. They argue that informative learning is about acquiring knowledge and skills leading to expertise, while formative learning is about socialising learners about values to produce professionals (Enkhtur and Yamamoto, 2017). Thus, we socialise students into social work values such as self-determination and respect for human rights. 'Transformative learning [the highest in the hierarchy], is about developing leadership attributes; its purpose is to produce enlightened change agents' (Enkhtur and Yamamoto, 2017, p.195) who can transform society.

However, some scholars have been sceptical about it due to its emphasis on the cognitive aspects of learning which makes it overlook other equally important aspects of transformative learning such as social and emotional. Behaviourists for instance argue that mental processes/cognitive aspects of behaviour are not observable and therefore cannot be measured objectively.

Since learning should bring about change in the learning experience, the change should be observable (Kasonde et al. 2021) and cognitive aspects cannot be observed to ascertain whether learning has taken place. Transformative learning also has roots in consciousness and empowerment (Illeris, 2014) which makes it important in social work practice. It therefore promotes social justice by raising awareness among the underprivileged.

Mezirow defined *transformative learning,* also known as *perspective transformation,* as a process of adult learning and change in which, as adults mature, they experience situations in which old coping mechanisms become ineffective (Damianakis et al., 2019) or completely fail. This makes individuals disoriented and thus, reflect on aspects of their lives that previously facilitated or hindered their learning. For instance, when still young, a learner can attend all classes, they have limited responsibilities other than themselves. But as an adult learner, they may have children, spouse, a job and other commitments adding to their responsibilities and possible distraction to their learning times. Thus, in reflecting on aspects of their life that previously facilitated their learning, such as limited access to and use of technology, the lack of responsibilities and disturbances in their early life, they may change their frame of reference. Learning therefore becomes a reflexive activity.

According to (Cranton, 1994; Mezirow, 1998), the learner is able to critically examine, question, validate and revise their taken-for-granted ways of knowing, believing and feeling (cited in Lee and Greene, 2008). This involves reflection of their beliefs, values, and cultural, cognitive and environmental systems. 'Critical self-reflection and reflective discourse are imperative in the process of transformative learning' (Lee and Greene, 2008, p.22). Beyond critical self-reflection, transformative learning is about developing learners that can bring about change.

The life course perspective (Elder, 1999) can complement this theory in explaining human experiences and how these would have lasting effects on their lives including learning. This perspective suggests that socio historical events have lasting effects on individuals, their relationships and their wellbeing overtime (Philips et al. 2010). For instance, poverty in early life may affect a person's learning outcomes. Poor education outcomes could in turn affect a person's income and other aspects of wellbeing later in life.

Transformative learning also draws from the works of three other scholars, namely; Paolo Freire, Larry Daloz and Robert Boyd (Dirkx, 1998). Freire emphasised conscientization or conscious-raising as one of the key concept to transformation. Other concepts in Freire's framework are praxis, codification and community engagement (Fleming, 2022). Freire was concerned with democratisation because authoritarianism, which according to him was on the rise, prevented citizens from expressing their experience (Fleming, 2022). Fleming argues that learning is not possible without expressing experience. The importance of experience in the learning process is emphasised in this chapter.

Boyd leaned towards psychosocial, emotional and spiritual aspects of learning (Enkhtur and Yamamoto, 2017). They argue that Boyd viewed transformative learning as a process of individuation, borrowed from Carl Jung in which a learner becomes aware of their unconscious self. Larry Daloz is credited for regarding transformative learning as a developmental process (Enkhtur and Yamamoto, 2017). These perspectives are all important in understanding transformative learning but space does not permit to discuss them in detail. However, Mezirow's perspective is more related to empowerment which is the main argument in this chapter. Hence, it is accorded more space.

Mezirow's articulation of transformation stands out in that it brings out the aspect of frame of reference which acts as a baseline against which learning can be measured. The most important of his arguments is meaning-making through reflection (Dirkx, 1998) and introspection. However, meaning-making may not always turn out to be positive. Some people may be thrown off balance through this process if the outcome is negative. For example, an adult who understands the importance of education but through reflection realise that they are running out of time with their age and therefore they would not make full use of the education they are pursuing. Such may not only be disorienting but also devastating.

According to Mezirow (1981), this theory has ten fundamental elements, namely; *a disorienting dilemma, the catalyst for self-examination, a critical assessment of one's internalised assumptions, exploration of new ways of behaving, competence building, planning of new action, and mobilise new resources, test the planned new course of action and implement the new course of action and integrate it with their new perspective* (cited in Damianakis et al., 2019). In general, the transformational approach encapsulates the implementation of policies and practices that integrate everyone into society so that they can benefit from societal resources and claim their rights (Sebates-Wheeler and Devereaux, 2009). It is a conscientising, redistributive and inclusive mechanism that promotes social justice. Thus, the hallmark of transformative social work education is empowerment.

Experiential Learning Theory

Experience is an important aspect of the learning process. It is for this reason that scholars in human learning and development such as Jean Piaget, John Dewey, Kurt Lewin, William James, Curl Jung, Carl Rogers and Paolo Freire among others gave it a central role in the learning process (Kolb and Kolb, 2011). Indeed 'experience is the best teacher' to emphasise the importance of first-hand experience and the learning people derive from interacting with phenomenon. This resonates well with constructivists view discussed earlier that people construct personal perspectives based on their experiences.

Kold and Kolb (2011) argue that social work training embeds experiential community-based learning. This field-based learning has been designated as a 'signature pedagogy' within social work to emphasise the importance of experience in fostering the learning process. Fieldwork practice is an important aspect of transformative social work education that allows learners to experience the phenomenon presented in practice. Thus, to integrate theory with practice, learners need to interact with phenomenon, interrogating theory on the basis of their field experiences and interpret these according to each one's learning style (Kolb and Kolb, 2011). Experiential learning involves learners participating or observing phenomenon to acquire knowledge through experience, cognitively and interactively and transform that experience into action.

Experiential learning derives its name from the emphasis placed on the role of experience in the learning process which also distinguishes it from other learning theories such as cognitive and behavioural theories (Kolb et al. 1999). According to these authors, while cognitive learning theories emphasise cognitive over affect, behavioural learning theories deny any role of subjective experience in the learning process. Behaviourists contend that cognitive processes cannot be observed and therefore cannot be measured objectively thus rendering their interpretations untenable. To behavioural theorists, stimulus-response conditioned and observed behaviour is more important in the learning process (Kasonde et al. 2013). However, behavioural theorists also acknowledge the importance of a favourable environment to the learning process. For instance, drawing from the concept of identity found in the work of Erik Erikson, Illeris (2014) notes the importance of the interaction between the individual and the social environment in influencing learning and the development of the individual.

Experiential Learning Theory 'is a dynamic view of learning based on a learning cycle driven by the resolution of a dual dialects of action/reflection and experience/abstraction' (Kolb and Kolb, 2011, p.43). These authors argue that it is grounded in six propositions thus; *learning as a process, learning is all re-learning, learning requires resolution of conflicts between dialectically opposed modes of adaptation to the world, learning is a holistic process of adaptation, learning results from synergetic transactions between the person and the environment and that learning is a process of creative knowledge*. From these propositions, we can deduce that learning is a process that involves adaptation and it thrives in a conducive interface between the learner and the environment to produce knowledge.

Experiential learning is also transformative and transformative learning is best achieved through experiential learning. That is, learning is easy when the learner interacts with phenomenon and its environment. Importantly, both transformational and experiential learning are empowering to the learner and that is likely to be reflected in the services they provide. It is for this reason that in this chapter, we argue that transformative education/ is the hallmark of empowerment. That is to say, the transformative process is inherently empowering. In the next section, we discuss empowerment and show how it is a transformative process and product.

Empowerment

Empowerment is one of the fluid concepts in social work in that it can mean different things to different people in different contexts. It can mean the process and /goal or outcome of participation, self-help, capacity building among others. While the process includes activities and actions such as capacity building involved in attaining empowerment, the outcome or goal entails self-reliant, independence. Empowerment is also a contested concept in social work partly because of its rationalistic undertones (Adams, 2003). Rationalism implicit it suggests that social work service users are rational and capable of self-advancement. Therefore, they would not need social workers. Therefore, the concept of empowerment must be constantly redefined and reconstructed by both professionals and service users especially the latter (Adams, 2003).

'Empowerment is the means by which individuals, groups and/or communities become able to take control of their circumstances and achieve their own goals thereby being able to work towards helping themselves and others to maximise the quality of their lives' (Adams, 2003, p. 8). In this context, empowerment is an end which justify the means. Whether the process is facilitated by outsiders or insiders (those affected) or both is irrelevant so long those involved can take charge of their affairs to improve their wellbeing and those of others.

According to Clark (2000) empowerment is more commonly used to describe service users being given 'meaningful choice' and 'valuable options' in order to gain greater control over their lives and their circumstances (cited in Trivithick, 2005:219). Meaningful choices can only apply to rational people as alluded to above. But this also assumes that they have all the valuable options at their disposal and information relating to the options. Without information on options, choices cannot be said to be 'meaningful'.

Guiterez (1990) identifies five (5) techniques that make empowerment a process, thus: *service user's definition of the problem or need; identifying and building upon service user's strength; engaging in a power analysis of the service user's situation; teaching specific skills; and mobilising resources and advocating for the service user* (cited in Trivithick, 2005). As adage goes, 'a problem well defined is a problem half-solved'. As social workers, we facilitate the service user's solving of their own problems. Therefore, service users should be clear from their own perspectives as to what problem they are embarking on to solve.

Rogers (2020) asserts that the client's problem and the clarity thereof is a catalyst for change. Once they are clear with the problem or need, a social worker needs to analyse their strengths in solving the problem by *'starting where the client is'*. This is the essence of the strengths perspective which entails assessing the client's goals, skills, strengths, abilities and other resources (Rogers, 2020. Rogers argues that the central tenet of the strengths perspective is the idea of shifting the focus from the problem to the strengths and resources that the client has. According to Rogers (2020), shifting the focus empowers the client to even confront future challenges. This is because it transforms the client's beliefs and values. In the strengths perspective, all human beings are considered capable of growth, change and adaptation (Weick et al. 1989) all of which are important aspects of the learning and transformation process. While all the five techniques given by Guiterez (1990) above are important and useful, the first two techniques are particularly critical to the empowerment process and social work practice in general.

Social work is an empowering profession in that it aims at enhancing problem-solving capacities of client systems while fostering transformation and enhancing their wellbeing. Empowerment is itself a transformational activity (Adams, 2003) in that it makes people take charge of their situations to achieve their goals. It makes people perceive their situations differently and moves them from a position of dependence to that of independence. Thus, social work is ontologically, epistemologically and methodologically empowering. It entails learning from experience or using experience of a situation to model solutions for future similar situations and actions. Thus, it is reflexive. Since social work is empowering and empowerment is transformational, it follows that social work is transformational. This linkage is discussed in details later.

'Social workers need empowerment to render their practice transformational' (Adams, 2003, p.3). Without being empowered social workers cannot bring about change (transformation) in the lives of the people they serve in whom the currency of empowerment revolves. Thus, after empowering social workers, they can, in turn empower those who use their services. However, there are exceptions to empowerment when dealing with certain vulnerable categories such as children, people with disabilities, older people, victims of war and disasters among others. As Adams (2003) notes, risk management can be disempowering and therefore inimical to independence and social justice which social work strives to promote.

Empowerment reduces dependence on hand outs or other actions that bring about and perpetuate dependence thus enabling some of the poor people to attain sustainable livelihoods (Sebates-Wheeler and Devereaux, 2009). Central to empowerment is participation of service users, at least in articulating their needs or defining their problems. It therefore raises people's consciousness. People need to participate in choices that affect their lives in order for them to gain greater control over their lives and livelihoods (Smale, Tuson, Stathan, 2000). Therefore, Social work need to enhance participation of service users in order to render their services empowering and transformational.

The Importance of Empowerment in Social Work

Foremost, the history of empowerment is rooted in mutual aid, self-help, liberation movements, rights and social activism, anti-racism and feminism among others all of which relate to the development of the social work profession (Adams, 2003). As noted earlier, social work fosters empowerment to make service users to take charge of their situations whether individually or in groups. Empowerment is a concept that relates so well to all methods of social work (Adams, 2003) be it working with individuals, groups, communities or organisations. It is also an outcome of the transformation process much as it also fosters transformation.

Social work is aimed at transforming service users' perspectives and situations. In so doing, service users are able to perceive their situations differently and to control their own affairs. It is thus a transformative and empowering profession. As Adams (2003) notes, 'empowerment in all domains and sectors of practice should be, if it has not already become the central, energising feature of social work' (p.6). It is for this reason that we refer to it in this chapter as the hallmark of transformation since social work is transformational.

The Transformative and Empowering Nature of Social Work

Social work education seeks to foster student transformation (Archer-Kuhn et al. 2021) both in their self-perception and their perception of the world. In turn, social workers are preoccupied with transformation of systems to empower social work service users and even transform these. Transformative education should bring about self-awareness and reflection to one's values and beliefs and make a person perceive themselves and the world around them differently. As discussed earlier, social work is inherently a transformative and empowering profession. Its historical association with and use of the PIE approach in dealing with service users is proof of empowerment. In this approach, the focus is on the transactions between people and their immediate environment (Weick et al. 1989). The PIE approach has been reliable in both the education and practice of social workers. It focuses on transforming and empowering a person facing a challenge to function optimally where they are with the resources they have. Transformation, as discussed earlier, is moderated by environmental factors which influence what we learn and how we choose what to learn.

Both empowerment and transformation involve reflexivity, criticality and conscious-raising which are important in changing the lives of social work students and social work service users. The three (reflexivity, criticality and consciousness) are particularly important for field practice done by social work students. Social work field education (field experience) is regarded as the signature pedagogy (Homonoff, 2008), because it socialises and transforms students to becoming practitioners. True transformation is assumed to have been attained upon completion of the field practicum. This critical education practice (Archer-Kuhn et al. 2021) signifies the real learning in social work in which concrete field experience is transformed into knowledge.

Fieldwork practice experience is intended to make students make reflective observations on theory but also on their fieldwork experience in order to inform practice. It is this concrete experience and critical reflective observations that is transformed into knowledge about social work practice. By and large, it is at this stage of training that social work students are transformed into practitioners. As Archer-Kuhn et al. (2021) observe, it is the new experiences that catalyses students into transformation. It is therefore empowering because it makes students practice competently and independently.

Navigating the relationship between theory and practice in the field can be disorienting thereby triggering critical reflections on long held assumptions, beliefs and values. Faced with such dilemma, a student will be prompted to explore new options and roles from which to build self-efficacy to act. It can therefore be argued that transformation and empowerment are what social work students are trained to do and use to improve their environment, their learning and their practice. While empowerment is the central feature of social work theory and practice (Adams, 2003), we argue that transformation is the hallmark of empowerment. Adams asserts that without empowerment, something is missing from that type of social work practice.

Social work is a profession that aims at enhancing the capabilities of client systems at various levels to acquire resources for meeting basic needs or the actual attainment of these. It helps people to manage their challenges, achieve meaningful change, and promote social justice. It thus transforms and empowers people by capacitating them to take charge of their lives. The change agents (social workers) should be empowered themselves. They should be transformed and be competent in bringing about change in other people's lives. The global definition of social work (IFSW, 2014) reverberates this argument. The IFSW and IASSW adopted definition states that:

'Social work is a practice-based profession and academic discipline that promotes social change and development, social cohesion and the empowerment and liberation of people.'

Both transformation (social change and development) and empowerment are clear in the above definition. This entails that social work is transformative and empowering.

Although social work also employs remedial measures at individual, family, group and community levels when necessary, it is mainly focused on facilitating sustainable social and behaviour change among service users. Behaviour change is a complex process that requires the use of transformational approaches, strategies and tactics. Such approaches include but are not limited to social development and the social work. The former incorporates social and economic issues to promote human wellbeing (Midgley, 1995) while the latter fosters transformation at training level to become a social worker and at professional level to bring about meaningful change at individual, family, group and community levels.

CONCLUSION

This chapter sought to discuss transformative social work education and how it transforms social workers and empowers them and those who use their services. Transformation addresses issues of structural inequalities, social justice, consciousness, criticality, reflexivity, perspective change, and empowerment. Critical in this transformative endeavour is experiential learning. Experiential learning, mainly through fieldwork practice is central to professional social work education (Archer-Kuhn et al. 2021). Thus, field work practice experience is the main transformative component in social work training. Experience is critical in that it influences and is influenced by transformation and empowerment. Classroom-based social work education can be said to be informative and formative.

While social work serves remedial and other important functions and roles in society, it is fundamentally transformational and empowering to both professional social workers and the people they serve. Thus, in our view, social workers should advocate for, and strengthen the empowering role that social work can play to learners and service users. This, we believe, can change and sustain the welfare of vulnerable people served by the profession. We suggest that future research and scholarship should aim at further exploring environments in which the transformative role of social work education can be nourished to foster social justice and promote equity of opportunities while recognising diversity among service users. This would make the profession more empowering.

REFERENCES

Adams, R. (2003). *Social Work and Empowerment*. Palgrave Macmillan.

Archer-Kuhn, B., Samson, P., Damianakis, T., Barrett, B., Matin, S., & Ahern, C. (2021). Transformative learning in field education: Students bridging the theory/practice gap. *British Journal of Social Work*, 51(7), 2419–2438. 10.1093/bjsw/bcaa082

Bell, K. (2012). Towards a post-conventional philosophical base for social work. *British Journal of Social Work*, 42(3), 408–423. 10.1093/bjsw/bcr073

Damianakis, T., Barrett, B., Archer-Kuhn, B., Samson, P. L., Matin, S., & Ahern, C. (2020). Transformative learning in graduate education: Masters of social work students' experiences of personal and professional learning. *Studies in Higher Education*, 45(9), 2011–2029. 10.1080/03075079.2019.1650735

Dirkx, J. M. (1998). Transformative learning theory in the practice of adult education: An overview. *PAACE Journal of Lifelong Learning*, 7, 1–14.

Drolet, J. L., and Nicholas, D. B. (2023). Welcome to the first issue of Transformative Social Work: A special issue on the impacts of the COVID-19 pandemic. *Transformative Social Work, 1*(1).

Elder, G. (1999). *Children of the Great Depression: Social change in life experience*. University of Chicago press.

Enkhtur, A., & Yamamoto, B. A. (2017). Transformative Learning Theory and its Application in Higher. *PAACE Journal of Lifelong Learning*, 7, 1–14.

Fleming, T. (2022). Mezirow's theory of transformative learning and Freire's pedagogy: Theories in dialogue. *Adult Education Critical Issues*, 2(2), 7–19. 10.12681/haea.32302

Frenk, J., Chen, L., Bhutta, Z. A., Cohen, J., Crisp, N., Evans, T., Fineberg, H., Garcia, P., Ke, Y., Kelley, P., Kistnasamy, B., Meleis, A., Naylor, D., Pablos-Mendez, A., Reddy, S., Scrimshaw, S., Sepulveda, J., Serwadda, D., & Zurayk, H. (2010). Health professionals for a new century: Transforming education to strengthen health systems in an interdependent world. *Lancet*, 376(9756), 1923–1958. 10.1016/S0140-6736(10)61854-521112623

Gray, M., & Coates, J. (2018). Changing gears: Shifting to an environmental perspective in social work education. In *Environmental Justice* (pp. 48–58). Routledge.

Gray, M., & Lombard, A. (2008). The post-1994 transformation of social work in South Africa. *International Journal of Social Welfare*, 17(2), 132–145. 10.1111/j.1468-2397.2007.00545.x

Homonoff, E. (2008). The heart of social work: Best practitioners rise to challenges in field instruction. *The Clinical Supervisor*, 27(2), 135–169. 10.1080/07325220802490828

Illeris, K. (2014). Transformative learning and identity. *Journal of Transformative Education*, 12(2), 148–163. 10.1177/1541344614548423

International Federation of Social WorkersInternational Association of SchoolInternational Council on Social Wel. (2012). The global agenda for social work and social development: Commitment to action. *Journal of Social Work Education*, 48(4), 837–843. 10.1080/10437797.2012.10662225

International Federation of Social Workers (IFSW), (2014). *Global Definition of social work*. Global Definition of Social Work – International Federation of Social Workers (ifsw.org).

Jonassen, D. H. (1994). Thinking Technology: Toward a Constructivist Design Model. *Educational Technology*, 34(4), 34–37. https://www.learntechlib.org/p/171050/

Kasonde, N., Hambulo, F., Haambokoma, N., & Tomaida, M. (2013). The Contribution of Behaviourism Theory to Education. *Journal: Zambia Journal of Education*, 4(1), 58–74.

Kolb, A. Y., & Kolb, D. A. (2011). Experiential learning theory: A dynamic, holistic approach to management learning, education and development. *The SAGE handbook of management learning, education and development*, 7(2), 42-68.

Kolb, D. A., Boyatzis, R. E., & Mainemelis, C. (2014). Experiential learning theory: Previous research and new directions. In *Perspectives on thinking, learning, and cognitive styles* (pp. 227–247). Routledge. 10.4324/9781410605986-9

Lee, M. Y., & Greene, G. J. (2004). A teaching framework for transformative multicultural social work education. *Journal of Ethnic & Cultural Diversity in Social Work*, 12(3), 1–28. 10.1300/J051v12n03_01

Lorenzetti, L., Dhungel, R., Lorenzetti, D., Oschepkova, T., & Haile, L. (2017, June). A transformative approach to social work education. In *Proceedings of the 3rd International Conference on Higher Education Advances* (pp. 801-809). Editorial Universitat Politècnica de València. 10.4995/HEAD17.2017.5422

Mezirow, J. (1978). Perspective transformation. *Adult Education*, 28(2), 100–110. 10.1177/074171367802800202

Midgley, J. (1995). *Social Development: The developmental perspective in social welfare*. Sage publications.

Minahan, A. (1981). Purpose and objectives of social work revisited [Introduction to Special Issue]. *Social Work*, 26, 5–6.

Moonga, F. (2018). Social protection and social work practice in Zambia. In Gray, M. (Ed.), *The Handbook of Social Work and Social Development in Africa* (pp. 72–83).

Noyoo, N. (2021). *Social Welfare and Social Work in Southern Africa*. African Sun Media. 10.18820/9781928480778

Phillips, J., Ajrouch, K., & Hillcoat-Nalletamby, S. (2010). *Key concepts in social Gerontology*. Sage publications. 10.4135/9781446251058

Rogers, A. T. (2020). *Human behavior in the social environment: Perspectives on development, the life course, and macro contexts*. Routledge. 10.4324/9781003025382

Sebates-Wheeler, R., & Devereaux, S. (2009). Transformative Social Protection: The currency of social justice. In Barrientos, A., & Hulme, D. (Eds.), *Social Protection for the Poor and Poorest: Concepts* (pp. 64–84). Policies and Politics.

Smale, G., Tuson, G., & Statham, D. (2000). *Social work and social problems*. Macmillan Press. 10.5040/9781350392618

Trevithick, P. (2005). *Social work skills*. Open University Press.

Twikirize, J., & Spitzer, H. (2019). Indigenous and innovative social work practice in Africa: Evidence from East Africa, In Twikirize and Spitzer (Eds), *Social work practice in Africa: Indigenous and Innovative approaches*. Fountain Publishers

Weick, A., Rapp, C., Sullivan, W. P., & Kisthardt, W. (1989). A strengths perspective for social work practice. *Social Work*, 34(4), 350–354. 10.1093/sw/34.4.350

Weiss-Gal, I. (2008). The Person-in-Environment Approach: Professional Ideology and Practice of Workers in Israel. *Social Work*, 53(1), 65–75. 10.1093/sw/53.1.6518610822

Wilson, J. M., Goodman, P. S., & Cronin, M. A. (2007). Group learning. *Academy of Management Review*, 32(4), 1041–1059. 10.5465/amr.2007.26585724

Chapter 2
A Conceptual Analysis on Transformational Learning Theory and Social Work Education

Özge Kutlu
https://orcid.org/0000-0002-4774-7326
Burdur Mehmet Akif Ersoy University, Turkey

ABSTRACT

Transformational learning theory is a perspective that focuses on understanding the learning process from individuals' experiences. According to this theory, learning interacts not only with external influences, but also with the individual's inner thoughts, feelings, and experiences. In social work education, transformational learning theory is used as an important tool to support individuals' personal and professional development. Using this theory, social workers can help their clients discover their strengths and realize their potential. At the same time, this theory encourages social work students to recognize their own biases and approach social problems from a critical perspective. In this way, social work professionals can develop more effective strategies to ensure social justice and equality.

INTRODUCTION

Transformation involves learning to look from a different window and internalizing it and integrating it into life permanently. Transformational learning theory is a framework that provides a structure and process that sheds light on the conscious and logical aspect of adult learning. This theory argues that frames of reference

DOI: 10.4018/979-8-3693-2407-3.ch002

influence and shape individuals, whether they are aware of it or not. It sheds light on how individuals become conscious of their previous assumptions, how they critically reflect on these assumptions, and how they develop strategies and actions to transform themselves. Thus, individuals can create their own frames of reference and create their own unique worldviews (Şahin, Erisen, & Çeliköz, 2016). Transformational learning is the process in which students not only receive information passively, but also question, criticize, personally interpret and internalize this information. This learning model focuses on the process of transforming and developing individuals' values, beliefs, and perspectives. Transformational learning promotes personal growth and social change. Transformational learning is very important for social work education. Because social workers need critical thinking and reflexivity skills when they face complex social problems. Transformational learning helps students develop these skills and provides the opportunity to continually question and evaluate their own values, attitudes, and practices. Social work is the process of interacting with and understanding people. Transformational learning helps students develop empathy skills and understand different life experiences. Social work undertakes the task of fighting for social justice and equality. Transformational learning helps students develop sensitivity to social justice issues and build strong motivation to combat these issues (Shishov, Popey-Ool, Abylkasymova, Kalnei, & Ryakhimova, 2022). Social workers support the transformation of individuals and society. Transformational learning enables social workers to be effective change agents. The use of transformational learning theory in social work education has a catalytic effect in terms of students gaining professional skills. For this reason, it is important to use transformational learning theory effectively in social work education.

In this chapter, the aim is to explore the essence of transformational learning theory, its stages, opportunities, and challenges, as well as the roles of teachers and students. Additionally, it seeks to examine how this theory can be integrated into social work education, drawing upon a literature analysis. Furthermore, the chapter aims to unveil the diverse perspectives that this theory brings to social work education.

A CONCEPTUAL GLANCE AT TRANSFORMATIONAL LEARNING

Transformational learning is the process of transforming an individual's frame of reference, meaning the process of questioning and making meaningful changes in emotions, thoughts, beliefs, culture, habits of mind, assumptions and experiences (Mezirow, 2000). Mezirow's transformational learning theory focuses on people internalizing their experiences completely and interpreting them in detail, making sense of them with different mindsets, and at the end of this psychological process, gaining a different perspective on the experience and experiencing a structural change in their thoughts, feelings and actions. In other words, Mezirow (1991, 1978) tries to explain with transformational learning theory how people attach meanings to their experiences, how they make sense of experiences holistically, the nature of the structures that affect the way they live the experience, the dynamics that play a role in changing the meanings attributed to the experience, and how meaning structures change when they find them dysfunctional. The aim of transformational learning theory is to liberate the mind of the individual in order to get rid of uncertainty/complexity by questioning the dilemmas, events, problems, emotions, thoughts, experiences, assumptions and values she/he encounters (Şen & Şahin, 2017).

Transformational learning process involves the individual criticizing his/her own assumptions, gaining awareness in the context of the beliefs and emotions he/she has, evaluating alternative perspectives, deciding to abandon the old by adopting the new perspective or synthesizing the old and new perspectives, acting according to the new perspective and this new perspective. It involves integrating the perspective into one's life as a whole (Mezirow, 1994; Cranton, 2002). According to Mezirow's (1996) point of view, the individual develops a new interpretation using her/his own experience or creates a gradual guide for how her/his future behavior will be by correcting and reshaping the errors of the existing interpretation, which is only possible through learning. Mezirow (1991), underlines that with transformational learning, the individual will experience developmental change at the end of the process and the individual will gain a new world view. In other words, the transformational learning process leads to an increase in the personal and developmental potential of the learner. Transformational learning is the individual's learning to question and reshape his/her own beliefs, assumptions, emotions, feelings, mindset, stereotypes and perspectives in accordance with a specific purpose and to look at them critically as a whole in order to achieve intellectual accumulation and personal development. Transformational learning is a holistic process that gains meaning in the context of various components by bringing together many concepts.

Meaning Schema

Meaning schema is a set of psychological assumptions, also expressed as reference frames on which a person bases his or her world views (Bartlett, 1958). Mezirow (1994) defines the semantic schema as "the constellation of concepts, beliefs, judgments, and emotions that shape a particular interpretation." Although the individual has the potential to gain critical awareness and change the meaning schemes completely, the new information can be rejected in the context of the existing meaning schemes, accepted by changing it slightly, or adapted to the existing scheme (Mezirow & Marsick, 1978).

Meaning Perspective

Meaning perspective refer to learning how one re-encounters one's own past and relives an event that occurred in the past. The individual learns to be critically aware of the cultural and psychological assumptions that influence the way he sees himself and his relationships and the way he shapes life. Meaning perspective is a set of personal values associated with thoughts, feelings and will that enable a person to understand herself/himself and his relationships, expressing the structure of cultural assumptions by which new experience is assimilated and transformed by past experience. Each individual has meaning perspectives shaped by the influence of the culture of the society in which he/she lives (Mezirow, 1985; Mezirow, 1994).

Frame of Reference

Frames of reference are structures in which expectations, perceptions, information and emotions are shaped and limited. Transformational learning aims to change the frames of reference, which are the assumption structures through which experiences are given meaning (Cranton, 1994; Cranton, 1996). According to Mezirow (2003) frames of reference can include fixed interpersonal relationships, political orientations, cultural bias, ideologies, schemas, stereotypes and practices, habits of mind, moral ethical norms, psychological preferences and schemas, paradigms in science and mathematics, frames in linguistics and social sciences, aesthetic values and standards.

Critical Reflection

Critical reflection guides people's actions during their transformative experiences (Tusting & Barton, 2011). As a matter of fact, Mezirow sees critical reflection as a conscious and explicit re-evaluation of meaning structures (Taylor, 2008). According to Mezirow (1994), in critical reflection, individuals look critically at their beliefs, which are usually acquired in childhood through the influence of the society and family members, to determine whether they are functional in adulthood.

Critical Self-Reflection

Critically reflecting on one's assumptions is key to transforming an accepted frame of reference, an essential dimension of learning to adapt to change. Self-reflection can lead to significant personal transformations (Mezirow, 1997). Kegan (2000) emphasizes that adults need to be able to engage in critical self-reflection in order to push the limits of their developmental capacities. Critical self-reflection requires the individual to question and develop a discourse on her/his own thoughts and life (Erden & Yıldız, 2020).

Critical Discourse

Discourse is verifying how one understands something and arriving at the best decision about a belief, idea, or perspective. Saying that learning is a social process, Mezirow (1997), argues that discourse is at the center of giving meaning and that learners must be helped to participate effectively in discourse. Critical discourse is necessary to test the validity of a transformed frame of reference in transformational learning, which involves critical reflection of assumptions.

STEP-BY-STEP TRANSFORMATIONAL LEARNING

Transformational learning refers to a process that involves individuals gaining awareness of the habits in their minds, evaluating alternative views, and deciding to replace the old view with a new one or make a synthesis of the old and new, resulting in more reliable information to guide action (Gravett, 2004). During the learning process of the transformational model, differences occur in the structural behavior and thoughts of the individual. In order for the learner to learn in line with his/her targeted goals, he/she must acquire critical thinking skills by benefiting from experiences as well as cognitive processes. Thus, the learner shows different discourses and behaviors by attributing various meanings to the achievements she/he has achieved. In doing this, the individual is active and the teacher is the person who learns with the individual. The learning environment, where the teacher is both a guide and a learner with the individual, is seen as a transformational learning model as a joint activity and is defined as the first place where experiences are experienced (Akpınar, 2010).

The ten stages defined by Mezirow and Marsick (1978) help understand how the transformational learning process occurs. These stages are:

- Creating a dilemma,
- Questioning the negative emotions in her/his own life,
- The individual critically evaluates assumptions,
- Accepting the individual's reaction and change process,
- Carrying out studies for relationships, actions and tasks,
- Planning for what to do,
- The individual has the necessary knowledge and skills to implement the plans,

- Trying new roles,
- Individuals embrace their new roles,
- Becoming aware of the change and transformation in the individual's life (Mezirow, 2000; Mezirow & Marsick, 1978).

For transformational learning to occur, the individual does not always have to start from the first step. In some cases, the individual may have already gone through certain stages. For this reason, the stages can occur in different ways or orders, and individuals can be involved in the transformation process at any point of these stages (Brock, 2010). However, it is stated that the stages of experiencing dilemmas and critical evaluation, which are confusing, prompt the person to think deeply, and literally change the individual's life direction, are necessary for the transformational learning process (Taylor, 1998). The stages of transformational learning and what these stages include are defined in ten stages.

Creating a Dilemma

The first requirement that stimulates the individual to transformational learning is an internal, personal crisis. In transformational learning theory, this crisis is defined as the individual creating a dilemma (Mezirow & Taylor, 2009). Dilemma formation occurs when an individual encounters an experience that does not match her/his expectations and meaning structures. This first stage can also be defined as the trigger of transformational learning. Events that deeply affect people and are turning points such as natural disaster, death of a valued relative, divorce, accident, war, job loss or retirement can cause an individual to experience a dilemma (Mezirow, 1997).

Questioning the Negative Emotions in Her/His Own Life

The individual's self-evaluation with fear, anger, and guilt is the stage in which the individual examines her/his old perspective after creating a dilemma. At this stage, the individual begins to evaluate herself/himself while struggling with the negative emotions she/he experiences.

The Individual Critically Evaluates Assumptions

The most important element of the transformational learning model is individuals' self-criticism (Çimen & Yılmaz, 2014). This stage is a critically oriented comprehensive process that involves thinking about and explaining one's current ideas and actions, seeking answers by asking questions to oneself, and confronting one's own thoughts and behaviors. After the individual's self-assessment, he/she evaluates his/her assumptions from a critical perspective.

Accepting the Individual's Reaction and Change Process

As a result of critical self-evaluation, the individual realizes that she/he has entered a transformation process. She/He can also share this situation with her/his environment. At this stage, the individual realizes and understands that other individuals around her/him have similar experiences, that they, too, have entered the transformational process like her/him, and that they are thinking about the changes on the way to transformation.

Carrying Out Studies for Relationships, Actions, and Tasks

After entering the transformation process, the individual begins to explore new roles, relationships and new options for actions.

Planning for What to Do

It is the stage where a consistent and effective action plan is created to include, internalize and adopt the radical changes that will result in transformation, and to act for these purposes. The action plan, which is based on a logical framework and is in line with the character of the changes, is designed by the individual in full detail and planned to be implemented.

The Individual Has the Necessary Knowledge and Skills to Implement the Plans

It is the stage where the individual acquires the knowledge and skills necessary to implement her/his plans. At this stage, the individual acquires the knowledge and skills that will enable her/him to implement the action plan required for the transformation process. At this stage, the individual begins to look for a new role and behavior style in order to solve the dilemma he experienced in the first place (Şen & Şahin, 2017).

Trying New Roles

Bu aşamada birey yeni rolleri bir süreliğine geçici olarak denemektedir. Birey bu aşamada önceden oluşturduğu yerleşik anlam yapılarını değiştirmeye çalışmaktadır.

Individuals Embrace Their New Roles

At this stage, the individual temporarily tries out new roles for a while. At this stage, the individual tries to change the established meaning structures she/he has previously created.

Becoming Aware of the Change and Transformation in The Individual's Life

It is the stage where the individual establishes self-efficacy, self-confidence and self-perception in new roles and new relationships. It is the stage in which new roles and self-confidence relationships are established between individuals and the development of a suitable self. At this stage, the individual understands and gives meaning to life with the new perspective she/he has acquired, and thus begins to integrate this new perspective into her/his own life (Şahin, 2023).

The stages in the transformational learning process are closely related to the development of individuals/groups. Especially the strategies followed keep the individual active in the transformational learning process in the learning environment. All of these affect the experiences and cultures of individuals/groups. At the end of all these processes, where the new conditions resulting from the transformation in the life of the individual/group will provide new roles in practices and this will bring new experiences, they gain the ability to achieve their goals in different ways with new perspectives and a new consciousness (McWhinney & Markos, 2003). In essence, the transformational learning model starts with dilemmas and as a result of other stages, new situations, events and information are formed. The first five stages focus on exploration through dilemmas and critical thinking, while the later stages focus on transformation, integration, and action.

TEACHER AND STUDENT ROLES IN THE TRANSFORMATIONAL LEARNING MODEL

In the transformational learning model, the roles of teacher and student are different from traditional learning models. Transformational learning emphasizes students' active participation and directing their own learning processes. In the transformational learning model, the teacher acts as a "catalyst". While the transformational learning process is defined as a "joint activity", the teacher in this process is defined as someone who "has gone on a joint discovery with his students" rather than as "an authority that informs uninformed students" or a guide (Akpınar, 2010).

According to Mezirow (2003) eacher roles in the transformational learning process are as follows:

- Preparing a safe environment for ideal learning conditions.
- Using effective teaching methods that support the learner-centered approach.
- Identifying issues with alternative personal perspectives and using activities that promote critical reflection.
- Providing a democratic environment and rationality.

In transformational learning theory, the teacher assumes a role of guiding students rather than just being a figure who transmits information. It guides students on how they should learn and provides support throughout the process. Providing students with a variety of learning opportunities, the teacher allows students to enrich their learning experiences through project-based studies, discussion groups, field studies and other interactive methods. The teacher strives to motivate and inspire students, and this motivation enables students to focus on their own goals and objectives. According to this theory, the teacher should be open to different ways of thinking, cultures and perspectives. Because being open to differences encourages diversity in the classroom and supports students learning from each other. The teacher offers students the opportunity to develop their questioning skills and use their creative thinking skills, thus increasing their critical thinking capacity. In the transformational learning model, the teacher should provide a learning-teaching environment, have learners do activities to help them gain the ability to question what they think, apply strategies that increase communication between individuals, provide a free and democratic environment for individuals to express their ideas easily, and give the individual the opportunity to express her/his ideas easily (Şen & Şahin, 2017).

In the transformational learning process, the student has the responsibility of participating in learning activities and communicating with other students and the teacher. Because the student who wants to realize the transformation has to share the responsibility with his class. If students and their group are not willing to collaborate and share responsibility, transformational learning will not occur (Taylor, 1998).

According to Mezirow (2003) göre, the roles of student in the transformational learning process are as follows:

- Critically evaluate the validity of one's own and others' assumptions.
- Using critical thinking to evaluate a belief or point of view, learning to participate fully, effectively, and freely in reflective conversation and discussion.
- Being hopeful about the results of acting from a transformational perspective.
- Providing emotional support for others to engage in transformational learning through empathy.

In the transformational learning process, the student actively participates in her/his own learning process. It processes information in a way that is not only receptive but also productive. The student, who sets her/his own learning goals, strives to achieve these goals. This effort allows the student to personalize the learning process. By participating in group activities, students learn from different perspectives and interact with each other. Interaction also supports the student's social learning experience. The student evaluates information from a critical perspective and develops thought processes by considering various perspectives. In essence, the transformational learning model reflects an approach in which teacher and student are in a more equal partnership, where students are more directing their own learning and strive for continuous improvement.

OPPORTUNITIES AND CHALLENGES IN TRANSFORMATIONAL LEARNING

As a result of transformational learning, some behaviors occur in the student. These can be expressed as a deep change in consciousness structure, perspective and world view (Stuckey, Taylor, & Cranton, 2013). Since the transformations that occur in the student's frame of reference lead the individual to think more clearly and comprehensively, differences are also observed in their behavior (Mezirow, 2003). In some studies, it has been observed that as a result of transformational learning, students' sense of self-confidence increases, their sense of compassion towards others increases, they are able to empathize more, and they take action more quickly to control their lives and make more functional decisions (Courtney, Merriam, & Reeves, 1998; Taylor, 1998). In addition, positive changes occur in personal beliefs, perceptions, attitudes and values. Because they can think more logically by becoming aware of the situations that limit their understanding of the events they experience.

As the individual continues to learn with a creative and discovery-oriented attitude, they begin to question more and understand what their experiences mean. This encourages the student to think in a more open and inclusive way (King, 2011). In other words, the moment the student puts aside black and white thinking and starts questioning, he encounters more opportunities. Therefore, they learn not only the content but also metacognitive awareness and thinking skills in new ways. Transformational learning strengthens critical thinking skills as a lifelong learning feature (Jonassen, Howland, Moore, & Marra, 2003).

Changes in students' understanding and belief structure cause changes in their lifestyles and behaviors (Reisinger, 2013). As a result of the research, an increase was observed in students' environmental awareness and environmental belief levels

(Thomas, 2009), leadership qualities (Fullerton, 2010), critical thinking tendencies and metacognitive awareness (Koç Akran & Epçaçan, 2018) through transformational learning.

Transformational learning theory posits that adults learn more from experience rather than from typical pedagogical training. There are also some challenges and criticisms of transformational learning. These criticisms are:

- Transformational learning focuses on individual transformation rather than social transformation (Collard & Law, 1989; Cunningham, 1992; Newman, 1994). It has been criticized that transformational learning is overly subjectivist and emphasizes ideas and values based on personal experiences. This situation can ignore objective reality and make the learning process biased.
- Transformational learning does not adequately consider the context (Clark & Wilson, 1991; Kovan & Dirkx, 2003). The transformational learning model may encounter some difficulties in practice. It is difficult to encourage and support individual transformation, especially in large classes or standardized learning environments.
- Transformational learning emphasizes cognition and rationality rather than emotions (Dirkx, 2006; Illeris, 2004; Sands & Tennant, 2010).
- Transformational learning is difficult to apply to different cultures (Hoggan, Malkki, & Finnegan, 2017).
- Changes arising from the normative development cycle of adults cannot be explained by transformational learning theory alone (Tennant, 1993).
- Transformational learning minimizes or ignores the impact of power relations that exist in the formal education process (Pietrykowski, 1998).

KEEPING UP WITH THE TIMES: ONLINE TRANSFORMATIONAL LEARNING PRACTICES

With developing technologies, transformational learning in online learning environments provides a more effective and powerful learning environment (Bolger, Rowland, Reuning-Hummel, & Codner, 2011). nline transformational learning practices include tools and methods used in the online environment to support students' personal and professional development, develop critical thinking skills and contribute to social change.

Transformational learning focuses on improving students' understanding of alternative perspectives and experiences on an individual basis, but also increases students' awareness (Johnson Bailey & Alfred, 2006). The transformational learning approach aims to fundamentally and respectfully change students' attitudes and analytical skills. Many tools are offered to facilitate communication, collaboration, and information exchange in the online learning environment, helping students critically examine their assumptions, seek additional perspectives, grapple with social issues, and create change. In this way, the online learning environment supports transformational teaching (Meyers, 2008). Online classes and discussion forums provide students with the opportunity to share different perspectives, think critically, and reflect on social issues. Students can interact with each other and share their learning experiences through these platforms.

Online learning environments are necessary to support transformational learning. Hamlin (2015) stated that transformational learning environments should be supported with online discussions, videos and especially blogs. He also stated that blogs are very effective in terms of critical discourse and self-critical reflection, which are the basic elements of transformational learning. Online mentoring programs support students' personal and professional development by connecting and receiving mentoring from experienced professionals in a virtual environment. Using online mentoring practices in social work education can accelerate the transformational learning process. Similarly, online simulations and role plays allow students to virtually experience real-world scenarios. These simulations can be effective in putting social work skills into practice and increasing students' confidence in dealing with various situations. Online transformational learning applications enrich social work education by providing students with flexibility, interaction and personal learning experiences and support students to contribute to transformation.

INTEGRATION OF TRANSFORMATIONAL LEARNING INTO SOCIAL WORK EDUCATION: WHY AND HOW?

The transformational learning model is based on the idea that it empowers students by enabling them to motivate themselves, enable them to make effective evaluations, move away from known thought patterns, empathize, and get rid of the reasons that prevent the individual from learning (Akçay, 2012). Transformational learning can be used as a framework in social work education and can provide students with a more in-depth learning experience. However, at this point, it is necessary to draw attention to some issues regarding how to use transformational learning theory in social work education.

Transformational learning cannot be done in traditional classrooms where students sit front to back. Classes should be divided into small groups of four or five students and students should work collaboratively on the assigned project. Additionally, students should be encouraged to think critically and ask reflective questions about what they see and think in in-class and out-of-class practices. Transformational learning emphasizes the individual questioning his or her own thoughts, values and experiences and reflecting deeply in this process. In education, students should be provided with the opportunity to question and evaluate themselves regularly. Students should be given the opportunity to relate their experiences to social work practice and learn from these experiences.

In transformational learning, students should be directed to think about rights, ethics, and cooperation rather than typical topics. If any subject or skill learned is applied in the family and society, transformation is achieve (Bivens, Moriarty, & Taylor, 2009). Transformational learning takes place in environments that include methods that enable students to think and actively participate (McCadden, 2020). As a matter of fact, transformational learning encourages a learning process based on interaction. In social work education, students should be provided with opportunities to come together through interactive methods such as group work, role plays and case analyses. Interaction supports students to share their experiences with each other and learn from each other.

In transformational learning environments, it is necessary to expose students to new perspectives and experiences, encourage critical reflection, enable group discussion, offer students various opportunities to become individuals, and help them acquire the necessary knowledge and skills (Mezirow & Taylor, 2009). Transformational learning emphasizes social justice and social change. In this context, in social work education, students should focus on issues related to social problems, inequalities and social change. Focusing on these issues can strengthen students' understanding of making an impact not only on an individual level, but also on a societal level.

Cranton (2006) conducted various studies on how the transformational learning process can occur, but stated that there is no teaching method that will guarantee the formation of transformational learning. The basic feature underlying transformational learning is the creation of an environment that will enable change. There are various suggestions on how to create an environment that will enable transformation and how such learning can be achieved. For example, creating a motivating event, encouraging students to make assumptions, providing critical self-reflection, being open to alternatives, actively involving students in a particular discourse, revising assumptions and taking actions as a result of these revised assumptions can provide transformational learning. However, providing students with practical experience opportunities such as mentoring and internships with experienced social workers in social work education can accelerate the transformational learning process. Mentoring gives students the opportunity to learn from real-world experiences.

Dirkx (2006) mentioned various strategies that can be used in a group environment for learning to occur. For example, active imagination activities and metaphors can be used for transformational learning. He also stated that deep and potentially creative approaches to emotion and behavior can be used as a tool to advance transformational learning experiences.

Romano (2018) listed the learning activities that can be used in transformational learning as follows:

- Critical thinking assignments: Term papers/essays, personal journals, assigned readings, and personal reflection.
- Discussions: Class and group projects, discussion of concerns.
- Students' self-evaluation: Self-evaluation in lessons and evaluation of personal learning.
- Discovering one's voice: Writing about concerns, classroom discussions, and personal journals.
- Support: Teacher, counselor, student, classmate, or other person.
- Discovering your own voice: Diaries.
- Various learning activities: Experimental workshops and laboratory experiences.

In order to support transformational learning, students should be given sample situations in which they will be in dilemmas during in-class activities, and they should be encouraged to interpret and try different situations and events through in-class creative drama activities. Additionally, students writing learning diaries at the end of the course will allow them to evaluate their in-class experiences. In social work education, students should be provided with opportunities to regularly question their own thoughts and values, develop a critical perspective, and think about how to integrate these values into social work practice. Methods that encourage reflexivity, such as writing tasks, group discussions, or journaling, should be used. By providing students with a reassuring environment, the teacher should prepare environmental conditions that will enable students to cooperate with various projects and presentations and to critically evaluate their experiences through mutual interactions. In social work education, students should be encouraged to actively participate in social change by offering courses and projects that focus on social justice issues. Transformational learning supports a student-centered learning process. Students should be given opportunities to direct their own learning journeys and active participation of students should be encouraged. Social work practices generally require interaction and communication. In social work education, methods such as role plays, case studies, group studies and simulations should be used to provide students with interactive learning experiences. These methods give students the opportunity to interact with each other and understand different perspectives.

The learning environment is critical for the integration of transformational learning theory into social work education. The learning environment should have features where the adult can feel good, where they can come together as a team with other participants, and where there will be no conflict, especially with the trainer. Since transformational learning is reconstructive in nature and requires the adult to reach new knowledge and skills by reinterpreting old experiences, it is inevitable that the learning environment is suitable for this structure.

Education and training materials have a great impact on making the learning process more effective and permanent (Okçabol, 2006). Educational materials are not just a textbook, ruler or globe, but also materials such as overhead projectors, films, posters, brochures and models that will be a source of learning and help reinterpret old experiences, with pictures, audio or as a guide to practice. Geray (2002) classifies such materials as visual, auditory and both visual and auditory materials. Visual materials such as charts, tables, maps, models, learning cards, slides and brochures are most preferred during the learning process due to their ease of use and economy. It is inevitable that such materials will be in the quantity and quality that an adult would need. Since the transformational learning process is often not a process in which the teacher conveys what he knows and the adult just listens, such materials must be compatible with the adult learning model. Because the adult learning environment can often be a laboratory, workshop or application class rather than a table and chairs.

Since adult learning often requires sharing or reinterpreting its own previous acquisitions through dialogue with other participants, the classroom seating arrangement should also be appropriate. It makes no sense for adults' learning environments to consist of tables and chairs lined up in a row. For this reason, the seating arrangement in the adult learning environment should generally be in an "O" or "U" shape, that is, in an arrangement that allows mutual communication, sharing and critical evaluation. Since adult learning is a learning model in which mutual dialogue and sharing of experiences occur frequently, it is important for participants to have a physical structure where they feel comfortable, can develop empathy, and tend to cooperate rather than compete. Güçlü (2000) lists the obstacles to transformational learning expected in the adult learning environment, stating that the adult and the facilitator/coach/trainer/guide must be compatible with each other, the environment must have sufficient capacity in terms of nutrition, shelter and learning, and it must not be excessively cold, hot, humid, dark or bright.

CONCLUSION

Transformational learning theory is an adult learning theory that focuses on the perspective transformations experienced by adults as a result of thinking critically, intensively and deeply about their own life experiences (McGuire, 2020). Transformational learning theory is very important for social work education. Because social work education focuses on developing students' understanding and practice towards transformation at the individual and social levels (Archer-Kuhn, et al., 2020). Transformational learning emphasizes the individual questioning, criticizing and changing his or her/his own thoughts and values. Using transformational learning in social work education can provide opportunities for students to understand their own value systems and biases. The reflection of this on social work practices is the realization of more effective social work interventions. Social work education enables students to focus on issues of social justice, contribute to systemic change, and develop skills to fight for social transformation. In addition, social work education offers students the opportunity to develop interactive skills, develop empathy and develop healthy relationships with clients. Transformational learning emphasizes that the individual's learning process should lead to a concrete transformation in practice. Social work education offers students the opportunity to apply the knowledge they learn to real-world situations and improve their skills in dealing with social problems. In fact, the relationship between social work education and transformational learning theory has a very complex structure. The use of transformational learning in social work education aims to make students more effective, sensitive and transformation-oriented social work professionals at the individual and social levels. Integrating transformational learning theory into social work education can contribute to social workers being more effective by encouraging students to think more critically, be sensitive to social justice and change issues, and continually improve themselves.

REFERENCES

Akçay, C. (2012). Dönüşümsel Öğrenme Modeli ve Yetişkin Eğitiminde Dönüşüm. *Milli Eğitim Dergisi*, 5-19.

Akpınar, B. (2010). Transformatif Öğrenme Kuramı: Dönüşerek ve Değişerek Öğrenme. *Anadolu Üniversitesi Sosyal Bilimler Dergisi*, 185-198.

Archer-Kuhn, B., Samson, P., Damianakis, T., & Barrett, B., MAtin, S., & Ahern, C. (2020). Transformative Learning in Field Education: Students Bridging the Theory/Practice Gap. *British Journal of Social Work*, 2419–2438.

Bartlett, F. (1958). *Thinking: An Experimental and Social Study*. Basic Books.

Bivens, F., Moriarty, K., & Taylor, P. (2009). Transformative Education and Its Potential for Changing The Lives of Children in Disempowering Contexts. *IDS Bulletin*, 40(1), 97–108. 10.1111/j.1759-5436.2009.00014.x

Bolger, B., Rowland, G., Reuning-Hummel, C., & Codner, S. (2011). Opportunities for and Barriers to Powerful and Transformative Learning Experiences in Online Learning Environments. *Educational Technology*, 36–41.

Brock, S. (2010). Measuring the importance of precursor steps to transformative learning. *Adult Education Quarterly*, 60(2), 122–142. 10.1177/0741713609333084

Çimen, O., & Yılmaz, M. (2014). Dönüşümsel Öğrenme Kuramına Dayalı Çevre Eğitiminin Biyoloji Öğretmen Adaylarının Çevre Sorunlarına Yönelik Algılarına Etkisi . *Bartın Üniversitesi Eğitim Fakültesi Dergisi*, 339-359.

Clark, M., & Wilson, A. (1991). Context and Rationality in Mezirow's Theory of Transformational Learning. *Adult Education Quarterly*, 41(2), 75–91. 10.1177/0001848191041002002

Collard, S., & Law, M. (1989). The Limits of Perspective Transformation: A Critique of Mezirow's Theory. *Adult Education Quarterly*, 39(2), 99–107. 10.1177/0001848189039002004

Courtney, B., Merriam, S., & Reeves, P. (1998). The Centrality of Meaningmaking in Transformational Learning: How HIV-Positive Adults Make Sense of Their Lives. *Adult Education Quarterly*, 48(2), 65–84. 10.1177/074171369804800203

Cranton, P. (1994). *Understanding and Promoting Transformative Learning: A Guide for Educators of Adults*. Jossey-Bass.

Cranton, P. (1996). *Professional Development as Transformative Learning: New Perspectives for Teachers of Adults*. Jossey-Bass.

Cranton, P. (2002). *Teaching for Transformation. New Directions for Adult and Continuing Education: No. 93. Contemporary Viewpoints on Teaching Adults Effectively*. Jossey-Bass.

Cranton, P. (2006). Fostering Authentic Relationships in The Transformative Classroom. *New Directions for Adult and Continuing Education*, 2006(109), 5–13. 10.1002/ace.203

Cunningham, P. (1992). From Freire to Feminism: The North American Experience with Critical Pedagogy. *Adult Education Quarterly*, 42(3), 180–191. 10.1177/074171369204200306

Dirkx, J. (2006). Engaging emotions in adult learning: A Jungian Perspective on Emotion And Transformative Learning. *New Directions for Adult and Continuing Education*, 2006(109), 15–26. 10.1002/ace.204

Erden, Ş., & Yıldız, A. (2020). Dönüştürücü Öğrenme Kuramı: Kavramlar, Kökenler ve Eleştiriler. *Yetişkin Eğitimi Dergisi*, 97-118.

Fullerton, J. (2010). *Transformative Learning in College Students: A Mixed Methods Study*. University of Nebrask.

Geray, C. (2002). *Halk Eğitimi*. İmaj Yayınevi.

Gravett, S. (2004). Action Research and Transformative Learning in Teaching Development. *Educational Action Research*, 12(2), 259–272. 10.1080/09650790400200248

Güçlü, N. (2000). Öğretmen davranışları. *Millî Eğitim Dergisi*, 21-23.

Hamlin, M. (2015). *Technology in Transformative Learning Environments*. IGI Global. 10.4018/978-1-4666-8571-0.ch004

Hoggan, C., Malkki, K., & Finnegan, F. (2017). Developing the Theory of Perspective Transformation: Continuity, Intersubjectivity, and Emancipatory Praxis. *Adult Education Quarterly*, 67(1), 48–64. 10.1177/0741713616674076

Illeris, K. (2004). Transformative Learning in the Perspective of a Comprehensive Learning Theory. *Journal of Transformative Education*, 2(2), 79–89. 10.1177/1541344603262315

Johnson Bailey, J., & Alfred, M. (2006). Transformational Teaching and the Practices of Black Women Educators. *New Directions for Adult and Continuing Education*, 2006(109), 49–58. 10.1002/ace.207

Jonassen, D., Howland, J., Moore, J., & Marra, R. (2003). *Learning to Solve Problems With Technology*. Merrill Prentice.

King, K. (2011). Teaching in An Age of Transformation: Understanding Unique Instructional Technology Choices Which Transformative Learning Affords. *Educational Technology*, 4–10.

Koç Akran, S., & Epçaçan, E. (2018). Dönüşümsel Öğrenme Modelinin 6. Sınıf Fen Bilimleri Dersinde Öğrencilerin Eleştirel Düşünme Eğilimlerine ve Bilişötesi Farkındalıklarına Etkisi. *Necatibey Eğitim Fakültesi Elektronik Fen ve Matematik Eğitimi Dergisi*, 538-571.

Kovan, J., & Dirkx, J. (2003). Being Called Awake: The Role of Transformative Learning in the Lives of Environmental Activists. *Adult Education Quarterly*, 53(2), 99–118. 10.1177/0741713602238906

McCadden, T. (2020). Book Review: Transformational Learning in Community Colleges: Charting a Course for Academic Success by Hoggan, C. D., & Browning, B. *Adult Learning*, 136–137.

McGuire, D. (2020). *Adult Learning Theories*. SAGE Encyclopedia of Higher Education.

McWhinney, W., & Markos, L. (2003). Transformative Education Across The Threshold. *Journal of Transformative Education*, 1(1), 16–37. 10.1177/1541344603252098

Meyers, S. (2008). Using Transformative Pedagogy When Teaching Online. *College Teaching*, 56(4), 219–224. 10.3200/CTCH.56.4.219-224

Mezirow, J. (1985). A critical theory of self-directed learning. *New directions for continuing education*, 17-30.

Mezirow, J. (1991). *Transformative Dimensions of Adult Learning*. Jossey-Bass.

Mezirow, J. (1994). Understanding transformation theory. *Adult Education Quarterly*, 44(4), 222–232. 10.1177/074171369404400403

Mezirow, J. (1996). *Faced Visions and Fresh Commitments: Adult Education's Social Goals*. National Louis University.

Mezirow, J. (1997). *Transformative learning: Theory to Practice*. P. Cranton içinde, *Transformative Learning in Action: Insights from Practice*. Jossey-Bass.

Mezirow, J. (2000). *Learning tothinklike an adult: transformation theory: core concepts*. J. Mezirow, & Associates içinde, *Learning as transformation: Critical perspectives on a theory in progress*. Jossey-Bass.

Mezirow, J. (2003). Transformative Learning as Discourse. *Journal of Transformative Education*, 1(1), 58–63. 10.1177/1541344603252172

Mezirow, J., & Marsick, V. (1978). *Education for Perspective Transformation: Women's Re-entry Programs in Community Collages*. Columbia University.

Mezirow, J., & Taylor, E. (2009). *Transformative Learning in Practice: Insights from Community, Workplace, and Higher Education*. Jossey-Bass.

Newman, M. (1994). Response to Understanding Transformation Theory. *Adult Education Quarterly*, 44(4), 236–242. 10.1177/074171369404400405

Okçabol, R. (2006). *Halk eğitimi (Yetişkin eğitimi)*. Ütopya Yayınevi.

Pietrykowski, B. (1998). Modern and Postmodern Tensions in Adult Education Theory: A Response to Jack Mezirow. *Adult Education Quarterly*, 49(1), 67–70. 10.1177/074171369804900108

Reisinger, Y. (2013). Transformation and Transformational Learning Theory. *Transformational tourism: Tourist perspectives*, 17-26.

Romano, A. (2018). Transformative Learning: A Review of the Assessment Tools. *Journal of Transformative Learning*, 53-70.

Şahin, İ. (2023). *Dönüşümsel Öğrenme ve Pozitif Psikoloji Kuramı Temelinde Spritüel Turizm Deneyimine Yönelik Ölçek Geliştirme ve Yapısal Modelleme Çalışması*. Akdeniz Üniversitesi Sosyal Bilimler Enstitüsü.

Şahin, M., Erisen, Y., & Çeliköz, N. (2016). The Transformational Learning of Three Adult Academicians. *Online Submission*, 299-307.

Sands, D., & Tennant, M. (2010). Transformative Learning in the Context of Suicide Bereavement. *Adult Education Quarterly*, 60(2), 99–121. 10.1177/0741713609349932

Şen, E., & Şahin, H. (2017). Dönüşümsel Öğrenme Kuramı: Baskın Paradigmayı Yıkmak. *Tıp Eğitimi Dünyası*, 39-48.

Shishov, S., Popey-Ool, S., Abylkasymova, A., Kalnei, V., & Ryakhimova, E. (2022). Transformational learning of teachers. *Revista on line de Política e Gestão Educacional*, 1-10.

Stuckey, H., Taylor, E., & Cranton, P. (2013). Developing A Survey of Transformative Learning Outcomes and Processes Based on Theoretical Principles. *Journal of Transformative Education*, 11(4), 211–228. 10.1177/1541344614540335

Taylor, E. (1998). *The theory and practice of transformative learning: A critical review. Information Series 374*. ERIC Clearinghouse on Adult, Career, and Vocational Education.

Taylor, E. (2008). Transformative Learning Theory. *New Directions for Adult and Continuing Education*, 2008(119), 5–15. 10.1002/ace.301

Tennant, M. (1993). Perspective Transformation and Adult Development. *Adult Education Quarterly*, 44(1), 34–42. 10.1177/0741713693044001003

Thomas, I. (2009). Critical Thinking, Transformative Learning, Sustainable Education, And Problem-Based Learning in Universities. *Journal of Transformative Education*, 7(3), 245–264. 10.1177/1541344610385753

Tusting, K., & Barton, D. (2011). *Öğrenme Kuramları ve Yetişkin Öğrenme Modelleri Üzerine Kısa Bir İnceleme*. Dipnot Yayınları.

ADDITIONAL READING

Cranton, P. (2002). Teaching for Transformation. *New Directions for Adult and Continuing Education*, 93(93), 63–72. 10.1002/ace.50

Mezirow, J. (1991). *Transformative Dimensions of Adult Learning*. Jossey-Bass.

Taylor, E. W. (2008). Transformative Learning Theory. *New Directions for Adult and Continuing Education*, 119(119), 5–15. 10.1002/ace.301

KEY TERMS AND DEFINITIONS

Accepting Change: Recognizing and embracing the transformational process, often shared with others undergoing similar experiences.

Creating a Dilemma: The initial stage in transformational learning where an individual encounters an experience that challenges their existing meaning structures.

Critical Discourse: Engaging in reflective conversation to verify and validate understanding and perspectives, central to transformational learning.

Critical Reflection: The conscious and explicit re-evaluation of one's beliefs, often leading to transformative change.

Critical Self-Reflection: The process of questioning one's own assumptions and developing a discourse about one's thoughts and life, essential for personal

Frames of Reference: Structures comprising expectations, perceptions, and emotions that shape and limit one's experiences and understanding.

Meaning Perspective: The way individuals re-encounter and reinterpret their past experiences, influenced by cultural and psychological assumptions.

Meaning Schema: A set of psychological assumptions or reference frames that form the basis of an individual's worldview.

Planning for Action: Developing a consistent and effective action plan to adopt new perspectives and implement changes.

Questioning Negative Emotions: A stage where individuals evaluate their old perspectives in light of the negative emotions triggered by a dilemma.

Transformational Learning: A process where individuals critically examine their existing beliefs, assumptions, and perspectives, leading to a profound change in their worldview and behavior.

Chapter 3
Transformational Teaching:
Learning That Extends Beyond the Walls of the Classroom

Kimberly Mudd-Fegett
https://orcid.org/0000-0001-9136-9206
Campbellsville University, USA

ABSTRACT

Transformational teachers join students in a life-long learning process that involves commitment, passion, transparency, and a shared belief that students desire to learn to improve themselves. Transformational leaders motivate their followers by inspiring them to perform at their highest level. Likewise, transformational educators motivate their students to excel academically and always to be attuned to opportunities for personal growth. When educators take students outside the classroom walls, they present students with learning opportunities that far exceed what the words on the pages of a book can teach. One can lecture on the Coliseum's cobblestone streets or Dachau's gas chambers. However, it is vastly different to travel to Munich and stand before the furnaces of Dachau or to walk on the streets of Rome where Caesar once walked. When unique learning opportunities transform students, they become excited about learning. They develop newfound motivation, self-efficacy, and a larger vision of their education and goals.

DOI: 10.4018/979-8-3693-2407-3.ch003

Copyright © 2024, IGI Global. Copying or distributing in print or electronic forms without written permission of IGI Global is prohibited.

THROUGH THE LENS OF TRANSFORMATION

Transformational teachers join students in a life-long learning process that involves commitment, passion, transparency, and a shared belief that students desire to learn to improve themselves. Transformational leaders motivate their followers by inspiring them to perform at their highest level. Likewise, transformational educators motivate their students to excel academically and always to be attuned to opportunities for personal growth (Yuner, 2020). When educators take students outside the classroom walls, they present students with learning opportunities that far exceed what the words on the pages of a book can teach. One can lecture on the Coliseum's cobblestone streets or Dachau's gas chambers. However, it is vastly different to travel to Munich and stand before the furnaces of Dachau or to walk on the streets of Rome where Caesar once walked. Experiential learning events transform the lives of students and educators alike. These unique opportunities give students a rich and meaningful view of the natural world outside of course content (Kolb & Kolb, 2017). When unique learning opportunities transform students, they become excited about learning. They develop newfound motivation, self-efficacy, and a larger vision of their education and goals (Yuner, 2020). Good educators strive to empower, inspire, and encourage students to reach their potential. Service-learning trips allow students to apply practice skills in real-life environments. It gives them the unique opportunity to build skills while serving others in the world around them. Transformational teaching includes inquiry-learning, project-based, and service learning, in which the learning is flexible, and the professor and learners are highly invested in the learning process (Fuglei,2021).

Since birth, individuals desire to understand the world around them through questioning and exploration. This desire to better understand their environment, gain knowledge, explore, and engage with materials formally in a classroom setting is known as inquiry-based learning (Wheatley, 2018). Furthermore, this learning approach allows students to work with peers, collaborate, learn communication skills, construct new knowledge, and gain investment in their learning process. Traditional teaching skills involve students sitting through long lectures without being involved or allowing them to reach their conclusions. As students become engaged in learning and develop the ability to think critically, they ultimately obtain skills they will need as they enter professional practice. This approach places questions at the center of the curriculum, placing as much value on research skills as on understanding the content (Parker, 2007). When educators commit to an inquiry-based approach, they provide their students with a rich experience to provoke critical thinking, curiosity, discovery, and investigation. Additionally, students can have ownership over their learning to draw connections between their academic content and their lives, which is particularly important for diverse learners.

One further learning approach in transformational is project-based learning. This collaborative inquiry-based teaching method intends to help students address complex problems by applying an integrated, constructed knowledge (Markula & Aksela, 2022). Furthermore, project-based learning refers to problem-oriented and student-centered learning, which occurs around projects that students carry out in group settings. Students must practice this in school as this is an essential skill in the work environment. Students can develop and practice problem-solving, decision-making, and negotiation skills. These skills are as necessary in the classroom as in everyday life. The learning environment of project-based learning builds trusting relationships where professional learning opportunities can be transformed to create reflective, empowered students (De Vivo, 2022).

Rather than being content-focused, this approach involves students in the learning process that includes critical thinking, goal-setting, and deep reflection. Through this process, students are far more likely to retain content as it becomes a lived experience. Active learners are excited to come to class to engage in learning and become world-changers. Educators use this approach to generate excitement in the learning process, thus maintaining students' focus, encouraging student involvement, and upholding university retention. However, transformational teaching is far more than a shared body of knowledge. It creates a dynamic relationship between teacher and student, promoting personal growth and development. A shared vision is built from within and outside the classroom walls, and through reflection, students can more readily articulate learning (Slavich & Zimbardo, 2012). The goal of teaching is to inspire and guide students. Transformational teaching aids students in retaining knowledge, gaining a sense of ownership of the knowledge, and, most importantly, helping to create lifelong learners.

One of the most crucial points in the transformational learning process is experimental learning, in which the teacher and student are both actively involved in the learning process. Experimental learning is hands-on learning rather than learning through a book or secondary research. Experiential learning can include simulations, interviews, expert panels, field trips, or acts of service. These learning acts engage the student, making the learning experience more relevant and immersed in the world around them (White & Nitkin, 2014). Furthermore, these unique experiences allow students to engage in significant personal insights, improve awareness, evaluate people's experiences, reflect, and deeply evaluate the world around them (Kolb & Kolb, 2017). As this ongoing act of reflection occurs, the true magic of experimental learning for the educator is the relationship that develops with the learner during the educational experience. All parties benefit from information during the learning experience, gaining new insight and challenging their viewpoint even if the destination, service, or experience has been previously experienced.

In this chapter, the author will highlight the value of transformational teaching, explicitly focusing on integrating practice in the classroom. This approach concentrates on empowering and motivating students to be their best version as they engage in the learning process. This chapter will discuss the value of the unique opportunities provided through practice experiences, service opportunities, and exceptional learning tools. This author will offer a unique transformational teaching guide that can be used in the classroom to engage students in learning partnerships. This guide outlines five teaching components that engage, empower, and transform students, hoping they leave the classroom a better version of themselves.

TRANSFORMATIONAL THEORY

The term "transformational teaching" was first introduced to describe the belief that educators could promote meaningful changes in the lives of their students if they presented their courses as life-changing opportunities (Slavich, 2005). Looking back on education over the last fifty years, we have seen an evolution in education. This evolution includes developing and appreciating student-centered, experimental, and collaborative learning in which unique partnerships between the educator and learner are formed (Slavich & Zimbardo, 2012). In this dynamic, the educator becomes an intellectual coach guiding students and facilitating key concepts. Through this relationship, students become challenged, encouraged, and transcend beyond the classroom walls. Far more than the lessons of the course room, transformational teaching is the ability for students to engage in self-discovery, challenging and changing their fundamental beliefs. Thus, educators' vast role in transforming students' thoughts, beliefs, and attitudes is questioned.

To better understand transformational theory, one must comprehend its theoretical basis. They begin with the social cognitive theory, which explores how learning occurs, stating that students are agents holding intentional influence over their learning and actions. Furthermore, this learning experience is significantly impacted by one's belief in one's capabilities and others' faith in that individual, including the educator, parents, caregivers, and peers. To succeed, educators must believe in success while encouraging, challenging, and supporting their students (Bandura, 2012). The second theory is the transformative learning theory, which states that students increase their understanding of the world by "revising their frame reference ."Initially, this frame is shaped by experience and culture. Their frame can be molded or reshaped over time through learning, challenges, new habits, and a new point of view. Through this theory, the educator is the "facilitator" during this process, providing the opportunities and experiences for this growth. The third and final theory is the intentional change theory, in which a change in an individual's feelings or behavior is involved through five steps. First, the individual must develop their ideal self, whom they desire to be. Second, they must assess their "real self," identifying their strengths and weaknesses. Third, individuals must develop a tailored learning plan to bridge the gap between their ideal and "real self ."The fourth and final step is to create and maintain close relationships with individuals who will support their growth (Boyatzis, 2006).

As outlined in the above theories, trust between the educator and students is one of the foundations of the transformational classroom for growth. There must be a level of respect in which students are willing to "risk what they do not know ."Keen & Woods (2016) highlight that using humor in the classroom is critical to building this trusting relationship. Engaging in meaningful dialogue where their ideas and experiences are explored is paramount in their transformational growth. Being authentic as an educator builds the context for critical reflection and self-reflection from students. Students should view their educators as trusted partners in their learning experience, one that expands far beyond the classroom walls. This meaningful, authentic engagement is outlined visually in the figure below (Lincoln Center, 2022, Fig. 1). This outline illustrates the genuine connection between educator and student through curiosity, stimulation, and academic performance.

Figure 1. TLC transformational education

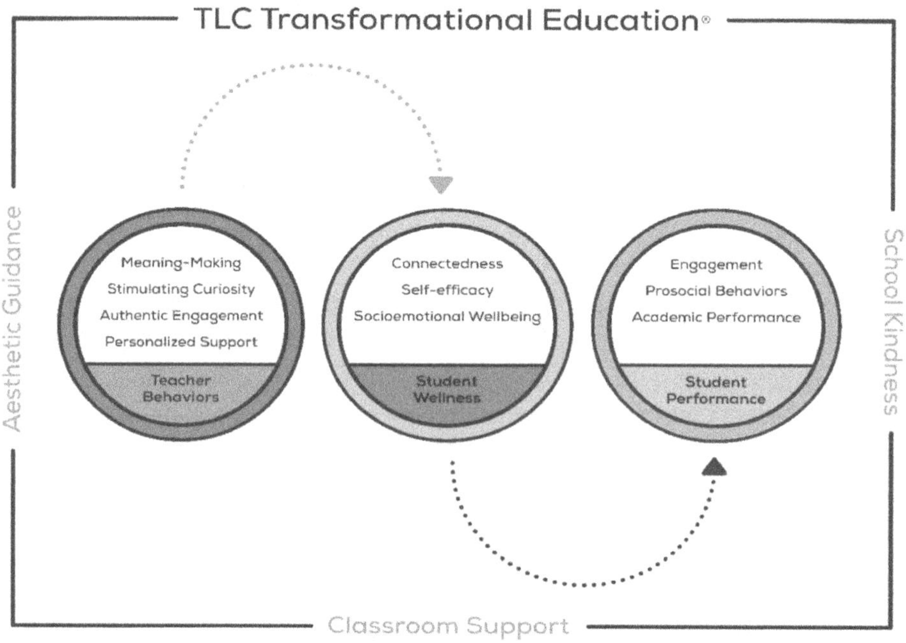

(Lincoln Center, 2022)

Transformational Teaching

FROM THE VOICES OF STUDENTS

The most impactful aspect of transformational teaching is its impact on the students. The opportunity to allow students to experience, service, and transform is life-altering. Below are the words of students who have traveled, served, and shared this transformation through experimental learning trips:

- "This week has been one of my social work career's most eye-opening and rewarding weeks. I took a trip with Campbellsville School of Social Work to the Texas/Mexico trip border to work with children and families who have immigrated to the US. We participated in children's ministry at a mission church, volunteered at McAllen Catholic Charities Humanitarian Respite Center Awareness, painted a house with Buckner Rio Grande Valley, and assembled senior food boxes for Food Bank RGV INC. I have experienced every emotion with tears of both sorrow and gladness. I have seen what is real and had deep conversations on immigration and humanitarian relief. Above all else, I have a deeper understanding of what my students and families may have gone through when they immigrated to the US for a better and safer life. Please pray for the people of Penitas, Texas, the people of the Rio Grande Valley, and all those who are crossing the border to seek safety and refuge in the US."
- "The most impactful trip for me was the service/mission trip to Houston, Texas. We went to help clean up from the hurricane, and it stood out to me because I made so many connections and relationships with my team and other individuals we came in contact with."
- "The social work department took us to Texas to do flood relief. This was my first time working with people who had experienced a disaster such as this one, and it was truly eye-opening. I have been on many trips with CU, and this was by far the best. I loved this trip because I got to know the people on the trip so much better and formed more relationships with them. I also learned more about my passion for serving others."
- "The most impactful trip for me was to the Navajo reservation in New Mexico. We engaged in building projects and conducted Bible studies for the children. This trip showed me a culture that I was unfamiliar with and allowed me to bond with peers amazingly."

Responses from students when transformational learning is used directly in the classroom through lectures, activities, case scenarios, and service:

- "The instructor challenged my thinking and improved my desire to learn."

- "The instructor was interested in the progress of the students."
- "Has helped me grow as a person. I do not want to be a social worker, as these courses were not part of my major. However, she made me feel competent in applying for a job."
- "Favorite so far- so nice and helpful."
- "Was a professor who assisted me during a time when I experienced many hardships with so much happening with my family. When I first reached out, I was unsure how to approach her to ask for assistance because I could not retain the information I was reading. However, she provided as much support as she could, being in another state. I am grateful to have had the experience and information shared within this course to help me in the future."

In the transformational process, the educator understands and appreciates that their purpose is far greater than simply delivering information. Instead, the goal is to assist the student in critical thinking, goal setting, and transformation that allows the student to arrive at a place of growth. As seen through the above testimonies, this can occur in direct service of experimental learning trips or the classroom walls as the instructor takes students on the adventure of expanding their knowledge. The possibilities of transformation are endless when you have a professor willing to join their students in the partnership of growth, experience, and engagement.

THEMES FROM STUDENTS' VOICES

The impact is apparent when students are taught through the lens of transformation. A unique learning partnership is developed in which they are heard, encouraged, and challenged to think critically and grow. Students will likely not remember the question to every homework assignment you gave, but they will reflect how you made them feel. They will place the educator who inspired them to achieve their goals and encouraged them to expand their knowledge and expectations of themselves. They will remember the educators who took learning beyond PowerPoints and lectures to unique opportunities that brought them beyond their comfort levels and questioned their experiences. The themes in the above testimonies are that my professor was interested in me as a person, my professor challenged me, and this experience changed me. The transformational process engages educators and students in a learning experience. Whether walking the streets of Paris together, serving in a local food pantry side by side, or processing role play in the classroom, when, as an educator, you are invested in the learning and development of your students, there are no limits to the learning experiences you can create.

EXAMPLES OF TRANSFORMATIONAL LEARNING

- **Role-playing: Human Behavior, Practice, Human Diversity, Child Abuse & Introduction to Social Work**—Engage students in a case scenario where they improve a practice scenario and then debrief the experience. Examples of this activity include having students role-play clinical situations in which they engage in practice situations with children, adolescents, families, and in group settings. Students are asked to display practice skills both as client and practitioner.

INTERVIEWING, SKILL BUILDING, QUESTIONING

- **Process Questions**: Human Behavior, Practice, Human Diversity, Child Abuse & Introduction to Social Work- Assist students in finding the source of an assumption or belief and processing their response.

What were the gender roles in your family of origin? How is this similar to others?

- **Content Questions:** Human Behavior, Practice, Human Diversity, Child Abuse & Introduction to Social Work- Raise students' awareness of an assumption or belief and process their response.

Why Do You Believe Individuals Abuse or Neglect Their Children?

- **Journaling:** Human Behavior, Human Diversity, Child Abuse—Ask students to write their feelings/thoughts about a specific subject matter and then process them. Examples of this activity include having students provide dialogue on their reaction to course material, practice situations, and journal situations they encounter outside of the classroom to discuss with their peers.

SELF-CARE, ADOLESCENT REFLECTION, SELF-REFLECTION QUESTIONNAIRE

- **Guest Lecturers:** Human Behavior, Practice, Human Diversity, Child Abuse & Introduction to Social Work- Invite professionals to speak to the class on a specific topic related to the course material.

Police Officer (K-9 Unit), School Social Worker, Clinical Social Worker

- **Peer Teaching:** Human Behavior, Practice, Human Diversity, Child Abuse & Introduction to Social Work- Allow students to lead the lecture using a method of their choice. Examples of this activity include having students complete a timeline, PowerPoint, or Poster Board of the required reading material for the class lecture.

Timeline, PowerPoints, Group Activities, Advocacy

- **Service-Learning Activities:** Human Behavior, Practice, Human Diversity & Introduction to Social Work- Students engage in service-learning opportunities in group and individual settings. Examples of this activity include having students select a social justice activity and present the stages of advocacy to their peers.

Serve Meal at Food Bank, Hurricane Clean Up (Texas)

- **Experimental Learning:** State, national, and global trips with students to engage in active learning outside of the classroom. Examples of this activity would include preparing and serving food to individuals at a local food pantry.

15-Day Trip to Europe With Students (Five Countries)

Each of these examples is an opportunity to engage the student in learning opportunities beyond the traditional lecture that encourages them to think critically, engage, analyze, and broaden their learning environment. Through these learning

Transformational Teaching

opportunities, you, as the educator, transform their learning experience, challenging them to seek more profound understanding.

Value of Transformational Leadership

Leadership is vital to the organization, particularly for the transformational teacher. It is the cornerstone of its operation and the main driver of change (Deng, Gulseren, Isola, Grocutt, & Turner, 2023). Transformational leadership highlights the performance and well-being of employees while offering support, encouragement, empowerment, and promoting self-growth. A deep trust is developed between the transformational leader and follower that benefits both the follower and the organization, highlighting growth, creativity, and outcomes. When transformative leaders are influential in their role, their followers are deeply committed to the mission, organization, and leader, as they are most often deeply invested in their work. Due to the strong emotional connection between leader and follower, as well as the passion felt for the mission of the organization, lower rates of burnout and dissatisfaction within their position. The value and support of transformational leadership will be explored further in-depth later in this textbook.

Value of Transformational Teaching

The students' statements above show the value of impact, empowerment, empathy, genuineness, and honesty. Within the walls of the transformational classroom, students are heard, understood, meaningful, and, most importantly, valued. They enter as students and leave as members of a transformed community where growth, learning, and elevation occur. Figure three (below), labeled *Transformational Teaching in Mudd-Fegett Classroom,* outlines the critical components of transformational teaching. The left side of the model is the components the professor brings to the classroom, demonstrating to students the teaching and academic excellence. The right side of the model is the components students take from the transformational teaching approach.

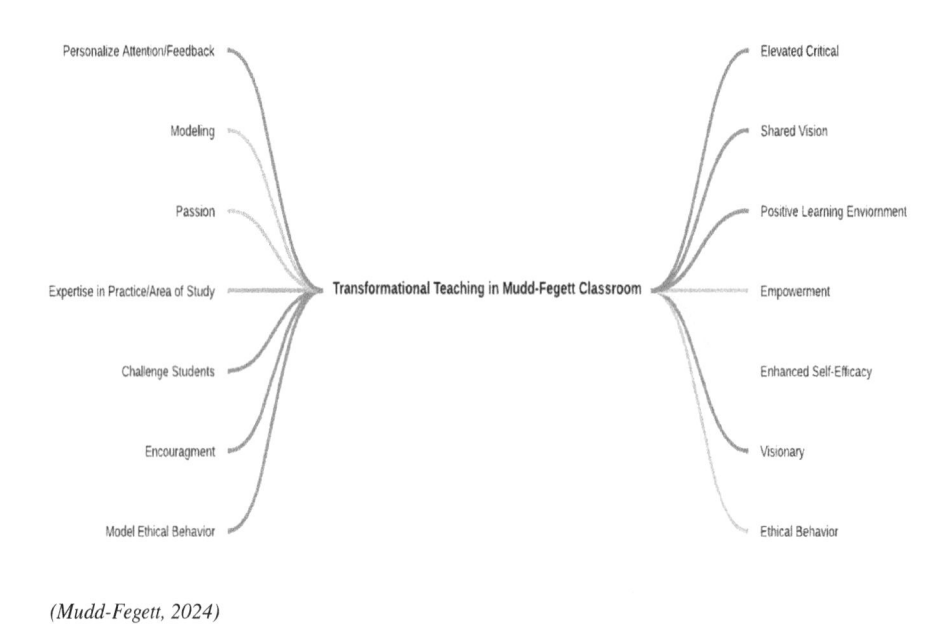

Figure 2. Transformation teaching in Mudd-Fegett classroom

```
Personalize Attention/Feedback ─┐                        ┌─ Elevated Critical
                                │                        │
            Modeling ───────────┤                        ├─ Shared Vision
                                │                        │
             Passion ───────────┤                        ├─ Positive Learning Enviornment
                                │                        │
Expertise in Practice/Area of Study ──── Transformational Teaching in Mudd-Fegett Classroom ──── Empowerment
                                │                        │
    Challenge Students ─────────┤                        ├─ Enhanced Self-Efficacy
                                │                        │
         Encouragment ──────────┤                        ├─ Visionary
                                │                        │
  Model Ethical Behavior ───────┘                        └─ Ethical Behavior
```

(Mudd-Fegett, 2024)

Through qualitative research methods, students were engaged in telling their narratives, allowing the impact of transformational teaching to be told through their experience. Allowing students to share their lived experiences, shared qualities, and beliefs regarding the classroom setting is imperative to understanding the impact it holds (Tomaszewski et al., 2020). Promoting authenticity and allowing others to express themselves freely are critical components of transformational learning. Encouraging growth, self-expression, and the ability to learn in an environment that grows to meet the student rather than making the student fit the environment is central to supporting and valuing each individual (Baumgardner, 2019). Thus, allowing students to voice the impact of this teaching style was crucial in this project as it spoke to the meaningfulness of student relationships and the passion felt for student success.

Challenges of Transformational Teaching

Transformational teaching comes with its challenges. First and foremost, for students that struggle in a "community-led" or group setting environment. The transformational classroom often fosters critical thinking and group assignments and encourages student involvement. Students who learn best in "content-based courses" may have anxiety or struggle to adjust to the concept of the transformed classroom (Baumgartner, 2019). Once in practice, students must adapt to various settings, including the ability to change to individual and group-based projects. Therefore, they must have a skill base to excel and apply critical thinking skills in various applications. Thus, encouragement must be used to empower these students to view this new learning opportunity as a way to build their confidence to explore beyond their traditional experiences.

Additional criticism of transformational teaching includes the need for more priority on critical thinking skills. The ability to incorporate concrete nonfiction perspective activities (autobiographies, essays, etc.) should be incorporated to address issues with applicability and over-generalization that many feel occur in the transformational classroom (Southworth, 2022). Incorporating procedural problems can assist students with knowledge transfer as they move into professional settings, as they will recognize the complexity of applying real-life problem-solving skills. The ability to prepare students with deep-rooted skill bases in open-mindedness, critical thinking, and real-life application best prepares them for the professional setting they will face.

In addition to the classroom setting, additional challenges to transformational teaching are the administration's support of experimental and service-based learning projects. Implementing such projects takes significant planning, funding, and, most importantly, the support of leadership and administration. These individuals must appreciate the value and significance of these learning experiences in students' lives. Taking students outside the classroom walls to service and experience culture in their community, nation, and abroad is life-changing.

Unique Perceptive

Educators with a unique perspective of practice bring invaluable skills to their classrooms. Using the knowledge from their practice, they can engage students in each of the suggested activities above, such as role-play, skill-building, content questioning, service learning, and guest lecturers, with a current lens of practice. In addition, their ability to challenge students with case scenarios and practice examples keeps students engaged and intrigued with a pulse on the recent trends of today's practice culture. Social work is an ever-evolving revolution that requires constant involvement, accuracy, and knowledge. Rokach (2016) highlights educators' meaningful and influential interaction with students, impacting their desire to study to excel both inside and outside the classroom. Furthermore, self-disclosure in the school of professional practice, personal experiences, and personal views increases this intimate relationship. The ability to fully engage students in the classroom affects them psychologically while decreasing anxiety and stress, increasing curiosity, and improving self-esteem.

When students are intrigued, engaged, and passionate about the subject matter they are presented, their attendance and performance will reflect their efforts—educators who are passionate about their profession and bring this to their classroom. In recent studies, students highlight the importance of educators who are life-long learners who are willing to engage in active learning in the classroom alongside their students. Likewise, educators who are involved, humorous, and motivated to challenge their students (Nushi, Momeni, & Roshanbin, 2022). This partnership will soon be transformed into a unique learning opportunity between educators and students.

White & Nitkin (2014) demonstrate the underpinnings of transformational teaching in the chart below. Using this illustration, it is apparent through this learning perspective that the educator needs to promote discovery, learning, critical thinking, and shared vision in the course. Likewise, the educator's responsibility should be noted to provide students with personalized feedback, encouragement, challenge, and reflection. It is clear that transformational teaching is an ongoing process that is built on an educational partnership. This partnership takes empathy, honesty, trust, and, most importantly, the shared goal of success.

Table 1. Transformation teaching theoretical underpinnings

Transformational Teaching Theoretical Underpinnings
Promote individual Challenge habits of mind Realize ideal self and Transcend self and collective self-efficacy and Points of view vision of future interest to achieve shared goals
Basic Principles
Facilitate Acquisition and Enhance strategies and skills Promote positive learning Mastery of Key course concepts for learning and discovery related attitudes, values, and beliefs
Core Methods
Establish Provide Challenge Personalize Create Promote shared vision modeling and and encourage attention and experiential prelections and or course mastery students feedback lessons reflection experiences

(White & Nikin, 2014, Fig. 2)

Called to Serve

One of the underlying themes in transformational theory is the genuine relationship that must be formed between the educator and their students. In higher Christian education, you are not just employed to teach; you are called to serve. Likewise, social workers are called to aid in healing the weak, feeding the poor, and loving the wounded. How educators use their practice experience can encourage, motivate, and ultimately empower students to change the world around them. The practice experience of educators has a tremendous ability to take students beyond the classroom walls. Christian servant professors can collaborate using transformational teaching and practice experience, including Christian compassion, to empower individuals, families, and communities. Social work was built on Christian servants' successes and failures as a grassroots profession. Professional programs must prepare students with knowledge and confidence to enter their chosen profession. When professors share their professional wisdom, knowledge, and experience, they can extend students' learning experience beyond the classroom walls (Wrenn & Wrenn, 2009). When Christian servant leaders (professors) share their experiences, they can demonstrate Christian compassion in practice scenarios that extend beyond the textbook. Matthew 9:36 states, "When he saw the crowds, he had compassion for them, because they were harassed and helpless, like sheep without a shepherd" (New International Version, 2023). In the classroom, as students witness the professor's Christian compassion for serving others, the student's desire to solve problems and alleviate the pain of others is heightened (Berkowicz & Meyers, 2015). Students gain awareness from the professor's practice and experience that will aid their development as social workers. Most importantly, they can see the passion professors have for serving others.

Hutchinson (2016) outlines that teaching is a highly challenging yet rewarding profession; professors see the profession's future in the classroom. As educators, students must learn theoretical knowledge from the school. However, it is imperative that through instruction and integration of practice, they also gain the ability to apply theories to practice. When professors integrate theory and their practice experience into the course curriculum, students can understand the curriculum more profoundly and meaningfully (Wrenn & Wrenn, 2009). Social work practice is a moving target that has and should continue to prove, disprove, and ensure professional activities occur (Farley et al., 2009). Some essential skills professors teach students include overcoming adversity, learning from challenges, and critically and professionally applying knowledge. These skills can be most adequately modeled in the classroom through practice experience. Self-awareness is a fundamental skill in the social work profession, and the ability to teach this in school is imperative to the success of students (Feize, 2018). When professors humble themselves to acknowledge successes and failures, future leaders of our profession are empowered. Proverbs 11:12 states, "When pride comes, then comes disgrace, but with humility comes wisdom" (New International Version, 2023). Likewise, engaging in self-reflectiveness is a practice competence that aids in professional communication, maintaining professional boundaries, and preventing burnout (Urdang, 2018). Halbert (1923), when defining the social work profession, states that part of civilization is to educate people on how to perform in complex enterprises when families, schools, and churches fail to accomplish this. This remains true; social workers inform students on how to comfort the hurt, heal the wounded, and love those we are entrusted to protect.

When the transformational process occurs, and students feel called to serve alongside their educators, their passion is evident. Students provided the following statements after being asked, "What does being called to serve mean to you?"

- "I know what it feels like to be abused. I feel it is important for kids to have someone to connect with. It is easier to talk to those who went through the same thing. I was called for this because I wanted to help kids get out of my situation."
- "I think everyone is called to serve and help others, but not everyone answers to the phone. It has a lot to do with morals and how you were raised, I feel. It is easier for some to help others than it is for some people."
- "I feel called to serve in social work because I have the heart for it. I care deeply about the well-being of others, but I can also keep it professional. I have always been empathic and trustworthy and always loved to help people as much as possible."
- "I feel called to serve because I know what is it like to be a scared, defenseless little kid that feels like they do not have a safe place and just wants someone to care about them. I think it is my calling to help kids by using my experience."
- Being called to serve comes with a passion for helping others. I believe God is where our passion comes from and ultimately, he is the reason we serve. Being called to serve could be serving children, adults, or seniors but we need to have the passion for serving them."

Mudd-Fegett Model of Transformational Teaching

Figure 3. Mudd-Fegett model of transformational teaching

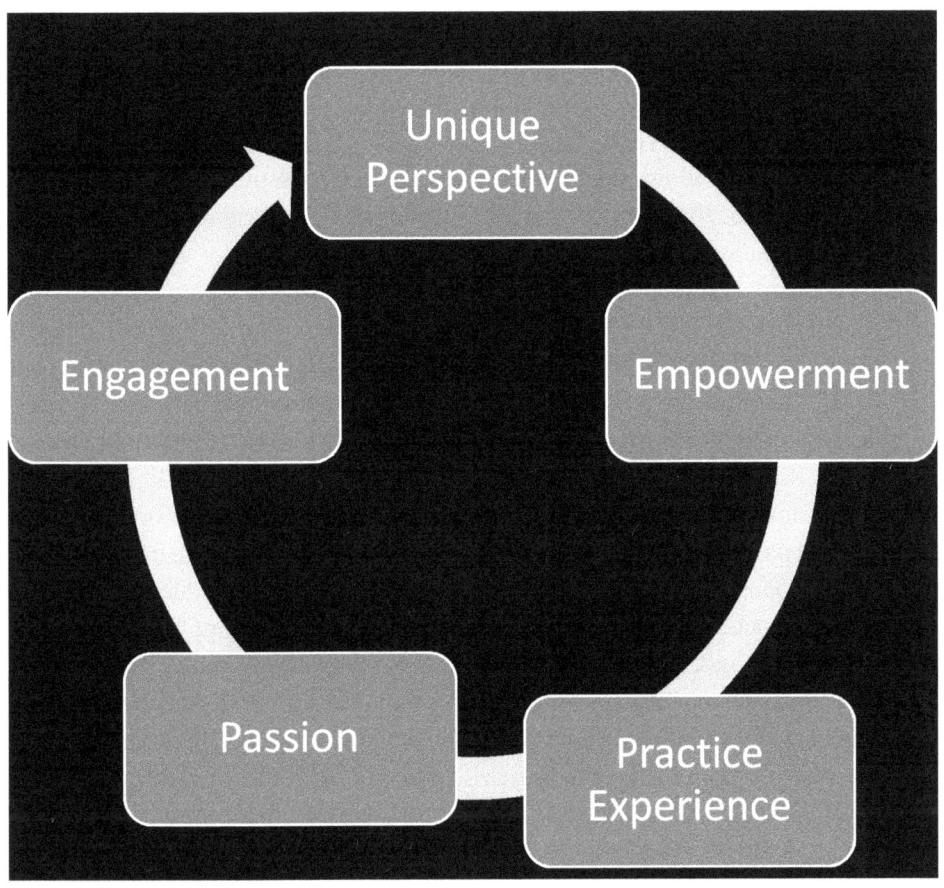

(Mudd-Fegett, 2024)

The Mudd-Fegett Model of Transformational Teaching outlines five key components essential to students' classroom experience. Each component adds richness and value to their learning, transforming the learning environment and creating a partnership between educator and student. The first component is each student's unique perspective to the classroom. Faculty and student interaction are paramount to retention and graduation rates amongst universities nationwide. The ability of students to have a genuine, caring relationship with their educator directly impacts their academic performance and their ability to thrive, particularly during times of crisis (Guzzardo et al., 2021). Supported and prepared academically, students will develop their capabilities regardless of their initial circumstances. Educator relationships are essential, and student's perspectives of their capabilities, value, and intellect are paramount. The second component is empowerment, creating a learning environment where students feel appreciated for their strengths and abilities. Likewise, students are encouraged to grow their self-esteem to impact their environment positively and desire to invoke change (Broom, 2015). All successful educators' goal is for their students to leave their classrooms feeling optimistic, emotionally engaged, transformed, and inspired. The third component is bringing practice to the school. When educators have practice experience, they can get to the classroom. This allows their students to have the value of firsthand knowledge that awards richness beyond the textbook. This practice experience bridges the gap between expectations and reality (Yin, 2019).

Furthermore, this gives students the richness of reflective lessons from current practice, opportunities for guest lectures, and firsthand knowledge from a practicing practice/practitioner. The fourth component is passion; it cannot be taught, but rather, the student must possess and bring it to the classroom. One's well-being significantly affects the psychological impact of one's work (Cabrita & Duarte, 2023). Specifically, the passion one feels toward one's work is directly linked to one's overall physical, psychological, and social well-being. The ability for one to feel satisfied and passionate about one's work increases one's ability to be motivated and significantly decreases negative symptoms such as burnout. An educator's passion for social work and ability to assist students in finding their calling is paramount in achieving their long-term professional success and overall well-being. The fifth and final component is student engagement. Effectively engaging students in the learning environment offers new opportunities to motivate and challenge their learning and transform them (LImniou, Sedghi, Kumari, & Drousiotis, 2022). Student engagement is directly linked to classroom performance, well-being, emotions, and belonging. Educators' ability to offer new learning opportunities and challenges for student engagement to incorporate flexibility, stimulate interaction, facilitate learning, and enhance emotional engagement increase short and long-term outcomes.

TRANSFORMED TO INSPIRE

Inspired by a desire to invoke critical thinking, passion, change, and knowledge, educators stand before their classes, hoping to transform them. Using transformational theory, educators have the unique opportunity to engage learners in engagement that is genuine, supportive, empowering, and challenges them to grow intellectually. Through a vast avenue of learning, transformational educators allow their students to question themselves to analyze themselves, their experiences, and their thought processes. Through this process, they emerge at growth and are better prepared

Transformational Teaching

to enter practice. Experiencing and accepting your calling is not easy, but with a transformational educator's support, guidance, and patience, students can be better prepared for the practice field that lies before them.

REFERENCES

Bandura, A. (2012). On the functional properties of perceived self-efficacy revisited. *Journal of Management*, 38(1), 9–44. 10.1177/0149206311410606

Baumgardner, L. (2019). *Fostering transformative learning in educational settings*. Adult Literacy Education. 10.35847/LBaumgartner.1.1.69

Berkowicz, J., & Myers, A. (2015). Compassion in the classroom: A "real strength" for education. *Education Week*.

Boyatzis, R. (2006). An overview of intentional change for a complexity perspective. *Journal of Management Development*, 25(7), 607–623. 10.1108/02621710610678445

Broom, C. (2015). Empowering students: Pedagogy that benefits educators and learners. *Citizenship, Social. Economics & Education*, 14(2), 79–86.

Cabrita, C., & Duarte, A. (2023). Passionately demanding: Work's passion's role in the relationship between work demands and affective well-being at work. *Frontiers in Psychology*, 14.

Center, L. (2022, January 09). *TLC Transformational Education*. TLC. https://tlcacademies.com/tlc-transformational-education/

De Vivo, K. (2022). A new research base for rigorous base project-based learning. *Connecting Education Research, Policy, and Practice*.

Deng, C., Gulseren, D., Isola, C., Grocutt, K., & Turner, N. (2023). Transformational leadership effectiveness: An evidence-based primer. *Human Resource Development International*, 26(5), 627–641. 10.1080/13678868.2022.2135938

Farley, A., Feaster, D., Schapmire, T., D'Ambrosio, J., Bruce, L., Oak, S., & Sar, B. (2009). The challenges of implementing evidence based practice: ethical considerations in practice, education, policy, and research. *Social Work and Society International Online Journal*, 7(2).

Feize, L., & Faver, C. (2018). Teaching self-awareness: Social work educator's endeavors and struggles. *Social Work Education*, 38(2), 159–176. 10.1080/02615479.2018.1523383

Fuglei, M. (2021). *Transformational teaching: A learning revolution*. Medium.

Guzzardo, M., Khosia, N., Adams, A., Bussmann, J., Engekman, A., Ingnaham, N., & Taylor, S. (2021). The ones that make a difference: Perspective on student-faculty relationships. *Innovative Higher Education*, 46(1), 41–58. 10.1007/s10755-020-09522-w33012971

Halbert, L. A. (1923). *What is Professional Social Work.* Kansas City. *Survey (London, England).*

Hutchings, T. (2016). *Teachings as a high-risk profession.* Protecting the Professional-Professional Ethics in the Classroom.

Keen, C., & Woods, R. (2016). Creating activating events for transformative learning in a prison classroom. *Journal of Transformative Education,* 14(1), 15–33. 10.1177/1541344615602342

Kolb, A., & Kolb, D. (2017). Experiential learning theory as a guide for experiential educators in higher education. *Experiential Learning & Teaching in Higher Education,* 1(1).

LImniou, M., Sedghi, N., Kumari, D., & Drousiotis, E. (2022). Student engagement, learning engagements and the Covid-19 pandemic: A comparsion between psychology and engineering undergraduate students in the UK. *Education Sciences,* 12(10).

Markula, A., & Aksela, M. (2022). The key charateristics of project-based learning: How teachers implement projects in K-12 science education. *Disciplinary and Interdiscplinary Science Education Research,* 4(2).

New International Version. (2023). Biblica.

Nushi, M., Momeni, A., & Roshanbin, M. (2022). Characteristics of an effective university professor from students' perspective: Are the qualities changing? *Frontiers in Education,* 7, 842640. 10.3389/feduc.2022.842640

Parker, D. (2007). *Planning for inquiry; Its not an oxymoron.* Center for Inquiry-Based Learning.

Rokach, A. (2016). The impact professors have on college students. *International Journal of Studies in Nursing,* 1(1), 9. 10.20849/ijsn.v1i1.80

Slavich, G. (2005). Tranformational teaching. *Excellence in Teaching,* 5.

Slavich, G., & Zimbardo, P. (2012). Transformational teaching: Theoretical underpinnings, basic principles, and core methods. *Educational Psychology Review,* 24(4), 569–608. 10.1007/s10648-012-9199-623162369

Southworth, J. (2022). Bridging critical thinking and transformative learning: The role of perspective-taking. *Theory and Research in Education,* 20(1), 44–63. 10.1177/14778785221090853

Tomaszewski, L., Zarestky, J., & Gonzalez, E. (2020). Planning qualitative research: Design and decision making for new researchers. *International Journal of Qualitative Methods*, 19. 10.1177/1609406920967174

Urdang, E. (2010). Awareness of self- A critical tool. *Social Work Education*, 5.

Wheatley, K. (2018). Inquiry-based learning: Effects on student engagement. *Student Scholarship*, 417.

White, S., & Nitkin, M. (2014). Cceating a transformational learning experience: Immersing students in an intensive interdisciplinary learning environment. *Teaching and Learning*, 8(2).

Wrenn, J., & Wrenn, B. (2009). Enhancing Learning by Integrating Theory and Practice. *International Journal on Teaching and Learning in Higher Education*, 21(2).

YIn, J. (2019). Connecting theory and practice in teacher education: English-as-a-foreign-language pre-service teachers' perceptions of practicum experience. *Innovación Educativa (México, D.F.)*, 1(4).

Yuner, B. (2020). Transformational teaching in higher education: The relationship between the transformational teaching of academic staff and students' self-efficacy for learning . *Educational Policy Analysis and Strategic Research*, 15(4).

Chapter 4
Transformational Leadership

Kimberly Mudd-Fegett
https://orcid.org/0000-0001-9136-9206
Campbellsville University, USA

Helen K. Mudd
https://orcid.org/0000-0002-2588-6886
Campbellsville University, USA

ABSTRACT

Transformational leadership is the process in which leaders play an idealized role model, stimulate and encourage innovative work behavior, provide inspirational motivation, engage in supporting and mentoring followers to achieve the organization's shared vision and goals, and create a connection that raises the level of motivation and morality in both the leader and the follower. This type of leader is attentive to the needs and motives of followers and supports each follower in reaching their fullest potential. The authors' experiences and success as transformational leaders and educators provide evidence of the truth of these findings. The authors will highlight personality characteristics, behaviors, and effects on practitioners, professors, and students of transformational leadership. The authors will show how transformational leaders and educators move followers from unquestioningly accepting provided information and directives to reflective, goal-oriented, critical thinkers.

DOI: 10.4018/979-8-3693-2407-3.ch004

INTRODUCTION TO TRANSFORMATIONAL LEADERSHIP

Transformational leadership, a process where leaders embody an idealized role model, stimulate innovative work behavior, provide inspirational motivation, and mentor followers to achieve shared vision and goals, has the transformative power to elevate motivation and morality in both the leader and the follower (Bass & Avolio, 1994; Bednall et al., 2018; Northouse, 2021; Suifan et al., 2018). This type of leader is not just attentive to the needs and motives of followers but also supports each follower in reaching their fullest potential. Bass and Riggio (2006) characterized transformational leadership as including four theoretically distinct components: idealized influence, inspirational motivation, intellectual stimulation, and individualized consideration. Fernsler (2015) challenged leaders interested in making significant and long-lasting changes to look within before they look outside themselves. He encouraged leaders to analyze situations, deepen their consciousness, learn to be fully present, build relationships, and improve communications if they wanted to influence human systems. Northouse (2001) found in 39 studies of transformational literature that individuals who exhibited transformational leadership were more effective leaders with better work outcomes.

Transformational leaders foster a culture of continuous improvement, innovation, and resilience by creating an environment where information is shared, and learning extends from individuals to groups and organizations. This, in turn, leads to sustainable success and competitive advantage for the organization. According to Hariharan and Anand (2023), transformational leadership is a key driver of learning within organizations, underlining the importance of supporting and nurturing individual learning to enhance organizational capabilities. Through their charismatic behaviors, transformational leaders influence their subordinates to emulate and learn from them. These leaders are considerate and provide their subordinates with support, mentoring, and coaching (Vera & Crossan, 2004). Organizations that invest in developing their employees tend to have higher levels of employee satisfaction and engagement. Buttigieg, Daher, Cassarc, and Guillaume (2023) emphasized the impact of transformational leadership in driving sustainable organizational change. They found that engagement is higher and burnout is lower under this leadership style. A commitment to learning helps organizations build resilience by preparing them to handle unexpected disruptions and crises. By continuously updating their knowledge and skills, they are better equipped to navigate uncertainties and sustain their operations over the long term.

The authors' experiences and success as transformational leaders and educators provide evidence of the truth of these findings. The authors will use over 40 years of leadership experience in educational and practice settings as the underpinning of this chapter. The authors will highlight personality characteristics, behaviors, and effects on practitioners, professors, and students of Transformational Leadership. The authors will show how transformational leaders and educators move followers from unquestioningly accepting provided information and directives to reflective, goal-oriented, critical thinkers. In and out of the classroom, transformational leaders work to build partnerships by creating a shared vision of the importance of life-long learning.

THE HISTORY AND THEORETICAL UNDERPINNINGS OF TRANSFORMATIONAL LEADERSHIP

James V. Downton coined the term transformational leader in 1973. Burns (1978), building on Downton's ideas, noted the stark differences between transactional and transformational leadership styles. Burns recognized that transformational leaders raised the level of human contact and ethical aspiration of both the leader and followers. Burns saw leadership as a process that raised the followers' motivation and morale. Burns highlighted the importance of transformational leaders heavily relying on charisma, inspiration, and clear communication of high expectations.

Tichy and Ulrich (1984), building on Burns's work, described a transformational leader as one with the capability to a) help the organization envision what it can become, b) mobilize the organization to work toward achieving the identified goal, and c) lead the organization to institutionalize the changes that must last over time. Tichy and Ulrich named Lee Iacocca, the chairman of Chrysler Corporation, one of the most dramatic examples of transformational leadership and organizational revitalization in the early 1980s. They emphasized that transformational leaders must understand equity, power, freedom, and decision-making dynamics. In addition to modifying systems, transformational leaders realigned cultural systems within the organization.

Beginning as a collaborative team in the mid-1980s, Bass and Avolio have co-authored numerous publications that have shaped the understanding of transformational leadership. Their joint efforts have advanced theoretical frameworks, measurement tools, and empirical research. Bass and Avolio developed the Multi-factor Leadership Questionnaire (MLQ) for measuring transformational leadership behaviors in 1985. This questionnaire has since become one of the most widely used instruments for assessing transformational leadership behaviors in research and organizational settings.

Inspired by the work, research, and theories of those before him, Bernard Bass (1990) added that transformational leaders express authentic and focused energy to inspire their followers to become more like them. Bass said followers must feel trust, admiration, loyalty, and respect for their leader (Ugochukwu, 2023). The ability to create these emotions creates a work environment in which followers are willing to work harder than they ever thought possible.

For the last 30 years, Peter Northouse has researched and written about various leadership styles, including transformational leadership, building on the work of other leadership scholars before him. Northouse's first edition of "Leadership: Theory and Practice" was published in 1997. This seminal text in leadership, published in 13 languages, is now in its 8th edition. Bass and Avolio's theories and works are prominently featured in Northouse's leadership book. In addition to Bass and Avolio, Northouse (2019) credits Bennis and Nanus (2007) and Kouzes and Posner (2002, 2017) as having significantly contributed to the knowledge and understanding of transformational research. Bennis and Nanus (2007) identified four common strategies leaders use in transforming organizations: clear vision, social architects creating shared meanings, trust, and creative deployment of self. Kouzes and Posner (2002, 2017) developed a transformational leadership model. Their model consists of five fundamental practices: model the way, inspire a shared vision, challenge the process, enable others to act, and encourage the heart.

Transformational leadership has revitalized the field of leadership studies (Hunt, 1999). What initially were only two researchers publishing a handful of articles has grown to an entire field of study on the moral foundation and legitimate use of transformational leadership across various fields of study, thus greatly influencing the research, influence, and practice of leadership practice (Spector, 2013). Transformational leadership has changed the field of leadership by shifting the focus from mere transactional exchanges to inspiring and empowering followers to achieve outcomes beyond expectations. Its emphasis on vision, charisma, motivation, and individualized consideration has redefined conventional notions of effective leadership, fostering a more holistic and empowering approach to leading organizations.

COMPARING LEADERSHIP APPROACHES TO TRANSFORMATIVE LEADERSHIP

In leadership studies, various theories and approaches have emerged to explain the complexities of leading individuals and organizations toward shared goals. Among these, transformational leadership is a compelling framework emphasizing the leader's ability to inspire and empower followers to achieve exceptional outcomes. Other leadership models, such as authentic, servant, and transactional, offer distinct perspectives on how leaders influence their followers and shape organizational dynamics. In this comparative analysis, the authors highlight the similarities and differences between transformational leadership and these alternative models, examining their underlying principles, key characteristics, and implications for organizational effectiveness.

The authentic leadership approach is often seen as an extension of transformational leadership, stressing that leaders do what is "good" or "right" for their followers and society. The four dimensions of authentic leadership include self-awareness, relational transparency, balanced information processing, and internalized moral perspective (Duarte, Ribeiro, Sernedo, & Gornes, 2021). Authentic leaders reinforce their followers' positive attitudes and behaviors, thus creating benefits for a specific workgroup and the entire organization. Authentic leaders promote creativity, fresh ideas, and valuable solutions, creating a dynamic in which followers enhance skill development and autonomy (Banks, McCauley, Gardner, & Gular, 2016).

Transformational leadership strongly emphasizes creating a compelling vision and mobilizing followers to pursue it. In contrast, authentic leadership prioritizes the leader's genuine expression of values and beliefs, fostering trust and credibility. While transformational leaders often seek to instill a sense of shared purpose and collective identity among followers, authentic leaders prioritize individual authenticity and personal integrity, encouraging followers to stay true to themselves. Authentic leadership emphasizes genuineness and ethical behavior, while transformational leadership focuses on vision, inspiration, and motivating followers toward a collective goal. Furthermore, authentic leadership focuses on personal integrity and building a trusting relationship between leader and follower. The starkest contrast between these two leadership theories is that transformational leaders focus on developing their followers for leadership roles.

In contrast, authentic leaders are more concerned with creating their followers' sense of self. Authentic leaders are not necessarily charismatic or inspirational. Instead, they are driven, creative visionaries processing information to illustrate consistency between their words and deeds (Banks et al., 2016). Acquiring to know and expose their true self, authentic leaders uphold high moral standards through self-development and self-awareness (Ford & Harding, 2017).

James Downton, who coined the phrase transformational leadership, and Robert Greenleaf were colleagues who contributed significantly to the understanding and promoting of servant leadership principles. In 1970, Robert Greenleaf published his essay *The Servant as Leader, establishing the underly*ing philosophy for servant leadership (Greenleaf, 1970). Servant leadership has a strong moral dimension, making altruism and caring for others the central components of this leadership process. The specified behaviors of a servant leader are respect for colleagues, being willing to listen, self-restraint, humility, and genuine willingness to serve others. Unique to servant leadership in this particular form of leadership, the leader puts their followers' needs before their own to help them reach their maximum potential in hopes of achieving personal success (Langof & Guldenberg, 2019). The goal of servant leadership is to meet the needs of followers, aiding them in obtaining autonomy to eventually becoming servants themselves.

Servant leadership prioritizes followers' development and well-being, while transformational leadership focuses on organizational goals through inspirational and shared vision. Unlike transformational leadership, servant leadership focuses on followers' needs while obtaining organizational success. Servant leaders put their followers before themselves, placing service at the center of their leadership philosophy. Servant leaders expect the best out of their people, creating a respectful, fair, and selfless environment. In contrast, transformational leadership emphasizes emotional intelligence, improved communication, follower participation, and inclusion (Lindberg, 2022). Transformational leaders inspire followers towards a common goal; however, servant leaders take time to develop each follower. Servant leaders are highly motivated to improve humanity, while transformational leaders aim to enhance people and organizations more generally.

Transactional and transformational leadership are contrasting models that offer distinct approaches to leading organizations and motivating followers. Transactional leadership focuses on exchanging rewards and punishments to influence follower behavior. In contrast, transformational leadership inspires and motivates followers by articulating a compelling vision, fostering a sense of collective purpose, and empowering individuals to achieve exceptional outcomes. Transactional leadership is based on the philosophy that followers require specific motivation and structure to produce desired results. Transactional leaders use punishment when they find work poor and rewards when they find work positive. This leadership philosophy is often criticized for being more management-oriented than strategic (Thanh & Quang, 2022; Western Governor University, 2021). Transactional leaders focus on maintaining stability and achieving predetermined goals. Transactional leaders do not encourage creativity but maintain a status quo under close supervision. Transactional leaders do not desire to create organizational growth, reframe the situation, or inspire followers to transform. Instead, they strive to maintain productivity (Xenikou, 2017).

Transformational, authentic, servant and transactional leadership represent different leadership models, each offering unique perspectives on how leaders influence followers and shape organizational dynamics. While transformational, authentic, and servant leadership emphasize empowerment, ethics, and inspiration, transactional leadership relies more on compliance and control. Despite their differences, each leadership model contributes to our understanding of effective leadership practices and offers valuable insights for those seeking to understand transformative leadership practices.

THE IMPACT OF CULTURAL FACTORS ON TRANSFORMATIONAL

Understanding the influence of cultural differences on leadership style and approach is intricate and multifaceted. Uniting diverse followers has become more important as organizations become increasingly culturally diverse (Mendenhall, Reich, Bird, & Osland., 2012). It is crucial for effective leadership in a multicultural or global setting to acknowledge these differences and adjust one's leadership style and approach accordingly. Culture is a system of awareness humans form as they confront challenges and adapt to social development. It influences behavior and psychological needs. Culture refers to fundamental assumptions, practices, and beliefs that are shared by group members and which influence their perceptions and reactions (Giorgi, Lockwood, & Glynn, 2015, p.3).

Na, Dongjian, and Yun (2021) conducted a study of 31 independent pieces of research (N 6474) and discovered that cultural differences have an impact on leadership behavior and the effectiveness of leadership. Western culture promotes individualism, while Eastern culture advocates collectivism. In cultures with high power distance, followers often expect a clear hierarchy and may be less open to participative leadership styles. In low-power cultures, followers prefer egalitarian relationships and are more receptive to empowerment and participative decision-making. In individualistic cultures, transformational leadership can appeal to personal development and individual achievements. In collectivist cultures, leaders need to emphasize group goals and community. Masculine cultures and individuals value competitiveness and achievement. While feminine cultures prioritize relationships and quality of life. Thus, the leader appeals to the masculine culture by emphasizing joining together for success. The leader appeals to the feminine culture or individual by prioritizing relationships, support, and collaboration.

Caza, Caza, and Posner (2021) conducted a study to determine if transformational leadership behaviors were universal by a) examining if leaders and followers perceive transformational leadership behaviors the same way across cultures and b) determining if the magnitude of satisfaction that followers derive from transformational leadership behavior was the same across cultures. Survey data from 71,537 leaders and their direct reports (n = 203,027) from 77 countries and hundreds of organizations were analyzed. Cultural universality was examined by comparing internal reliability scores and using multilevel mixed coefficient models to assess the similarity of effect sizes across cultures. Caza, Caza, and Posner (2021) found that regardless of culture, when interacting with leaders from their own culture, followers were universally alike in their perceptions of transformational leadership behavior and their satisfaction with such behavior. From this massive study, one can infer that transformational leadership appears to be a universally satisfying leadership style. Followers worldwide reported similar levels of increased satisfaction in response to transformational leadership behavior and showed similar tendencies in recognizing such behavior from their leaders. Caza, Caza, & Poser (2021) replicated and extended previous findings of the GLOBE study (House et al. 2004), which found that followers worldwide positively endorsed transformational leadership. The GLOBE study based its results on 65 societies, including 17,300 middle managers from 951 organizations in the food processing, financial services, and telecommunications services industries. At least in terms of follower satisfaction, it appears that transformational leadership is a "safe bet" for how leaders should behave. The results suggest that leaders' efforts at transformational behavior will be recognized and appreciated similarly by most followers (Caza et al., 2021, p. 9).

ETHICAL LEADERSHIP

At its core, ethical transformational leadership combines the principles of transformational leadership with a solid commitment to moral values, integrity, and ethical decision-making, fostering positive organizational change and sustainable success. Ethical theories fall into two broad categories for studying leadership: theories about leaders' conduct and theories about leaders' character (Northouse, 2019, p. 339). Northouse (2021) reminds us that leadership is employed by individuals with worthy intentions and also by those with self-serving motivations. Leaders with good intentions include Mother Theresa, Martin Luther King Jr., and Nelson Mandela. Unethical and destructive leaders include Hitler, Pol Pot, and Idi Amin. Leaders, whether ethical or unethical, use the power and influence of leadership to move toward and accomplish goals. Bass (1998) coined the term pseudotransformational leadership. This term refers to leaders who are self-consumed, exploitive, and power-oriented, with warped moral values (Bass & Riggio, 2006). Northouse (2021) points out that ethical leaders set clear expectations for ethical behavior, communicate ethical values and standards, and hold themselves and others accountable for upholding these principles. They create a supportive ethical climate where ethical behavior is valued, encouraged, and rewarded (Northouse, 2021). Likewise, Barsky (2019) underscores the importance of ethical leadership in promoting organizational integrity, trust, and sustainability. He emphasizes that ethical leaders are committed to upholding ethical standards and equipped with the knowledge, skills, and resources to address ethical dilemmas and promote ethical conduct in their organizations. According to Barsky (2019), ethical leadership encompasses several key components, including moral awareness, moral reasoning, moral courage, and ethical action. Barsky contends that ethical leadership involves promoting ethical conduct and equipping leaders with the skills and tools to identify, analyze, and resolve ethical issues in their organizations (Barsky, 2019).

The core values of ethical transformational leadership mirror those of social work: integrity, competency, service, dignity, and worth of the individual, the value of human relationships, and social justice. The social work professional code of conduct promotes respecting, protecting, and serving others. Likewise, ethical leaders are responsible for developing and enforcing solid ethical standards within their organizations (Engelbrecht, Van Aswegen, & Theron, 2005). Decisions based on these values put followers' best interests foremost, contributing to their leadership transformation (Whiteman, 2018).

ATTRIBUTES OF TRANSFORMATIONAL LEADERS IN THE EDUCATIONAL ENVIRONMENT

Transformational leaders aim to cultivate authentic relationships with individuals, fostering a sense of value, acceptance, and purpose. Gaining the trust of their followers through competence, good communication skills, sound judgment, and confidence, transformational leaders are reliable leaders upon whom their followers depend for guidance. Transformational leaders are committed to creating a better work environment for themselves, colleagues, students, and the institution. Consistency, growth, and self-awareness are integral components of this process. Transformational leaders acknowledge and recognize others' successes, motivating followers to reach their potential (Saputra et al., 2022). The leader encourages the follower to excel despite the individual gain or motive of the leader. This raising of morale and expectations, in turn, will raise the organization's values, priorities, and standards. (Saputra, Rini, & Hariri, 2022). Transformational leaders must be self-motivated and make difficult decisions in the best interest of the organization and followers, even if they conflict with their interests. Transformational leadership has an additive effect; it moves followers to accomplish more than what is usually expected of them. They become motivated to transcend their self-interests for the good of the group or organization (Bass & Avolio, 1990a). Collaborative efforts among team members, facilitated by creativity, self-expression, and a shared vision and led by transformative leadership, can increase productivity, motivation, self-confidence, and overall success (Gunawan, 2020).

Transformational leaders must be humble and willing to adapt to their followers' needs, taking calculated risks when required. Being proactive, inspiring, and innovative, transformational leaders do not shy away from seeking ideas from their followers or empowering them to seek alternative solutions when necessary. Transformational leaders build deep levels of mutual trust with their followers.

Transformational leaders demonstrate their professional and organizational passion by working towards goals built on a framework of shared vision, values, and trust. (Alessa, 2021). Transformational leaders push followers to attain higher morals and motivation through charismatic leadership and visionary goals. Transformational leaders are authentic in their actions and care deeply for their followers, concerned about their long-term success and well-being. From a strength-focused perspective, they motivate their followers to identify with the organization's mission. Transformational leaders inspire commitment from followers, creating a collaborative environment for service, change, and self-empowerment.

As social workers, we create partnerships with clients to bring about change. Similarly, leaders within the University community promote collaboration to enhance the learning environment. Transformational leaders engage followers in a sense of vision, fostering trust and gaining their respect. Followers can share their concerns, knowledge, and feedback and grow as individuals (Vinh, Hien, & Do, 2022). Transformational leaders generally can correct and reprimand while maintaining a positive relationship with the one being corrected. While understanding delegation, transformational leaders recognize and believe that one should only delegate a task that one would be willing to undertake. Collaboration, shared purpose, accountability, and responsibility are critical in transformational leadership. Transformational leaders recognize and appreciate that decision-making in an organization is complex. They acknowledge that accountability and responsibility require one to take ownership of leadership decisions.

Professors and students have diverse backgrounds. Leaders should model mastery by presenting practical examples, intellectually challenging individuals, creating safe learning experiences, and encouraging individuals to articulate their learning. Individuals succeed best in environments where they feel heard, empowered, and valued. As Maya Angelou (1928) reminds us, "Children may not remember what you said, but they will remember how you made them feel." Transformational leaders embrace Angelou's message.

Transformational leadership is most effective when it engages followers in shared visions, hope, change, and common goals. Transformational leaders inspire followers to develop long-term vision, self-awareness, and a desire to lead others. By encouraging followers to push beyond their perceived limitations, transformational leaders can help them grow and achieve more than they ever thought possible. Transformational leaders are emotionally aware and considerate of their followers, yet they are authentic and display strong ethical standards. They manage their empathy, compassion, and emotions in a controlled manner that speaks to their emotional intelligence (Mencl, Wefald, & Ittersum, 2018). Effective leadership and shared passion create personal interactions and positive relationships, leading to organizational transformation. Transformational leaders are engaged with their followers, attuned to their needs, and willing to sacrifice for the organization's good. Transformational leaders offer their team members essential support, encouragement, compassion, empathy, and coaching to help them grow and develop professionally and personally.

Transformational leaders recognize and appreciate their followers' leadership skills, empowering and mentoring them. Lancefield and Rangen (2021) describe transformational leaders as focused on achieving organizational goals through teamwork, clear expectations, and a willingness to take risks. To empower their followers, transformational leaders set forth their actions to give their followers the skills, tools, and encouragement to transform into the best version of themselves. The outcome is systematic trust, change, and growth.

Challenges and Limitations of Transformational Leadership

One single leadership theory cannot be expected to encompass all aspects of leadership behavior. Therefore, it is essential to acknowledge and discuss the limitations of transformational leadership while crediting the overwhelming impact and benefits it brings to its followers and the organization. Transformational leadership is an emotional form of leadership that actively engages, supports, empowers, and empathizes with followers. A significant limitation of transformational leadership is the lack of task-oriented behaviors. These behaviors include expected task goals, operational planning, coordinating activities, and allocating resources (Lai, Tang, & Lin, 2020) One charismatic, transformational leader can be instrumental in leading their followers to success. However, they must acknowledge the trust, responsibility, and faith placed on them to ensure the well-being and growth of their followers. Ultimately, the influence given in leadership takes emotional maturity, integrity, and devotion to followers to invest in their growth and success. In the real world, transformational leaders most likely behave only intermittently in a transformational manner. For instance, transformational leaders have been accused of being unethical because some scholars have observed that transformational leaders sometimes behave out of personal interests instead of promoting followers' needs or organizational values (Bass and Steidlmeier, 1999). Hay (2006) argues that transformational leaders must assume moral responsibility to "avoid dictatorship and oppression of a minority by a majority" (p. 10). When transformational leaders force their ideology onto their followers, employees may perceive their leaders as egotistical. As mentioned earlier in this chapter, ethical leaders are responsible for developing and enforcing solid ethical standards within their organizations (Engelbrecht, Van Aswegen, & Theron, 2005). In human service organizations, ethical transformational leaders honor the core values of social work and adhere to the NASW Code of Ethics. Resisting the urge to be the heroic figure in transformational leadership is necessary to keep followers aligned with the mission and goal of serving others.

Eisenberg, Post, and DiTomaso (2019) studied 53 innovation teams to examine the relationship between team performance and geographic dispersion. Their findings suggest that when teams are geographically dispersed, transformational leadership may be less effective in improving team performance. This is particularly significant given the rise of remote work in educational and human service organizations.

Other limitations include fit with bureaucratic organizations, focus on long-term vision, which may lessen attention to the daily operational needs of the organization, geographic location of followers, and focus on self-motivation and autonomy, which may not be a good fit for all employees. The leadership literature has indicated that transformational leadership relies on building relationships, inspiring and developing others, and emphasizing the team approach - all of which are characteristics traditionally associated with femininity (Bass, 1999; Lai, 2011; Pounder & Coleman, 2002). Further research is necessary to examine each of these limitations.

The Impact of Transformational Leadership on Organizations

Leadership has a powerful influence on learning and development in today's organizations. Various types of leadership are conducive to building a learning organization. In terms of learning, Lam (2002), in a cross-nation sample, found that transformational leadership positively influences the process and results of organizational learning. Xie (2020) likewise found that transformational leadership has a significant and positive relationship with learning organizations. Scholars view long-term vision as a primary characteristic of transformational leaders. Their vision creates empowering conditions that increase followers' job commitment, enhance job performance, and promote long-term learning and development in various cultural and organizational settings (Triana, Richard, & Yucell, 2017). Xie (2020) encouraged HR departments to design and implement transformational leadership coaching programs systematically. From a resource perspective, transformational leadership creates a supportive environment for followers, which, in turn, fosters positive resource accumulation while reducing stress and work-family conflict (Arnold, 2017).

Evidence suggests that followers worldwide prefer leaders who demonstrate transformational leadership behaviors (House et al., 2004). Transformational leadership has a significant impact on the behavior, thinking, and overall performance of its followers. It also fosters transformational learning that focuses on the intellectual discussion of the problems at hand. This, in turn, promotes learning and innovation (Choudhary, Akhtar, and Zaheer, 2013). Bass and Riggio (2006) suggested that transformational leadership's popularity may be due to its emphasis on intrinsic

Transformational Leadership

motivation and follower development, which fits with the needs of today's work groups, who want to be inspired and empowered to succeed. According to Northouse (2019), transformational leadership has several strengths. These include the fact that it has been widely researched, it makes intuitive sense to people, it recognizes leadership as a collaborative process between leaders and followers, it complements other leadership models, it prioritizes the needs, values, and morals of followers, and it is highly effective.

According to Kouzes and Posner (2017), transformational leadership helps leaders motivate and inspire followers through five key practices:

1. Model the Way: Transformational leaders clarify values, set a clear example, and align their values with their followers and the organization.
2. Inspire a Shared Vision: These leaders encourage followers to voice their aspirations and motivations, and recognize that they are part of something meaningful that can only be achieved through teamwork.
3. Challenge the Process: Transformational leaders seek opportunities for improvement, question the status quo, and support experimentation.
4. Enable Others to Act: They build relationships, promote cooperation, provide autonomy, and enhance competencies.
5. Encourage the Heart: Transformational leaders create a community by recognizing both group accomplishments and individual contributions.

In conclusion, transformational leadership significantly impacts organizations by promoting learning, innovation, and follower development through modeling, inspiring, challenging, enabling, and encouraging.

Transformational Leadership Process Mapping Organizational

Leadership process mapping involves identifying, analyzing, and visualizing the various organizational processes and interactions influenced or directly driven by leadership actions. The authors present a transformational leadership process map that can be applied across educational and other human service organizations. See Figure 1.1 for more details. The Mudd-Fegett and Mudd Transformational Leadership Process Map identifies core social work values and professional attributes that ground leadership's four theoretical distinct components, resulting in desired organizational behaviors. The core social work values and professional attributes have been identified and examined earlier in this chapter.

The authors propose the Mudd-Fegett and Mudd Transformational Leadership Process Map from their extensive experience in practice and educational leadership. Bass and Riggio (2006) characterized transformational leadership as including four theoretically distinct components: idealized influence, inspirational motivation, intellectual stimulation, and individualized consideration. The Mudd-Fegett and Mudd Transformational Leadership Process Map illustrates how each theoretical component, grounded in the core values of social work and identified professional attributes, leads to the identified behaviors within the organization. Idealized influence is exemplified through followers who are committed to the organization's mission statement, adhere to the NASW Code of Ethics, and remain loyal to the leader and the organization. Inspirational Motivation is shown through followers who demonstrate a passion for the profession and organization, profess a commitment to serve, integrate spirituality in practice and teaching, and verbalize a clear vision of their calling. Intellectual Stimulation is confirmed by followers embracing transformational teaching, increasing their intellectual productivity footprint, and a heightened intellectual synergy within the department or organization. Individualized Consideration is displayed in empowered followers, freedom of intellectual creativity, increased self-efficacy, and appreciation for mentorship.

The Mudd-Fegett and Mudd Processing Mapping of Transformational Leadership in Social Work is in its development stage and is considered a conceptual framework. The development of the conceptual map included an extensive literature review, the summation of which has been provided in this chapter. The authors will employ concept mapping (structured conceptualization) as the primary methodology for validating the Mudd-Fegett/Mudd Processing Mapping of Transformational Leadership in Social Work. Concept mapping is a methodology for organizing the ideas of a group on any topic of interest and representing those ideas visually in a series of interrelated maps. It is a formal group process tool that includes a sequence of structured group activities linked to a series of multivariate statistical analyses that process input and generate maps. The authors will fine-tune the Mudd-Fegett and Mudd Processing Mapping of Transformational Leadership in Social Work conceptual map based on feedback from the concept mapping. Analysis of the mapped processes will allow authors to identify gaps, redundancies, or inefficiencies in the mapping process.

The authors encourage readers of this chapter to contribute their input to finalizing the Mudd-Fegett and Mudd Processing Mapping of Transformational Leadership. Readers can participate by answering the questions posed to the focus group participants

1. A leader should have the following essential attributes to ensure excellence in transformational leadership.
2. A leader should have the following core values to ensure excellence in transformational leadership.
3. The qualities of employees led by a transformational leader are

Transformational Leadership

Answers to the provided questions can be sent to hkmudd@campbellsville.edu or knmudd-fegett@campbellsville.edu

Figure 1. Mudd-Fegett/Mudd processing mapping of transformational leadership in social work

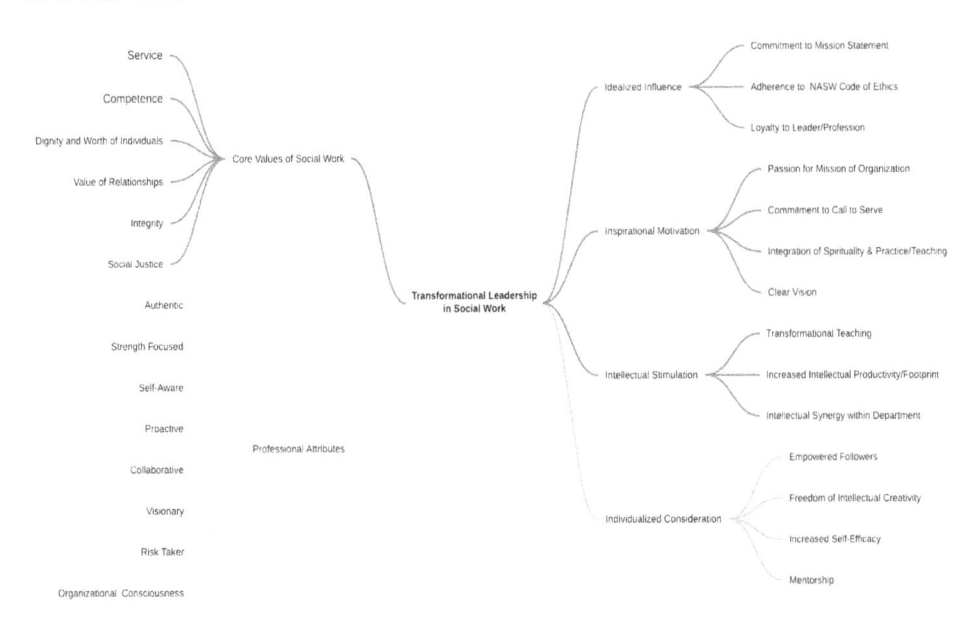

SUMMARY

Transformational leadership is the process in which leaders play an idealized role model, stimulate and encourage innovative work behavior, provide inspirational motivation, engage in supporting and mentoring followers to achieve the organization's shared vision and goals, and create a connection that raises the level of motivation and morality in both the leader and the follower (Bass & Avolio, 1994; Bednall et al., 2018; Northouse, 2021; Suifan et al., 2018). Transformational leadership is a process that changes and transforms individuals and organizations. (Northouse, 2021). The defining characteristic of transformational leadership is the leader's ability to inspire, motivate, and empower followers to achieve exceptional outcomes (Bass & Riggo, 2006). Transformational leadership empowers people to accomplish positive change through idealized influence, inspirational motivation, intellectual stimulation, and individualized consideration. Leaders enable change by emotionally connecting with their audience and inspiring them to achieve something greater than themselves.

REFERENCES

Alessa, G. (2021). The dimensions of transformational leadership and its organizational effects in public universities in Saudi Arabia: A systematic review. *Frontiers in Psychology*, 12.34867578

Angelou, M. (1928, April 4).

Arnold, K. A. (2017). Transformational leadership and employee psychological well-being: A review and directions for future research. *Journal of Occupational Health Psychology*, 22(3), 381–393. 10.1037/ocp000006228150998

Banks, G., McCauley, K., Gardner, W., & Gular, C. (2016). A meta-analytic review of authentic and transformational leadership: A test for redundancy. *The Leadership Quarterly*, 27(4), 634–652. 10.1016/j.leaqua.2016.02.006

Barsky, A. E. (2019). *Ethics and values in social work: an integrated approach for a comprehensive curriculum* (2nd ed). Oxford University Press.

Bass, B. M. (1999). Two decades of research and development in transformational leadership. *European Journal of Work and Organizational Psychology*, 8(1), 9–32. 10.1080/135943299398410

Bass, B. M., & Avolio, B. J. (1993). Transformational leadership and organizational culture. *Public Administration Quarterly*, 17(1), 112–121. https://www.jstor.org/stable/40862298

Bass, B. M., & Riggio, R. E. (2006). *Transformational leadership*. Psychology Press. 10.4324/9781410617095

Bass, B. M., & Steidlmeier, P. (1999). Ethics, character, and authentic transformational leadership behavior. *The Leadership Quarterly*, 10(2), 181–217. 10.1016/S1048-9843(99)00016-8

Baumgartner, L. (2019). *Fostering transformative learning in educational settings*. Adult Literacy Education. 10.35847/LBaumgartner.1.1.69

Bednall, T. C., & Rafferty, E., A., Shipton, H., Sanders, K., & J. Jackson, C. (. (2018). Innovative behavior: How much transformational leadership do you need? *British Journal of Management*, 29(4), 796–816. 10.1111/1467-8551.12275

Bennis, W. G., & Nanus, B. (2007). *Leaders: The strategies for taking charge*. Harper Publishers.

Burns, J. (1978). *Leadership*. Harper.

Buttigieg, S. C., Daher, P., Cassar, V., & Guillaume, Y. (2023). Under the shadow of looming change: Linking employees' appraisals of organizational change as a job demand and transformational leadership to engagement and burnout. *Work and Stress*, 37(2), 148–170. 10.1080/02678373.2022.2120560

Caza, A., Caza, B. B., & Posner, B. Z. (2021). Transformational Leadership across Cultures: Follower Perception and Satisfaction. *Administrative Sciences*, 11(1), 32. 10.3390/admsci11010032

Choudhary, A. I., Akhtar, S. A., & Zaheer, A. (2013). Impact of transformational and servant leadership on organizational performance: A comparative analysis. *Journal of Business Ethics*, 116(2), 433–440. 10.1007/s10551-012-1470-8

Duarte, A., Ribeiro, N., Sernedo, A., & Gornes, D. (2021). Individual performance: Affective commitment and individual creativity's sequential mediation. *Frontiers in Psychology*, 12(06), 675749. 10.3389/fpsyg.2021.675749

Eisenberg, J., Post, C., & DiTomaso, N. (2019). Team dispersion and performance: The role of team communication and transformational leadership. *Small Group Research*, 50(3), 348–380. 10.1177/1046496419827376

Engelbrecht, A., Van Aswegen, A., & Theron, C. (2005). The effect of ethical values on transformational leadership and ethical climate in organizations. *South African Journal of Business Management*, 36(2), 9–26. 10.4102/sajbm.v36i2.624

Fernsler, T. (2015). Transformational leadership. *Nonprofit World*, 33(1), 17–17.

Ford, J., & Harding, N. (2017). The impossibility of the "true self" of authentic leadership. *Sage Journals*, 7(4).

Giorgi, S., Lockwood, C., & Glynn, M. A. (2015). The many faces of culture: Making sense of 30 years of research on culture in organization studies. *The Academy of Management Annals*, 9(1), 1–54. 10.5465/19416520.2015.1007645

Greenleaf, R. (1970). *The Servant as Leader*. Center for Applied Studies.

Gunawan, G. (2020). The influence of transformational leadership, school culture, and work motivation on school effectiveness in junior high school in Medan. *Budapest International Research and Critics Institute Humanities and Social Sciences*, 3(1), 625–634. 10.33258/birci.v3i1.824

Hariharan, K., & Anand, V. (2023). Transformational leadership and learning flows. *The Learning Organization*, 30(3), 309–325. 10.1108/TLO-09-2021-0115

Hay, I. (2006). Transformational leadership: Characteristics and criticisms. *E-Journal of Organizational Learning and Leadership*, 5(2). http://www.weleadinlearning.org/ejournal.htm

Hogg, B. (2024, February 22). *10 Characteristics of Transformational Leaders*. Billhogg. https://www.billhogg.ca/10-characteristics-of-transformational-leaders/

House, R. J., Hanges, P. J., Javidan, M., Dorfman, P. W., & Gupta, V. (Eds.). (2004). *Culture, leadership, and organizations: The GLOBE study of 62 Societies*. Sage Publications.

Kareem, J., Patrick, H., Prabakaran, N. B. V., Tantia, V., Kumar, P., & Mukherjee, U. (2023). Transformational educational leaders inspire school educators' commitment. *Frontiers in Education*, 8. 10.3389/feduc.2023.1171513

Kouzes, J. M., & Posner, B. Z. (2017). *The leadership challenge* (3rd ed.). Jossey-Bass.

Lai, A. (2011). Transformational-transactional leadership theory. *2011 AHS Capstone Projects*. Digital Commons. http://digitalcommons.olin.edu/ahs_capstone_2011/17

Lai, F.-Y., Tang, H.-C., & Lin, C.-C. (2020). Transformational leadership and job performance: The mediating role of work engagement. *SAGE Open*, 10(1). 10.1177/2158244019899085

Lam, Y. J. (2002). Defining the effects of transformational leadership on organizational learning: A cross-cultural comparison. *School Leadership & Management*, 22(4), 439–452. 10.1080/1363243022000053448

Lancefield, D., & Rangen, C. (2021). *4 Actions Transformational Leaders Take*. Business Management.

Langof, J., & Guldenberg, S. (2019). Servant leadership: A systematic literature review- toward a model of antecedents and outcomes. *Sage Journals*, 34, 4.

Lindberg, C. (2022). *Transformational Leadership vs. Servant Leadership*. Webinar Recording: https://www.leadershipahoy.com/transformational-vs-servant-leadership

Mencl, J., Wefald, A., & Ittersum, K. (2018). Transformational leader attributes: Interpersonal skills, engagement, and well-being. *Leadership and Organization Development Journal*, 37(5), 635–657. 10.1108/LODJ-09-2014-0178

Mendenhall, M. E., Reiche, S. B., Bird, A., & Osland, J. S. (2012). Defining the 'global' in global leadership. *Journal of World Business*, 47(4), 493–503. 10.1016/j.jwb.2012.01.003

National Association of Social Workers. (2021). *NASW Code of Ethics*. NASW. https//www.socialworkers.org/About/Ethics/Code-of-Ethics/Code-of-Ethics-English

Northouse, P. (2021). *Leadership: Theory and practice* (9th ed.). Sage Publications, Inc.

Pounder, J. S., & Coleman, M. (2002). Women – Better leaders than men? In general and educational management it still "all depends.". *Leadership and Organization Development Journal*, 23(3), 122–133. 10.1108/01437730210424066

Saputra, I., Rini, R., & Hariri, H. (2022). Principal's transformational leadership in the education era. *International Journal of Current Science Research and Review*, 5(8). 10.47191/ijcsrr/V5-i8-07

Slavich G.M & Zimbardo P. G. (2012). Transformational teaching: Theoretical underpinnings, basic principles, and core methods. *Educ Psychol Rev*, 24(4), 569-608. .10.1007/s10648-012-9199-6

Spector, B. (2013). Lee Iacocca and the origins of transformational leadership. *Leadership*, 10(3), 361–379. 10.1177/1742715013514881

Suifan, T. S., Abdallah, A. B., & Al Janini, M. (2018). The impact of transformational leadership on employees' creativity. *Management Research Review*, 41(1), 113–132. 10.1108/MRR-02-2017-0032

Thanh, N., & Quang, N. (2022). Transformational, transactional, laissez-faire leadership styles and employee engagement Evidence from Vietnam's public sector. *SAGE Open*, 12(2), 2022. 10.1177/21582440221094606

Tichy, N., & Ulrich, D. (1984). The leadership challenge: A call for transformational leader. *Sloan Management Review*, 26(1).

Triana, M. D. C., Richard, O. C., & Yucel, I. (2017). Status incongruence and supervisor gender as moderators of the transformational leadership to subordinate affective organizational commitment relationship. *Personnel Psychology*, 70(2), 429–467. 10.1111/peps.12154

Vera, D., & Crossan, M. (2004). Strategic leadership and organizational learning. *Academy of Management Review*, 29(2), 222–240. 10.2307/20159030

Vinh, N., Hien, L., & Do, Q. (2022). The relationship between transformation leadership, job satisfaction, and employee motivation in the tourism industry. *Administrative Sciences*, 12(4), 161. 10.3390/admsci12040161

Western Governor University. (2021). *Retrieved from Defining Transactional Leadership*. EGU. https://www.egu.edu/transactional-leadership2103.html

Whiteman, M. (2018). *Ethics in Life and Vocation*. Milne.

Xenikou, A. (2017). Transformational leadership, transactional contingent reward, and organizational identification: The mediating effect of perceived innovation and goal culture orientations. *Frontiers in Psychology*, 8, 8. 10.3389/fpsyg.2017.0175429093688

Xie, L. (2020). The impact of servant leadership and transformational leadership on learning organization: A comparative analysis. [Servant and transformational leadership and learning]. *Leadership and Organization Development Journal*, 41(2), 220–236. 10.1108/LODJ-04-2019-0148

Zhao, N., Fan, D., & Chen, Y. (2021). Understanding the Impact of Transformational Leadership on Project Success: A Meta-Analysis Perspective. *Computational Intelligence and Neuroscience*, 2021, 1–12. 10.1155/2021/751779134707652

Chapter 5
International Field Education Through the Lens of Cultural Humility:
Transformational Learning Abroad

Lisa M. B. Tokpa
Uganda Christian University, Uganda

ABSTRACT

With the challenges facing our society today, it is critical that opportunities be provided for social work students to learn about difference, and how to work effectively with diverse populations. International field education is one important way to provide these opportunities to students in an immersive setting. The Uganda Studies Program provides experiential knowledge in this through a framework of cultural humility. Grounded in educational standards, the author presents considerations, challenges, and learning opportunities within cross-cultural exchanges. Power dynamics embedded in such exchanges are explored, and a challenge is presented to move towards active participation in redressing inequalities through mutually beneficial partnerships. A case is made, and a guide provided for American social work programs to adhere to its ethical mandate and responsibility to decolonize international field education in ways that support indigenous social work, local supervisors, and academicians, while simultaneously providing quality, competency-based student learning outcomes.

DOI: 10.4018/979-8-3693-2407-3.ch005

International Field Education Through the Lens of Cultural Humility

INTRODUCTION

Turn on the news today and the overwhelming challenge is this: We struggle to get along with those who are different than us. Social work stands out among other fields of study for its unparalleled emphasis on embracing diversity as a fundamental cornerstone of the profession. The role of a social worker has perhaps never been more needed, but how are we training social work students to be leaders in this critical pursuit within our nation and around the world? Are we giving them opportunities to practice and gain supervisory feedback before they are expected to take on a caseload of diverse clients or meet with a community that has been shaped by vastly different life experiences? Universities need to invest in, and give priority to, training the next generation of social workers to work effectively and humbly within diverse populations. International field education is one important way to provide these opportunities to students in an immersive setting (Healy & Thomas, 2020). This pursuit requires social work programs to demonstrate the profession's values of increasing critical consciousness around power dynamics, especially inherent in study abroad and cultural immersive learning, particularly in the Global South[1] (Jönsson & Flem, 2018).

"Transformative learning is significant learning experience that engages the learner intellectually, emotionally, and socially" and is a critical component of international field education (Ali et al, 2022 p. 29; Giles, 2014). International collaborations have the potential to create opportunities for learning that help students translate theory into practice, widen their perspectives of helpful interventions, develop greater self-awareness in working with diverse populations, and centralize relationships in social work practice (Lager et al., 2010; Ali et al., 2022; Roe, 2015). International field placements also help students recognize the impact of imperialism, colonialism, and modernization (Hay et al., 2018; Nadan, 2017) and "redress inequalities in a global context" (Bell & Anscombe, 2012, p. 1033).

Acknowledging the importance of cross-cultural learning opportunities, particularly international field education, is just the first step. The next is designing them in a way that upholds the values of the social work profession. The first three competencies within the Council on Social Work Education's (CSWE) 2022 Educational Policy and Accreditation Standards help guide the way:

1. Demonstrate Ethical and Professional Behavior
2. Advance Human Rights and Social, Racial, Economic, and Environmental Justice
3. Engage Anti-Racism, Diversity, Equity, and Inclusion in Practice

One way in which CSWE operationalizes the third competency is this:

Demonstrate cultural humility by applying critical reflection, self-awareness, and self-regulation to manage the influence of bias, power, privilege, and values in working with clients and constituencies, acknowledging them as experts of their own lived experiences (p. 10).

Further, the National Association of Social Workers Code of Ethics (2021), section 1.05 highlights the importance of cultural humility as it states, "Social workers should demonstrate awareness and cultural humility by engaging in critical self-reflection (understanding their own bias and engaging in self-correction); recognizing clients as experts of their own culture; committing to life-long learning; and holding institutions accountable for advancing cultural humility" (NASW, 2021). The importance of cultural humility in study abroad and cultural immersion is gaining traction as a credible framework for engagement with diverse communities (Ferranto, 2015; Isaacson, 2014; Luciano, 2020; Zhu et al., 2023). Further, the emphasis on cultural humility within these existing educational guidelines provides a guidepost for the design of ethical, cross-cultural engagement.

This chapter will examine methods for establishing international student opportunities that align with the tenets of cultural humility, foster student competency development while simultaneously centralizing the needs of local communities. This can be a challenging endeavor, so this too will be discussed, and solutions provided.

The Uganda Studies Program

Much of my learning and many of the examples presented in this chapter are derived from the Uganda Studies Program (USP), a study abroad program at Uganda Christian University. USP has been providing cross-cultural learning for students since 2004, and social work emphasis since 2009, utilizing an experiential learning model that incorporates culturally immersive components in school, work, and family settings. The program is based on the belief that the best way to learn about identity, culture, and navigating difference effectively is by building authentic relationships *within* diversity. USP has built strong partnerships with local partner agencies over time and many cups of tea. The mutually beneficial relationships between USP, the host university (UCU), agency supervisors, and the students provide the foundation for learning for all involved in the partnership.

USP's approach to field education embraces cultural humility through several key elements, including an interactive seminar that provides the space to prepare for, process, and assess experiences, focusing on critical self-reflection and awareness. The social work program is embedded in the larger USP experience, which includes a core course that gives further opportunity for students to reflect on their own values in light of their various experiences in Uganda. USP social work students live with host families and African peers on the UCU campus and conduct internships under the supervision of Uganda professionals. It is through these relationships that students learn what it means to be a part of a community that holds values and norms different than their own.

The Challenge

It is part of American's DNA to achieve greatness and value the work of striving to be the best at a personal, community, and national level. This competitive backdrop can become dangerous when it creates a false narrative about other countries, especially those in the Global South. When these narratives are internalized, cross-cultural engagement is bound to fail before it has started. Three pervasive myths I have seen in international social work programming that need to be confronted are (1) Social work ethics don't apply when traveling to the Global South, (2) American education is best, and (3) It is our role to help.

Modeling Ethics

While institutions of higher education desire to use the tool of education to fight these widespread inaccuracies, perceptions of the Global South invade even the halls of social work programs. An author of the article, "#WhiteSaviorComplex: Confidentiality, Human Dignity, Social Media, and Social Work Study Abroad" retells the controversy over faculty displaying photos of clients during their short-term trips to countries in the Global South, failing to recognize the ethical violation because they wanted to share their significant experience with others (p. 5).

During faculty trips to the Uganda Studies Program, the ethical policies of taking photos along with sharing identifying stories must be enforced and faculty must be reminded throughout, as the temptation to capture their experience to share with others can be strong. Why do we hold such a double standard when in countries with people who are Black and Brown? Self-reflection, a marker of cultural humility, is critical of all who take part in cross-cultural experiences, including leaders of these trips. When faculty model cultural humility and provide ethical policies before the exchange, students will be much more likely to follow their lead.

Contextualizing Student Learning

Trusting the expertise of local professionals is also something that trickles down to the students' approach abroad. When U.S. social work programs maintain a rigidity to the way competencies are operationalized in a U.S. context, for example, this can easily set students up for frustration and an elitist approach to their experience and relationship with their foreign supervisor/coworkers. If there is unconfronted misinformation about the context in which the student is learning, assumptions are easily made by faculty that reflect a notion of, "I need to control a lot of their experience since they won't be meeting our standards of education there." Perhaps unintentional, this academic rigidity and control, which is based on stereotypes and assumptions, is neo-colonialism masked in social work jargon.

Deconstructing "The Helper"

Many students who complete field placements through the Uganda Studies Program often go through a process of deconstructing their expectations about their role as a "helper" and then reconstructing their understanding of their role as a "learner." Field directors have a key role in preparing students for their international field placement to lessen the dissonance between what students expect and what they encounter in regard to the student's role in Uganda.

Much has been written about the dangers of "voluntourism," (Wearing, 2001; Bandyopadhyay & Patil, 2017), "poverty porn," (Dortonne, 2016), and the "white savior complex" (Cole, 2012), as well as the importance of "decolonization" in our approach (Delgado & Mulder, 2017). A study conducted with students from Sweden and Norway who completed internships in the Global South revealed their focus on underdevelopment and legitimizing interventions that are seen as making necessary changes, and even "rescuing" communities and people living there (Jönsson & Flem, 2018). Social work programs should be leading the way in confronting paternalistic approaches in international programming rather than contributing to their destructive impact. Conversations about these approaches – and how to avoid them -- should start early, well before students engage in the exchange.

Unpacking Cultural Humility

Given the powerful false narratives, the American ethnocentric impulse (Storti, 2001), and cultural bias that exists in our society, it is imperative that leaders return to the basic tenets of cultural humility when envisioning, planning, designing, implementing, and evaluating international exchanges. At its core, cultural humility is an "accurate awareness of self (including limitations), honesty in self presentation, and orientation to others rather than to self "(Worthington et al., 2017, p. 4). Further clarified, it is a "change in overall perspective and way of life" (Foronda et al., 2016, p. 214). A conceptual study conducted by Bibus and Koh (2021) furthered the discourse on cultural humility to include the relational nature of social work, adding that the concept is more accurately *intercultural* humility as a social worker's "ethical responsibilities flow from all human relationships from the personal and familial to the social and professional" (NASW, 2021, Purpose of the NASW Code of Ethics).

A study on transformational learning and cultural humility in study abroad identified three major themes in the student learning process: 1) confusion and discomfort, 2) remolding, and 3) humility in action (Zhu et al., 2023). If the goal is for the cross-cultural exchange to propel students to be more effective bridge-builders across difference, challenges need to be embraced, discussed, and reflected upon. Close supervision is needed to keep students moving through these stages. Without guidance, students can get stuck within the frustration that marks the first stage, risking a deepening of held, Western-centric beliefs and a repeating of damaging approaches abroad. Or they could stagnate in the remolding process, which can be inward and reflective. While important, many approaches stop at the analysis of social problems highlighted by stepping outside one's own culture, rather than "challenging situations of inequality, oppression and social change at the structural level or 'undoing of privileges' at the individual" (Jönsson & Flem, 2018; Pease, 2010).

Five pillars of cultural humility that this chapter will focus on are 1) Utilizing self-reflection; 2) Acknowledging privilege and the power associated with it; 3) Viewing local professionals as experts in their context; 4) Becoming a life-long learner; and 5) Creating mutually beneficial partnerships (Bennett & Gates, 2019; Fisher-Borne et al., 2015; Gottlieb, 2020; Tervalon & Murray-Garcia, 1998; Zhu et al., 2023). We will consider these pillars of cultural humility, ways to incorporate them into programming, common challenges to prepare for, and ways to overcome those challenges.

Self-Reflection

Both the Council on Social Work Education and the National Association of Social Workers underscore the importance of "critical reflection, self-awareness, and self-regulation to manage the influence of bias, power, privilege, and values in working with clients and constituencies…" (CSWE, 2022, p. 10). Incorporating exercises that promote self-reflection, awareness, and regulation are a critical place to start when conceptualizing a successful international learning experience for social work students. If these are not intentionally integrated into the design of the program, the default approach marked by bias and false narratives will go unchallenged (Ali et al., 2022; Dunlap & Mapp, 2017; Sewpaul & Henrickson, 2019). Furthermore, if intentional efforts to increase critical consciousness are not integrated throughout the program – from preparation to debrief – implicit bias will not only go unchecked, but may grow deeper roots.

Journals

Journaling is one common way in which self-reflection, awareness, and regulation can be intentionally integrated into the international program curriculum. At USP, journals follow the goals and methodology presented in the book, Charting A Hero's Journey, by Linda A Chisholm (2000):

Journals are not simply a telling of thoughts, feelings, and daily goings on, according to Chisholm, "...it is a developed form of literature that teaches you the art of careful observation, accurate reporting and in this case, cross-cultural analysis. A journal commands the writer and invites the reader into the very process through which new thinking is derived and change occurs. Journals, at their best, are a vehicle for the student to examine, direct, and document the transformation of the self." (xi)

Journals are evaluated based on observation/reflection, knowledge/values/skill development of and within the host culture, self, and social work profession, integration of learning, and academic writing. Students are encouraged to read their journals aloud in the seminar so other students can give feedback and encouragement. They are used as a jumping-off point for further reflection and discovery.

Seminar

In seminar/group discussions, as well as during one-on-one supervision meetings with both US-based faculty and local supervisors, opportunities for self-reflection should be provided. For example, students might come to a seminar frustrated about something they observed or experienced in the cross-cultural practice setting. They should be encouraged to express their raw emotions (unless offensive to others in the class), and then utilize this opportunity to explore any implicit bias that might be at play. "Why do you think that frustrated you?" "What did you expect and then what did you find?" and then explore the dissonance between expectations (often based in what is known) and reality (what may still be unknown). Utilizing experiences that give rise to emotions and reactions, which are then explored to reveal a deeper self-awareness, can be a very impactful lesson that students will remember far into their careers. Likewise, curricula that successfully weave experiences with opportunities for reflection (and challenge) are critical ways in which a social work program can achieve its goal of preparing social workers for the challenges in bridging rifts of difference in the future. Other ways to incorporate self-reflection are through student evaluations, which could include sections that note self-evaluation. Also, process-recordings can be particularly beneficial in cross-cultural settings, especially if local supervisors/faculty provide feedback as well. Self-reflection should be noted throughout the discussion recorded.

Power and Privilege

CSWE and NASW (2021) clearly state that self-reflection is not just for self-actualization, but is important in order to "...*manage the influence of bias, power, privilege, and values in working with clients and constituencies...*" (CSWE, 2022, p. 10). Unearthing power and privilege dynamics is an important goal of self-reflection and the concept of cultural humility, which recognizes "that culture is often used as a tool of social, economic, and political power of one group over another" (Pon, 2009). If left unaddressed, the cultural oppression can be perpetuated in professional encounters between service providers and recipients (Zhu, et al., 2023, p. 4; Mapp & Rice, 2019).

Caron (2020) notes three elements necessary for international social work programs: 1) anti-imperialist practice frameworks that include understanding colonialism; 2) anti-oppressive practice perspectives which promote equity, inclusion, change, and social justice, and 3) a critical approach to practice that entails understanding one's own beliefs, privileges, power dynamics, and oppressions. These aspects are still often missing in many international exchanges – relationships may be formed and respect offered, but an awareness and understanding of the complex power dynamics at play in such exchanges is too often overlooked.

To start, leaders need to explore these questions: What is the historical background of the country, tribe, and people group that we are engaging? What are current perceptions within the community of those from the U.S. and what are those perceptions based on? How do the perceptions differ towards the various races and ethnicities of Americans? What role did oppression play in its history and who were the main actors? How can this program work towards dismantling existing power inequalities?

Gaining as much information as possible about the context in which students are engaging is critical, noting the diversity and intersectionality that often exists within all layers of society (i.e., countries, communities, tribes, families, etc.). Further, research the impact that American travelers may have on these host communities. Are they typically welcomed or is there suspicion? Again, what is the historical backdrop to these perceptions? Studies have shown more emphasis is needed to prepare students in global inequalities and privileges. Without this backdrop, along with an intentional focus throughout their time abroad on critical reflections around issues of social justice and human rights, "students risk reproducing the notion of 'the other' in need of (white, western) development interventions (Escobar, 1995; Jönsson & Flem, 2018; Pease, 2010; Goudge, 2003). If possible, preparation for international exchanges should include a unit on global inequalities which particularly highlight the specific realities of racism and its role in the communities involved in the exchange.

In Uganda, there is a long history of colonialism, religious missions, and tourism that dramatically impacts the perceptions of foreigners from the West. While Ugandan culture tends to be welcoming and hospitable to all guests, the power dynamics that exist play an important role in many interactions, and hence they need to be a part of the preparation for student engagement. Just as in all worker-client relationships, power needs to be considered (CSWE, 2022). If a social worker asks a client if they can take their photo, the client cannot be assumed to have agency to respond authentically. Therefore, no-photo policies are in place to avoid this ethical conflict. Likewise, depending on the disparity of power between the visitor and host, asking permission may not cover concerns about the ethics of a request. At the same time, when power dynamics are assumed, agency is taken away. For example, a student refusing to accept something given because they are perhaps overly sensitive to the power dynamics they assume led to the gift, or a student refusing to take a photo with a host sibling because she doesn't feel she can trust when they say it is acceptable to do so.

To understand how to properly engage despite power disparities, those with cross-cultural experience – especially within the context where students are going – should be relied upon. Additionally, cross-cultural relationships formed and strengthened over time and through honest conversation will lead to a deeper understanding of the intricacies of power dynamics within relationships. This should first be modeled through the relationships between leaders of the exchange, and then encouraged between students and their peers/coworkers/supervisors. For example, USP students often bring up an uncomfortable situation during home visits in which the client or coworkers give the student a chair to sit in while everyone else sits on the floor. This example sheds light on the complexities within these exchanges and provides an opportunity for deeper discussions on what cultural humility might look like in action. Does acknowledging power imbalances require students to confront the imbalance and refuse the honored seat? Was the chair given because the student was White? From the US? Male? Or just because they were a visitor, and all visitors are given an honored seat? Would it be offensive to refuse such a gesture? These dynamics are discussed in the seminar, but the conclusion is always the same – students are encouraged to talk with their Ugandan supervisor and/or coworkers about it. Utilizing such situations to build cross-cultural relationships in which there is an honest exchange of ideas and a shift toward mutual benefit is an important part of redressing existing power imbalances.

In addition to these experiences providing opportunities to learn about the depths and complexities of power dynamics, they also provide opportunities to focus on dismantling any sense of entitlement and can bring about a greater awareness of student privilege. Powerful, practical, and personal experiences are bound to happen when students are abroad, and these need to be properly debriefed to maximize their learning potential. For some White students, traveling to the Global South may be the first time they are not in the racial group majority, and this gives rise to new situations in which they experience privilege that they would not otherwise have (Zhu et al., 2023). For example, a dress code or other policy might be strictly enforced for local or even students of color on the program by the agency/institution, but not for the White students. White students might be offered better food, more grace when learning something new in the culture, or given easier tasks in the home or practicum setting. Similarly, male students may be afforded obvious advantages and respect, as may all students to some degree because they are educated, speak English well, come from a wealthy nation, and are perceived to be wealthy or have connections with those who are, etc. These situations can be extremely uncomfortable and even disturbing to students who may not have recognized their power in ways that translate to obvious privilege.

It is important to acknowledge the vastly different experience American students of color may have from their White peers within these global exchanges. It is critical for program leaders to anticipate and plan for this reality, preparing students of color and providing resources throughout the program to help them process their experiences in safe and supportive environments. For Latino/a, Black and Asian students, the study abroad experience may motivate them to connect (or reconnect) with their origin, better understand themselves and where their ancestors came from (Zhu et al., 2023). For all students on these exchanges, countless opportunities exist to better see and understand complex and intersecting power and privilege dynamics. The goal of the program should be to help students translate these experiences and new realizations beyond the study abroad opportunity and allow it to propel them towards wider social change, dismantling racism, gender inequality, etc. at all levels and within all spheres. The task might feel overwhelming for students, but the opportunity is to start somewhere. USP students are asked, "What can you do to chip away at the sometimes-massive power imbalances that you are walking into?" Responses come such as, "I can ask my supervisor/coworkers questions" and "I can withhold judgement and approach with curiosity when I don't understand something happening at my site." The curriculum should give space for these critical conversations to turn experiences into learning and action.

While the program should support students to process and learn from these complicated power dynamics, it is also imperative that it also focuses on the wider impact of having Western students at partners agencies semester after semester, work towards redressing power imbalance and creating more equitable partnerships towards greater structural change. For example, when supervisors and/or community members are confused by the placement of a student of color instead of a White student, USP has joined with UCU faculty and more seasoned supervisors to elevate the awareness and training around diversity and combating the "whiteness of power"

(Goudge, 2003). The genuine relationships formed over time between international volunteers and host communities, or in our case, USP and its partner supervisors, can increase critical consciousness of all involved (Lough & Carter-Black, 2015; Loftsdóttir, 2002; Moncrieffe, 2009). These particular race dynamics in international volunteering, which could include study abroad, is described by Lough & Carter-Black (2015) as the "white elephant in the room" as they studied the perceptions of Kenyans towards international volunteers. The study highlighted a perceived connection between whiteness and wealth, resources, knowledge/competency, trust, and esteem in the community.

At USP, we have seen individual and community perceptions challenged by engaging students as learners, under the authority and guidance of Ugandan supervisors. Community members and clients are sometimes surprised when they first see a Western student learning from their local social worker, but over time have come to understand that the USP interns are students and have traveled across the globe to learn from the expertise of Ugandan professionals. More research needs to be conducted on the program's impact, but it is our hope that over time, USP students' presence in these communities as learners will challenge destructive power imbalances and racial denigration, while elevating the esteem and influence of local social workers (Fox, 2012). Lough & Carter-Black (2015) summarize the goal well, "Although neocolonial power structures are difficult to shift at the macro level, strengths-based dialogue, decentralized decision making, enhancing the mutuality of international exchange, and promoting culturally immersive relationships are micro steps toward greater racial equality in development practice" (p. 13).

Respecting and Involving the Expertise of Local Professionals

CSWE's 3rd competency: "Engage Anti-Racism, Diversity, Equity, and Inclusion in Practice" notes that clients and constituents should be acknowledged as "experts of their own lived experiences" (2022, p. 10). NASW also highlights social workers "recognizing clients as experts of their own culture" as an important part of cultural humility." (2021, 1.05c). Likewise, local social work professionals and supervisors also deserve this same recognition and respect. NASW further states, "Social workers should treat colleagues with respect and should represent accurately and fairly the qualifications, views, and obligations of colleagues" (2021, 2.01a). Respect and involvement are not always afforded to social work professionals in the Global South. However, to do so is an ethical mandate of the profession (Parker et al., 2015). Additionally, local expertise and active participation of host communities is paramount in creating exchanges that are rooted in the important social work value of context shaping effective practice, self-determination, as well as ensuring long-term sustainability (Sossou & Dubus, 2013). Fisher and Grettenberger's (2015) community-based participatory study abroad model supports the idea of participants as both teachers and learners, honoring local knowledge and removing the dichotomy of outside expert and recipient of their knowledge (Mapp & Rice, 2019).

What would happen if we *started* the process of engaging in international field placements with local professionals? What often occurs is an organization is located, a local supervisor agrees to oversee the student, and they are trained on what the US based faculty think they should learn when abroad. This colonial approach is widely accepted and rarely challenged. It's vital to include supervisors and local professionals in the design of the exchange – not just "fitting them in" once the program is established (Lough & Toms, 2017; Fisher & Grettenberger, 2015; Ouma & Dimaras, 2013). What do they want to offer and receive in the exchange? From their expertise, what do they see as the most important lessons that their supervision and context have to offer and receive from this exchange? And using a strengths-based perspective, what are the strengths of the culture and community within international exchanges? In Uganda, supervisors have intentionally utilized Uganda's communal culture to teach translatable skills in community development and the formation of relationships to build human resilience. There is also an emphasis on Uganda's problem solving and innovative approaches amidst a lack of formal resources, as well as advocating for clients through partnerships and networking. In Ghana, a study found that students had a reorienting towards human connection and the "resisting of the culture of waste, consumerism, materialism, and convenience back home" (Zhu et al., 2023, p. 15). Through relationships with local professionals, the strengths of the context should be explored and highlighted in the design of the program.

Context matters – this social work value needs to be modeled to students. Too often academicians can hold too tightly to the way in which standards and expectations are articulated and understood, thus missing out on a wider perspective, which is vital to contextualizing social work standards. This approach can unwittingly impose Westernized methods at the expense of indigenous models (Mathiesen & Lager, 2007; Cleak et al., 2016). Research cautions "importing Western values to assist marginalized ethnic groups may result in new forms of inequity" (Ali et al., 2022; Greenfield et al., 2012; Law & Lee, 2016). To avoid this, field directors should ask, "How is competency development operationalized in this new context?" "How might it be articulated?" For example, local supervisors should be asked what it looks like at their agency and within their cultural context to "demonstrate ethical and professional behavior" among other competencies and practice behaviors. The responses can then be added to the framing of the competency-based experience. For example, the feedback we were given by Ugandan supervisors was that some of the CSWE competencies were written (or at least understood by American students and faculty) as too individual-focused for the Ugandan context. Together, we created and edited practice behaviors that reflected the communal spirit of the supervisors, staff, organizations, and communities that students worked with, while still holding true to universal principles embedded in each competency. As another example, Ravulo (2018) created a new model for engagement based upon the local community's epistemologies in the Pacific Islands, where social work is not yet fully recognized as a profession, yet social work skills and knowledge abound. The result was personal and professional growth among students, and partnerships that were upheld by underlying social work values of dignity and worth of all people and communities. By highlighting and utilizing indigenousness knowledge, students learn new and innovative ways to foster empowerment and justice applicable to various cultural contexts (Ravulo, 2018; Kincheloe et al., 2008).

Because knowing the context is such a key part of achieving outcomes in social work practice, utilizing local supervision is critical in any exchange in which students engage in field work. Intentionally and continuously empowering local supervisors in the exchange is one of the most critical pieces in creating mutual benefit and maintaining an approach of cultural humility. Due to societal power dynamics, implicit bias, etc. when working in the Global South, even though supervisors should have authority over and respect from their student, this is unfortunately not always the case. Leaders of these exchanges need to model this respect first and foremost by deferring to the opinions and supervision expertise of local supervisors and presenting to students this alignment with their local supervisor. It is important to recognize that respecting local voices, especially when students feel confused, stressed, or uncomfortable with their field experience, may not be the student's default. This makes it even more critical for Western program leaders to empower local supervisors in all phases of the exchange. When conflicts or different ideas arise (and they will, due to vastly different cultural backgrounds and ideas), it is important to come to agreement with supervisors on the messages given to students, and then presenting an aligned approach.

One lesson learned at the Uganda Studies Program was that providing training to local supervisors, when done well and with mutual respect and participation, helps empower supervisors to regain footing in the often imbalance of power in the local supervisor – American student dynamic. These trainings too are part of the benefit that local supervisors gain from the exchange, especially when conducted in collaboration with a local social work academic program. In Uganda, supervisors are eager to learn, but sometimes cannot afford higher education, so the trainings that offer certificates from a local university are well received. To create a collaborative approach to these trainings, it is beneficial to incorporate local professionals and seasoned supervisors as trainers, in addition to local academicians.

Lessons students implicitly and explicitly learn through these exchanges can be far-reaching in their social work practice. If they learn to listen to and respect the work and voices of local professionals, they will be more likely to replicate this approach in their practice when working with diverse communities and clients. Cultural humility is like any other skill -- if practiced over time, it becomes second nature. Respecting and elevating local voices, working towards mutual benefit when designing programs, etc. can take time and "muscle" – but muscle memory will be achieved and will then become the default of students-turned-professional when working across differences. However, it is important to note that perfecting "cultural humility" is not the goal and is counter to its essence based in humility, which brings us to another pillar: life-long learning.

Life-Long Learning

This is perhaps the key to true cultural humility: a commitment to life-long learning (NASW, 2021, 1.05c). If one sets out to gain mastery of this skill and approach, the primary element is lost. Humility can be worked on, practiced, and one can be held accountable to, but its essence is this: We will always have more to learn. *Always*. Especially when it comes to engaging with different people groups. We will never fully grasp or understand someone's life and experience unless we have walked in their shoes. Cultural humility must be viewed as an ongoing process as opposed to an outcome (Ortega & Faller, 2011).

Learning anything new or unique can lead to an arrogance that "I now 'get it'" with a slippery slope to the assumption that "you don't get it" as others are judged. We have experienced this from and towards other Westerners in Uganda. For example, together with a Ugandan colleague, we approached a refugee agency looking for internship partners. The leader was from the U.S. and her skepticism was obvious from the start. She was unpersuaded to partner even as the Ugandan head of department explained how semester-long internships are important to teach the next generation of both Ugandan and foreign social work students. She was blinded by her "progressive" way of engaging and thought she was "protecting her clients" from short-term relationships, but was just another example of deciding what was best for a group of people she didn't fully understand and becoming a block in empowering Ugandans to learn how to effectively work with other Africans in need.

A commitment to life-long learning requires an intentional look at the role that cynicism plays when lessons are learned across cultures. Battling cynicism is perhaps one of the greatest challenges USP students face as their perspective shifts, their understanding of the world grows, and they then return to their home context. Programs need to be aware of this temptation and intentionally counter the damage of cynicism paired with arrogance, one way is through key times of reflection. The Uganda Studies Program, for example, conducts a four-day debrief at the end of the semester that provides the students with tools to help prepare them to translate and integrate their learning in Uganda, including utilizing the same cultural humility they worked on in Uganda, when they return home.

Mutually Beneficial Partnerships

An inherent foundation of cultural humility is that of mutual benefit. It is also a piece that is easily diminished when there are more or louder voices from the West. Mapp and Rice (2019) argue that social work study abroad programs must be designed to center "the needs of the community and not that of the students" (p. 427). According to a recent overview of international social work practicums, the 2000-2010 research showed an increase in critical questions about the reciprocity of approaches (Ali et al., 2022). Lough (2009) expressed concerns about the unidimensional nature of international exchanges. Furthering this important discourse, research has emerged that provide models that support reciprocity within international field education within the past decade (Thampi, 2017; Sossou & Dubus, 2013). An approach that resonates with the USP model is the asset-based justice learning model which focuses on the needs of the host community and redressing social injustices at all levels of engagement (Butin, 2007; Donaldson & Daughtery, 2011; Sossou & Dubus, 2013), as well as Fisher and Grettenberger's (2015) community-based participatory study abroad model, which emphasizes the needs of the community and their participation in developing projects that affect them (Mapp & Rice, 2019). Seeing faculty model the importance and commitment to establishing equal partnerships across differences is perhaps the greatest lesson students will learn from such an exchange, and an ethical imperative towards a social justice model of engagement. The partnerships that are forged between faculty, institutions, agencies, and professionals can be the student's model for their partnership with peers, and their respect for their local supervisors. Countering the hierarchy so often modeled in exchanges with the Global South, and the action taken to foster mutuality, will speak louder than any words written in a text. In summary, the following are a few critical ways in which creating mutually beneficial partnerships can be achieved:

- Engaging with a goal to elevate the voices of indigenous social work professionals is an important starting point. Ravulo (2018) notes, "There is an ongoing need to recognize the importance of indigenous peoples around the world and their ontologies and epistemologies in social work practice" (p. 57). One way to do this in international programming is to establish professional partnerships in research, training of local supervisors, teaching collaborations, and the development of student learning goals and curriculums.
- Leaders of these exchanges should always ask "How is this benefitting the host country and its people?" and deriving answers to this from local leaders

- throughout the exchange, and then incorporating their ideas regarding what could be done to make it more equal in its benefit.
- As mentioned, incorporating local leaders in all stages of the programming to ensure that a local approach is being heard and acknowledged throughout the exchange, not just at the beginning.
- Always asking, "What is our impact?" Is it positive, negative, or neutral? Are we unintentionally disadvantaging local students or other local populations simply with our program's presence, students, money (real and perceived), etc.?
- In collaboration with local academicians and professionals, create a list of benefits that both sides of the exchange are to receive. Return to it and add on to it, acknowledging that the students (who are traveling for the purpose of their learning) will benefit the most unless intentional consideration and action is taken to counter this imbalance of benefit.

As a department within Uganda Christian University, it is important that USP collaborates with the university's social work program in its common goal of providing quality social work education, including field practicums. One successful way we have accomplished this is through a cross-cultural social work group that meets several times throughout the semester and is made up of an equal number of UCU and USP students. These group meetings are led by the UCU Social Work Head of Department and the USP Social Work Coordinator who facilitate discussions about diversity and difference in practice. Students learn both the similarities and differences in social work academia, how social workers are perceived in different cultures, how ethical decision making is influenced by culture (especially confidentiality, boundaries, etc.), individual versus communal culture implications, the differing roles of government, faith and religion and many other topics that maximize the diversity of student experiences toward the shared goal of increased cultural and self-awareness. The prevailing realization from these student engagements is that context must shape practice in order for it to be effective. Bibus and Koh (2021) note that "studies have found that participants in structured intergroup dialogue groups experience reductions in prejudice, gains in knowledge about other cultures or social groups, and improvements in understanding others (Dessel et al., 2012, Rodenborg & Boisen, 2013, Rodenborg & Bosch, 2009). While ideal to have in-person groups, many goals can be accomplished through the formation of virtual peer-to-peer learning groups, including the goal of mutual benefit.

Skepticism certainly exists among scholars and faculty regarding the possibility of achieving mutual benefit given the existing power dynamics and the ease in which a partnership can turn exploitive. This is especially true when placing American undergraduate university students at agencies in the Global South. Similarly, but perhaps with less complexity, controversy exists when any student is placed at a domestic, under-resourced agency. Efforts to quantify and further define "benefit" have been made with this concern in mind and should continue to be explored. Differing opinions on this complicated subject should be welcomed, supported by the value of life-long learning. To note, some of the benefits that Ugandan supervisors have reported in the USP exchange include increased English language proficiency of staff and clients, assistance with technology, a new and outside perspective to difficult casework and administrative tasks, a boost to the program image in the community with the inclusion of international student learners (which is not without complexity as discussed in this chapter, but is nevertheless consistently noted as a benefit by supervisors), trainings and professional development, contributing to the field of global social work, being an extension of the quality higher education of Uganda Christian University, and the assistance of students who are motivated, committed, and willing to help where needed. However, it has been my experience that often the greatest benefit that I witness in these cross-cultural exchanges is difficult to quantify accurately because the benefit is the relationship itself. There is transformative power in genuine, reciprocal human connection, bridging the vast differences in our identities.

What Cultural Humility is Not

Now that we have taken a closer look at what cultural humility is and how it can be used as a framework for program design, it is important to also discuss what it is not. It can be tempting, especially when uncomfortable, to use cultural humility as a reason for not leaning into the discomfort of difference. For example, USP students often will claim that the reason they have not brought up a hard conversation with their supervisor or are not fully participating in the activities at their agency is because they are trying to practice cultural humility. Statements such as "Who am I to say or do anything in this context?" or "I don't know enough to participate well, so I will just observe" can often be heard. Cultural humility does not mean perfect engagement, but it does require effort. It requires us to try – recognizing that we will probably make mistakes, but the effort in *trying* speaks volumes about the desire to grow, learn, and develop. Trying – and making mistakes – shows the host culture that those awkward interactions are worth it to develop genuine connections across difference. These efforts also help chip away at power imbalances – *we need the help of local expertise*, and this vulnerability is important to demonstrate to establish reciprocity in relationships abroad. Further, participation within a community is of high value within many Global South contexts. Therefore, it is even more important for students to engage in activities, even when lacking confidence. It is important to recognize when students are using cultural humility as a justification for avoiding discomfort and to help them explore what they are feeling, redefining cultural humility as active not passive. Cultural humility should propel social workers towards social justice; it should propel us to "confront imbalances [in power] rather than just acknowledge that they exist." (Fisher-Born et al., 2015, p. 177)

Through my international experiences, I too have used the justification of "cultural humility" when I lacked confidence in sharing my thoughts, offer my assistance, or be an effective leader. I have needed my African peers, coworkers, and supervisors to help me see the difference between humility and a lack of courage. This can be a complicated tension to explore, especially for students at the start of their social work career, and it depends on many factors. It is still something I am exploring and is a topic a Ugandan university colleague will often challenge me and USP students on. He and other Ugandan professionals challenge USP staff and students to not be so consumed with fear that we are violating the values of cultural humility and encourages us to "be free" (as Ugandans say). The main point being, while approaching difference with humility is paramount, we need the ongoing feedback from our cross-cultural relationships to ensure we are operationalizing cultural humility in ways that are mutually beneficial and, ultimately, creating authentic connections across difference.

With cultural humility providing a framework, let us build upon it by discussing the creation of quality and ethical curriculums, and then policies that help program participants adhere to the values of cultural humility.

Decolonizing Curriculums

According to Razack (2012), one major problem for students doing international field training in the Global South is the West-centric frames of reference they obtain through their educations in the Global North. This has been described as "professional imperialism" which replicates itself in different global contexts while ignoring existing power structures. (Nuttman-Shwartz & Berger, 2012, p. 229).

"New horizons are needed for an international field training responding appropriately to local concerns while critically aware of the impact of West-centric discourses on local activities. This requires new pedagogical practices and educational tools to envision possibilities for change within the dominant discourses (such as neo-liberalism, colonization, imperialism, and Third world development) that influence the contexts of international field training" (Jönsson & Flem, 2018).

Engaging in the process of decolonizing curriculums should be a priority for social work educators, and involves many steps and approaches, but an important one for the purpose of this chapter is recognizing who is "at the table". International exchanges can have the best intentions, but if the curriculums are not created within the diversity it seeks to teach about, the exchange can be easily weighted towards Western student benefit, overshadowing, or becoming completely devoid of voices from the other side of the exchange, and even becoming exploitive. Part of cultural humility is a recognition of one's own limited perspective, experiencing the world through one lens (Bibus & Koh, 2021). Therefore, it is imperative to incorporate – at all points in the planning, designing, implementing, and evaluating phases – the perspectives of those engaging in the exchange. Questions should be asked such as "What voices are being heard in leadership positions in this exchange?" "What research, authors, and texts are we incorporating into the curriculum, and do they reflect the perspectives of those involved in this exchange?" and as mentioned previously, "How are competencies being operationalized in the cultural context of engagement, and are those differences highlighted for students?"

When students are given lenses to see beyond their single narrative of the world, they can become more critical of the predominantly White social work theories and interventions (Tascón & Ife, 2019) and can continue important efforts to decolonize social work education. This can be seen at USP when social work students learn from interactions with their Ugandan peers at UCU that culture must impact practice, but then recognize - and become troubled - that it is predominately Western textbooks that provide the curricular backdrop at the school.

Educators and leaders who offer assignments such as case studies, process recordings, and research projects can have good intentions towards teaching valuable skills to social work students. However, if these assignments are not crafted and guided with the values of cultural humility in mind, they can do damage to the relationships within the cross-cultural program, including (and most concerning) relationships between local social workers and their clients.

First, Do No Harm

While "First, do no harm" is known more widely as an oath for health care professionals, the concept is foundational in learning abroad as well. As discussed, the predominant form of study abroad and international social work pedagogy can create harm by perpetuating stereotypes or colonial perspectives in the Global South (Mapp & Rice, 2019; Razack, 2009). It can create an experience that can be categorized as a 'colonial gaze', even when students are connected to Global South contexts through histories of migration and/or colonization (Sosa & Lesniewski, 2020).

Returning to the CSWE EPAS (2022), the first competency states: "Demonstrate Ethical and Professional Behavior," but are we cognizant of what that means in a foreign context before we send and oversee students practicing in that context? It is important to explore the established codes of ethics that are specific to the countries in which the cross-cultural exchange takes place and add these to the curriculum as required reading and studying, ideally in collaboration and discussion with local social work academicians. Additionally, the integration of the International Federation of Social Workers (IFSW) Code of Ethics into course curriculum and guidelines is important to broaden the scope of global ethical decision-making. IFSW as well as the International Association of Schools of Social Work (IASSW) have adopted the Global Agenda for Social Work and Social Development in 2010 which is another foundational framework for curriculum development (Ali et al., 2022).

When providing opportunities for social work study in foreign contexts, it is important to anticipate the potential situations that could occur that may create ethical conflicts, potential harm to the host community, or exploitation. Making promises (whether intentional or not), certain assignments, and insufficient supervision are just some of the common examples of potential harm that both leaders and students should be aware of.

Promises

When confronted by human suffering, sometimes for the first time or in a new way, it is natural to want to stop the suffering immediately – especially if it seems we have the resources to do so. While it might seem obvious, sometimes emotions can take over what may have been discussed inside the walls of a classroom and promises can be made by students to help. Sometimes promises are not made with words, but the actions taken can unintentionally lead clients, families, or community members to believe that the commitment to help has been established. Taking photos of the seemingly dire situation or even a Westerner asking certain questions of clients served by the local agency can give the illusion that they intend to help -- especially upon the backdrop of perceived notions that foreigners have more wealth, resources, and are often offering aid (Lough & Carter-Black, 2015). When this help does not come, usually expected in the form of money, donations, or sponsorship, clients can blame the local social workers and agency, thus causing a rift in the relationships that are vital for sustainable impact.

It can be tempting for social work students, especially when unfamiliar with the context, to miss the complexity of situations they encounter. On the surface, a student may perceive the problem faced by a client to solely be a lack of money, when they may not make this simple deduction in their own context. For example, USP students often come to Uganda with a desire to help and serve those they see as "less fortunate." They may be tempted to give money for the surgery needed, a new pair of shoes, buyers for their hand-woven baskets or carefully crafted necklaces, or even a promise of sponsorship. While generosity is not the problem, just like in the US, giving or promising gifts (especially without knowledge of the context or people and when the stay is short-term) creates ethical dilemmas and damaged relationships. But when faced with a combination of an unfamiliar context and heart-wrenching situations, social work principles can be all too often overlooked.

In Uganda, USP students have made promises (sometimes unintentionally) to clients and when the reality of fulfilling these promises becomes difficult or impossible, the promise may be forgotten by the student but held closely by the client, sometimes for years to come. The most harmful part of this scenario is that the local agency is left to try to explain what may have happened. Due to desperation, the agency social workers may not be believed and could even be blamed for the unfulfilled promise. Rather than being a support to the agency and fostering a deeper connection between local workers and clients that could lead to more sustainable impacts, the student (even while unintentional) can easily hinder these goals.

Assignments

Assignments given to students to accomplish during their study/placement abroad or within cross-cultural exchanges need to be well thought out and in collaboration with local professionals, as they also have the potential to harm clients and communities. As discussed, Westerners need to evaluate closely the power dynamics at play when agreeing to assignments with local agencies. A mutually beneficial relationship with local professionals needs to be forged to ensure that assignments are not in any way hindering their mission and work. At times, a local supervisor may put the learning needs of the student above those of the clients because they are caught between the values of helping clients and helping guests/honored faculty/partners achieve their goals. This is a difficult dilemma to put on local supervisors. Consultation within mutually beneficial partnerships, including local social work academicians, is imperative in assignment creation.

Ensuring students are following ethical principles in research assignments, for example, can be difficult when the context is familiar, and even more difficult in unfamiliar contexts. When in a foreign context, it is vital to collaborate with local professionals and academicians throughout the research project (Guth & Asner-Self, 2017), and abide by the protocols that often have been established at partner institutions to protect vulnerable populations. As has been discussed regarding general international field curriculums can also be applied to research: "It is important for academics in the Global North to de-center their own values and humbly seek to learn, and work within, the parameters of the local Afro- centric value system" (Hodge & Kibirige, 2021, p. 4). Only local expertise will be able to answer critical questions in research approaches, such as: What research questions unintentionally promise support? What research questions are too personal or will bring offense? Local knowledge is essential to ensure that actions do not become harmful to clients and communities. As a rule of thumb, a student who is new to a cultural context is probably not the best person to be carrying out any research directly with clients but could be helpful in data analysis or other behind-the-scenes tasks. Even Western faculty should see themselves as "junior partners in the research enterprise" that is conducted in a foreign context (Hodge & Kibirige, 2021, p. 5). For a more in-depth look at cross-cultural research, an article written specifically from the Uganda Christian University context is: *Addressing the Global Inequality in Social Work Research: Challenges, Opportunities, and Key Insights and Strategies in Sub-Saharan Africa* by David R. Hodge and Kasule Kibirige (2021).

Case studies are a common assignment for social work students, as they provide an opportunity for in-depth study of one case, client, or community, often throughout the course of a semester. These too, have the potential for harm unless closely supervised by home university faculty, as well as local social work academicians. Local supervisors should be given the authority to decide what client could benefit from such an assignment and when it is acceptable for a student to engage directly or indirectly with a client. Giving local supervisors this authority requires ongoing collaborative meetings and trainings to ensure that national and international ethical principles are being upheld in the process, especially given complicated power dynamics. These trainings are also imperative to ensure that students are being given direction on these high-risk assignments from a common approach.

Just as it is important in domestic placements, field directors need to consider the amount of supervision a student requires in each given assignment. In a foreign context, the supervision required is significantly greater due to the cultural differences. "Harm" can take the form of asking the student to accomplish too many assignments at their site (or confusing assignments not adequately explained to supervisors) that take the supervisor away from their clients, especially when the supervisor is already taking on more responsibility given that their student often needs ongoing cultural training and translation support. While evaluations are important, programs need to consider the time required for local supervisors to complete complicated and frequent field evaluations of the students, as well as what technology is accessible and reliable to complete these evaluations. If possible, these evaluations are best conducted if based upon the contextualized competencies that have been formulated in partnership with local supervisors, thus avoiding any confusion as to what is being asked of them regarding the student's progress, and giving supervisors a sense of ownership of student learning goals. In conclusion, assignments given to students should be done in collaboration with local supervisors where mutually beneficial relationships have been established. Careful consideration needs to be taken to ensure that each assignment that engages time and energy of local staff is done so within the scope of mutual benefit.

What is communicated to clients, whether intentional or not, as well as what practicum assignments are given to students while abroad are just some of the considerations leaders need to explore when designing and implementing study abroad opportunities. The risk of potential harm should be well understood through mutually beneficial partnerships, as well as inform the establishment of program policies.

Policies

Study abroad policies are critical to create ethical engagement based in the values of cultural humility. Policies regarding safety, health, and relationships have proven to be key elements of a sustainable international program at UCU. For the purposes of this chapter, policies regarding photos and social media will be examined as it highlights the impact of cultural humility in policy development and implementation.

Photos and Social Media

Policies regarding social media must evolve with the quickly shifting digital landscape. Country-specific ethical principles need to be researched to see if they include the use of technology, social media, and/or photo ethics. Photo ethics have already been mentioned in this chapter, as unfortunately, there is a tendency for those traveling to the Global South from the North to overlook the same ethical standards that would be standard in a domestic context. Unearthing the reasons for this tendency is important and are detailed in the article, "#WhiteSaviorComplex: Confidentiality, Human Dignity, Social Media, and Social Work Study Abroad" (Hamilton et al., 2021). Confronting the lax standards of photo and social media ethics is part of a larger process of unlearning colonialist paradigms, particularly rampant when traveling to and learning from within the Global South.

During orientation, USP conducts a social media skit in which real posts made by former USP students that have sensationalized their experience are shared. Then USP staff members read fictitious, but possible, responses from online community members, such as sending school faculty, friends, and family. The result is some laughs and an increased awareness of the importance of recognizing that the various people who read these posts might easily have misperceptions about Ugandans, and the posts of the students might well lead others to draw incorrect conclusions about the program. Finally, we have a basic social media policy that is included in the student handbook that all students read and sign, acknowledging that they have read it and understand its contents—including the disciplinary procedures that students can expect if they do not abide by the policy. The policy clearly states that students are not allowed to take any photos of clients at their practicum sites or during site visits, and not allowed to share personal stories of clients on any internet platform.

Any exceptions to this must go through USP coordinators. Outside of practicums, the statement advises students to ask themselves the following questions before posting anything about their time in Uganda: *Do I have a relationship with the people I'm taking a picture of? Do I know their names? Would I take that same photo at home? How would I feel if someone took a picture of me in that manner? Am I posting something that will send unclear or untrue messages about my safety or health? What message am I sending about my experience, myself, and the people of Uganda when I post this?*

The orientation sessions and policies provide a starting point to our conversations that happen throughout the semester regarding accurate/appropriate messaging: What message do you want to send about your time in Uganda, and does it honor the dignity and worth of Ugandans? To have a policy is the first step, but giving students an intrinsic motivation to consistently do this throughout their time in Uganda (and their career in social work) takes much more time and attention.

It is through cultivated-over-time, authentic relationships that policies evolve and respond to the context where the program is located. For example, USP's "no photos of clients" policy was established based on ethical standards in a North American context as well as a program commitment to redress power imbalances and avoid unintended financial commitments. However, when the policy was discussed at field supervisor training, it was met with some questions and disagreements from Ugandan supervisors. *What if the photos are taken by USP students with an organizational camera? What if the student has a better camera or is more skilled at photography and we need higher-quality photos for our donors?* If a Ugandan supervisor does not have a problem with a student taking photos of clients and even posting them on social media, what should the response be as a cross-cultural program?

One could easily take the route of creating and enforcing a USP policy in the name of upholding "ethical standards," but this is a slippery slope back into Western neocolonial tendencies to tell Ugandans what is "right" and "good" without seeking their perspectives in the creation of the policy. Three considerations have guided USP's response to these questions: (a) It is important to come to agreement on a case-by-case basis *in relationship* with Ugandan supervisors/faculty, (b) *all* perspectives are needed to navigate complicated ethical dilemmas, and (c) embrace nuance. Often the solution is not the easiest route (i.e. "the Ugandan supervisor is always right" or "this is how the NASW Code of Ethics is interpreted at home"). While the Ugandan cultural perspective must always be honored and power dynamics redressed, in a cross-cultural partnership all perspectives need to be heard and considered. For example, a supervisor might be advocating for students to take photos and post them because (a) that is what foreigners have always done—it is expected and not questioned, or (b) it can lead to much needed income for the organization. These conversations are more complicated than just submitting to the supervisor's judgment in all situations involving American students. A partnership with the local social work department is critical in these dilemmas to determine how best to navigate universal social work ethics within a country's context. Joining with local social work program leaders is also critical in communicating controversial policies so it is clear that they are mutually agreed-upon across cultural perspectives.

This process requires a return to the basic tenets of cultural humility, including always being a learner (no matter if one is a student or leader). Once we start to believe that we have the most progressive, well-researched, most effective approaches to conducting ourselves and programs cross-culturally, we fall back into our neocolonial tendencies without notice or challenge. Just as we encourage our students to do, we must approach every interaction as a learner, determined to develop study abroad partnerships that honor all clients and their stories.

Types of International Exchanges

While this chapter provides examples and a background knowledge of semester abroad programming, much of this can be applied to other program designs for international learning. Even if the time abroad for students is not in a semester increment, the relationships established among leaders can model cultural humility that has been, or has the potential to be, cultivated over time. Mapp & Rice (2019) argue that short-term trips, if done well, can help student to achieve CSWE (2022) established competencies, especially competency 2 and 3 regarding global oppression and marginalization, power and privilege, and cultural humility. The authors further outline a human rights-based approach as a helpful road map for both short-term and semester-long programming. The key components being human dignity, non-discrimination, participation, transparency, and accountability (Androff, 2016).

Due to financial constraints and degree requirements, a semester abroad may not be possible. However, due to the depth of learning that can be achieved through cross-cultural relationships and living abroad, a program's commitment to high quality and ethical international engagement may require a reconfiguration of the curriculum to allow for such opportunities. When there is a commitment on behalf of an institution to international field placements, there is usually a way to make it work for interested students. A program and its faculty need to frequently ask, "What will it require of us to do this well?" Despite challenges, international field placements are consistently found to provide transformative learning opportunities for social work students (Weibe, 2012; Bell & Ansconbe, 2013).

There is also certainly a place for non-travel international exchanges which, given technology advances, are much more realistic today. These exchanges can also be conducted within a framework of cultural humility and mutual benefit as discussed in this chapter. Examples of this include finding university social work program partners who also have an interest in cross-cultural skill building and knowledge. Within these partnerships, virtual classes could be held together, students could partner in joint assignments, guest lecturing or co-teaching opportunities could be established, and faculty development programs implemented that would benefit faculty from both universities. And just as students are asked during their field work, faculty should also ask "How are we chipping away at power imbalances through this program?" Perhaps this is a commitment to faculty, supervisor, and/or student scholarships and international opportunities for partner universities. At the very least, it requires a commitment to viewing local social work supervisors and academicians as experts of their context and giving them the authority and respect deserved in a cross-cultural exchange.

Notes on Author

Lisa Tokpa was the Social Work Coordinator and Faculty at USP from 2012-2023 and now the program's Director of Field Education, utilizing experiences in Uganda to build the capacity of community engagement efforts through internships across USP's academic emphases, which in addition to Social Work, include Global Health and Interdisciplinary.

REFERENCES

Ali, W., Drolet, J., Khatiwada, K., Chilanga, E., & Musah, M. N. (2022). The shifting landscape of international practicum in social work education. *International Journal of Social Work*, 9(1), 15–39. 10.5296/ijsw.v9i1.19129

Androff, D. (2016). *Practicing rights: Human rights-based approaches to social work practice*. Routledge.

Bandyopadhyay, R., & Patil, V. (2017). 'The white woman's burden' - the racialized, gendered politics of volunteer tourism. *Tourism Geographies*, 19(4), 644–657. 10.1080/14616688.2017.1298150

Bell, K., & Anscombe, A. W. (2013). International field experience in social work: Outcomes of a short-term study abroad programme to India. *Social Work Education*, 32(8), 1032–1047. 10.1080/02615479.2012.730143

Bennett, B. (2019). LGBTQI Aboriginal communities in Australia. *Social Work Education: The International Journal*, 38(5), 604-617. doi:10.1080/02615479.2019.158887210.1080/02615479.2019.1588872

Bibus, A. A., & Koh, B. D. (2021). Intercultural humility in social work education. *Journal of Social Work Education*, 57(1), 16–27. 10.1080/10437797.2019.1661925

Butin, D. W. (2007). Justice-Learning: Service-learning as justice-oriented education. *Equity & Excellence in Education*, 40(2), 177–183. 10.1080/10665680701246492

Caron, R. (2020). Anti-imperialist Practice and Field Placements. "Researcher/educator/practitioner" Model for International Social Work Practice. *Journal of Teaching in Social Work*, 40(1), 71–85. 10.1080/08841233.2019.1694619

Christholm, L. A. (2000). *Charting and hero's journey*. International Partnership for Service Learning.

Cleak, H., Anand, J., & Das, C. (2016). Asking the critical questions: An evaluation of social work students' experiences in an international placement. *British Journal of Social Work*, 46(1), 389–408. 10.1093/bjsw/bcu126

Cole, T. (2012, March 21). The white-savior industrial complex. *The Atlantic*. https://www.theatlantic.com/international/archive/2012/03/the-white-savior-industrial-complex/254843/

Confraria, H., Godinho, M. M., & Wang, L. (2017). Determinants of citation impact: A comparative analysis of the global south versus the global north. *Research Policy*, 46(1), 265–279. 10.1016/j.respol.2016.11.004

Council on Social Work Education. (2022). *Educational policy and accreditation standards*. CSWE. https://www.cswe.org/getmedia/bb5d8afe-7680-42dc-a332-a6e6103f4998/2022-EPAS.pdf

Delgado, L., & Mulder, L. (2017). Eliminating racism, decolonizing education and building an inclusive society: The role of universities in the Kingdom of the Netherlands. *Race Equality Teaching*, 34(2), 15–20. 10.18546/RET.34.2.04

Dessel, A., Bolen, R., & Shepardson, C. (2012). Hopes for intergroup dialogue: Affirmation and allies. *Journal of Social Work Education*, 48(2), 361–367. 10.5175/JSWE.2012.201100091

Donaldson, L. P., & Daughety, L. (2011). Introducing asset-based models of social justice into service learning: A social work approach. *Journal of Community Practice*, 19(1), 80–99. 10.1080/10705422.2011.550262

Dortonne, N. (2016). *The dangers of poverty porn*. CNN. https://www.cnn.com/2016/12/08/health/poverty-porn-danger-feat/index.html

Dunlap, A., & Mapp, S. C. (2017). Effectively preparing students for international field placements through a pre-departure class. *Social Work Education*, 36(8), 893–904. 10.1080/02615479.2017.1360858

Escobar, A. (1995). *Encountering development: The making and unmaking of the third world*. Princeton University Press.

Ferranto, M. L. G. (2015). A qualitative study of baccalaureate nursing students following an eight-day international cultural experience in Tanzania: Cultural humility as an outcome. *Procedia: Social and Behavioral Sciences*, 174, 91–102. 10.1016/j.sbspro.2015.01.631

Fisher, C. M., & Grettenberger, S. E. (2015). Community-based participatory study abroad: A proposed model for social work education. *Journal of Social Work Education*, 51(3), 566–582. 10.1080/10437797.2015.1046342

Fisher-Borne, M., Cain, J. M., & Martin, S. L. (2015). From mastery to accountability: Cultural humility as an alternative to cultural competence. *Social Work Education*, 34(2), 165–181. 10.1080/02615479.2014.977244

Foronda, C., Baptiste, D. L., Reinholdt, M. M., & Ousman, K. (2016). Cultural humility: A concept analysis. *Journal of Transcultural Nursing*, 27(3), 210–217. 10.1177/1043659615592677726122618

Fox, G. R. (2012). Race, power, and polemic: Whiteness in the anthropology of Africa. *Totem: The University of Western Ontario Journal of Anthropology*, 20(1).

Gottlieb, M. (2020). The case for a cultural humility framework in social work practice. *Journal of Ethnic & Cultural Diversity in Social Work*, 9(1), 1–19. 10.1080/15313204.2020.1753615

Goudge, P. (2003). *The whiteness of power: Racism in third world development and aid*. Lawrence & Wishart.

Greenfield, E. A., Davis, R. T., & Fedor, J. P. (2012). The effect of international social work education: Study abroad versus on-campus courses. *Journal of Social Work Education*, 48(4), 739–761. 10.5175/JSWE.2012.201100147

Guth, L. J., & Asner-Self, K. K. (2017). International group work research: Guidelines in cultural contexts. *Journal for Specialists in Group Work*, 42(1), 33–53. 10.1080/01933922.2016.1264519

Hamilton, L., Tokpa, L., McCain, H., & Donovan, S. (2021). #WhiteSaviorComplex: Confidentiality, human dignity, social media, and social work study abroad. *Journal of Social Work Education*, 59(4), 1–11. 10.1080/10437797.2021.1997685

Hay, K., Lowe, S., Barnes, G., Dentener, A., Doyle, R., Hinii, G., & Morris, H. (2018). 'Times that by 100': Student learning from international practicum. *International Social Work*, 61(6), 1187–1197. 10.1177/0020872817702707

Healy, L. M., & Thomas, R. L. (2020). *International social work: Professional action in an interdependent world*. Oxford University Press.

Hodge, D., & Kasule, K. (2022). Addressing the global inequality in social work research: Challenges, opportunities, and key insights and strategies in Sub-Saharan Africa. *Social Work Research*, 46(1), 84–92. 10.1093/swr/svab020

Isaacson, M. (2014). Clarifying concepts: Cultural humility or competency. *Journal of Professional Nursing*, 30(3), 251–258. 10.1016/j.profnurs.2013.09.01124939335

Jönsson, J. H., & Flem, A. L. (2018). International field training in social work education: Beyond colonial divides. *Social Work Education*, 37(7), 895–908. 10.1080/02615479.2018.1461823

Kincheloe, J. L., Steinberg, & Shirley, R. (2008). Indigenous knowledges in education: Complexities, dangers, and profound benefits. In N. K. Denzin, Y. S. Lincoln, & L. Tuhiwai Smith (Eds.), *Handbook of critical and indigenous methodologies* (1st ed., pp. 135–156). Thousand Oaks, CA: Sage.

Lager, P., Mathieson, S., Rodgers, M., & Cox, S. (2010). *Guidebook for International Field Placements and Student Exchanges Planning, Implementation, and Sustainability*. CSWE Press.

Law, K. Y., & Lee, K. M. (2016). Importing Western values versus indigenization: Social work practice with ethnic minorities in Hong Kong. *International Social Work*, 59(1), 60–72. 10.1177/0020872813500804

Loftsdóttir, K. (2002). Never forgetting? Gender and racial-ethnic identity during fieldwork. *Social Anthropology*, 10(3), 303–317. 10.1111/j.1469-8676.2002.tb00061.x

Lough, B. (2009). Principles of effective practice in international social work field placements. *Journal of Social Work Education*, 45(3), 467–479. 10.5175/JSWE.2009.200800083

Lough, B., & Carter-Black, J. (2015). Confronting the white elephant: International volunteering and racial (dis)advantage. *Progress in Development Studies*, 15(3), 207–220. 10.1177/1464993415578983

Lough, B. J., & Toms, C. (2017). Global service-learning in institutions of higher education: Concerns from a community of practice. *Globalisation, Societies and Education*. 10.1080/14767724.2017.1356705

Luciano, D. (2020). An immersion experience in China: Cultivating cultural humility among social work students. *Journal of Ethnographic and Qualitative Research*, 14(3), 199–215.

Mapp, S., & Rice, K. (2019). Conducting rights-based short-term study abroad experiences. *Social Work Education*, 38(4), 427–438. 10.1080/02615479.2018.1560403

Mathiesen, S., & Lager, P. (2007). A model for developing international student exchanges. *Social Work Education*, 26(3), 280–291. 10.1080/02615470601049867

Moncrieffe, J. (2009). Intergenerational transmissions and race inequalities: Why the subjective and relational matter. *IDS Bulletin*, 40(1), 87–96. 10.1111/j.1759-5436.2009.00013.x

Nadan, Y. (2017). Rethinking 'cultural competence' in international social work. *International Social Work*, 60(1), 74–83. 10.1177/0020872814539986

National Association of Social Workers. (2021). *Code of ethics*. National Association of Social Workers. https://www.socialworkers.org/About/Ethics/Code-of-Ethics/Code-of-Ethics-English

Nuttman-Shwartz, O., & Berger, R. (2012). Field education in international social work: Where we are and where we should go. *International Social Work*, 55(2), 225–243. 10.1177/0020872811414597

Ortega, R., & Faller, K. C. (2011). Training child welfare workers from an intersectional cultural humility perspective: A paradigm shift. *Child Welfare*, 90(5), 27–49.22533053

Ouma, B., & Dimaras, H. (2013). Views from the global south: Exploring how student volunteers from the global north can achieve sustainable impact in global health. *Globalization and Health*, 9(1), 1–6. 10.1186/1744-8603-9-3223889908

Parker, J., Crabtree, S. A., Azman, A., Carlo, D. P., & Cutler, C. (2015). Problematising international placements as a site of intercultural learning. *European Journal of Social Work*, 18(3), 383–396. 10.1080/13691457.2014.925849

Pease, B. (2010). *Undoing privilege: Unearned advantage in a divided world.* Zed Books. 10.5040/9781350223738

Pon, G. (2009). Cultural competency as new racism: An ontology of forgetting. *Journal of Progressive Human Services*, 20(1), 59–71. 10.1080/10428230902871173

Ravulo, J. (2018). Australian students going to the Pacific Islands: International social work placements and learning across Oceania. *Aotearoa New Zealand Social Work*, 30(4), 56–69. 10.11157/anzswj-vol30iss4id613

Razack, N. (2009). Decolonizing the pedagogy and practice of international social work. *International Social Work*, 52(1), 9–21. 10.1177/0020872808097748

Razack, N. (2012). International Social Work. In Gray, M., Midgley, J., & Webb, S. (Eds.), *The Sage handbook of social work* (pp. 707–722). Sage. 10.4135/9781446247648.n46

Rodenborg, N., & Boisen, L. A. (2013). Aversive racism and intergroup contact theories: Cultural competence in a segregated world. *Journal of Social Work Education*, 49(4), 564–579. 10.1080/10437797.2013.812463

Rodenborg, N., & Bosch, L. (2009). Intergroup dialog: Introduction. In Gitterman, A., & Salmon, R. (Eds.), *Encyclopedia of social work with groups* (pp. 78–83). Routledge.

Roe, E. P. (2015). *Exploring the influence of international social work practicums on career choices and practice approaches.* [Doctoral (PhD) thesis, Memorial University of Newfoundland]. https://research.library.mun.ca/9735/

Sewpaul, V., & Henrickson, M. (2019). The (r)evolution and decolonization of social work ethics: The global social work statement of ethical principles. *International Social Work*, 62(6), 1469–1481. 10.1177/0020872819846238

Sosa, L. V., & Lesniewski, J. (2020). De-colonizing study abroad: Social workers confronting racism, sexism and poverty in Guatemala. 40(2), 1-18. *Social Work Education*. 10.1080/02615479.2020.1770719

Sossou, M. A., & Dubus, N. (2013). International social work field placement or volunteer tourism? Developing an asset-based justice-learning field experience. *Journal of Learning Design*, 6(1), 10–19. 10.5204/jld.v6i1.113

Storti, C. (2001). *The Art of Crossing Cultures* (2nd ed.). Intercultural Press.

Tascón, S. M., & Ife, J. (Eds.). (2019). *Disrupting Whiteness in social work*. Routledge. 10.4324/9780429284182

Tervalon, M., & Murray-García, J. (1998). Cultural humility versus cultural competence: A critical distinction in defining physician training outcomes in multicultural education. *Journal of Health Care for the Poor and Underserved*, 9(2), 117–125. 10.1353/hpu.2010.023310073197

Thampi, K. (2017). Social work education crossing the borders: A field education programme for international internship. *Social Work Education*, 36(6), 609–622. 10.1080/02615479.2017.1291606

Wearing, S. (2001). *Volunteer tourism: Experiences that make a difference*. Oxon: CABI. Wiebe, M. (2012). Shifting sites of practice, field education in Canada. *Social Work Education*, *31*(5), 681-682. https://doi.org/10.1079/9780851995335.0000

Zhu, R., Olcoń, K., Pulliam, R. M., & Gilbert, D. J. (2023). Transformative learning and the development of cultural humility in social work students. *Social Work Education*, 42(5), 694–709. 10.1080/02615479.2022.2056158

ENDNOTE

[1] For the purposes of this chapter, we are using the most common definition of the "global south" as the region consisting of Africa, Latin America, and the developing nations in Asia (Confraria et al., 2017)

Chapter 6
Transformational Learning Abroad:
Social Work Students and NGOs

Jennifer Lanham
Campbellsville University, USA

Elizabeth Ann Moore
Campbellsville University, USA

ABSTRACT

Partnering non-governmental organizations (NGOs) and social work students is effective in helping conflict-affected communities. It offers valuable knowledge, hands-on practice, and a fresh NGO perspective. However, it presents obstacles, such as personal biases and cultural barriers. To overcome these, social work students must prioritize mental wellness, keep unbiased views, and learn about local cultures. Transformative learning is an essential aspect of this partnership. NGOs assist folks facing significant life challenges, enabling students to understand difficulties beyond textbooks. Together, they positively impact communities by tackling complex issues, spreading awareness, and fostering inclusivity.

INTRODUCTION

Partnering with social work students and Non-governmental Organizations (NGOs) proves to be a winning formula for helping conflict-affected communities. Collaboration has several benefits: The students gain valuable knowledge, direct practice, and experience, and they see the world from new angles, expanding their worldviews. Although there may be challenges and hurdles, the rewards are un-

DOI: 10.4018/979-8-3693-2407-3.ch006

doubtedly valuable. This alliance goes beyond academic theories and is not just about textbook knowledge; passion ignites learning within the student. However, there is a catch: Passion alone cannot dig deep enough into understanding. We need more than just surface-level involvement. Students' lenses of viewing the world become more polished, which sharpens their perspectives; their empathy deepens significantly. Working shoulder-to-shoulder does not just craft skills—it cultivates compassion and instills responsibility.

Collaboration can yield many benefits, but it can also present obstacles. Choosing a side is a significant pitfall, especially in conflict-affected communities, where deep-seated historical and ideological divisions exist. Being mindful of biases and neutral words and actions can help students to prevent unintended disputes and avoid sparking conflicts. Dealing with personal leanings, cultural barriers, and political subtleties is just scratching the surface; social work students must also grasp all facets of conflict complexities, confront local resistance, and even battle homesickness and burnout. Therefore, taking care of mental and physical health is crucial. All these factors impact collaborations and put collaborations at risk if not managed carefully under expert guidance to navigate cultural variances or politics. Therefore, painting an idealistic picture is unrealistic; obstacles must be tackled head-on by keeping unbiased views intact and doing homework about local culture before diving into new experiences while prioritizing mental wellness.

Transformative Learning is essential to this partnership. It involves a shift in the students' perception of themselves and their perceived world. Social work students are encouraged to rethink their assumptions and expand their lens of the world through study, paving the way for self-growth and encouraging them to think about how this may benefit the communities they serve. Transformative Learning is a journey where one's view of oneself and everything around them undergoes profound changes. This process requires deep introspection and an expansive understanding of one's new surroundings, a needed skill for studying and practicing abroad. As part of students' study abroad program, social work students are encouraged to evaluate their convictions while acknowledging societal impacts that mold their career choice. This results in huge wins like challenging their mindset, seeing the world in new ways, and personal development that can cause broader community change. Social work students are not just learning—they are evolving, gaining fresh skills, and creating positive changes. Their education abroad provides priceless real-world experience.

Partnering with non-governmental organizations (NGOs) provides a life-changing experience for social work students. It is a chance to extend practice, change beyond classroom boundaries, and see real-world issues firsthand. NGOs assist folks who have faced significant life challenges, enabling students to understand the difficulties others face beyond textbooks and stepping into others' shoes to feel life's challenges. This is the essential empathy booster; real-world exposure breeds empathy among students studying abroad. Social initiatives are not just about doing our part—they are fights for justice and equality. It is not a one-way street; the partnership between social work students and NGOs is mutually beneficial. NGOs gain from fresh perspectives that students bring on board and from abroad. Through spearheading initiatives, social work students lead projects that promote community engagement, reinforcing and strengthening bonds within these communities. As a united front, both groups positively impact conflict-affected communities by tackling complex issues headfirst, spreading awareness, raising public consciousness, and fostering a sense of belonging. This nurtures inclusivity and solidarity among people navigating adversity. Studying abroad plus practical application equals lasting change to reach a sustainable and peaceful future.

Understanding Conflict-Affected Communities In an ever-changing and evolving world where politics, religion, and general life grow evermore complex, communities can be conflict-affected for several reasons. Regardless of the reasons for strife and conflict, some general themes and characteristics exist for those living in such communities. Such communities find themselves living in fear and confusion. There is poor communication and usually a lack of clarity about who is in charge when the issue is a civil or international conflict, the hostility, attacks, and revenge attacks are terrifying for those trying to survive it.

Families and individuals are left to grapple with whether they leave their homes and the lives they have always known for the unknown in hopes of safety. Remaining where their safety is uncertain is traumatic, but so is fleeing to unknown parts in hopes of a better life. Whether they stay or leave, they are living with few resources, poor facilities, and much uncertainty, creating significant stress and anxiety (Gargan, 1993).

When the upheaval is political, this often leads to an environment and culture of rape, murder, false imprisonment, torture, and displacement. Those living and surviving in this environment often suffer feelings of guilt, helplessness, and inadequacy. They want to impact change towards peace but are powerless to do so. There are spontaneous crimes and vigilantism. There is little trust in the legal system, and often, things devolve into ethnic conflict (Hartoyo, 2016).

Indonesia provides an interesting case of how this usual environment was averted despite internal conflict. In this case, social capital contributed to violence prevention and conflict resolution. "Muakhi" tradition in Lampung (Hartoyo, 2019), "Pela Gandong" tradition in Mauku (Bakri, 2015), and the "Tepung Twawar" tradition in South Sumatra (Alfitri & Hambali, 2013). According to Widyaningsih and Kuntarto (2019), local wisdom is shared by all ethnic groups. Pancasilar, as the state ideology, is an instrument of increasing tolerance between the ethnic groups in Indonesia (Singgih, 2016). Karo Batak people use customary laws to resolve conflicts (Kaban & Sitepu, 2017).

These examples suggest the power of strong cultural traditions and beliefs. Unfortunately, most progressive societies do not have such cohesive and peace-focused traditions from which to draw. Therefore, most conflicts across modern societies lead to individual and community chaos and trauma. The impact of such trauma is tremendous, and when considering reconciliation and peacebuilding, one must look at individual and community reconciliation.

Let us consider the idea of transitional reconciliation as it applies to transitional societies, which is how most conflict-affected communities can best be described (Daly & Sarkin, 2007). There is little capital or financial resources in transitional societies, and people need more patience. Therefore, reconciliation must target specific problems.

For individual reconciliation and peace to occur, adverse events must be absent. There must be a belief that reoccurrence is unlikely, and nightmares must subside. For physical and psychological wounds to heal, people must understand what happened and why. To feel human again, they must have a sense of safety and a time to mourn and remember those lost individuals and places and reconnect. For the community to find reconciliation and peace, its individuals must find peace. Whatever affects the community's individuals affects the community as a whole (Daly & Sarkin, 2007).

No country or community can replicate another's reconciliation or peacebuilding process. Each community is the expert on their situation. They must trust their judgment on what will and will not work. Each place has its unique resources: financial, social, cultural, and traditional. Each also has its own specific needs and priorities: physical, psychological, and material. One common thread is the need for government to play a significant role in developing and maintaining peace. Otherwise, powerful independent forces can prey on weaker groups despite these groups' importance and potential contributions. Reconciliation efforts should cross sectors of any community.

Once peace has been obtained, the effort to sustain it is ongoing. One example of such a sustaining effort is peace museums. In the mid-1990s, Dr. Sultan Somjee and an ethnographer built and funded a peace museum in Kenya. There were two objectives for the museum. The first was to give exposure to African peace heritage. The second was facilitating community access to resources and managing traditional peace materials. It was intended to be a repository of knowledge on peace culture (Walter & Laven eds.,2017). It is a constant reminder of how peace was won and the value of maintaining it. Somjee's (Schweinitz, 1984) definition of peace is the Swahili word "utu," which means humanistic values ingrained in the fabric of oral tradition and material culture.

Role of Social Work in Peacebuilding Peacebuilding is a process involving conflict resolution at all levels. A host of theories can drive the process of peacebuilding. One such theory is Constructive Conflict Transformation, which was put forth by Adam Curle (1994), added to by Johan Galtung (1996), and further revised by Jean-Paul Lederach (1997). The theory addresses the ongoing process of achieving change in relationships, behaviors, attitudes, and structures from adverse to positive cooperation, with local partners being the key to success.

There are six fundamental steps in Constructive Conflict Transformation. First is the engagement of actors contextual to local needs. Second, the conflicts relating to goals are known and dealt with openly. Third, goals are reliable, and small successes are acknowledged and celebrated. Fourth, risks are known and clarified. Fifth, a commitment to not harm. Finally, the strategies are tailored to the environment and culture (BMZ, 2013, pp. 16-17).

Various Social Theories have applications for peacebuilding. Systems theory is another relevant theory as it applies to conflict resolution. Systems theory emphasizes that the relationship between individuals and groups is not simply the sum of its parts. Instead, the interconnected nature of such relationships results in developing entities with their own culture, norms, values, and ways of communicating. The system that develops has unique parts and roles. The different components develop expectations that people have of themselves and others. The result is a system in which the components are interdependent (Kirst-Ashman & Hull, 2015; Martin, 2015).

The application of Social Constructionism to reconciliation is most relevant. At its core, the theory posits that people build their constructs or realities in coordination with others and the events and circumstances most relevant to them (Berger & Luckman, 1967; Neimeyer, 2006). People develop narratives they tell themselves and others based on their experiences, which are also embedded in their cultures and social relationships (Winslade & Monk, 2008). Therefore, how a person interprets an event or interaction is more important than the event itself (Lightman, 2004). This interpretation is critical when bringing various actors together to resolve conflict. We should not judge or speak for others. We must allow them to tell their stories (Denborough, 2014).

Social Exchange Theory addresses the heart of how conflict resolution and peacebuilding develop. This theory views negotiation as an exchange of resources (Homans, 1974). Like systems theory, the fundamental premise is that people are interdependent. Individually, they have tangible and intangible assets that are valuable to one another (Corcoran, 2013). Individuals and social systems can improve their situation by trading resources such as food, housing, labor, respect, information, trust, and other resources (Murdach, 2008). Essentially, people are viewed as mutually responsive. They reciprocate when someone provides them with something of benefit or treats them well. The basic assumption of the theory is that people are rational and tend to seek rewards and avoid punishments.

While understanding relevant theories is critical when formulating an approach to conflict resolution and peacebuilding, implementation is always unique. Examining various peacebuilding experiences across situations and cultures can educate and inform future conflict resolution efforts.

Local peacebuilding necessitates more than liberal values and the absence of conflict. It is a continuous process of changing relationships, behaviors, and attitudes. There must also be a change in the structure of the environment from negative to positive to instill meaningful and lasting peace. The role of external actors, that is, NGOs and social workers in various forms, is to support local actors (Paffenholz, 2015, p. 859). Considering post-structuralism and postcolonial theories, the local actors must be the starting point for peacebuilding (MacGinty & Richmond, 2013, p. 772).

Postcolonialism is the attempt of entities under colonial rule to return to precolonial states. Under colonial rule, imperialist states assumed authority over resources. These ideologies and insatiable resource demands lead to a total breakdown of traditional practices. Postcolonialism is an attempt to return to precolonial traditions. This includes returning to traditional conflict resolution approaches (Oyeniyi, 2017). Similarly, post-structuralism attempts to move away from the structure imposed upon entities.

The local actors' viewpoints are critical if local ownership is to occur in the process. The essential role of social workers in the process is crisis prevention, reducing violence in the conflict, and building structures and institutions after the violence has ended (Konsortium, ZFD 2010, p. 9).

A meaningful study by Auer-Frege (2010) tracks 40 German organizations engaging in civil conflict transformation. All organizations worked on projects in other countries and collaborated only with actors in those countries. The German organizations sent in Civil Peace Service (CPS) workers, who are social workers. The CPS workers saw themselves as neutral, independent, and supportive and attempted to intervene extraordinarily little with the peace process. Their role was to create a constructive environment for peace, strengthen positive elements in the conflict, and limit negative factors. Contact with the target group on-site was viewed as critical for success. The study was a series of interviews to explore what CPS workers learned from the process after the work was completed.

All projects first established a dialogue between local and external actors. Next, they created a structure that allowed local society to contribute to planning, management, implementation, supervision, and monitoring. They then focused on expanding tangible and non-tangible resources. Finally, they promoted community ownership (Erasmus, 2001, pp. 249-250).

Fascinating insights were gained from work in Sierra Leone and Liberia. The CPS workers were supervised by seconded personnel in the relevant local organizations. The roles of the local partners were made clear to all, and there was an iterated understanding of everyone's distinct roles. It was made noticeably clear what the project role of the CPS workers was and what financing they brought through NGOs.

The second personnel were social workers who were not local but came to live in the country and build relationships and stay for an undetermined amount of time to see the project through to sustained peace. They would train, accompany, advise, and strengthen local staff and structures. They assisted locals in working on a solution from within (Zilviler Friedendienst, 2014, p. 5). The local partners supervised the seconded personnel and assisted them in integration into the community. The key for the CPS and seconded personnel was to accept that they are always outsiders, even when they became integrated. They could not become insiders, as their impartiality would be lost. They needed to remember that they do not come from the conflict region and require help understanding the dynamics.

Studying Abroad and Transformational Experiences As educators with experience in leading study abroad programs, we passionately believe that international travel offers social work students an invaluable chance to have life-altering experiences. We have witnessed how this opportunity allows students to view the world from different perspectives, broadening their understanding and exposing them to diverse approaches to addressing critical societal issues like conflict and inequality. As students embark on this transformative journey, being exposed to diverse backgrounds and worldviews sparks a global awareness in students; it challenges their preconceived notions and biases while fostering the creation of innovative ideas. By immersing themselves in communities, students gain a deeper appreciation for our world's rich diversity and are empowered to establish meaningful connections with individuals from various cultural backgrounds (Strange & Gibson, 2017).

According to Mezirow (1978), transformative learning is the process in which learners interpret and reinterpret their experiences to create meaning and facilitate learning, leading to a shift in their worldview through critical reflection. Transformative learning goes beyond knowledge acquisition; it delves into how learners find significance and understanding in their lives. Learners question what they previously knew or believed and approach things from fresh perspectives to accommodate new insights and information. It is emancipatory if we can be freed from the constraints and distortions that are a part of each person's frame of reference (Fleming, 2018).

Therefore, transformational learning becomes the conduit when students explore unfamiliar places and leave their comfort zones. Studying abroad is a viable way to promote adaptability, resilience, and independence, which are essential qualities for social work practice (Bogo & Patterson, 2005). As students immerse themselves in a community's culture, they learn how diverse cultures address challenges and develop innovative practices and solutions. These insights can then be applied in their current practice and future careers, making a positive impact.

Students must first learn how to connect with individuals and communities from diverse backgrounds to embrace ambiguity and think creatively to solve problems. In the spirit of Mezirow (1978), Berdan et al. (2013) emphasize an aspect of this connection, suggesting that international experiences can transform individuals by expanding their perspectives, sparking curiosity, and fostering a global mindset essential for personal growth. This reflective approach allows for self-discovery and a deeper appreciation of the complex diversity of cultures.

Studying abroad can lead to transformative learning by immersing students in environments that encourage them to question assumptions and foster meaningful transformation for self-identity (Onosu, 2021). Studying in another country offers an educational experience by exposing students to different perspectives firsthand. Students who engage with cultures unlike theirs are encouraged to reassess their preconceived notions and expand their worldview. For example, a student from North America who studies in the Czech Republic may encounter contrasting values, traditions, and ways of communicating. Educators often encourage students to challenge their assumptions and embrace various new viewpoints. Studying abroad offers an opportunity for students to face and overcome challenges beyond their environment. These challenges contribute to growth by instilling confidence and adaptability beyond academic matters (Deardorff et al., 2014: Domakin, 2019).

Students who initially struggle with language barriers while abroad may find that overcoming these obstacles enhances their communication skills and fosters a lasting sense of self-assurance (Strange & Gibson, 2017). The transformative power of studying broadens perspectives and sharpens cultural understanding, enabling students to adapt to diverse environments adeptly. Students cultivate genuine respect for our interconnected world by immersing themselves in cultures and prioritizing empathy over preconceived notions. They develop an awareness and humility through experiences and genuinely appreciate the rich tapestry of local cultures, fostering a mindset that goes beyond borders.

As we support the growth of students, they can truly discover their identities. When students are taken out of their surroundings, they can redefine who they are and explore previously unexplored aspects of themselves. For example, a student studying trade disruptions in Northern Ireland following Brexit might find a newfound passion for sustainable practices, prompting a shift in their area of social work concentration and personal values. Traveling abroad pushes students to step outside their comfort zones, allowing for profound emotional and intellectual growth that is often hard to achieve within familiar surroundings. Students immersed in diverse cultures are challenged to adapt to unfamiliar communities, question assumptions, and better understand themselves and the world around them (Domakin, 2019).

We strongly encourage students to explore their beliefs while considering society's influence on their career paths, which is essential in a study abroad program. This experience offers benefits such as challenging their perspectives, gaining fresh insights into the world, and fostering personal growth that can positively impact community transformation (Berdan et al., 2013). Social work students are not simply acquiring knowledge but evolving as individuals, developing skills, and driving positive change. Exposure to global environments provides invaluable real-life experiences, but most students need encouragement to question norms actively. As educators, we acknowledge that exposing them to structures and promoting critical thinking helps them challenge assumptions and broaden their horizons. Students should approach their encounters and experiences with intentionality, reflection, and an open mind. Before traveling, we guide our students on principles that can enhance their overall experience:

- engage in self-awareness and self-critique;
- learn from and listen to the people and their communities;
- avoid stereotypes, generalizations, and judgments;
- acknowledge and address power dynamics and inequalities;
- be open to feedback, learn from mistakes, and adapt; and
- continue to learn and grow from the experience and apply the insights and skills gained to one's life.

However, personal growth requires more than just exposure to international settings. Trevalon and Murray-Garcia (1998) emphasized the significance of exposure in fostering humility and pioneered the concept of "cultural humility." When students study abroad, they gain experiences that expose them to the vastness and diversity of the world and make them realize the limits of their understanding. Foronda et al. (2016, p. 214) concluded that cultural humility is "a way of being" and "involves a change in all perspectives." These experiences help students to appreciate and respect others' perspectives, leading to a lifelong commitment to intercultural understanding.

According to the Council on Social Work Education Educational Policy and Accreditation Standards (CSWE, 2022), social workers must demonstrate cultural humility by critically reflecting on themselves, being self-aware, and regulating their biases, power dynamics, privileges, and values when collaborating with clients and communities. This way, we set an example for our students by demonstrating the importance of self-reflection and cultural understanding. Humility involves acknowledging individuals as experts in their lived experiences, so it becomes essential to personal growth and effective social work practice. It facilitates connections and respectful communication with individuals from diverse backgrounds, encouraging students to engage in deeper intercultural understanding through reflection—an experience that leads to effective global citizenship (Fleming, 2018). International exposure, personal growth, and cultural humility are potent tools to challenge one's assumptions, broaden one's worldview, and increase empathy and respect for others (Mizrahi, 2017; Tervalon & Murray-García, 1998).

COLLABORATION BETWEEN SOCIAL WORK STUDENTS AND NON-GOVERNMENTAL ORGANIZATIONS

Global partnerships between social work students and non-governmental organizations (NGOs) are crucial in promoting peacebuilding and revitalization efforts. By collaborating, students with innovative ideas and academic knowledge and NGOs with organizational infrastructure and expertise can develop sustainable peace strategies that bridge the gap between theoretical knowledge and practical experience. This collaboration helps to better understand the complexities involved in peacebuilding efforts (Liu & Zhang, 2018).

Social work students historically established partnerships with NGOs in conflict-affected regions in the United States by studying abroad. This approach has allowed students to understand the community's history marred by conflicts, including its cultural and political complexities and the daily challenges those affected by the conflict face (Gabel, 2022).

However, collaborations between social work students and NGOs lead to challenges and require guidelines to be effective (Green, 2016). One major challenge is the difference in resources and expertise between social work students and well-established NGOs. While students offer perspective and energy, NGOs provide invaluable expertise and organizational infrastructure. To be successful, best practices involve incorporating cultural sensitivity training and cross-cultural communication workshops and demonstrating a commitment to learning from and adapting to local customs and practices.

Establishing sustainability and lasting effects is another challenge arising from the collaboration between social work students and NGOs. This is because students' involvement may be temporary due to commitments or time limits, disrupting the continuity of initiatives. To address this issue, following practices such as comprehensive project planning, clear transition strategies, and empowering local communities to sustain these initiatives becomes crucial even after student involvement concludes (Wang & Watts, 2017).

Another significant challenge is ensuring that social work students' contributions align with the needs and priorities of the communities NGOs serve. Partnerships should prioritize community-driven approaches rather than imposing external agendas. To achieve this, it is recommended to conduct needs assessments involving stakeholders and engage community members in decision-making processes.

Miscommunication or a lack of confidence can hinder progress and negatively impact outcomes. To address this, it is crucial to establish communication channels such as meetings, progress reports, and feedback sessions to promote transparency and mutual understanding. Building trust requires time, listening, open dialogue, and reliability. Students are responsible for adhering to guidelines, being accountable, and maintaining standards in their contributions.

Following practices, including establishing clear goals and expectations, cultivating mutually beneficial relationships, embracing continuous learning and adaptation, reflecting, building capacity, and empowering communities, is essential to overcoming these challenges effectively.

In conclusion, partnerships between social work students and NGOs have the potential for positive change, but they also come with challenges. However, by adhering to established guidelines and prioritizing communication, cultural sensitivity, community involvement, ethical considerations, and ongoing learning, these partnerships possess the potential to generate meaningful and enduring changes when addressing societal issues (Sleegers, 2019).

Initiatives and Strategies for Revitalizing Communities We aim to highlight successful approaches for revitalizing conflict-affected communities in Ukraine and Northern Ireland through our personal transformative learning experiences abroad. We will focus on how social work students teamed up with NGOs to partake in initiatives that promote peace and reconciliation, helping to rebuild communities.

A relevant example of a collaboration between a Ukrainian NGO and a U.S. university provides an excellent overview of meaningful collaborative work and its limitations. In the late 1990s, a grant-funded group of professionals from a U.S. university traveled to Ukraine to work in partnership with an NGO there. The problem to address was substance abuse. The Ukrainian government would not provide funds for treatment, and there were no other ways to support treatment for those who have a substance use disorder. The culture, in general, viewed addiction as a moral issue. Therefore, the support for this group needed to be improved within the government and across all potential resource levels. The NGO recognized that their belief that those who have an addiction should have the opportunity to change was a minority view. The United States has had a self-sustaining model for treatment since the 1960s. This is the Therapeutic Community model of habilitation and rehabilitation. The ultimate collaboration was training provided by social workers for recovery staff who worked in a therapeutic community for Ukrainians who were prepared to implement such a program in Kyiv, Ukraine. Prior to the training, the two groups met to educate each other. Ukrainian staff educated the social workers on the drug problem, potential resources, efforts tried, and cultural considerations. The U.S.

social workers educated the Ukrainians on how Therapeutic Communities work in the United States. From this upfront work, the training could be tailored to what was feasible in Ukraine. The main limitation of this project was minimal follow-up. There was some follow-up between the NGO and the social workers regarding the progress of the Ukrainians, but there needed to be direct contact between the trainers and the trainees. A more sustained effort could have allowed the social workers to learn more about potential resources and assist the Ukrainians with developing a unified plan for sustainability efforts.

From 2013 to 2017, our social work program engaged in a significant partnership with Crosscare, a prominent NGO based in Dublin. This collaboration was aimed at bolstering peacebuilding initiatives across Ireland and Northern Ireland, serving as a testament to the power of cooperative efforts in addressing complex social issues. These regions had suffered from a long and violent conflict, known as the Troubles, between pro-UK Protestants (unionists) and pro-Irish Catholics (nationalists), which ended with the Good Friday Agreement in 1998. This agreement established a power-sharing system and a peaceful resolution for Northern Ireland. However, peacebuilding remained a crucial goal for social work, as many issues and challenges persisted, such as trauma, division, inequality, and intolerance.

Crosscare and our students worked together through various programs and initiatives to address the issues and challenges that hindered peacebuilding in Ireland. Crosscare took a holistic and responsive approach that met Dublin's diverse communities' economic, educational, cultural, and health needs. The organization also partnered with local and global actors, such as other NGOs, government agencies, and academic institutions, to enhance collaboration and solidarity. Crosscare demonstrated how peacebuilding efforts are interconnected and require collective action. Moreover, McEvoy-Levy (2001) supports the role of youth in peacebuilding and conflict transformation in Northern Ireland and other post-conflict societies. The author argues that youth are often marginalized and excluded from formal peace processes but can also be active and creative agents of social and political change.

Our students engaged with humility and an eagerness to learn, actively contributing, and playing a crucial role in the support and enhancement of the peacebuilding initiatives led by Crosscare's youth workers. They participated in various activities, such as job training, education support, community development, cultural events, and festivals. Through these activities, they helped empower marginalized groups, strengthen community bonds, promote dialogue, celebrate diversity, foster unity, and break down barriers. They also learned from the challenges and opportunities of peacebuilding in Ireland and gained valuable skills and insights for their future practice.

Cultural humility was one of the primary skills and insights our students developed through collaboration with Crosscare. As we have seen, cultural humility means trusting and learning from clients with diverse cultural backgrounds and experiences. It requires us to be aware of our limitations and biases, to be open-minded and curious, and to collaborate with clients to find the best solutions for their needs (Belliveau, 2019; Loya & Peters, 2019). Cultural humility also entails a lifelong commitment to self-reflection and learning and a willingness to challenge and change oppressive structures and systems. Our students exhibited cultural humility during their interactions, embracing the rich diversity of communities and cultures, such as in Finglas, a historically underserved area of Dublin. They did not assume that they knew everything about their culture, nor did they impose their views or judgments on the community. Instead, they asked questions, sought feedback, and learned from their stories and experiences. Students were able to learn how youth workers raise awareness among young people, encouraging them to challenge the stereotypes and labels that society often imposes on them. They also acknowledged and addressed the power dynamics and inequalities between them and the community and tried to reduce the barriers and gaps that hindered effective communication and collaboration. By doing so, students built trusting and meaningful relationships with the Finglas community and enhanced their intercultural competence and awareness.

Our students actively participated in the HEROS program which is instrumental in uniting youth across Ireland, fostering a culture of connection and relationship-building. Working side by side with experienced youth workers, they actively contributed to a celebration of cultural diversity, embodying the spirit of collaboration and mutual learning. The HEROS program, a beacon of sports' role in peacebuilding and social cohesion, unites young individuals from Northern Ireland, Ireland, and Scotland through ice hockey. This sport serves as a conduit for developing friendships, teamwork, leadership, and respect. Participation in the program equips young people with life skills and confidence, preparing them for future success.

As part of their fieldwork with Crosscare, our social work students immersed themselves in the HEROS program, which has been a collaborative partner since 2007 alongside Army Welfare Services and the Ballynafeigh Community Development Association. Crosscare's commitment to recruiting and supporting youth from Finglas and Swords has allowed participants to reap the program's benefits. Our students additionally played a supportive role, assisting with planning and providing mentorship, thereby enhancing the young participants' experience through various activities, including ice hockey sessions and cultural workshops.

The collaboration extended to learning from and contributing to international partners like HEROS Canada, the program's primary organizer and benefactor. This partnership provided our students with exposure to global best practices in leveraging sports for peacebuilding and social inclusion, enriching their perspectives as emerging social work professionals.

Cultural and creative endeavors are potent tools for social inclusion, capable of dismantling barriers and forging unity among communities. Our engagement with the HEROS program has been a profound educational journey, contributing significantly to peacebuilding and social cohesion efforts in Ireland. Our students gained firsthand experience and insights while working with youth from diverse and conflict-impacted backgrounds, harnessing the power of sports to drive positive societal change. They cultivated cultural humility, critical thinking, and reflexivity, confronting various realities and challenges during their fieldwork.

The transformative power of the HEROS program, evidenced by the empowerment and life-changing experiences of its young participants, has been an invaluable source of inspiration. The stories of achievement and the unwavering commitment of all partners and volunteers have left an indelible mark on our students.

The HEROS program exemplifies the profound impact of collaborative efforts in peacebuilding, underscoring the necessity of collective action for sustainable peace. These partnerships underscore the vital role of cooperation between academia and international NGOs in fostering enduring peace and social justice. By uniting forces, we can leverage our unique strengths to forge a more equitable and peaceful world. Addressing economic disparities, championing education, celebrating cultural diversity, and prioritizing mental health are integral to creating a harmonious society, as outlined by O'Grady et al. (2018).

Impact and Outcomes Measuring the impact of peacebuilding initiatives is crucial for assessing the effectiveness and sustainability of these endeavors (Church & Rogers, 2006). One significant approach to measuring impact involves using quantitative indicators to evaluate tangible outcomes. This includes metrics such as the number of individuals reached, changes in community behaviors, reductions in conflict-related incidents, or improvements in socio-economic indicators. For instance, tracking the percentage decrease in reported violence cases or an increase in the number of individuals taking part in conflict resolution workshops provides measurable data indicative of progress. Qualitative methods encompass gathering narratives, stories, and testimonials from community members directly affected by these initiatives. Conducting interviews, focus group discussions, or participatory evaluations enables the collection of personal accounts and beliefs, illuminating the subjective experiences and changes within communities resulting from the peacebuilding efforts. Involving community members in the evaluation process ensures that their voices are heard, perspectives are considered, and their role in the peacebuilding process is acknowledged. Participatory methods, such as community scorecards or participatory impact assessments, empower communities to assess and reflect on the impact of initiatives based on their lived experiences and beliefs.

Baseline data provides a reference point for comparison, enabling measuring changes or improvements over time. Regular monitoring and evaluation help to track progress, identify challenges, and make prompt adjustments to enhance the effectiveness of peacebuilding initiatives (Lederach, 2015).

Moreover, a theory of change or logic model framework can help map the causal pathways between activities, outputs, outcomes, and impacts (Anderson, 2005). This structured approach aids in finding key indicators, clarifying the expected results, and understanding the mechanisms through which initiatives contribute to peacebuilding efforts. It enables a systematic approach to measuring short-term and long-term impacts, facilitating comprehensive evaluation. Additionally, assessing the sustainability and long-term effects of peacebuilding initiatives is essential. Evaluating whether changes are enduring and whether initiatives have led to lasting shifts in attitudes, behaviors, or institutional practices is crucial for understanding sustained impact.

Measuring the impact of peacebuilding initiatives requires a multifaceted approach that combines quantitative and qualitative methods, participatory approaches, continuous monitoring, and frameworks that capture both short-term outcomes and long-term changes (Paffenholz, 2015). By employing comprehensive evaluation strategies, social work students and international NGOs can assess their peacebuilding effectiveness, sustainability, and transformative effects, enabling continual improvement and informed decision-making in advancing peace and social cohesion (Lederach, 2015; Schirch, 2011).

In communities worldwide that have been impacted by conflict, there are many more powerful stories of change and testimonials from the efforts of American social work students and international NGOs (Ungar & Hadfield, 2019). Take, for example, the story of a refugee family in the Middle East who received support from an NGO working in partnership with social work students. Despite facing displacement and trauma, this family found solace through the support provided by these initiatives. The mother, who once experienced the horrors of war, shares how counseling sessions helped her manage anxiety and provided a space to share her experiences (Khoury-Kassabri & Benbenishty, 2018).

In another account from an African nation grappling with conflict challenges, a young woman recounts her journey towards empowerment through collaborations between NGOs and social work students. After enduring gender-based violence, she found refuge in programs designed to empower women. Leadership workshops, vocational training opportunities, and survivor support groups allowed her to discover her strength and voice. Now an enthusiastic supporter of gender equality, she advocates for women in her community. Her inspiration stems from the transformation she experienced through collaborative initiatives (Zhao et al., 2005).

Stories from conflict-affected regions in South America further testify to the impact of peacebuilding efforts focusing on youth. One young man, previously trapped in a cycle of violence and despair, discovered a path through programs facilitated by these partnerships. He unearthed his potential to create positive change by engaging in initiatives, art therapy sessions, and community projects. Today, he leads initiatives that promote peace and empower people, drawing from his experiences to guide others toward a brighter, more peaceful future (Sanchez & Garvin, 2016).

The stories and accounts of transformation presented above demonstrate the strength, empowerment, and healing that result from the collaboration between social work students and NGOs. They also highlight how such initiatives create a positive impact by bringing people together across divides and fostering solidarity. These stories underscore the significance of education, psychosocial support, and community-driven efforts. However, some challenges need to be addressed. The testimonials also shed light on these initiatives' goals for resources, complexities arising from norms, and the long journey toward achieving sustainable peace.

Despite these challenges, the narratives reflect resilience, empowerment, and optimism from efforts focused on healing and promoting peace during such times. They highlight how these partnerships impact individuals while displaying their determination to pave a path toward a more peaceful future filled with promise.

Collaborations have produced valuable lessons and highlighted areas for improvement. One significant lesson learned is the importance of cultural humility and contextual understanding. "Cultural humility is a lifelong process of self-reflection and learning that supports cultural competence and challenges power imbalances in cross-cultural relationships" (Gotlieb, 2020, p. 114). Recognizing the diversity of cultural norms, beliefs, and historical backgrounds within communities affected by conflict is crucial. Furthermore, these collaborations have highlighted the significance of community engagement and participatory approaches. Involving local stakeholders, including community leaders, grassroots organizations, and affected individuals, is essential for the success and sustainability of initiatives. Social work students have learned that community-driven approaches empower locals to take ownership of interventions, ensuring relevance, sustainability, and long-term impact (Truell, 2021).

Partnerships between students and NGOs have underscored the importance of ethical considerations and reflexivity. Truell (2021) highlighted the ethical challenges faced by social workers in conflict situations:

Social workers often face complex ethical dilemmas in conflict, violence, and human rights violations. They must balance their professional values and principles with the realities and constraints of their work contexts. They also must consider their actions, risks, and benefits for themselves, their clients, and their organizations.

Social workers must know their positionality, biases, and emotions and conduct critical reflection and supervision to ensure ethical and practical practice. (p. 284)

Understanding power dynamics, maintaining confidentiality, and upholding ethical standards when working with vulnerable populations is paramount. Social work students have learned the necessity of continuous self-reflection, acknowledged their biases, and critically evaluated their roles and impact within these partnerships. Moreover, valuable insights have been gained regarding implementing all-encompassing and integrated interventions. Addressing the complex needs of communities affected by conflict requires multifaceted approaches. One key area is the need for enhanced sustainability and capacity-building efforts. Social work students and NGOs can improve by building local capacities, fostering partnerships with local institutions, and devising strategies for the continued impact of initiatives after student involvement ends. Improving monitoring and evaluation frameworks is essential. Rigorous data collection methodologies, establishing baseline indicators, and conducting longitudinal studies can enhance impact measurement, ensuring evidence-based approaches and informed decision-making.

The collaborations between social work students and international NGOs in conflict-affected communities have provided invaluable lessons and showed areas for improvement. Emphasizing cultural humility, community engagement, ethical considerations, holistic interventions, sustainability, and robust evaluation methodologies can enhance the effectiveness and sustainability of future initiatives. These lessons are guiding principles to refine and strengthen collaborations, contributing to more impactful and sustainable interventions in conflict-affected regions.

Ethical Considerations and Challenges There are widely accepted humanitarian principles. These values are designed to guide decision-making despite limited resources, competing interests, and ethical dilemmas. Social workers are expected to operationalize and embody principles and stick to a moral code to navigate the complexities embedded in emergency response in conflict areas. An added challenge is that social workers must employ fidelity to social work efforts and values, and even if they differ from other professionals, they find themselves working beside them (Barbar, 2023).

The fundamental humanitarian principles coincide very well with social work values and ethical principles as well as the General Assembly of the International Association of Social Workers principles. There are four fundamental principles. First, the principle of humanity, which is to prevent and alleviate human suffering wherever it may be found. We are to protect life and health and ensure respect for all humans. Second is the principle of impartiality. This means protecting life and alleviating human suffering based on need and individual suffering. There is to be no discrimination based on nationality, race, religion, social class, or political opinions. The priority is to serve the most vulnerable and urgent in need. The third principle is neutrality. We cannot take sides or engage in political, racial, religious, or ideological controversies. The fourth principle is independence. We must maintain autonomy from states, combatants, or other local or international authorities (Wise et al., 2021).

The NASW Code of Ethics (2021) puts forth four values and corresponding ethical principles that align with humanitarian principles. The first is the value of service, with the ethical principle of our primary goal being to help people in need and address social problems. Next is the value of social justice. The corresponding ethical principle is that social workers should challenge social injustices. The third value is honoring the dignity and worth of a person. This goes with the ethical principle of social workers respecting a person's inherent dignity and worth. Finally, there is the value of the importance of human relationships. The correlating ethical principle is that social workers recognize the vital importance of human relationships (NASW, 2021).

The General Assembly of the International Association of Social Work and the International Federation of Social Work (2018) establish nine guiding principles. Several of these align closely with the humanitarian principles discussed above. First, the recognition of the inherent dignity of humanity. Second, is promoting human rights. Third is promoting social justice. Then, promoting the right to self-determination. Finally, treating people as whole persons.

The core of most Western humanitarian efforts is the *Dunantist tradition*, named for Henry Dunant of the Red Cross. His premise was principles of respect for the dignity, agency, and autonomy of individuals receiving care, avoiding harm, and committing to the just application of resources (General Assembly of the World Medical Association, 2015). Interestingly, this medical perspective also coincides with social work values and ethics.

There are emerging issues in current conflict settings where humanitarian efforts are made: accountability to the affected population, decolonization of humanitarianism, intersectional diversity, and evolving interpretation of maleficence or "do no harm" (Barbar, 2023). There are significant growing challenges for humanitarian efforts and organizations. A quickly changing operational and political context demands ever-increasing accountability. The growth of digital media and its role in conflicts has increased the scrutiny of decision-making. Furthermore, global funding has increased, creating new actors, and expanding response capacity, modern technology, and digital tools (Welsh, 2023). With this increased exposure, there is pressure from entities that may not have context for the decisions. The increased accountability may seem positive through one lens. However, it means more reporting measures, resulting in increased time spent reporting versus providing services.

Core humanitarian principles of humanity and impartiality promote assistance and services based on need. However, there is a growing imbalance for the forgotten in crisis. Often, the need is prioritized based on the donor preference and the media. This creates an ethical dilemma for those providing the services who are aware of the actual priorities of need. Ethical decision-making also involves ensuring that local communities and civil society have opportunities to determine local humanitarian priorities. This situation may present challenges for humanitarian aid providers striving to maintain neutrality, as local communities often form alliances that facilitate their access to funding and acceptance. Such dynamics can complicate the providers' efforts to deliver aid impartially (Barbar, 2023).

Conclusion As we discussed earlier, communities that are affected by conflict face a variety of issues, which often include fear, confusion, hostility, helplessness, trauma, and limited resources. However, each community finds its unique way to achieve peace and sustainability and move forward. Fundamental steps can be taken to achieve peacebuilding, such as engaging with all actors, addressing conflicts and goals openly, ensuring reliability in the goals, celebrating small successes, recognizing risks, and tailoring strategies to the environment and culture.

We have also explored several theories that can be useful in developing strategies for peacebuilding, including conflict transformation, systems theory, social construction theory, and social exchange theory. Students working alongside NGOs in peacebuilding can experience transitional learning, which involves interpreting and reinterpreting their experiences to create meaning and facilitate learning. This can lead to a shift in their worldview through critical reflection and help them develop innovative ideas and academic knowledge to contribute to sustainable peace strategies.

The collaboration between students and NGOs can bridge the gap between theoretical knowledge and practical experience. Students need to respect and understand the expertise and resources that well-established NGOs bring to the process.

REFERENCES

Alfitri, A., & Hambali, H. (2013). Integration of national character education and social conflict resolution through traditional culture: A case study in South Sumatra Indonesia. *Asian Social Science*, 9(12), 1250135. 10.5539/ass.v9n12p125

Anderson, A. A. (2005). *The community builder's approach to theory of change: A practical guide to theory development*. Aspen Institute.

Auer-Frege, I. (2010). *Wege zur Gewalt Freiheit: Methoden der internationalen zivilen Konfliktbearbeitung*. Büttner Verlag.

Bakri, H. (2015). Conflict resolution toward local wisdom approach of pela gandong in Ambom City. *The Politics: Jurnal Magistar Ilmu Politik Universitae Hasanuddin*, 18, 51–59.

Barbar, A. (2023). *Challenges for ethical humanitarian health responses in contemporary conflict*. Research Gate.

Belliveau, M. (2019). "I need to learn from you": Reflections on cultural humility through study abroad. *Reflections: Narratives of Professional Helping, 25*(1), 70-81.

Berdan, S. N., Goodman, A. E., & Taylor, M. (2013). Preparing for the 21st century: The global imperative. *International Educator*, 22(6), 12–17.

Berger, P., & Luckman, T. (1967). The Social Construction of Reality: A Treatise in the Sociaology of Knowledge. Harmonsworth, Penguin Books.

BMZ. (2013). *Entwicklung fur Frieden und Sicherheit: Entwicklungpolitisches Engagement im Kontext von Konflikt, Fragilität und Gewalt*. BMZ—Strategiepapier.

Bogo, M., & Paterson, J. (2005). Promoting self-awareness in beginning social work students. *Social Work Education*, 24(4), 409–423.

Brannelly, L., & Novelli, M. (2012). The role of non-governmental organisations in education for peacebuilding: A case study of Northern Ireland. *Compare: A Journal of Comparative Education*, 42(1), 53–76.

Church, C., & Rogers, M. M. (2006). *Designing for results: Integrating monitoring and evaluation in conflict transformation programs*. Search for Common Ground.

Corcoran, K. E. (2013). Divine exchanges: Applying social exchange theory to religious behavior. *Rationality and Society*, 25(2), 335–369. 10.1177/1043463113492306

Council on Social Work Education. (2022). *2022 educational policy and accreditation standards*. CSWE.

Curle, A. (1994). New challenges for citizen peacemaking. *Medicine and War*, 10(2), 96–105. 10.1080/07488009408409148

Daly, E., & Sarkin, J. (2007). *Reconciliation in divided societies: Finding common ground*. University of Pennsylvania Press. 10.9783/9780812206388

Deardorff, D. K., Hunter, L. E., & Wallace, M. J. (2014). The impact of study abroad on college students' intercultural competence. *Frontiers: The Interdisciplinary Journal of Study Abroad*, 24, 239–251.

Denborough, D. (2014). Michael White and adventures downunder. *Australian and New Zealand Journal of Family Therapy*, 35(1), 110–120. 10.1002/anzf.1049

Dolan, P., & Connolly, J. (2017). Cultural and creative activities as a means of social inclusion and community cohesion: A case study of Ireland. *International Journal of Cultural Policy*, 23(5), 567–581.

Domakin, A. (2019). Experiential learning: Transforming theory into practice. *Social Work Education*, 38(2), 141–154.

Dundonald International Ice Bowl. (2023, August 24). *The HEROS programme glides back to Dundonald International Ice Bowl*. DIIB.

Erasmus, V. (2001). Community mobilization as a tool for peacebuilding. In Reychler, L., & Paffenholz, T. (Eds.), *Peacebuilding: A field guide* (pp. 246–257).

Fleming, J. (2018). Transformative learning in social work education: A review of the literature. *Social Work Education*, 37(6), 688–702.

Foronda, C., Baptiste, D. L., Reinholdt, M. M., & Ousman, K. (2016). Cultural humility: A concept analysis. *Journal of Transcultural Nursing*, 27(3), 210–217. 10.1177/1043659615592677726122618

Friedendienst, Z. (2014). *Grundlagen, Akteure und Verfahren des ZFD*. https://www.ziviler-friedensdienst.org/sites/default/files/media/file/2022/zfd-ziviler-friedensdienst-zfd-kompakt-2264_23.pdf

Gabel, S. G., & Yang, N. (2022). Transnational advocacy at the United Nations for social workers. *Journal of Human Rights and Social Work*, 7(4), 417–427. 10.1007/s41134-022-00216-135971383

Galtung, J. (1996). Peace by peaceful means: Peace and conflict, development, and civilization. *Sage (Atlanta, Ga.)*. Advance online publication. 10.4135/9781446221631

Gargan, E. A. (1993, January 14). Refugees Fleeing Tajikistan Strife. *New York Times*.

General Assembly of the International Association of Social Workers & International Federation of Social Workers. (2018). Global Social Work Statement of Ethical Principles. General Assembly of the International Association of Social Workers & International Federation of Social Workers.

Green, D. (2016, October 19). Academics and NGOs can work together in partnership but must do so earlier and with genuine knowledge exchange. *Impact of Social Sciences.*

Hartoyo, H., & Fahmi, T. (2018). Towards a new village development paradigm in Lampung province, Indonesia. *Journal of Legal, Ethical and Regulatory Issues, 21.*

Homans, G. (1974). *Social behavior: Its elementary forms* (2nd ed.). Harcourt Brace Jovanovich.

Kaban, M., & Sitepu, S. (2017). The efforts of inheritance dispute resolution for customary land on Indigenous peoples in Karo North Sumatra, Indonesia. *International Journal of Private Law*, 8(3/4), 281–298. 10.1504/IJPL.2017.087364

Kanyangale, P., & Mwaura, N. K. (2019). Social work students' engagement with non-governmental organizations in conflict-affected communities: A case study of Malawi. *International Social Work*, 62(6), 1587–1601.

Khoury-Kassabri, M., & Benbenishty, R. (2018). Social work education in conflict and post-conflict countries: An exploratory study among Palestinian and Israeli students. *British Journal of Social Work*, 48(1), 1–19.

Kirst-Ashman, K., & Hull, G. (2015). *Generalist practice with organizations and communities* (6th ed.). Cengage.

Lederach, J. (1997). *Building peace: Sustainable reconciliation in divided societies.* United States Institute of Peace Press.

Lederach, J. P. (2015). Measuring impact in peacebuilding: Looking beyond the sum of the parts. *Journal of Peacebuilding & Development*, 10(1), 14–27. 10.1177/1542316614555755

Lightman, D. (2004). *Power optimism: Enjoy the life you have…create the success you want.* Power Optimism.

Liu, J., & Zhang, Y. (2018). Exploring the partnership strategies between social work education and non-governmental organizations: A systematic literature review. *Social Sciences*, 7(8), 131. 10.3390/socsci7080131

Loya, M., & Peters, K. (2019). Critical literacy: Engaging students to enhance cultural humility in study abroad. Reflections. *Narratives of Professional Helping*, 25(1), 82–94.

MacGinty, R., & Richmond, O. (2013). The local turn in peacebuilding: A critical agenda for peace. *Third World Quarterly*, 34(4), 763–783. 10.1080/01436597.2013.800750

Martin, M. E. (2015). *Advocacy for social justice: A global perspective*. Pearson.

McEvoy-Levy, S. (2001). Youth as social and political agents: Issues in post-settlement peace building. *Kroc Institute Occasional Paper, 21*(OP:2), 1-36.

Mezirow, J. (1978). Perspective transformation. *Adult Education*, 28(2), 100–110. 10.1177/074171367802800202

Murdach, A. D. (2008). Negotiating with antisocial clients. *Social Work*, 53(2), 179–182. 10.1093/sw/53.2.17918595451

National Association of Social Workers. (2021). *Code of Ethics*. NASW. https://www.socialworkers.org/About/Ethics/Code-of-Ethics/Code-of-Ethics-English

Neimeyer, R., Herrero, O., & Botella, L. (2006). Chaos to Coherence: Psychotherapy Integration of Traumatic Loss. *Journal of Constructivist Psychology*, 19(2), 127–148. 10.1080/10720530500508738

O'Doherty, J., McKeown, S., & Gallagher, T. (2019). The impact of a cross-community music project on young people's attitudes to peacebuilding in Northern Ireland. *Music Education Research*, 21(4), 375–389.

O'Grady, K., & Mannion, G. (2018). Crosscare's peacebuilding initiatives in Dublin: A case study in community-based approaches to conflict transformation. *Journal of Peacebuilding & Development*, 13(2), 32–47.

Onosu, O. (2021). The impact of study abroad on the self-identity of social work students. *Journal of International Social Work*, 64(1), 67–82.

Oyeniyi, A. (2017). Conflict resolution in the Extractives: A consideration of traditional conflict resolution paradigms in post-colonial Africa. *Williamette Journal of International Law and Dispute Resolution*, 25(1), 56–77.

Paffenholz, T. (2015). Beyond the normative: Can women's inclusion really make for better peace processes? *International Affairs*, 91(3), 537–554.

Paffenholz, T. (2015). Unpacking the local turn in peacebuilding: A critical assessment towards an agenda for future research. *Third World Quarterly*, 36(5), 857–874. 10.1080/01436597.2015.1029908

Sánchez, G., & Gavin, L. (2016). Youth and peacebuilding: From the margins to the center. *Journal of Peacebuilding & Development*, 11(1), 26–40.

Schirch, L. (2011). *Measuring the impact of peacebuilding: A review of current practice*. USIP. https://www.usip.org/publications/2011/11/measuring-impact-peacebuilding-review-current-practice

Schweinitz, K. (1984). Political Capacity in Developing Societies A. H. Somjee. *Economic Development and Cultural Change*, 33(1), 182–185. 10.1086/451452

Singgih, E. (2016). Suffering as grounds for religious tolerance: An attempt to broaden Panikkar's insight on religious pluralism. *Exchange*, 45(2), 111–129. 10.1163/1572543X-12341396

Sleegers, P. (2019). Understanding school-NGO partnerships. *Journal of Educational Administration*, 57(4), 322–328. 10.1108/JEA-03-2019-0053

Streden, P. (1997). A.H. Somjee Development Theory: Critique and Explorations. *Economic Development and Cultural Change*, 41(1), 207–211. 10.1086/452004

Tervalon, M., & Murray-García, J. (1998). *Cultural humility versus cultural competence: A critical distinction in defining physician training outcomes in multicultural education.*

The General Assembly of the World Medical Association. (2015). *Ethical principles of health care in the times of armed conflict and other emergencies*. WMA. https://www.wma.net/wp-content/uploads/2016/11/4245_002_Ethical_principles_web.pdf

Truell, R. (2021). The role of social workers in conflict situations. *International Review of the Red Cross*, 103(912), 277–2911.

Ungar, M., & Hadfield, K. (2019). The differential impact of environment and resilience on youth outcomes. *Canadian Journal of Behavioural Science, 51*(2), 135-146.

Walter, D., & Laven, D. (Eds.). (2017). *Heritage and Peacebuilding*. The Boyell Press. 10.1515/9781782049951

Welsh, J., Wise, P., & Sepúlveda, J. (2023). Preface. *Daedalus*, 152(2), 6–12. 10.1162/daed_e_01988

Widyaningsih, R., & Kuntarto, B. (2019). Local Wisdom approach to develop counter radicalization strategy. In Proceedings of 1st International Conference on Life and Applied Sciences for Sustainable Rural Development. *IOP Conference Series. Earth and Environmental Science*, 255(1), 20–49.

Winslade, J., & Monk, G. (2008). *Practicing narrative mediation: Loosening the grip of conflict*. Jossey-Bass.

Wise, P. H., Shiel, A., Southard, N., Bendavid, E., Welsh, J., Stedman, S., Fazal, T., Felbab-Brown, V., Polatty, D., Waldman, R. J., Spiegel, P. B., Blanchet, K., Dayoub, R., Zakayo, A., Barry, M., Martinez Garcia, D., Pagano, H., Black, R., Gaffey, M. F., & Bhutta, Z. A. (2021). The political and security dimensions of the humanitarian health response to violent conflict. *Lancet*, 397(10273), 511–521. 10.1016/S0140-6736(21)00130-633503458

Zhao, Y., Lei, J., Yan, B., Lai, C., & Tan, H. S. (2005). What makes the difference? A practical analysis of research on the effectiveness of distance education. *Teachers College Record*, 107(8), 1836–1884. 10.1177/016146810510700812

Chapter 7
Affectagogy:
Learning With Heart - Nurturing Knowledge Through Emotional Bonds

Ken Nee Chee
http://orcid.org/0000-0003-3732-604X
Faculty of Computing and Meta-Technology, Sultan Idris Education University, Malaysia

ABSTRACT

This chapter unveils Affectagogy, a transformative pedagogical approach that bridges the emotional and cognitive realms of learning. Recognizing the undeniable influence of emotions on knowledge acquisition, Affectagogy emphasizes the concept of learning with the heart to nurture knowledge through emotional bonds. It explores the synergistic relationship between affect (emotions and feelings) and pedagogy (teaching methods). The chapter introduces "human-touch learning," highlighting the significance of empathy, social interaction, and resilience-building in fostering deeper student engagement, motivation, and well-being. Practical guidelines are provided for implementing Affectagogy across educational levels, encompassing the thoughtful integration of educational technology. Ultimately, this chapter advocates for a holistic approach to education, emphasizing the cultivation of both emotional and intellectual intelligence. This balanced approach aims to prepare learners for success in an emotionally intelligent world, fostering resilience, empathy, and a lifelong love of learning.

DOI: 10.4018/979-8-3693-2407-3.ch007

INTRODUCTION

Affectagogy, signifying "touching the emotions" (D'ambrosio, 2020), revolutionizes education by emphasizing the crucial role of emotional connections in learning (Torres et. al., 2022). It aims to create a more profound, engaging, and effective learning experience by moving beyond solely transmitting knowledge. This chapter explores the foundational aspects of Affectagogy, its biological underpinnings, the core principles of Human-Touch Learning, and its practical applications across diverse educational settings. By delving into the intricate interplay between affective experiences and cognitive processes, Affectagogy offers insights into optimizing pedagogical practices for fostering deep understanding, emotional engagement, and lasting knowledge retention in learners of all ages and backgrounds.

Affectagogy, a term derived from "affect" (emotion) and "agogos" (leading), signifies a shift in educational philosophy. It emphasizes the importance of emotions in learning, emerging in response to the limitations of purely cognitive approaches.

The growing body of research on emotional intelligence (EQ) highlights its significant impact on various aspects of student development, including academic achievement, well-being, and classroom dynamics (Matthews, 2020; Polak et al., 2015; Iram, 2021). This recognition has fueled the rise of Affectagogy, which advocates for a holistic approach that integrates EQ with teaching strategies.

Affectagogy fosters a learning environment where emotional and intellectual growth are equally valued. By cultivating emotional intelligence among both students and teachers, educational institutions can create a more supportive and effective learning environment. This ultimately translates to enhanced academic performance, positive classroom dynamics, and nurtured student well-being. The increasing focus on EQ in education paves the way for Affectagogy to become an essential component of a thriving learning environment.

Imagine a classroom where the emotional and intellectual needs of students are harmoniously balanced. This vision is not just a theoretical ideal but a lived experience for educators like myself. My journey with Affectagogy began years ago when I noticed the profound impact of incorporating emotional intelligence into my teaching practice. Just as a song sets the tone at the beginning of a lesson as induction set, Affectagogy introduces an empathetic approach that resonates throughout the learning experience.

In-Depth Analysis and Prior Research

Affectagogy is grounded in the principles of emotional intelligence, first popularized by Daniel Goleman. Goleman's work highlighted the critical role of self-awareness, self-regulation, motivation, empathy, and social skills in personal

Affectagogy

and professional success. Building on these foundations, Affectagogy incorporates these elements into educational frameworks.

Research by Mayer and Salovey (1997) on emotional intelligence provides a solid foundation for Affectagogy. Their ability model of emotional intelligence emphasizes the importance of perceiving, using, understanding, and managing emotions. Integrating these abilities into teaching practices enhances students' emotional and academic outcomes.

Additional studies, such as Durlak et al.'s (2011) meta-analysis on social and emotional learning programs, provide empirical evidence supporting the benefits of incorporating emotional intelligence into education. These programs have shown significant improvements in students' social behaviors, attitudes, and academic performance, reinforcing the relevance of Affectagogy.

The Neurological Foundations of Emotional Learning

Understanding Affectagogy's impact necessitates exploring the intricate dance between our emotions and cognitive processes. Neuroscience has illuminated a complex network of neural pathways where feelings and thoughts converge, demonstrating the significant influence emotions hold on our cognitive abilities (Matthew et. al., 2018). This intersection underscores the importance of considering emotional factors in educational contexts, as they can profoundly shape learning outcomes. By acknowledging the symbiotic relationship between affect and cognition, educators can design pedagogical strategies that harness the power of emotions to enhance understanding, retention, and overall educational experiences, thereby optimizing learning environments for diverse learners across various educational settings.

Key Points

- **Emotions and Cognition:** Research underscores the profound impact of emotions on cognitive functions like attention, memory, and decision-making (Venkatesh & Fischer, 2019). Emotions can either enhance or impair these functions, highlighting the critical need for educational strategies that positively engage students' emotions (Purcia et. al., 2023).
- **The Amygdala's Role:** This brain structure plays a central role in both emotional learning and memory formation (Yang & Wang, 2017). The amygdala governs our emotional responses and significantly impacts memory, especially for emotionally charged experiences (Zhang, 2022). This dual role underscores the importance of emotional engagement in facilitating deeper understanding and information retention (Silva et. al., 2020).

Human-Touch Learning: The Essence of Affectagogy

At the heart of Affectagogy lies Human-Touch Learning, a pedagogical approach prioritizing emotional bonds among educators, learners, and learning material (Kjersti, 2023). This approach emphasizes the cultivation of meaningful connections within educational settings, fostering a supportive and empathetic environment for students to thrive. Human-Touch Learning recognizes the significance of emotional engagement in the learning process, acknowledging that when students feel valued and understood, they are more motivated to learn and achieve academic success. By placing students' emotional well-being at the forefront, educators can create a nurturing space where learning becomes not only intellectually stimulating but also deeply enriching on a personal level.

Key Principles

- **Empathy and Warmth:** The foundation of Human-Touch Learning rests on fostering empathy, warmth, and genuine interest in students' learning journeys. By prioritizing these values, educators cultivate a nurturing environment that facilitates deeper learning and promotes students' emotional well-being (David et. al., 2022).
- **Engagement and Motivation:** Emotional connections significantly enhance students' engagement and motivation (Terence et al., 2022). When students feel emotionally invested in their learning, they are more likely to actively participate, demonstrate higher levels of curiosity, and retain information more effectively (Matthew et. al., 2023).

Core Concepts

- **Emotional Engagement:** Creating a classroom environment where students feel emotionally connected and engaged.
- **Empathy:** Understanding and responding to students' emotional states and needs.
- **Reflective Practice:** Encouraging self-awareness and self-regulation among students and educators.
- **Social Interaction:** Fostering positive relationships and collaborative learning experiences.
- **Resilience Building:** Helping students develop coping strategies and resilience in the face of challenges.

Affectagogy

Implementing Affectagogy in Educational Settings

Adopting Affectagogy marks a transformative leap in educational philosophy, demanding a profound shift towards emotionally-integrated pedagogy. Grounded in research by Mihaela et al. (2022), this approach requires educators to transcend traditional knowledge transmission. Instead, they become orchestrators of emotional engagement, as highlighted by Joshua et al. (2020). This paradigm acknowledges that effective learning isn't solely about disseminating information but fostering profound connections between learners and subject matter. Educators embracing Affectagogy evolve into facilitators of emotional resonance, nurturing environments where students not only comprehend but deeply connect with the material. In essence, Affectagogy redefines the educator's role, placing emotion at the core of the teaching and learning experience.

Strategies for Implementation

- **Fostering Positive Relationships:** Establishing a classroom culture based on mutual respect, understanding, and emotional support is critical. This can be achieved by actively responding to students' emotional needs, offering encouragement, and maintaining open lines of communication (Konstantinos & Stavros, 2022).
- **Emotionally Engaging Materials:** Designing learning experiences that resonate emotionally with students can significantly enhance engagement (Chaitali et. al., 2022). This may involve integrating real-world applications, stories, or challenges relevant to students' lives and evoking emotional responses (Luisa-Marie et. al., 2021).
- **Active Emotional Engagement:** Encourage students to express their emotions and reflections related to the learning material. Techniques such as reflective journals, group discussions, and emotional intelligence activities can help students connect with the material on a deeper level, fostering a more meaningful learning experience (Mystakidis, 2021).

Practical Strategies

- **Emotionally Intelligent Teaching:** Incorporate activities that promote emotional awareness and regulation, such as mindfulness exercises and reflective journaling.
- **Empathetic Communication:** Use active listening and empathetic responses to create a supportive classroom atmosphere.

- **Collaborative Learning:** Design group activities that encourage cooperation and empathy among students.
- **Resilience Training:** Implement programs that teach students how to manage stress and adversity.

The Power of Empathy in Education

Empathy, the profound capacity to comprehend and resonate with another's emotions, lies at the heart of Affectagogy. This pedagogical approach, highlighted by Ode et. al. (2023), underscores the pivotal role empathy plays in educational dynamics. By embracing empathy, educators cultivate profound bonds with their students, transcending mere instruction to create an atmosphere of genuine care and understanding. Such empathetic connections not only enhance student-teacher rapport but also nurture a nurturing learning milieu where students feel valued and supported. In this symbiotic relationship, empathy becomes the guiding light, illuminating paths toward enriched educational experiences and holistic student development.

Empathy in Action

- **Understanding Student Needs:** An empathetic teacher is adept at recognizing the diverse emotional and academic needs of their students. This understanding allows for tailored support that addresses individual challenges and aspirations, fostering a sense of belonging and personalized learning experiences (Heather et. al., 2023).
- **Creating an Inclusive Classroom:** Empathy fosters an environment where all students feel valued and included (Yunfei, 2022). Recognizing and celebrating diversity in learning styles, backgrounds, and emotional expressions strengthens the classroom community, promoting respect and belonging for all learners.

Expanding Affectagogy Across Educational Spectrums

The principles of Affectagogy resonate profoundly across all educational stages, transcending boundaries to cultivate emotional engagement and address the multifaceted needs of learners. From early childhood education to higher academia, the ethos of empathy-driven teaching permeates, fostering inclusive and supportive environments where every learner can thrive. Whether guiding young minds in foundational learning or empowering advanced scholars in critical inquiry, Affectagogy

Affectagogy

remains a steadfast compass, navigating the complexities of emotional intelligence and interpersonal connection. Its universal relevance underscores a commitment to holistic education, where empathy serves as the cornerstone for nurturing not only academic prowess but also the socio-emotional well-being of learners at every stage of their educational journey.

Early Childhood Education

- **Creating a Secure Emotional Environment:** In early childhood settings, Affectagogy emphasizes the creation of a secure emotional environment where young learners feel valued, understood, and connected to their educators and peers (Ross et. al., 2020).
- **Emotional Literacy Activities:** Activities focused on emotional literacy, such as identifying and expressing feelings through stories, art, and play, lay the foundation for lifelong emotional intelligence (Seon et. al., 2022). This approach nurtures not only academic readiness but also social and emotional development, crucial for young children's overall well-being (Maciej, 2022).

Primary and Secondary Education

- **Integrating Emotional Engagement:** As students progress through their educational journey, Affectagogy can address the increasingly complex emotional and academic challenges they face (Ken et. al., 2007; Yun-Ching et. al., 2012). This involves integrating emotional engagement into the curriculum, promoting empathy, and fostering a classroom culture where students feel safe to express themselves and take intellectual risks (Alimul, 1921).
- **Collaborative Learning:** Projects that require collaborative problem-solving, peer feedback, and reflective practices encourage students to connect emotionally with the material and each other, enhancing learning outcomes and personal growth (Kim-Daniel, 2023).

Higher Education and Adult Learning

- **Relevance and Motivation:** The principles of Affectagogy are equally relevant in higher education and adult learning contexts, where emotional engagement can significantly impact motivation, persistence, and achievement (Jianhui et. al., 2020). Emphasizing the relevance of learning material to

students' personal and professional lives can foster deeper engagement and practical application of knowledge (Oliver et. al., 2018).
- **Self-Reflection and Community Engagement:** Creating opportunities for self-reflection, peer interaction, and community engagement within coursework can help learners connect emotionally with their studies, leading to a more meaningful and transformative educational experience (Therese, 2023).

Affectagogy and Inclusive Education

Affectagogy's emphasis on empathy and emotional connection holds particular significance in inclusive education settings, where students with diverse learning needs converge (Stuart, 2023). Customizing learning experiences to accommodate the spectrum of emotional and cognitive requirements ensures each learner feels esteemed and assisted. This inclusive paradigm cultivates an educational milieu where disparities are embraced, nurturing emotional and academic flourishing for all students (Farooq & Asim, 2018). By recognizing and honoring individual differences, Affectagogy promotes an environment where every student, irrespective of background or ability, can embark on a journey of learning and self-discovery, fostering a sense of belonging and empowerment within the classroom community.

Challenges and Opportunities

While the application of Affectagogy holds great promise, educators and institutions may face challenges in its implementation, including:

- **Resistance to Change:** Shifting pedagogical approaches can encounter resistance. Addressing concerns and providing support through professional development can help ease the transition.
- **Limited Resources:** Implementing Affectagogy may require additional resources for personalized learning and creating emotionally engaging environments. Creative solutions and collaboration can address these limitations.
- **Need for Professional Development:** Equipping educators with the necessary skills and knowledge to effectively implement Affectagogy necessitates ongoing professional development opportunities.

These challenges also present opportunities for innovation, collaboration, and the development of new pedagogical strategies that prioritize emotional engagement alongside academic excellence (Kjersti, 2023).

The Future of Affectagogy in Education

As we stand on the cusp of a new era in education, marked by rapid technological advances and changing societal needs, Affectagogy offers a visionary path forward (Reva, 2022). It emphasizes the enduring value of emotional connections in a world increasingly mediated by digital interfaces. The future of Affectagogy in education is not just about preserving the human touch but expanding its reach through innovative practices and technologies. By leveraging digital tools to enhance empathy-driven teaching and learning experiences, Affectagogy has the potential to revolutionize education, preparing students to thrive in an interconnected, emotionally intelligent global society.

Integrating Technology with Affectagogy

The integration of educational technology and Affectagogy presents exciting opportunities (Mehul, 2020). Digital platforms can facilitate emotional connections in ways previously unimaginable, from:

- **Virtual reality environments** that simulate real-life emotional experiences to promote empathy and understanding.
- **AI-driven analytics** that personalize learning based on emotional responses.

The challenge lies in harnessing technology to enhance, rather than replace, the human elements of teaching and learning. While digital tools offer unprecedented opportunities for engagement and personalization, they must complement, not overshadow, the vital role of human connection in education. Integrating technology judiciously within the framework of Affectagogy involves striking a delicate balance, where digital innovations serve as enablers rather than substitutes for authentic interactions between educators and learners. By prioritizing empathy and emotional intelligence in the design and implementation of educational technologies, we can ensure that technology enhances the human experience of teaching and learning, rather than detracting from it.

Preparing Educators for an Affectagogy-Centric Future

The role of educators will continue to evolve as Affectagogy gains prominence (Cekaite & Goodwin, 2023). Teacher education programs will need to equip future educators with the necessary skills and knowledge to effectively implement Affectagogy in their classrooms:

- **Training in Emotional Intelligence:** Fostering emotional intelligence (EQ) in educators is crucial. This involves developing competencies like self-awareness, self-regulation, social awareness, relationship management, and motivation (Nguyen et. al., 2022).
- **Designing Emotionally Engaging Learning Experiences:** Teacher education programs should incorporate training on designing curriculum and activities that actively engage students' emotions.
- **Creating a Culture of Empathy and Respect:** Fostering a classroom culture built on empathy and respect is essential for Affectagogy to thrive.

Professional Development for Existing Educators

Professional development opportunities are equally vital for existing educators. This can involve workshops, seminars, and online learning modules focusing on implementing Affectagogy strategies across diverse subject areas and grade levels. Educators also benefit from sessions dedicated to developing effective assessment methods that encompass both academic achievement and emotional engagement and growth. Moreover, practicing self-care strategies to safeguard emotional well-being and prevent burnout is essential. By investing in ongoing professional development tailored to the principles of Affectagogy, educators can continuously refine their skills, deepen their understanding, and ensure they remain equipped to create nurturing and effective learning environments for all students.

Building Resilient and Engaged Learners

The ultimate goal of Affectagogy is to cultivate learners who are not only knowledgeable but also emotionally intelligent, resilient, and engaged citizens (Lorraine et. al., 2019). By embedding emotional learning in the curriculum, students can develop the skills to:

- Manage their emotions effectively.
- Build healthy relationships with others.
- Make responsible decisions.
- Navigate the complexities of life with compassion and understanding.
- Develop a lifelong love of learning.

This holistic approach to education prepares students to face the challenges of the future with confidence, empathy, and a sense of purpose (Cekaite & Goodwin, 2023).

Case Scenarios and Real-World Examples

Consider a case scenario where a teacher, Ms. Katherine, notices that her students are disengaged and anxious about upcoming exams. By applying Affectagogy, she introduces mindfulness sessions to help students manage their stress and incorporates collaborative projects that build social bonds and peer support. Over time, students not only improve academically but also develop a stronger sense of community and emotional resilience.

CONCLUSION: A CALL FOR TRANSFORMATIVE EDUCATION THROUGH AFFECTAGOGY

Traditional education often prioritizes cognitive learning, neglecting the crucial emotional dimension. Affectagogy emerges as a powerful challenge to this status quo. By placing emotions at the core of learning, Affectagogy has the potential to revolutionize education (Mehul et. al., 2020).

This transformation goes beyond improved test scores. Affectagogy aspires to enrich the human experience itself (Streeter, 2022). Imagine a future generation equipped with:

- **Empathetic leadership:** Affectagogy fosters compassion and emotional intelligence, paving the way for leaders who prioritize the well-being of others.
- **Critical thinking with a heart:** Learners engage deeply with the world, critically analyzing issues while remaining attuned to the emotional dimensions.
- **Deep connections:** By fostering emotional connection in the classroom, Affectagogy cultivates a sense of belonging and connection, both within and beyond the classroom walls.

Widespread adoption of Affectagogy by educators, policymakers, and learners can make this vision a reality. Its principles can guide the development of inclusive, engaging, and effective educational practices that cater to the whole student. This is not just about improving educational outcomes; it's about creating a more compassionate, empathetic, and emotionally intelligent society.

Affectagogy compels us to integrate emotional intelligence into the very foundation of education. It envisions a future where learning with heart is not a mere aspiration, but the cornerstone of every educational experience. By fostering knowledge through emotional connection, Affectagogy offers a blueprint for nurturing compassionate and emotionally intelligent communities. This transformation has the power to ripple outwards, from classrooms to the world beyond.

Affectagogy advocates for a transformative approach to education, one that values emotional intelligence as much as intellectual achievement. This philosophy is rooted in the belief that education should nurture the whole person, preparing students not just for exams but for life. To achieve this, educators must embrace strategies that foster emotional and social growth alongside academic learning.

By integrating Affectagogy into educational practice, we can develop resilient, engaged, and empathetic students. This approach requires a shift in mindset and methodology, but the potential benefits make it a worthy endeavor. The time is ripe for educators to adopt Affectagogy and lead the way toward a more compassionate and effective educational future.

In conclusion, Affectagogy offers a promising pathway to a more holistic and effective educational system. By addressing the emotional and intellectual needs of students, we can create learning environments that are both supportive and stimulating. The principles and strategies outlined in this chapter provide a foundation for educators to begin implementing Affectagogy in their classrooms, paving the way for a transformative educational experience.

The call to action is clear: Embrace Affectagogy and transform education into a journey that nourishes both the intellect and the heart.

REFERENCES

Cekaite and, A., & Goodwin, M. H. (2023). Human Touch. *A New Companion to Linguistic Anthropology*, 391-409.

Chaitali, S. (2022). *Using Emotional Learning Analytics to Improve Students' Engagement in Online Learning*. ASCILITE Publications. 10.14742/apubs.2022.129

Chung, Y.-C., Carter, E. W., & Sisco, L. G.Yun-Ching. (2012, December). Chung., Erik, W., Carter., Lynn, G., Sisco. (2012). A Systematic Review of Interventions to Increase Peer Interactions for Students with Complex Communication Challenges. *Research and Practice for Persons with Severe Disabilities : the Journal of TASH*, 37(4), 271–287. Advance online publication. 10.2511/027494813805327304

D'ambrosio, M. (2020). Educating emotions: The pedagogical approach of emotional action. *Education Sciences & Society - Open Access, 11*(1). 10.3280/ess1-2020oa9292

David, B. (2022, August 29). Colm, McGuinness., Aiden, Carthy. (2022). Do educators value the promotion of students' wellbeing? Quantifying educators' attitudes toward wellbeing promotion. *PLoS One*, 17(8), e0273522. Advance online publication. 10.1371/journal.pone.0273522

Durlak, J. A., Weissberg, R. P., Dymnicki, A. B., Taylor, R. D., & Schellinger, K. B. (2011). The impact of enhancing students' social and emotional learning: A meta-analysis of school-based universal interventions. *Child Development*, 82(1), 405–432. 10.1111/j.1467-8624.2010.01564.x21291449

Farooq, M. S., & Asim, I. (2018). Nurturing inclusive education through cooperative learning as pedagogical approach at primary school level. *PJE*, 35(3). 10.30971/pje.v35i3.780

Goleman, D. (1995). *Emotional Intelligence: Why It Can Matter More Than IQ*. Bantam Books.

Heather, F. (2023, May 28). Jane, W., Davidson., Amanda, Krause. (2023). Examining the empathic voice teacher. *Research Studies in Music Education*, 1321103X2311720. 10.1177/1321103X231172065

Iram, A.Nasreen, A. (2021). Effect of teachers' emotional intelligence on student' involvement and task orientation in classroom learning environment at secondary school level. *Pakistan Journal of Educational Research*, 4(4). 10.52337/pjer.v4i4.353

Jianhui, Yu. (2020). *Changqin, Huang., Xizhe, Wang., Yaxin, Tu*. Exploring the Relationships Among Interaction, Emotional Engagement and Learning Persistence in Online Learning Environments., 10.1109/ISET49818.2020.00070

Joshua, K. (2020). *Classroom Culture: Stories of Empathy and Belonging*. IGI Global. 10.4018/978-1-7998-2971-3.ch011

Ken, G. (2007, July). Solvegi, Shmulsky. (2007). Meeting the Needs of Students with Complex Psychological and Educational Profiles. *College Teaching*, 55(3), 134–136. 10.3200/CTCH.55.3.134-136

Kim-Daniel, V. (2023). Students' experiences of peer feedback practices as related to awareness raising of learning goals, self-monitoring, self-efficacy, anxiety, and enjoyment in teaching EFL and mathematics. *Scandinavian Journal of Educational Research*, 1–15. 10.1080/00313831.2023.2192772

Kjersti, L. (2023). *107 Emotion in language education and pedagogy*. DEG. 10.1515/9783110795486-043

Konstantinos, B., & Stavros, S. (2022). Working with Students on Establishing a Student-Oriented Classroom Culture: A Teaching Initiative Designed to Build an Inclusive and Highly Engaging Learning Environment in Online and Face to Face Environments. In *Higher Education* (pp. 73–82). CRC Press. 10.1201/9781003021230-6

Lorraine, D. (2019). *Developing Employable, Emotionally Intelligent, and Resilient Graduate Citizens of the Future*. Springer. 10.1007/978-3-030-26342-3_6

Luisa-Marie. (2021). *Hartmann., Stanislaw, Schukajlow*. Interest and Emotions While Solving Real-World Problems Inside and Outside the Classroom., 10.1007/978-3-030-66996-6_13

Maciej, G. (2022). *Assessing Young Children's Emotional Well-Being: Enacting a Strength-Based Approach in Early Childhood Education*. 10.1007/978-981-19-5959-2_9

Matthew, A. (2018, February). Scult., Ahmad, R., Hariri. (2018). A brief introduction to the neurogenetics of cognition-emotion interactions. *Current Opinion in Behavioral Sciences*, 19, 50–54. 10.1016/j.cobeha.2017.09.014

Matthew, R. (2023, October 13). The relations between students' belongingness, self-efficacy, and response to active learning in science, math, and engineering classes. *International Journal of Science Education*, 45(15), 1241–1261. 10.1080/09500693.2023.2196643

Matthews, G. (2020). Developing emotionally intelligent teachers: A panacea for quality teacher education. *International Journal on Integrated Education*, 3(6), 92–98. 10.31149/ijie.v3i10.676

Mayer, J. D., & Salovey, P. (1997). What is emotional intelligence? In Salovey, P., & Sluyter, D. J. (Eds.), *Emotional development and emotional intelligence: Educational implications* (pp. 3–31). Basic Books.

Mehul, S. Vikas, Agarwal., Latika, Gupta. (2020). Human touch in digital education-a solution. *Clinical Rheumatology*. 10.1007/s10067-020-05448-y

Mihaela, M. (2022, April 11). Emotional and Social Engagement in the English Language Classroom for Higher Education Students in the COVID-19 Online Context. *Sustainability (Basel)*, 14(8), 4527. 10.3390/su14084527

Muniroh, A. (2021). Empathy Education Based Classroom Through Emotional Engagement during the Pandemic. *EDUTEC: Journal of Education And Technology*, 4(4), 644–650. 10.29062/edu.v4i4.226

Mystakidis, S. (2021). Deep meaningful learning. *Encyclopedia*, 1(3), 988–997. 10.3390/encyclopedia1030075

Nguyen, T., & Tu, A. N. (2022). Developing Emotional Intelligence for Education Innovation in Schools. *VNU Journal of Science: Education Research*. 10.25073/2588-1159/vnuer.4659

Ode, Y. (2023). Educator and Student Interaction in a Classroom Learning Atmosphere. AURELIA: *Jurnal Penelitian dan Pengabdian Masyarakat Indonesia*. 10.57235/aurelia.v2i1.309

Oliver, M. (2018). *Beyond CLIL: Fostering Student and Teacher Engagement for Personal Growth and Deeper Learning*. Springer. 10.1007/978-3-319-75438-3_16

Polak, A., Pavel, J., & Bajramlić, E. (2015). Approaches, methods and techniques used for developing emotional competency in the classroom. *Studia Edukacyjne*, 34, 325–344. 10.14746/se.2015.34.20

Purcia, E., Ygrubay, R. A., & Marbibi, A. M. (2023). Emotions as Language Learning Enhancers of Grade 11 Students. *American Journal of Multidisciplinary Research and Innovation*, 2(3), 9–14. 10.54536/ajmri.v2i3.1543

Y., Reva. (2022). Humanization of pedagogical communication is effective harmonious influence on student personality development educational process. *Osvìtnìj vimìr*. 10.31812/educdim.5708

Ross, C. (2020). *Building a Secure Learning Environment Through Social Connectedness*. Taylor & Francis. 10.4324/9780429027833-8

Seon, H. (2022). *The Effects of Emotional Expression Activities Using Picture Books on Young Children's Emotional Intelligence and Empathic Ability*. Korean Association For Learner-Centered Curriculum And Instruction. 10.22251/jlcci.2022.22.18.877

Silva, C. R. D., Veiga, F., Pinto, É. S., & Ferreira, I. (2020). Retention in school: Could student's affective engagement play an essential role in its prevention? *Millenium*, 14(2), 59–68.

Streeter, J. R. (2022). Humanizing the curriculum: Exploring the use of drama pedagogy in faculty development. In *The Routledge Companion to Drama in Education* (pp. 357–363). Routledge. 10.4324/9781003000914-38

Stuart, M. (2023). Inclusive Education for Students With Diverse Learning Needs in Mainstream Schools. *International perspectives on inclusive education*. Emerald. 10.1108/S1479-363620230000020009

Terence, . (2022, June). School connection through engagement associated with grade scores and emotions of adolescents: Four factors to build engagement in schools. *Social Psychology of Education*, 25(2-3), 675–696. 10.1007/s11218-022-09697-4

Therese, F. (2023). Reflecting on Students' Reflections: Exploring Students' Experiences in Order to Enhance Course Delivery. *The Qualitative Report*. 10.46743/2160-3715/2023.5868

Torres, I., Statti, A., & Torres, K. M. (2022). Emotion and online learning. In *Online Distance Learning Course Design and Multimedia in E-Learning* (pp. 81–113). IGI Global. 10.4018/978-1-7998-9706-4.ch004

Venkatesh, S., & Fischer, C. E. (2019). Cognitive factors associated with emotional intelligence. *International Psychogeriatrics*, 31(9), 1229–1231. 10.1017/S1041610219000917 34658311

Yang, Y., & Wang, J. Z. (2017). From structure to behavior in basolateral amygdala-hippocampus circuits. *Frontiers in Neural Circuits*, 11, 86. 10.3389/fncir.2017.00086 29163066

Yunfei, S. (2022). The Connection Between Empathy and Equity in Higher Education. 10.4018/978-1-7998-9746-0.ch001

Zhang, I. (2022). The impact of emotional arousal on amygdala activity, memory consolidation, and long-term potentiation in the hippocampus. *Journal of Student Research*, 11(2). 10.47611/jsr.v11i2.1614

Affectagogy

KEY TERMS AND DEFINITIONS

Affectagogy: A term derived from "affect" (emotion) and "agogos" (leading), emphasizing the role of emotional connections in learning to create engaging and effective educational experiences.

Amygdala: A brain structure that plays a central role in emotional learning and memory formation, influencing how emotionally charged experiences are remembered.

Emotional Engagement: The involvement of students' emotions in the learning process, which enhances motivation, participation, and information retention.

Emotional Intelligence (EQ): The ability to perceive, use, understand, and manage emotions, which is crucial for personal and professional success and is integrated into educational frameworks in Affectagogy.

Empathy: The ability to understand and resonate with the emotions of others, essential for creating meaningful connections in educational settings.

Human-Touch Learning: A pedagogical approach within Affectagogy that prioritizes emotional bonds among educators, learners, and learning materials, fostering a supportive and empathetic environment.

Neuroscience of Emotional Learning: The study of how emotions and cognitive processes interact within the brain, highlighting the significant impact of emotions on attention, memory, and decision-making.

Reflective Practice: Encouraging self-awareness and self-regulation among students and educators to improve learning outcomes and emotional well-being.

Resilience Building: Helping students develop coping strategies and resilience to manage stress and adversity effectively.

Social Interaction: Fostering positive relationships and collaborative learning experiences to enhance students' social and emotional development.

Chapter 8
Experiential Learning in the Digital Classroom to Improve Outcomes Related to Diversity, Equity, and Inclusion

Lauren Lunsford
Belmont University, USA

Amanda Nelms
https://orcid.org/0000-0002-9154-8607
Belmont University, USA

Sally Barton-Arwood
Belmont University, USA

ABSTRACT

The purpose of this chapter is to explore the utility and process for integrating an experiential service-learning experience that promotes diversity and inclusion into an online learning environment. Experiential education and service-learning opportunities have been found to be a successful means for students to interact with individuals from different backgrounds and improve their cultural awareness. Given the promise for experiential education to address and improve outcomes related to DEI, it is worthwhile to investigate ways to integrate these activities into online courses. This chapter aims to: (1) introduce the benefits of experiential education and rationale for its inclusion as a practice to improve outcomes related to diversity and inclusion, (2) provide an overview of the potential of e-service learning as a

DOI: 10.4018/979-8-3693-2407-3.ch008

Experiential Learning in Digital Classroom to Improve Diversity, Inclusion

means to do this, (3) share an example e-service-learning project

INTRODUCTION

Experiential education, when done authentically, can help students build relationships with individuals from different cultural backgrounds and help them become aware of issues faced by individuals from other cultures. Service-learning has been identified as a tool for enhancing what is taught in our coursework and fostering a deeper understanding of others (Salam, Ibrahim, & Farook, 2019). Experiential learning and service learning are often cited as high impact practices by the Association of American Colleges and Universities (AAC&U). These pedagogies improve student outcomes in a multitude of a ways. Experiential learning opportunities are grounded in hands-on opportunities that help students extend their learning beyond the more basic conceptual and into the applied realm. By integrating real-world situations into coursework students are able to see the concepts we are teaching in action and able to envision the utility of their work in their own future.

The purpose of this chapter is to explore the utility and process for integrating an experiential experience that promotes diversity and inclusion into an online learning environment. Experiential education and service learning opportunities have been found to be a successful means for students to interact with individuals from different backgrounds and improve their cultural awareness. In particular, Holsapple's review of the literature (2012) found that such activities facilitated students' confrontation of stereotypes that they held about the individuals, an increased knowledge of a new culture, and a stronger belief in the value of diversity (Eyler & Giles, 1999; Hughes, Welsh, Mayer, Bolay, & Southard, 2009). Given the promise for experiential education to address and improve outcomes related to diversity, equity, and inclusion, it is worthwhile to investigate ways to integrate these activities into online courses. This chapter aims to: (1) introduce the benefits of experiential education and rationale for its inclusion as a practice to improve outcomes related to diversity and inclusion, (2) provide an overview of the potential of e-service learning as a means to do this, (3) share an example e-service-learning project, and (4) provide practical recommendations for implementing such activities.

EXPERIENTIAL LEARNING

Experiential learning opportunities can take many forms, including internships, service learning opportunities, student teaching placements, volunteering opportunities and even study abroad opportunities. By paying attention to the critical and impactful tenets of experiential education an instructor can bring these experiential opportunities into their coursework in a variety of ways. Kolb's seminal work (1984) examines the means by which "experience is the source for learning and development." Experiential learning is built upon the ideals of educational psychologists like Piaget and Dewey. When examining this pedagogy under the lens of Piaget's cognitive theory it becomes clear that providing students with concrete experiences facilitates their ability to understand concepts more deeply and relate them back to their own lives in a more impactful way. Similarly, experiential learning allows students to refine their purpose at hand and "transforms the impulses, feelings, and desires of concrete experience into higher-order purposeful action" (p.22).

Experiential learning is cited as a central aspect of two high impact practices by AAC&U (Internships and Service Learning and Community Learning). Internships are likely the most commonly utilized form of experiential learning because of their direct correlation to a student's career goals. Internships are seen as a critical component to facilitating a students' successful transition from the academic world to their career. Internships often vary in length but always aim to provide the student with opportunities to apply their learned skills in the real world and thus reinforce their knowledge and development. This work surrounding internships is most often focused on helping students' become career ready and increase their earning potential and corporate skill set. However, work surrounding Service Learning and Community Learning aims to help students apply their skills to solve real world problems in their communities. These problems and situations are not necessarily tied to their major focus of study and are focused more on the development of model citizenship.

Experiential Learning and Diversity

A commitment to diversity and inclusion is a critical element of career readiness and is touted as essential by the National Associate of Colleges and Employers. In order to be career ready college students must "demonstrate the awareness, attitude, knowledge, and skills required to equitably engage and include people from different local and global cultures. They should engage in anti-racist practices that actively challenge the systems, structures, and policies of racism. Service-learning has been found to positively impact students' intercultural competence and attitudes related to diversity and inclusion (Borden, 2007; Buchanan, Correia, & Bleicher, 2010). Experiential education and service learning opportunities have been found to be a successful means for students to interact with individuals from different backgrounds and improve their cultural competence. In particular, Holsapple's review of the literature (2012) found that such activities facilitated students' confrontation of stereotypes that they held about the individuals, an increased knowledge of a new culture, and a stronger belief in the value of diversity (Eyler & Giles, 1999;

Antmann, 2004; Plann, 2002; Hughes, Welsh, Mayer, Bolay, & Southard, 2009). Service learning opportunities provide students with purposeful tasks that help them, among other things, build relationships with people different from themselves. These relationships can be the catalysts for important mindset shifts for students when they are developed thoughtfully. In particular, research has shown that deep, meaningful contact can result in lower levels of ethnocentrism for participating students (Borden, 2007). While ethnocentric attitudes vary for individuals they demonstrate a positive bias toward one's ingroup and a negative bias towards those they see as "the other". Ethnocentric individuals tend to have limited interaction and appreciation for other cultures (Nanda & Warms, 1998), and is a serious obstacle for a college student to develop a mindset of diversity and inclusion. Service-learning is a potentially powerful tool for addressing the ethnocentrism that our college students may bring to the classroom, but certain principles must be considered in order for this practice to reach its maximum potential. Utilizing a framework to analyze these considerations is an important element when designing impactful projects

Experiential Learning, Service Learning, and Contact Theory

Contact Theory (CT) is an important theoretical framework to take into account when implementing service learning opportunities that aim to improve the participants' intercultural competency and attitudes towards diversity and inclusion. Allport (1954) outlines five key elements of CT within service-learning as: (1) equal status contact, (2) pursuit of common goals, (3) intergroup cooperation, (4) support of authorities, custom, or law, and (5) sustained, long-term contact. Attending to these principles when implementing service-learning work has been found to improve individual's ethnocentricism and decrease one's stigma and biases towards another group (Conner & Erickson, 2017). These principles are important to keep in mind when designing service-learning opportunities that aim to improve diversity and inclusion outcomes. Establishing equal status and pursuit of common goals are important elements when designing the experience in that the task at hand should not succumb to a power deferential that would contribute to a sense of saviorism. Developing tasks that allow individuals to work side by side together establish a framework of equality and inclusion from the beginning. For example, the authors engaged in a project where freshman college students served as conversation partners for adult English Language (EL) learners. While the project clearly contributed heavily to providing the EL learners important conversation practice, the prompts that were developed for the conversations centered around getting to know the city that the college freshman just moved to. This allowed both parties to contribute to the project and for the benefits to be mutual, beyond expanding the college students' intercultural competencies. Another example shared by Borden

(2007) demonstrates how having college students work side by side with community members on a project to develop a proposal for a vacant lot created a task that required expertise from all members of the community. Establishing a clear for participants that require everyone's participation contributes heavily to the success of the service-learning project and is a prerequisite for intercultural growth. These common goals and tasks must require cooperation across the participating groups under a set of agreed upon norms in order for their task to be completed and thus garner success for all involved. Finally, in order for these interactions to move from the transactional to the transformational a successful project must be one that is ongoing and sustained. A one-and-done approach to service learning opportunities will not garner the intended outcomes of transforming an individual's perceptions of diversity and inclusivity.

E-Service Learning for Implementing Experiential Education in the Digital Classroom

COVID-19 presented an enormous challenge for those in education, particularly those implementing experiential learning opportunities. Strict social distancing kept learners from engaging in the hands-on activities that were the hallmark of experiential learning. As classes moved online more and more instructors found themselves without the key experiential activities that were so important to their courses. Since COVID-19, coursework is being delivered online, and the use of e-service-learning has risen as an important tool in the online world (Schmidt, 2021). Integrating experiential learning in the digital world is not without challenges. A large- scale study of students engaging in e-service-learning activities found that these activities were not as impactful as traditional in person service-learning activities (Ngai, Lau, & Kwan, 2023). However, the technologies expanded as a result of COVID do open up opportunities to utilize e-service-learning in new ways. By leveraging technology to implement experiential pedagogies in courses that did not previously include such experiences, we have the opportunity to introduce more experiences for more students. This chapter will provide an overview of e-service learning and examples of its use prior to the COVID-19 pandemic as well as its utilization since then in the digital classroom. Because utilizing digital space during COVID-19 took may forms took many forms the best way to begin to analyze this work is to begin with an effective framework to delineate different approaches and projects that use the digital space in different ways.

A Framework for Examining E-Service Learning

The analysis and comprehension of e-service learning can be significantly enriched by exploring it through various lenses. Waldner et al. (2012) have provided a valuable framework that delves into the implementation aspects of both the course and the service activity on a continuum of how much of the course and service are conducted in an online manner. Their framework categorizes e-service learning into four tiers, each with distinct characteristics and implications. Traditional service-learning (T-SL) encompasses traditional in-person courses coupled with in-person service learning activities. This tier facilitates direct interaction and engagement between students and the community, foster a deep understanding of real-world issues. This is the tier at which most of our research regarding service learning has occurred for the since service learning's inception as a powerful instructional strategy.

At Tier One, courses are fully online, combined with in-person service learning activities. This tier introduces the challenge of balancing online coursework with practical, hands-on experiences but a great deal of research has identified this as an effective means to execute service-learning (Bennett & Green, 2001; Burton, 2003).

In Tier Two, courses are conducted in person while service learning activities are executed online or virtually in some way. Many projects at this level involve having students develop products and resources for their community partners (Mosley, 2005; Lazar & Preece, 1999) but the online activities can involve direct virtual interactions for participants.

Tier Three courses involve situations where both the course and/or the service are both partially onside and partially online. Programs within this tier attempts to maximize the potential of opportunities in person and virtual environments (Killian, 2004, Blackwell, 2008). This tier highlights the potential for online platforms to facilitate both service learning experiences and coursework in both formats, albeit with considerations for logistical arrangements and communication methods.

Lastly, Tier Four involves both the course and the service learning activity being conducted online. Waldner et al (2012) term this "extreme e-service learning" and emphasize that 100% of the activities are conducted virtually. This tier presents unique opportunities for leveraging digital tools and collaborative platforms to engage students in service-oriented projects remotely. However, it also raises challenges related to maintaining a sense of community and ensuring effective communication and coordination among participants.

Each tier within this framework presents its own set of opportunities and challenges when implementing e-service learning pedagogy. By examining e-service learning through these tiers, educators and researchers can gain deeper insights into the dynamics of online learning environments coupled with community engagement, ultimately enhancing the effectiveness of this instructional approach.

Product Outcomes of E-Service Learning

The exploration of e-service learning pedagogy can be enriched by examining both its means of execution and the outcome it generates. Traditional engagement in service learning usually involves in-person interactions, as seen in Tier One of Waldner's framework. However, as projects transition to online platforms in tiers 2, 3, and 4, the nature and scope of the project outcomes can vary significantly. While a comprehensive framework encompassing the outcomes for e-service learning assignments is yet to be developed, researchers have employed diverse strategies and assignments in their service-learning projects. These strategies have led to the creation of valuable service and products that contribute to both community partners and student learning experiences.

The products and services resulting from e-service learning projects can take various forms, ranging from indirect service through the development of products for community partners to more direct interactions. For instance, Mosley (2005) assisted in creating websites for nonprofit organizaiotns, showcasing a form of indirect service delivery. Schmidt (2021) worked on developing vieos and reading books for preschool children, demonstrating another indirect delivery option. Lazar and Preece (1999) as well as Figuccio (2020) focused on developing and providing resources for community organizations, highlighting another avenue of indirect service. These examples illustrate the versatility of e-service learning opportunities where the interaction between the partners and the students can vary significantly. Even in scenarios with minimal direct interaction, students can gain valuable insights into the needs and dynamics of the population and organization that they are serving. This diversity in the execution methods and project outcomes underscores the adaptability and effectiveness of e-service learning as a pedagogical tool to foster community engagement and student learning.

As noted above a great deal of research has been done on the ways that e-service learning can be executed in an indirect manner. On the other hand, students can engage in more direct opportunities virtually by spending time online in a variety of ways. The project that we will share involved direct online engagement for students in an in person class (Tier Two). While Waldner's framework provides much promise for analyzing e-service learning, it has been underutilized as a framework for analyzing the outcomes of a project as well as the practical considerations one must consider in order to maximize the benefits of both the students and community partners.

An Example of e-Service Learning With Direct Service-Learning Virtual Opportunities

The authors' project integrated the use of e-service-learning by connecting freshman students with individuals participating in an English Learners course being held at a nonprofit off campus. Participating students served as online conversation partners for these English Learners and provided 15-20 minutes of conversation practice via Zoom each week. This project was developed collaboratively with a local nonprofit, and its implementation yielded several important lessons for those engaging in experiential learning in the digital space. The research project that we are presenting here involved an in person class participating in e-service learning by engaging directly and virtually, following the Tier Two model. Students attended a course twice a week, and as part of their service learning activities, they engaged in weekly 30-minute conversations with English language learners. Unlike some e-service learning projects that involve developing tangible products, the focus of this project was on fostering intercultural understanding and providing support to newcomers.

In this project, freshman college students served as conversation partners for individuals enrolled in an English Language Learners class, offering opportunities to practice and improve their English language skills. The students spent time researching and familiarizing themselves with the organization that they were working with and learning about the challenges that parents who are English Language Learners (ELLs) face. Parents of school age children who do not speak English proficiently have identified the language barrier as a primary obstacle to their engagement in their children's schools (Zarate, 2007).

Conversely, the ELL individuals were tasked with identifying ways to help the college students who were new to their city acclimate to their surroundings. Beyond language practice, the conversations also served as a platform for cultural exchange, where the adult EL students shared insights about their respective cultures and lives in the city that the college freshman had just moved to. The adult EL students shared their favorite spots in the city, enriching the experience with local knowledge and personal recommendations. Successful service learning occurs when individuals share a common goal and collaborate as equals towards that goal and these provided a task for each side of the partnership.

This project exemplifies how e-service learning can transcend boundaries of project development and instead focus on fostering meaningful connections and mutual learning between individuals from diverse backgrounds. By engaging in dialogue and sharing experiences, participants not only contribute to each other's growth but also promote a sense of community and inclusivity within educational settings.

Practical Recommendations

While a number of best practices can be identified in the research surrounding experiential education and service-learning, there are also a number of practical considerations to take into account when implementing such a project in the digital space. Projects should be guided by community partner needs while also maximizing benefits for the students engaging in the experiential opportunities. This can become increasingly challenging in the digital classroom and there are strategies and considerations to keep in mind to maximize benefits for all. First of all, while many of us are increasingly comfortable functioning in the digital space it is important to carefully guide all participants through each step of all aspects of the project related to technology. Conducting at least the first session with "live" hands-on support can go a long way in avoiding pitfalls and technological problems. Supplementing the sessions with detailed videos for connecting to zoom rooms is also a helpful support. Therefore, it is important to frontload a session for students regarding potential problem that they may encounter and how they might solve them. This can avoid frustrations and disconnect for all involved. To support the technological needs students may have it is also critical for the teacher or leader to regularly rotate through the zoom rooms to provide support.

Another consideration is tending to the fact that individuals will interacting "unsupervised" in breakout rooms at time and they will be interacting with other adults in the community. Because freshman may be as young as 17 years and older possibly minors it is important to be cognizant when creating groups of students to interact in these conversation groups. Individuals participating in these groups were vetted by both the community partner leader and the faculty member. Before sessions began behavioral expectations were covered and a rubric for their expectations was shared that would impact their participation grade in their respective classes. These expectations were important for ensuring respectful discussion as well as for fostering meaningful relationships for all involved.

Finally, it is important to build time to celebrate the relationships built. As most projects continue for an extended time it is important to nurture the relationships that the students and participants are developing and take time to celebrate that. An activity at the end of the semester is a great way to facilitate this celebration and leads nicely to a culminating reflection which is so critical. In sum, online activities are an incredibly powerful way to facilitate meaningful experiential learning activities, especially when designed thoughtfully and collaboratively.

REFERENCES

Allport, G. W. 1. (1954). *The nature of prejudice.* Cambridge, Mass., Addison-Wesley Pub. Co.

American Association of Colleges and Universities (2023). *High-impact practices.* AACU.

Amtmann, J. (2004). Perceived effects of a correctional health education service-learning program. *Journal of Correctional Education*, 55(4), 335–348.

Bennett, G. (2001). Promoting Service Learning Via Online Instruction. *Higher Education*, 20.

Blackwell, C. W. (2008). Meeting the objectives of community-based nursing education. In A. Dailey-Hebert, E. Donnelli-Sallee, & L. DiPadovaStocks (Eds.), *Service-eLearning: Educating for citizenship* (pp. 87-94). Charlotte, NC: Information Age Publishing.

Borden, A. W. (2007). The impact of service-learning on ethnocentrism in an intercultural communication course. *Journal of Experiential Education*, 30(2), 171–183. 10.1177/105382590703000206

Buchanan, M. C., Correia, M. G., & Bleicher, R. E. (2010). Increasing preservice teachers' intercultural awareness through service-learning. *The International Journal of Research on Service-Learning in Teacher Education*, 1(1), 1–19.

Burton, E. (2003). Distance learning and service-learning in the accelerated format. *New Directions for Adult and Continuing Education*, 2003(97), 63–72. 10.1002/ace.89

Conner, J., & Erickson, J. (2017). When does service-learning work? Contact theory and service-learning courses in higher education. *Michigan Journal of Community Service Learning*, 23(2), 53–65. 10.3998/mjcsloa.3239521.0023.204

Eyler, J., & Giles, D. E. (1999). *Where's the learning in service-learning?* Jossey-Bass.

Figuccio, M. (2020). Examining the efficacy of e-service learning. *Secondary Teacher Education*, (5).

Holsapple, M. (2012). Service-learning and student diversity outcomes: Existing evidence and directions for future research. *Michigan Journal of Community Service Learning*, 5–18.

Hughes, C., Welsh, M., Mayer, A., Bolay, J., & Southard, K. (2009). An innovative university-based mentoring program: Affecting college students' attitudes and engagement. *Michigan Journal of Community Service Learning*, 16(1), 69–78.

Killian, J. (2004). Pedagogical experimentation: Combining traditional, distance, and service learning techniques. *Journal of Public Affairs Education*, 10(3), 209–224. 10.1080/15236803.2004.12001360

Kolb, D. A. (1984). *Experiential learning: Experience as the source of learning and development*. Prentice-Hall.

Lazar, J., & Preece, J. (1999) Implementing Service Learning in an Online Communities Course. International Academy of Information Management.

Mosley, P. (2005). Redesigning web design. *Academic Exchange Quarterly*.

Nanda, S., & Warms, R. L. (1998). *Cultural anthropology* (6th ed.). Wadsworth.

Ngai, G., Lau, K.-H., & Kwan, K.-P. (2024). A Large-Scale Study of Students' E-Service-Learning Experiences and Outcomes During the Pandemic. *Journal of Experiential Education*, 47(1), 29–52. 10.1177/10538259231171852

Plann, S. (2002). Latinos and literacy: An upper-division Spanish course with service-learning. *Hispania*, 85(2), 330–338. 10.2307/4141094

Salam, M., Awang Iskandar, D. N., Ibrahim, D. H. A., & Farooq, M. S. (2019). Service learning in higher education: A systematic literature review. *Asia Pacific Education Review*, 20(4), 573–593. 10.1007/s12564-019-09580-6

Schmidt, M. E. (2021). Embracing e-service learning in the age of COVID and beyond. *Scholarship of Teaching and Learning in Psychology*. 10.1037/stl0000283

Waldner, L. S., Widener, M. C., & McGorry, S. Y. (2012). E-service learning: The evolution of service-learning to engage a growing online student population. *Journal of Higher Education Outreach & Engagement*, 16(2), 123–150.

Zarate, M. E. (2007). Understanding Latino Parental Involvement in Education: Perceptions, Expectations, and Recommendations. Los Angeles, California. The Tomás Rivera Policy Institute. University of Southern California.

Chapter 9
An Educationally-Beneficial Experience for Undergraduate Students:
A Service-Learning Mentoring Project With Native American Youth

Crystal S. Aschenbrener
Campbellsville University, USA

ABSTRACT

Service-learning has been an increasingly used high impact approach to facilitate applied learning. Mentorship between undergraduate students and youth is commonly utilized as a tactic to support one of the goals of service-learning: addressing and fulfilling community needs. A consistently underserved and underrepresented population of youth are Native Americans who reside on rural reservations who often experience community-wide social problems. While often the impacts of mentorship on youth are researched, this study examines the impact on undergraduate students' perceptions after completing a mentoring intervention with Native American youth. A mixed method approach was designed, using pre- and post-surveys as well as a final reflective comprehensive paper to collect data. The results concluded that by completing the service-learning project in partnership with the Native American youth, it created positive impacts on the undergraduate students' educational perceptions, such as with an underrepresented culture, mentoring intervention, and applied research.

DOI: 10.4018/979-8-3693-2407-3.ch009

INTRODUCTION

Experiential education, when done authentically, can help students build relationships with individuals from different cultural backgrounds and help them become aware of issues faced by individuals from other cultures. Service-learning has been identified as a tool for enhancing what is taught in our coursework and fostering a deeper understanding of others (Salam, Ibrahim, & Farook, 2019). Experiential learning and service learning are often cited as high-impact practices by the Association of American Colleges and Universities (AAC&U). These pedagogies improve student outcomes in a multitude of ways. Experiential learning opportunities are grounded in hands-on opportunities that help students extend their learning beyond the more basic conceptual and into the applied realm. By integrating real-world situations into coursework, students can see the concepts we are teaching in action and envision their work's utility in the future.

This chapter aims to explore the utility and process for integrating an experiential experience that promotes diversity and inclusion into an online learning environment. Experiential education and service learning opportunities successfully allow students to interact with individuals from different backgrounds and improve their cultural awareness. In particular, Holsapple's review of the literature (2012) found that such activities facilitated students' confrontation of stereotypes that they held about the individuals, an increased knowledge of a new culture, and a stronger belief in the value of diversity (Eyler & Giles, 1999; Hughes et al., 2009). Given the promise of experiential education to address and improve outcomes related to diversity, equity, and inclusion, it is worthwhile to investigate ways to integrate these activities into online courses. This chapter aims to (1) introduce the benefits of experiential education and the rationale for its inclusion as a practice to improve outcomes related to diversity and inclusion, (2) provide an overview of the potential of e-service learning as a means to do this, (3) share an example e-service-learning project, and (4) provide practical recommendations for implementing such activities.

EXPERIENTIAL LEARNING

Experiential learning opportunities can take many forms, including internships, service learning opportunities, student teaching placements, volunteering opportunities, and study-abroad opportunities. By paying attention to experiential education's critical and impactful tenets, an instructor can bring these experiential opportunities into their coursework in various ways. Kolb's seminal work (1984) examines how "experience is the source for learning and development." Experiential learning is built upon the ideals of educational psychologists like Piaget and Dewey. When reviewing this pedagogy under the lens of Piaget's cognitive theory, it becomes clear that providing students with concrete experiences facilitates their ability to understand concepts more deeply and relate them to their own lives in a more impactful way. Similarly, experiential learning allows students to refine their purpose at hand and "transforms the impulses, feelings, and desires of concrete experience into higher-order purposeful action" (p.22).

Experiential learning is cited as a central aspect of two high-impact practices by AAC&U (Internships and Service Learning and Community Learning). Internships are likely the most commonly utilized form of experiential learning because of their direct correlation to a student's career goals. Internships are critical in facilitating a student's successful transition from the academic world to their career. Internships often vary in length but always aim to provide the student with opportunities to apply their learned skills in the real world and thus reinforce their knowledge and development. This work surrounding internships often focuses on helping students become career-ready and increase their earning potential and corporate skill set. However, work surrounding Service Learning and Community Learning aims to help students apply their skills to solve real-world community problems. These problems and situations are not necessarily tied to their primary focus of study; they are focused more on the development of model citizenship.

Experiential Learning and Diversity

A commitment to diversity and inclusion is a critical element of career readiness and is touted as essential by the National Association of Colleges and Employers. To be career-ready, college students must "demonstrate the awareness, attitude, knowledge, and skills required to engage equitably and include people from different local and global cultures. They should engage in anti-racist practices that actively challenge the systems, structures, and policies of racism. Service-learning has positively impacted students' intercultural competence and attitudes related to diversity and inclusion (Borden, 2007; Buchanan et al., 2010). Experiential education and service learning opportunities successfully allow students to interact with individuals from different backgrounds and improve their cultural competence. In particular, Holsapple's review of the literature (2012) found that such activities facilitated students' confrontation of stereotypes that they held about the individuals, an increased knowledge of a new culture, and a stronger belief in the value of diversity (Eyler & Giles, 1999; Antmann, 2004; Plann, 2002; Hughes et al., 2009). Service learning opportunities provide students with purposeful tasks that help them, among other things, build relationships with people different from themselves. These relationships can catalyze important mindset shifts for students when they are developed thoughtfully. In particular, research has shown that deep, meaningful contact can result in lower levels of ethnocentrism for participating students (Borden, 2007). While ethnocentric attitudes vary for individuals they demonstrate a positive bias toward one's ingroup and a negative bias towards those they see as "the other". Ethnocentric individuals tend to have limited interaction and appreciation for other cultures (Nanda & Warms, 1998). This is a severe obstacle for a college student to develop a mindset of diversity and inclusion. Service-learning is a potentially powerful tool for addressing the ethnocentrism our college students may bring to the classroom. Still, certain principles must be considered for this practice's maximum potential. Utilizing a framework to analyze these considerations is essential when designing impactful projects.

Experiential Learning, Service Learning, and Contact Theory

Contact Theory (CT) is an essential theoretical framework to consider when implementing service learning opportunities to improve the participants' intercultural competency and attitudes toward diversity and inclusion. Allport (1954) outlines five critical elements of CT within service learning: (1) equal status contact, (2) pursuit of common goals, (3) intergroup cooperation, (4) support of authorities, custom, or law, and (5) sustained, long-term contact. Attending to these principles when implementing service-learning work has been found to improve an individual's ethnocentricism and decrease stigma and biases towards another group (Conner & Erickson, 2017). These principles are essential when designing service-learning opportunities to improve diversity and inclusion outcomes. Establishing equal status and pursuing common goals is crucial when designing the experience. The task should not succumb to a power deferential that would contribute to a sense of saviorism. Developing functions that allow individuals to work together establishes a framework of equality and inclusion. For example, the authors engaged in a project where first-year college students were conversation partners for adult English Language (EL) learners. While the project contributed heavily to providing the EL learners with critical conversation practice, the conversation' prompts centered on getting to know the city the college freshman had just moved to. This allowed both parties to contribute to the project and for the benefits to be mutual beyond expanding the college students' intercultural competencies. Another example shared by Borden (2007) demonstrates how having college students work side by side with community members on a project to develop a proposal for a vacant lot created a task requiring expertise from all community members. Establishing a clear for participants that requires everyone's participation contributes heavily to the success of the service-learning project and is a prerequisite for intercultural growth. These shared goals and tasks must require cooperation across the participating groups under a set of agreed-upon norms to complete their task, thus garnering success for all involved. Finally, for these interactions to move from the transactional to the transformational, a successful project must be ongoing and sustained. A one-and-done approach to service learning opportunities will not garner the intended outcomes of transforming an individual's perceptions of diversity and inclusivity.

E-Service Learning for Implementing Experiential Education in the Digital Classroom

COVID-19 presented an enormous challenge for those in education, particularly those implementing experiential learning opportunities. Strict social distancing kept learners from engaging in the hands-on activities that were the hallmark of experiential learning. As classes moved online, more instructors found themselves without the vital experiential activities essential to their courses. Since COVID-19, coursework has been delivered online, and e-service-learning has become a vital tool for the online world (Schmidt, 2021). Integrating experiential learning in the digital world is challenging. A large-scale study of students engaging in e-service-learning activities found that these activities were less impactful than traditional in-person service-learning activities (Ngai et al., 2023). However, the technologies expanded due to COVID-19, opening up opportunities to utilize e-service-learning in new ways. By leveraging technology to implement experiential pedagogies in courses that did not previously include such experiences, we can introduce more experiences for more students. This chapter will provide an overview of e-service learning, examples of its use before the COVID-19 pandemic, and its use since then in the digital classroom. Because utilizing digital space during COVID-19 took many forms, the best way to begin to analyze this work is to start with a practical framework to delineate different approaches and projects that use the digital space differently.

A Framework for Examining E-Service Learning

The analysis and comprehension of e-service learning can be significantly enriched by exploring it through various lenses. Waldner et al. (2012) have provided a valuable framework that delves into the implementation aspects of the course and the service activity on a continuum of how much the course and service are conducted online. Their framework categorizes e-service learning into four tiers, each with distinct characteristics and implications. Traditional service-learning (T-SL) encompasses traditional in-person courses and in-person service-learning activities. This tier facilitates direct interaction and engagement between students and the community, fostering a deep understanding of real-world issues. This is the tier at which most of our service learning research has occurred since service learning's inception as a powerful instructional strategy.

At Tier One, courses are entirely online, combined with in-person service learning activities. This tier introduces the challenge of balancing online coursework with practical, hands-on experiences. However, much research has identified this as an effective means to execute service-learning (Bennett & Green, 2001; Burton, 2003).

In Tier Two, courses are conducted in person, while service-learning activities are executed online or virtually in some way. Many projects at this level involve having students develop products and resources for their community partners (Mosley, 2005; Lazar & Preece, 1999), but online activities can involve direct virtual interactions with participants.

Tier Three courses involve situations where the course and the service are partially online and partially online. Programs within this tier attempt to maximize the potential of opportunities in person and virtual environments (Killian, 2004; Blackwell, 2008). This tier highlights the potential for online platforms to facilitate both service learning experiences and coursework in both formats, albeit with considerations for logistical arrangements and communication methods.

Lastly, Tier Four involves the course and the service learning activity being conducted online. Waldner et al. (2012) term this "extreme e-service learning" and emphasize that 100% of the activities are conducted virtually. This tier presents unique opportunities for leveraging digital tools and collaborative platforms to remotely engage students in service-oriented projects. However, it also challenges maintaining a sense of community and ensuring effective communication and coordination among participants.

Each tier within this framework presents opportunities and challenges when implementing e-service learning pedagogy. By examining e-service learning through these tiers, educators and researchers can gain deeper insights into the dynamics of online learning environments coupled with community engagement, ultimately enhancing the effectiveness of this instructional approach.

Product Outcomes of E-Service Learning

The exploration of e-service learning pedagogy can be enriched by examining both its means of execution and the outcome it generates. Traditional engagement in service learning usually involves in-person interactions, as seen in Tier One of Waldner's framework. However, as projects transition to online platforms in tiers 2, 3, and 4, the nature and scope of the project outcomes can vary significantly. While a comprehensive framework encompassing the outcomes for e-service learning assignments is yet to be developed, researchers have employed diverse strategies and assignments in their service-learning projects. These strategies have led to the creation of valuable services and products that contribute to both community partners and student learning experiences.

The products and services resulting from e-service learning projects can take various forms, ranging from indirect service through the development of products for community partners to more direct interactions. For instance, Mosley (2005) assisted in creating websites for nonprofit organizations, showcasing a form of indirect service delivery. Schmidt (2021) worked on developing videos and reading books for preschool children, demonstrating another indirect delivery option. Lazar and Preece (1999) and Figuccio (2020) focused on developing and providing resources for community organizations, highlighting another avenue of indirect service. These examples illustrate the versatility of e-service learning opportunities where the interaction between the partners and the students can vary significantly. Even in scenarios with minimal direct interaction, students can gain valuable insights into the needs and dynamics of the population and organization they serve. This diversity in the execution methods and project outcomes underscores the adaptability and effectiveness of e-service learning as a pedagogical tool to foster community engagement and student learning.

As noted above, a great deal of research has been done on how e-service learning can be executed indirectly. On the other hand, students can engage in more direct opportunities virtually by spending time online in various ways. The project we will share involves direct online engagement for students in an in-person class (Tier Two). While Waldner's framework provides much promise for analyzing e-service learning, it has been underutilized as a framework for analyzing the outcomes of a project and the practical considerations one must consider to maximize the benefits for both the students and community partners.

An Example of E-Service Learning With Direct Service-Learning Virtual Opportunities

The authors' project integrated e-service-learning by connecting first-year students with individuals participating in an English Learners course at a nonprofit off campus. Participating students served as online conversation partners for these English Learners and provided 15-20 minutes of conversation practice via Zoom each week. This project was developed collaboratively with a local nonprofit, and its implementation yielded several important lessons for those engaging in experiential learning in the digital space. The research project we present here involves an in-person class participating in e-service learning by engaging directly and virtually, following the Tier Two model. Students attended a course twice a week, and as part of their service learning activities, they engaged in weekly 30-minute conversations with English language learners. Unlike some e-service learning projects that involve developing tangible products, this project focused on fostering intercultural understanding and providing support to newcomers.

In this project, first-year college students served as conversation partners for individuals enrolled in an English Language Learners class, offering opportunities to practice and improve their English language skills. The students spent time researching and familiarizing themselves with the organization they were working with and learning about the challenges faced by parents who are English Language Learners (ELLs). Parents of school-age children who do not speak English proficiently have identified the language barrier as a primary obstacle to their engagement in their children's schools (Zarate, 2007).

Conversely, the ELL individuals identified ways to help college students new to their city acclimate to their surroundings. Beyond language practice, the conversations also served as a platform for cultural exchange, where the adult EL students shared insights about their respective cultures and lives in the city that the college freshman had just moved to. The adult EL students shared their favorite spots in the city, enriching the experience with local knowledge and personal recommendations. Successful service learning occurs when individuals share a common goal and collaborate as equals towards that goal, providing a task for each side of the partnership.

This project exemplifies how e-service learning can transcend the boundaries of project development and instead focus on fostering meaningful connections and mutual understanding between individuals from diverse backgrounds. By engaging in dialogue and sharing experiences, participants contribute to each other's growth and promote a sense of community and inclusivity within educational settings.

Practical Recommendations

While several best practices can be identified in the research surrounding experiential education and service learning, there are also several practical considerations to consider when implementing such a project in the digital space. Community partners should guide project needs while maximizing benefits for the students engaging in the experiential opportunities. This can become increasingly challenging in the digital classroom, and there are strategies and considerations to keep in mind to maximize benefits for all. First, while many of us are increasingly comfortable functioning in the digital space, it is essential to carefully guide all participants through each step of the project, including all technology-related aspects. Conducting at least the first session with "live" hands-on support can go a long way in avoiding pitfalls and technological problems. Supplementing the sessions with detailed videos to connect to Zoom rooms is also helpful. Therefore, it is essential to frontload a session for students regarding potential problems they may encounter and how they might solve them. This can avoid frustrations and disconnect for all involved. To support

An Educationally-Beneficial Experience for Undergraduate Students

students' technological needs, the teacher or leader must regularly rotate through the Zoom rooms to provide support.

Another consideration is tending to the fact that individuals will interact "unsupervised" in breakout rooms and interact with other adults in the community. Because first-year students may be as young as 17 years and older, possibly minors, it is essential to be cognizant when creating groups of students to interact in these conversation groups. The community partner leader and the faculty member vetted individuals participating in these groups. Before sessions began, behavioral expectations were covered, and a rubric for their expectations was shared that would impact their participation grade in their respective classes. These expectations were essential for ensuring respectful discussion and fostering meaningful relationships for all involved.

Finally, it is essential to make time to celebrate the relationships that have been built. As most projects continue for an extended time, it is necessary to nurture the relationships the students and participants are developing and celebrate them. Activity at the end of the semester is a great way to facilitate this celebration and leads nicely to a culminating reflection, which is critical. In sum, online activities are a compelling way to facilitate meaningful experiential learning, especially when designed thoughtfully and collaboratively.

REFERENCES

Allport, G. W. 1. (1954). *The nature of prejudice.* Cambridge, Mass., Addison-Wesley Pub. Co.

American Association of Colleges and Universities (2023). *High-impact practices.* AACU.

Amtmann, J. (2004). Perceived effects of a correctional health education service-learning program. *Journal of Correctional Education*, 55(4), 335–348.

Bennett, G. (2001). Promoting Service Learning Via Online Instruction. *Higher Education*, 20.

Blackwell, C. W. (2008). Meeting the objectives of community-based nursing education. In A. Dailey-Hebert, E. Donnelli-Sallee, & L. DiPadovaStocks (Eds.), *Service-eLearning: Educating for citizenship* (pp. 87-94). Charlotte, NC: Information Age Publishing.

Borden, A. W. (2007). The impact of service-learning on ethnocentrism in an intercultural communication course. *Journal of Experiential Education*, 30(2), 171–183. 10.1177/105382590703000206

Buchanan, M. C., Correia, M. G., & Bleicher, R. E. (2010). Increasing preservice teachers' intercultural awareness through service-learning. *The International Journal of Research on Service-Learning in Teacher Education*, 1(1), 1–19.

Burton, E. (2003). Distance learning and service-learning in the accelerated format. *New Directions for Adult and Continuing Education*, 2003(97), 63–72. 10.1002/ace.89

Conner, J., & Erickson, J. (2017). When does service-learning work? Contact theory and service-learning courses in higher education. *Michigan Journal of Community Service Learning*, 23(2), 53–65. 10.3998/mjcsloa.3239521.0023.204

Eyler, J., & Giles, D. E. (1999). *Where's the learning in service-learning?* Jossey-Bass.

Figuccio, M. (2020). Examining the efficacy of e-service learning. *Secondary Teacher Education*, (5).

Holsapple, M. (2012). Service-learning and student diversity outcomes: Existing evidence and directions for future research. *Michigan Journal of Community Service Learning*, 5–18.

Hughes, C., Welsh, M., Mayer, A., Bolay, J., & Southard, K. (2009). An innovative university-based mentoring program: Affecting college students' attitudes and engagement. *Michigan Journal of Community Service Learning*, 16(1), 69–78.

Killian, J. (2004). Pedagogical experimentation: Combining traditional, distance, and service learning techniques. *Journal of Public Affairs Education*, 10(3), 209–224. 10.1080/15236803.2004.12001360

Kolb, D. A. (1984). *Experiential learning: Experience as the source of learning and development*. Prentice-Hall.

Lazar, J., & Preece, J. (1999) Implementing Service Learning in an Online Communities Course. *14th Annual Conference*. International Academy of Information Management.

Mosley, P. (2005). Redesigning web design. *Academic Exchange Quarterly*.

Nanda, S., & Warms, R. L. (1998). *Cultural anthropology* (6th ed.). Wadsworth.

Ngai, G., Lau, K.-H., & Kwan, K.-P. (2024). A Large-Scale Study of Students' E-Service-Learning Experiences and Outcomes During the Pandemic. *Journal of Experiential Education*, 47(1), 29–52. 10.1177/10538259231171852

Plann, S. (2002). Latinos and literacy: An upper-division Spanish course with service-learning. *Hispania*, 85(2), 330–338. 10.2307/4141094

Salam, M., Awang Iskandar, D. N., Ibrahim, D. H. A., & Farooq, M. S. (2019). Service learning in higher education: A systematic literature review. *Asia Pacific Education Review*, 20(4), 573–593. 10.1007/s12564-019-09580-6

Schmidt, M. E. (2021). Embracing e-service learning in the age of COVID and beyond. *Scholarship of Teaching and Learning in Psychology*. Advance online publication. 10.1037/stl0000283

Waldner, L. S., Widener, M. C., & McGorry, S. Y. (2012). E-service learning: The evolution of service-learning to engage a growing online student population. *Journal of Higher Education Outreach & Engagement*, 16(2), 123–150.

Zarate, M. E. (2007). Understanding Latino Parental Involvement in Education: Perceptions, Expectations, and Recommendations. The Tomás Rivera Policy Institute. University of Southern California.

Chapter 10
Nurse Educators Answering the Call to Missions

Angie G. Atwood
Campbellsville University, USA

ABSTRACT

Educators can personally impact college students' lives by leading medical mission trips. The purpose of this chapter is to discuss accepting the call to missions, the role of the nurse educator in mission work, challenges and opportunities, and cultural preparedness. Beyond didactic instruction and clinical training, engaging in mission work provides a transformative experiential way for instructors to develop holistic learning experiences. The word 'transformative' is an adjective that means causing or able to cause an important and lasting change in someone or something. A transformative experience like this helps students learn in a manner that will foster life-long learning. Assuming the role of a mission team leader involves guiding college students through experiences that extend beyond the traditional classrooms.

INTRODUCTION

Educators can personally impact college students' lives by leading medical mission trips. The purpose of this chapter is to discuss accepting the call to missions, the role of the nurse educator in mission work, challenges and opportunities, and cultural preparedness. Beyond didactic instruction and clinical training, engaging in mission work provides a transformative experiential way for instructors to develop holistic learning experiences. According to Merriam-Webster.com (2024), the word transformative is an adjective that means causing or able to cause an important and

DOI: 10.4018/979-8-3693-2407-3.ch010

Nurse Educators Answering the Call to Missions

lasting change in someone or something. A transformative experience like this helps students learn in a manner that will foster life-long learning.

Assuming the role of a mission team leader involves guiding college students through experiences that extend beyond the traditional classrooms. This task also accepts responsibilities, bringing challenges and opportunities related to the educator's leadership abilities in medical mission trips. This chapter discusses the significance of fostering medical mission learning experiences, heeding the call to missions, and the internal motivation and ethical considerations that provoke nurse educators to take part in these impactful journeys of service and education.

ACCEPTING THE CALL

The decision to accept the call to missions often comes from a deep sense of a spiritual calling and a scriptural understanding of the importance of serving others. Christian missions must include a priority of sharing the Gospel of Jesus Christ or it is no longer a mission but rather a Samaritan work. Meeting the needs of mankind with medicine and holistic nursing care through medical mission work must encompass the Great Commission. Providing only physical needs to a non-Christian group of people neglects the opportunity to share the gospel, possibly impacting their eternal destiny. Nurse educators draw inspiration from biblical teachings that emphasize compassion, service, and the alleviation of suffering. The call to missions reflects the biblical focus of answering a higher calling and fulfilling a sacred duty to care for those less fortunate and vulnerable people living on the margin. Here are some scriptures to further explain:

1. **Jeremiah 1:5** (*King James Bible*, 1769/2017) "Before I formed thee in the belly, I knew thee, and before thou camest forth out of the womb, I sanctified thee, and I ordained thee a prophet unto the nations." This verse shares that individuals are given a specific purpose by God. Nurse educators accepting the call to missions may perceive their mission work as a fulfillment of a duty to serve and make a positive impact on the health and well-being of those in need.
2. **Isaiah 6:8** (*King James Bible*, 1769/2017) "Also, I heard the voice of the Lord, saying, Whom shall I send, and who will go for us? Then said I, Here am I; send me." This scripture reflects the willingness to respond to a call for service. Leaders who accept the call to missions, express their readiness to go where they are needed, recognizing the heartfelt potential of their skills and knowledge.
3. **Matthew 25:40** (*King James Bible*, 1769/2017) "And the King shall answer and say unto them, Verily I say unto you, inasmuch as ye have done it unto one of the least of these my brethren, ye have done it unto me." This verse emphasizes the

connection between service to others and service to God. Individuals engaging in mission work view their efforts as an expression of their faith, recognizing the significance of caring for the less fortunate and underserved populations.
4. **1 Peter 4:10** (*King James Bible*, 1769/2017) "As every man hath received the gift, even so minister the same one to another, as good stewards of the manifold grace of God." This scripture shares the concept of using one's gifts and talents to minister to others. Nurses, acknowledging their unique gifts in higher education, often see mission work as acts of the grace bestowed upon them, with a responsibility to share their knowledge and skills for the greater good.

By accepting the call to missions, educators not only align their actions with these biblical principles but also gain strength and inspiration from the wisdom found in the scriptures. The combination of faith and professional calling becomes a guiding force as they begin a journey of service, compassion, and transformative impact.

ROLE OF THE NURSE EDUCATOR AS MISSION LEADER

The role of the nurse educator in leading medical mission trips is complex and extends far beyond the traditional boundaries of the classroom. Northouse (2021) describes a leader as an individual who influences a group of people toward the achievement of a common goal. With each transformative event experienced by the student, the leader assumes an enormous amount of responsibility to facilitate the integration of education, service, and cultural competency. Among their responsibilities is the meticulous planning and coordination required to ensure the success the mission. From securing travel arrangements and accommodations to arranging medical supplies in resource-limited settings, nurse educators serve as servant leaders, ensuring a smooth medical mission trip experience filled with learning and service.

Securing travel arrangements and accommodations is a realm of mission work that one may not anticipate taking ample of time. With medical missions, traveling to countries outside of the United States involves sharing suggested immunizations for the area of travel, securing visas if required, booking modes of transportation, housing, correct money currency, and arrangements for meals.

The Centers for Disease Control and Prevention (CDC) provides vital information on travel health, including destination-specific recommendations for vaccinations, health advisories, and disease outbreaks. Their Travelers' Health website (https://wwwnc.cdc.gov/travel/) is a wonderful resource for travelers, including medical mission workers. The World Health Organization (WHO) is another organization that offers guidance on international travel and health. WHO provided recommendations for vaccinations, disease prevention, and travel advisories. Their International Travel and Health website (https://www.who.int/ith/en/) provides useful information for travelers regarding health risks in different regions of the world. The United States (U.S) Department of State has a website link https://travel.state.gov/content/travel/en/international-travel.html, that offers information on travel requirements, including visa regulations, for U.S. citizens traveling abroad. It also provides country-specific travel advisories and safety information. Mission team leaders are encouraged to use these resources in preparation for a mission trip to ensure the safety and health promotion of all team members.

Securing modes of transportation well in advance is best for favorable rates. The leader may be working with the educational institution to optimize resources to consider group bookings for special airfare rates to reduce team member costs. Coordinating ground transportation such as travel from the airport to the guest house and traveling during the mission will be less hectic if accommodations are secured weeks in advance.

Mission team leaders must reserve suitable accommodations that meet the needs of the mission team. This may include the number of team members, room assignments and special requests, accommodating the separation of males and females, and consideration of location, safety, amenities, and cost per night/week. A good resource of information is often a local native of the area, such as a missionary, who can give suggestions for accommodations.

It is common practice to carry a combination of cash, credit/debit, and the local currency when engaged in mission trips. Each team member can exchange currency in advance or upon arrival to ensure the availability of local currency for transactions. Meals for the mission team should be planned, considering dietary restrictions, cultural preferences, and availability of a food preparation team. A list of local restaurants with menus may also be helpful. Planning for the mission team's nutritional needs and proper hygiene standards will aid in a positive mission team experience.

It's essential to communicate effectively with everyone involved in the mission, including team members, local partners, and service providers, to ensure that transportation, housing, currency, and meals are arranged smoothly. Flexibility and planning are key elements, as unexpected challenges may arise during the mission trip.

Educationally, the mission leaders become creators of experiential learning, developing a plan that brings together didactic learning with hands-on clinical experience. Experiential learning is widely recognized for its effectiveness in promoting deep learning, critical thinking, problem-solving skills, and personal growth (Uzun & Uygun, 2022). They must balance the delivery of healthcare services with the educational level of the participants involved, creating a wonderful learning environment that fosters critical thinking, adaptability, and competency within the participating students. This includes designing and implementing learning activities with a focus on the unique opportunities presented by the mission setting. The nurse educator must be ready for unforeseen changes in plans and practice with the utmost flexibility. They serve as mentors and role models, guiding students through various challenges and ethical considerations while helping them provide quality healthcare in culturally diverse areas with limited resources. Their role extends to fostering cultural competence among students, including relativism, an appreciation for diversity, and a sense of humility and respect in the face of unfamiliar healthcare experiences. According to Merriam-Webster.com (2024), relativism is a theory that knowledge is relative to the limited nature of the mind and the conditions of knowing or a view that ethical truths depend on the individuals and groups holding them. In simplistic terms, relativism is understanding that cultures have a variety of views and truths as they know them.

By incorporating local knowledge and beliefs into health promotion efforts, nurses can foster trust and collaboration within communities. Throughout the mission, the nurse leaders play a crucial role in facilitating debriefing discussions to allow reflection, providing students with the opportunity to process their experiences, confront ethical dilemmas, and reflect on meaningful lessons. In doing so, they contribute to the personal and professional growth of students, helping them develop a new understanding of global health issues and a commitment to social responsibility. Debriefing helps team members process the psychological impact of challenging situations encountered during medical missions, thereby promoting resilience and wellness among participants (Fanning & Gaba, 2017).

In essence, the role of the nurse educator in leading medical mission trips is a combination of leadership, mentorship, and facilitator of learning. By blending education and service, navigating challenges, and fostering cultural competence, nurse educators shape a transformative educational experience. These experiences not only equip students with clinical skills but also empower them with a profound sense of spiritual empathy, cultural humility, and a commitment to making a positive impact globally. Grant et al. (2020) describe spiritual empathy as the capacity to understand and connect with another person's spiritual experiences, beliefs, and values encompassing the demonstration of compassion and support in their spiritual journey. Cultural humility is an approach to understanding and interacting with individuals from different cultural backgrounds, with acts of openness, self-awareness, and willingness to learn from others (Hook et al., 2019). Making a global impact through medical missions has a positive impact by providing essential healthcare services to underserved populations, improving health outcomes, and fostering cross-cultural understanding and collaboration (Crump et al., 2020). Often nursing students anticipate a focus on clinical skills and surprisingly gain a wealth of unanticipated knowledge in realms of global impact, spiritual empathy, and cultural humility.

CHALLENGES AND OPPORTUNITIES

Navigating the challenges of leading medical mission trips at the college level demands a steadfast commitment to planning, cultural sensitivity, and the integration of educational and healthcare objectives. Such challenges align with biblical principles that outline the importance of preparation, compassion, and a holistic approach to service. Numerous studies emphasize the importance of holistic approaches in medical missions, recognizing the impact of psychological, social, and spiritual factors on individuals' well-being (Puchalski, 2023).

Planning

Whether the trip is worth course credit or experiential knowledge, balancing the educational objectives of the mission trip with the primary goal of providing free healthcare services and fulfilling Matthew 28:16-20 (*King James Bible*, 1769/2017), the Great Commission, can be challenging. Finding opportunities for meaningful learning experiences while ensuring safe, quality patient care requires methodological planning.

The beginning step includes working with the Campus Missions Director. The director can directly answer questions and give details about previous mission trips, mission trip guidelines at the governing institution, fundraising ideas, travel insurance, and acquisition transportation. Collaborating with the Campus Missions Director parallels the biblical notion of seeking guidance and wisdom from those with experience as referenced in Proverbs 15:22 (*King James Bible*, 1769/2017). Engaging with experienced directors ensures a solid foundation for the mission, drawing on collective wisdom to overcome challenges.

Next, getting students involved is crucial, though it can be fun, but also exhausting. College students and their families have numerous questions. Providing an inclusive stakeholders meeting is a great way to share details with a large group. Informational handouts are helpful, allowing a way to reflect on the information discussed during the meeting. The process of engaging students aligns with the biblical principles of community and shared responsibility. Galatians 6:2 (*King James Bible*, 1769/2017) encourages believers to "Bear one another's burdens, and so fulfill the law of Christ." The collaborative effort of addressing numerous questions and concerns from students and their families fosters a sense of communal responsibility.

Furthermore, the task of balancing the educational goals of a mission trip and providing healthcare services echoes the biblical principle of stewardship. Nurse educators must carefully manage resources at their disposal—both educational and medical—to maximize their impact on the communities they serve. In the face of these challenges, nurse educators can draw inspiration from biblical narratives where in leaders, upon receiving mandates, meticulously planned and engaged in collaborative efforts in order to fulfill their own missions.

Lastly, therefore the planning phase becomes an opportunity for educators to enhance the biblical principles of stewardship, seeking counsel, and communal responsibility. As nurse educators navigate the trip details, cultural concerns, and educational focuses of the medical mission trip, their commitment to addressing these challenges, in a manner that aligns with biblical principles, becomes the foundational testament to their strategic approach to healthcare and education in the mission field. This methodological journey of planning and executing mission trips has now become a living demonstration of faith in action.

Cultural Preparedness

Cultural preparedness is a crucial aspect of medical mission trips, particularly for nurse educators leading students in diverse and unfamiliar cultural settings. It involves developing an understanding and sensitivity to the cultural differences, beliefs, values, and practices of the communities being served. Successfully navigating cultural differences within a mission environment enhances the effectiveness of healthcare delivery, fosters positive interactions with local populations, and promotes a more enriching educational experience for students (Kimberly, 2023). To be fully prepared a step-by-step approach becomes necessary.

First, nurse educators need to be aware of their own cultural biases and assumptions. This self-awareness is foundational for developing cross-cultural competence in not only themselves as leaders, but in the students they are leading. The nurse educator understands that acknowledging the diversity within the mission team itself is part of cultural preparedness. Team members may bring different cultural backgrounds and perspectives that, when addressed effectively, can aid in the mission's success (Kimberly, 2023). Nurses must seek a firm understanding of the impact of race, ethnicity, gender, sexual orientation, and socioeconomic status influence health outcomes. This awareness allows for a more comprehensive approach to patient care during mission trips into unfamiliar areas of the world. (Kimberly, 2023)

Following self-awareness, the nurse leader must gain an understanding of the local culture, traditions, and customs is essential (Červený et al., 2022). This knowledge helps in providing healthcare services and educational approaches to align with the cultural relativism of the population to be served. Adequate language skills, or access to interpreters, is another vital step in cultural preparedness that will foster effective communication between healthcare providers and patients who may not speak the same language. Clear communication helps in obtaining accurate medical histories, explaining diagnoses and treatment plans, and addressing any concerns or questions the patient may have. Miscommunication can lead to misunderstandings and compromise the quality of care. Awareness of non-verbal cues and body language is crucial, as these can vary significantly across cultures and may convey meanings different from verbal communication.

Another essential step in preparedness is to practice religious and spiritual sensitivity. Recognizing and respecting diverse religious and spiritual beliefs is crucial. This recognition includes understanding how certain beliefs may influence healthcare decisions and practices. Acknowledging and respecting local traditional healing practices alongside Western medicine is necessary for establishing a working relationship built on trust. Once established, the Biblical truths can be shared to promote a Christian worldview approach to spiritual needs.

Mission leaders may witness the implications of various modalities of healing. For example, Haitian people involved in Vodou may participate in self-harming practices, thus presenting to free medical clinics with burns and lacerations to the skin. As they seek care for their basic physical needs, members of the mission team are ready to meet their spiritual needs by telling tell them about the ultimate healer, Jesus, eventually sharing the plan of His salvation. Free medical clinics are commonly held at churches where large areas can be sectioned off to set up stations. The first area serves as the priority station, the prayer group. Team members listen to the individual's needs, share the gospel, pray with each patient and their families, provide free Bibles to new converts, and connect them with a local church and pastor to cultivate spiritual growth. Other stations may include the following: (a) a health assessment area to obtain the patient's vital signs and medication allergies, (b) an area for the physician's assessment, (c) a private area for medication administration, and (d) a table of gifts, often free supplies such as food items, toiletries, and/or articles of clothing.

Cultivating cultural humility is another demonstration of cultural preparedness. Cultural humility involves maintaining an open and humble attitude towards learning from the community (Hook et al., 2019). This approach recognizes that while educators may not fully understand the complexities of the local culture, they continuously and actively seek to improve cultural competence. For example, the Haitian people allow the men in the group to eat before the women and children. This practice may be difficult to watch, as often the women and children in third-world countries remain hungry due to water and food shortages. The mission team may not agree with this practice, but being adaptable to cultural differences, and a willingness to modify approaches to align with local norms contributes to successful engagement with the people being served. Simple modifications such as team members sharing their water and food with the women and children to prevent starvation, is one method of adaptation that honors both cultural beliefs.

Another significant cultural difference is Haiti's connection to Vodou practices. Vodou priests are viewed as accepted leaders, also known as Voodoo priests. This religion is practiced primarily in Haiti and parts of the Caribbean and emphasizes the importance of ancestor worship, spirits (lwa), and rituals for healing and spiritual guidance (Metraux, 2019). The Vodou priests treat patients but they can't treat complex situations or perform invasive surgeries (Dean, 2021). Spiritual empathy with humility entails one's own limitations to understanding the full deep of all religions and the needs of others. It is acknowledging that one may not have all the answers and not fully understand another individual's spiritual experience. This form of spiritual humility fosters respect and openness for learning from others as well as self-reflection and growth (Bekelman et al., 2007).

During medical missions, those providing care must acknowledge the ethical considerations for the people being served. Respecting patient autonomy is a fundamental ethical principle. This exercise involves recognizing that patients, even in different cultural contexts, have the right to be informed to make decisions about their healthcare (Beauchamp et al, 2017). Ensuring informed consent processes are culturally sensitive and crucial for ethical healthcare delivery. A need for an interpreter may be necessary. Once healthcare activities have ended, the mission leader should engage students in a post-trip debriefing session allowing the group to reflect on cultural experiences, discuss the challenges encountered, and to share individual insights. Post-trip debriefing is a crucial opportunity to process the experiences, challenges, and insights gained during the mission trip. The reflection sessions promote collective as well as individual reflection of the experiences. It allows participants to share their difficulties and brainstorm solutions for future missions. Continued and ongoing learning that will improve cultural preparedness for future mission trips. This method concentrates the focus of unity between spiritual and physical needs, by introducing how faith in the Lord, Jesus Christ, heals nations.

In summary, cultural preparedness is a dynamic and ongoing process requiring a commitment to continuous learning, a spirit of humility, and the ability to adapt. By prioritizing cultural preparedness, nurse educators facilitate more meaningful and respectful interactions with the communities they serve, contributing to the success and sustainability of medical mission trips.

Integration of Educational and Medical Mission Objectives

The integration of educational and medical mission objectives is a process that requires careful planning, collaboration, and a holistic approach to healthcare and education. This integration is essential, ensuring that medical mission trips not only provide valuable physical and spiritual needs, to underserved communities but they also contribute to the educational experience of the participating students. Here are a few steps to follow:

- Begin with identifying specific learning goals that students are expected to achieve during the mission trip. Goals may include improvement in cultural competence, demonstration of clinical skills, and an enhanced understanding of global health issues. Once identified, align these educational objectives with the overall purpose and goals of the mission so student competency can be verified. For example, if the overall goal of the mission trip is to share the Gospel of Jesus Christ, then the educational goals must include knowledge in the plan of salvation, how to witness to people with no Bible knowledge, along with clinical skills needed to provide safe and compassionate patient care.
- Encourage interdisciplinary collaboration by involving students from various healthcare disciplines. This fosters a collaborative approach to problem-solving and patient care. In third-world countries, medical mission team members often have an extra layer as they use translators when working with doctors, pharmacists, and other members of the healthcare team.
- Implement reflective practices to encourage students to critically analyze their experiences, challenges, and personal growth during the mission. Integrate debriefing sessions into the mission schedule. These sessions should not only focus on medical cases but also the cultural, ethical, religious, and personal aspects of the experience, fostering a deeper understanding of the mission's impact. Devotional time is one common method used by Christian medical mission teams. This method allows team members to share testimonials each day, giving focus to the goal of the mission.
- Incorporate discussion of ethical principles into the curriculum, emphasizing the importance of patient autonomy, informed consent, and the importance of respect and dignity for individuals with diverse perspectives. Further, ensure that the mission activities adhere to the highest ethical standards. This includes such things as obtaining informed consent, respecting patient autonomy, and addressing any ethical dilemmas that arise during healthcare delivery (Beauchamp et al., 2017)
- Identify specific clinical and non-clinical skills that students should develop during the mission, such as effective communication, teamwork, and adaptability. Structure mission activities to provide hands-on experiences that allow students to apply learned skills and enhance their understanding of skills they are learning in the classroom.
- Evaluate the long-term impact of the mission trip on students' careers, perspectives, and commitment to global health. Assess the sustainable impact

of the mission on the local community's healthcare system. This evaluation helps in refining future mission strategies and educational approaches.

By intentionally integrating these educational and medical mission objectives, nurse educators can create transformative learning experiences that not only benefit the communities being served but also contribute significantly to the professional and personal development of the participating students. This integration ensures a balance between healthcare services and the competent healthcare workforce.

CONCLUSION

In this comprehensive exploration of nurse educators' role in leading medical mission trips, the chapter emphasizes the impact nurse educators have on students' lives by guiding transformative experiences beyond traditional education. The discussion includes acceptance of the call to missions, the multifaceted role of nurse educators, challenges and opportunities occurring during mission trips, and the critical aspect of cultural preparedness. The chapter recognizes the biblical foundation inspiring nurse educators to accept the call to missions, drawing on scriptures such as Jeremiah 1:5, Isaiah 6:8, and Matthew 25:40. These scriptures explain the purpose, willingness to serve, interconnectedness of service to others and service to God, and the stewardship of one's gifts in ministering to others.

Nurse educators serve as mentors, orchestrators of experiential learning, and facilitators of cultural competence, shaping a transformative educational experience that extends far beyond the classroom. In summary, this chapter offers a comprehensive view of the profound impact of nurse educators as leaders of medical mission trips, combining both professional expertise and guiding with biblical principles with the cultural competence to create transformative experiences for both educators and students.

REFERENCES

Bekelman, D. B., Dy, S. M., Becker, D. M., Wittstein, I. S., Hendricks, D. E., Yamashita, T. E., & Gottlieb, S. H. (2007). Spiritual well-being and depression in patients with heart failure. *Journal of General Internal Medicine*, 22(4), 470–477. 10.1007/s11606-006-0044-917372795

Betancourt, J. R., Green, A. R., Carrillo, J. E., & Ananeh-Firempong, O. (2003). *Travelers' health*. CDC. https://wwwnc.cdc.gov/travel/

Červený, M., Kratochvílová, I., Hellerová, V., & Tóthová, V. (2022). Methods of increasing cultural competence in nurses working in clinical practice: A scoping review of literature 2011-2021. *Frontiers in Psychology*, 13, 936181. 10.3389/fpsyg.2022.93618136092120

Crump, J. A., Sugarman, J., & Barry, M. A. (2020). Ethical considerations for short-term experiences by trainees in global health. *Journal of the American Medical Association*, 324(7), 737–738. 10.1001/jama.300.12.145618812538

Dean, N. (2021, Sep 04). On a medical mission: Granville's Healing Art Missions helps Haiti through unrest, and earthquakes. *The Advocate*.https://www.proquest.com/newspapers/on-medical-mission/docview/2568860421/se-2

Fanning, R. M., & Gaba, D. M. (2017). The role of debriefing in simulation-based learning. *Simulation in healthcare. Simulation in Healthcare*, 2(2), 115–125. Retrieved January 12, 2024, from. 10.1097/SIH.0b013e318031553919088616

Hook, J. N., Davis, D. E., Owen, J., Worthington, E. L., & Utsey, S. O. (2013). Cultural humility: Measuring openness to culturally diverse clients. *Journal of Counseling Psychology*, 60(3), 353–366. 10.1037/a003259523647387

Kimberly, A. (2023). Promoting cultural competence in nursing: Strategies for providing inclusive patient care. *Opinion Journal of Advanced Practices in Nursing*, 8(6). https://www.hilarispublisher.com/open-access/promoting-cultural-competence-in-nursing-strategies-for-providing-inclusive-patient-care.pdf

King James Bible. (2017). King James Bible Online (Original work published 1769).

Metraux, A. (2019). Voodoo in Haiti. In *Voodoo in Haiti* (pp. 1-25). Routledge (Original work published 1959).

Moudatsou, M., Stavropoulou, A., Philalithis, A., & Koukouli, S. (2020). The Role of Empathy in Health and Social Care Professionals. *Healthcare (Basel)*, 8(1), 26. 10.3390/healthcare801002632019104

Northouse, P. G. (2021). *Leadership: Theory and practice* (9th ed.). SAGE Publications.

Puchalski, C. M. (2023). Integrating spirituality into patient care: An essential element of person-centered care. *Polish Archives of Internal Medicine*, 123(9), 491–497. 10.20452/pamw.189324084250

U.S. Department of State. (n.d.). *International travel*. US DoS. https://travel.state.gov/content/travel/en/international-travel.html

Uzun, C., & Uygun, K. (2022). The effect of simulation-based experiential learning applications on problem solving skills in social studies education. *International Journal (Toronto, Ont.)*.

Chapter 11
Toward a Transformational Learning:
Integrating Spiritual Diversity Practices in Social Work Classrooms

Pious Malliar Bellian
http://orcid.org/0000-0001-8543-4032
School of Social Work, Indiana University, Indianapolis, USA

ABSTRACT

There are inadequacies in the existing mode of instruction/pedagogical approaches in capturing sacred moments, diverse practices, and spiritual perspectives of multiple learners in social work classrooms. Diversification of social work discourse incorporating both secular and non-secular perspectives is a vital challenge that needs to be addressed. Recognizing this challenge, social work students and instructors needed a space to reach those 'sacred but transformative learning experiences,' producing new avenues and streams beyond acquiring new skills in the traditional sense of pedagogy. Therefore, this chapter proposes spiritual diversity practices and new strategies that can be applied in social work classroom settings for optimizing the transformational learning environment through non-traditional teaching methods. The chapter also proposes cultural humility as a spiritually-informed practice. Finally, potential recommendations are suggested.

DOI: 10.4018/979-8-3693-2407-3.ch011

INTRODUCTION AND BACKGROUND

This chapter invites social work educators and academicians to engage in a transformative social work conversation to enhance effectiveness and productivity. The chapter proposes spiritual diversity practices and new strategies that can be applied in social work classroom settings to optimize the transformational learning environment through non-traditional teaching methods. This will allow social work students to incorporate potential spiritual diversity practices into their professional development process to create a growth-oriented atmosphere. There are inadequacies in the existing mode of instruction/pedagogical approaches in capturing those sacred moments, diverse practices, and spiritual perspectives of multiple learners in social work classrooms. As we know, the interacting epistemologies of students and teachers have a more significant implication when engaged in collaborative learning in the educational setting. More specifically, in social work academia, while navigating the epistemological perspectives of the students, social work educators need to integrate spiritual practice and inquiry implicitly and explicitly into their classroom settings.

Diversifying social work discourse to encompass secular and non-secular perspectives is a significant challenge that demands attention. Acknowledging this challenge opens doors to those 'sacred but transformative learning experiences', which go beyond acquiring new skills in the traditional sense of pedagogy in social work. Therefore, this chapter aims to inspire growth by transcending our individual and collective limits. The chapter is structured to first delve into specific transformational learning theories, including the transformational theory of teaching. Next, it explores cultural humility as a spiritually informed practice to address structural inequalities. Finally, it presents contextually sensitive practices and innovative strategies that can be implemented in social work classroom settings to foster a transformational learning environment through non-traditional teaching methods.

Transformative Learning Approach

Integrating the transformative learning approach in social work education marks a breakthrough towards creating a space where holistic development can be stimulated. Along with the attitude of cultural humility and interdisciplinary approach, this makes it possible to work with people from different cultures and communities on a profoundly empathetic level (Archer-Kuhn et al., 2020). As defined by Robert et al. (2018), transformative learning prioritizes integrating experience, critical thinking, and dialogue as a tool for sparking internal and social transformation. For example, the "Social Work Week" experiential learning assignment intends to sharpen undergraduate students' group practice skills by collectively preparing, implementing, and evaluating a campus-wide project. This didactic approach emphasizes the need for adaptability to improve student learning, which, in turn, also imposes unique demands on educators and learners (Robert et al., 2018). Furthermore, as Damianakis et al. (2020) discussed, transformative learning involves five interrelated dimensions: emotional, cognitive, spiritual, physical, and social/environmental. This pluralistic approach underlines the usage of teaching methodologies that support student growth across all these dimensions, enabling the journey that is characterized by feelings of displacement, critical re-evaluation, and, finally, transformation (Damianakis et al., 2020; Tomaney et al., 2023).

Diverse Educational Approaches

The educational approaches given include the *Infusion Approach*, where spiritual content is integrated into existing courses; the *Specialization Approach*, which offers specialized courses on spiritual diversity; and *Experiential Learning*, which includes the use of reflective exercises and case studies in resolving spiritual issues (Morton et al., 2017). These models should elevate ethical competence, for example, through the awareness of one's ideology and prejudices, a client-oriented approach concerning individual spiritual views, and preparedness to find solutions in situations when professional ethics may conflict with spiritual values (Hodge et al., 2016). In addition, teamwork and intercultural skills are emphasized as fundamental elements (Hodge et al., 2016). This integration involves interdisciplinary collaboration with chaplains, clergy, and other professionals in order to help clients with their spiritual concerns, the development of a culturally sensitive perspective to understand these variations across cultures, and the enhancement of assessments skills to evaluate the spiritual resources and needs of the clients sensitively (Brady et al., 2021).

Integrating Faith and Spirituality

Clinically, spiritually sensitive interventions, narratives regarding a client's spiritual expression, and establishing a supportive environment where clients may express their spiritual concerns are paramount (Zgierska et al., 2016). Moreover, a focus on research and evidence-based practices, including empirical studies on the effect of integrating spirituality into social work practice as well as the creation of outcome measures to assess the impact of spirituality on social work practice, is an example of the significance of grounding educational practices in solid research foundations (Otaye-Ebede et al., 2019). Integrating faith and spirituality into social work academia, called 'Faith and Spirituality Integration,' comprises accepting spirituality as an essential aspect of human experience that affects well-being, coping, and resilience (Yun et al., 2019).

In order to alter learning, this chapter discusses incorporating spiritual diversity practices within the social work education curriculum. The contention is that the emotional, intellectual, spiritual, physical, social, and environmental domains are essential in student development. As future social workers engage in inclusive pedagogy that celebrates student diversity and provides equal learning opportunities, they will acquire the skills to assist clients with varying spiritual origins and spiritual tribes. As a result, suggesting changes to pedagogical theory that incorporate spirituality into human well-being contributes to the conversation surrounding social work education. Interestingly, this aims to improve the quality of care for multicultural people by bridging theory and practice.

THEORETICAL UNDERPINNINGS

Transformational learning encompasses a true spirit of integration. Further, it challenges people's perceptions, values, and assumptions, resulting in lasting changes in the lives of students, educators, and their environments. What gives people the confidence to alter their lives? What causes them to suffer such justifiable repercussions and fosters an open culture strong enough to overcome society's complexity and division? How can a classroom be changed to become a place of learning and independence? A theoretical comprehension would help inform the reader of the transformation process's epistemological perspectives and transformational implications. In this chapter, let us explore the transformational learning theory (TLT) and transformational theory of teaching (TTT) to engage in a transformative process of generating sustainable results by responding to the challenges of the systems and appreciating human potential and inner capacities.

Transformational Learning Theory

Transformative Learning Theory (TLT) is the basis for a profound explanation of educational processes' effect on people, especially in multicultural education and spiritual diversity practices like those found in social work classrooms (Damianakis et al., 2020). This concept of TLT is based on the thought that what makes individuals is not just the accumulation of knowledge but also the transformation of how they perceive things (Van Schalkwyk et al., 2019). To apply this theory in a practical setting, including multicultural spiritual diversity activities in curriculums can harness this transforming potential. For example, invite students to apply their critical thinking skills to their values and beliefs and how these determine their professional duty and practice.

The transformational learning process involves critical self-reflection and self-examination for the learning to be effective and cause a change in the learner's perspective (Kuriakou, 2023). In this context, social work education means getting the students to self-reflect on their beliefs and attitudes toward spirituality and diversity. Hence, the empathetic and inclusive approach to their profession will be enhanced (Kuriakou, 2023). Educators can facilitate this reflective process; hence, the students can appreciate and understand clients' spiritual diversity and points of view. This calls for including spiritual diversity practices into the curriculum as a natural component in harmony with the institutional strategy and disciplinary specialization. Recognizing language adoption as a means to achieve implementation stresses the necessity of developing a set of words for spiritual diversity. Hence, the educational medium perfectly absorbs the receptors for this concept. In classrooms, this implies an approach of teaching that is tolerant of the diversity of spiritual things, where students get different aspects of the presentation through which they will view their practice.

Transformational Theory of Teaching

According to the theory of transformational teaching, education should essentially be a vehicle that redirects students' ideas, modes of behavior, and emotional reactions for comprehensive development (Bellamkonda et al., 2023). As Kramer et al. (2018) assert, transformative teaching requires educators to engage in their own experience at a deep level, allowing the educator to approach learning more comprehensively and reflectively. The reflective role of teachers plays a vital role in the transformation of teacher effectiveness, as well as ensuring that such change spreads through the educational environment (Awkard, 2015). Baldachino (2015) has stressed a holistic view of learning, which relates closely to liberating students from the unthinking acceptance of experiences. This way of thinking furnishes the appropriate space for reworking perception, identity, and values, which are the very basis of spiritual diversity.

In addition, the teacher collaboration discussed by Ronfeldt et al. (2015) emphasizes the cooperative nature of various professional strategies, which further enriches the transformational learning experience through communication, trust, and respect. The Social Work Transformation Survey (SWTS) development by Isabel et al. (2023) to measure transformative learning in undergraduate social work education demonstrates the necessity of creative journaling as a transformative pedagogy. Moreover, social work field placements, as mentioned by Calderwood and Rizzo (2022), through the lens of student-supervisor relationships and transformative learning, also emphasize the magnitude of trust, respect, engagement, care, and humility. These components must be present in a teaching atmosphere aligned with transformative learning so that spiritual diversity practices are integrated.

CULTURAL HUMILITY AS SPIRITUALLY INFORMED PRACTICE

Cultural Humility (CH) is a virtue that allows one to balance out imbalances and rebuild dynamic partnerships with people from different backgrounds and cultures via continuous introspection and critique of beliefs, values, attitudes, and cultural identity (Tervalon & Murray-Garcia, 1998). CH involves dealing with the other person's situation and social transformation at different levels, adding meaning to the concept as we link it with social transformation (Abe, 2020). Three potential strategies to achieve this broad-spectrum goal in a classroom include discussing how cultural humility can be learned, valued, and practiced in social work classrooms; examining the advantages and disadvantages of CH in diverse practice settings; and considering how educators and trainees in social work might address structural injustices their future clients face by utilizing cultural humility as a *spiritually informed practice*. This overarching goal of establishing CH as a Spiritually Informed Practice could be navigated and functionalized under the following sections of transformative experiences, connecting culturally and critical self-awareness and self-examination by the instructors and the students.

Transformative Experiences

Figure 1. Spiritual diversity practices in social work classrooms

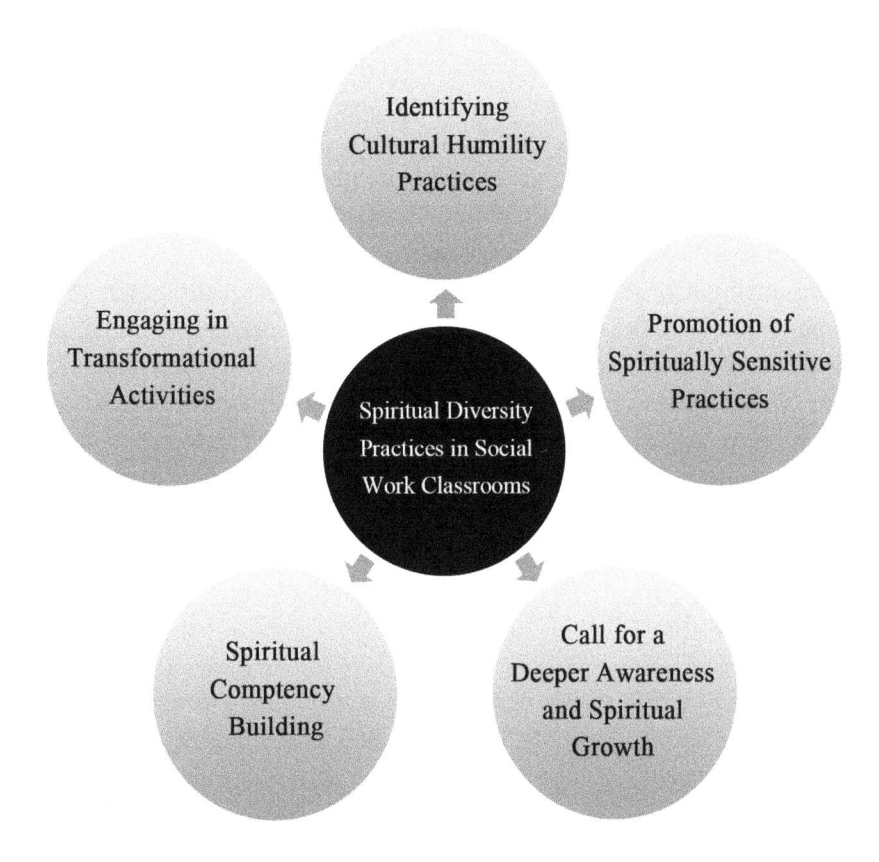

Figure 1 illustrates a framework for the spiritual diversity practices that advance a transformational learning environment: *identifying cultural humility practices, promoting spiritually sensitive practices, calling for deeper awareness and spiritual growth, building spiritual competency, and finally, engaging in transformational activities.* This framework will help to normalize and accept spirituality as a necessary component of completeness for intuitive investigation in a classroom setting. Educators have the capacity to enhance and transform students' power into an environment of growth and productivity rather than mere 'competition.'

Cultural humility's role in introducing spiritual diversity practices in social work classrooms might be seen as the core spiritual precept. That is to say, it emphasizes that a transformation stands at the center of the educational process that implies lifetime learning and self-knowledge (Rosen et al., 2017). According to Zhu et al.

(2022), the acquisition of cultural humility is a multi-stage phenomenon starting with confusion and discomfort, then re-shaping and ending in humility. This route can be seen as one of transformative learning; during this, the disorienting dilemmas make a possibility of meaningful connections between old beliefs and new cultural operations (Zhu et al., 2022).

Coppola and Taylor (2022) refine this conceptualization of cultural humility by adding ***intrapersonal, interpersonal, and transformative sidelines*** to the main idea. Suppose academicians promote the social work learning setting as a 'transformational arena' that embraces and fosters the synergistic relationship between spirit, soul, and body. This will create an intrapersonal, interpersonal, and transformative milieu in the social work classroom setting.

Paying attention to student's experiences of cultural identity, as explored by Sloane and Petra (2019), is a crucial step in achieving cultural humility. This approach enhances empathy and advocacy, stressing the need for the teacher to interact with the learners' narratives about religion/spirituality (Sloane & Petra, 2019). Such discussions help students comprehend their identities and first-hand experiences and promote cultural humility by confronting everyday religious experiences and biases. This method fosters critical consciousness, psychosocial support, and social justice-oriented pedagogies and behaviors.

Connecting Culturally

Cultural connectivity, firmly based on acknowledging and appreciating various spiritualities, is a way out of the transformative learning path (Lehtomäki et al., 2015). By connecting culturally, teachers and students begin a voyage beyond the confines of traditional educational principles, bringing an atmosphere where spiritual diversity is noticed and cherished, as it is one of the integral parts of the human experience (Rissanen et al., 2016). For example, the coursework within the preservice music education course exposes students' inner conflict, marking the complicated nature of fostering cultural humility.

Cole's (2020) conceptual model strengthens this conversation by advocating for the combined inclusion of spirituality through all fundamental social work courses. This model is founded on the person-environment formulation and shows the link between spirituality, social work education, and spirituality, which shows the multifaceted nature of spirituality and education (Cole, 2020). Additionally, the use of the arts-based methods discussed in the study by El-Lahib et al. (2020) makes an innovative and creative way to approach education. These techniques establish ties to social problems, allow the person self-development, and emphasize the usefulness of creative pedagogies in developing spiritual diversity (El-Lahib et al., 2020).

Developing cultural humility through active listening to stories of religious identity by Sloane and Petra (2019) is critical. This practice is a vital tool for bringing to the surface hidden biases and making critical conversations about various types of bias, for example, those related to race, gender, sexuality, and disability (Sloane & Petra, 2019). In addition, according to Limb et al. (2018), implementing *spiritual genograms* in social work practice is yet another example of the practical benefit of culturally competent tools that can be effectively used in therapy, particularly with individuals who have religiosity as part of their background. This procedure provides an understanding of clients' spiritual mindset while influencing the therapeutic relationship through cultural competence (Limb et al., 2018). These activities will reinforce as an integral part of normalizing the understanding that spirituality is intertwined with the mundane activities of life. Therefore, based on the core values of integrity and competence, the development of spiritual competencies enables the social worker to practice ethically in ways that honor contextual and cultural sensitivity.

Critical Self-Examination and Self-Awareness

As Stevens (2018) pointed out, spiritual diversity is crucial when discussing self-awareness. He suggested a 'life tasks' model of discovery, testing, and integration phases. These tasks, in which experiential exercises play a significant role, are needed to develop self-awareness in spiritual care, consequently improving the quality of care (Stevens, 2018). The model also emphasizes the importance of self-exploration in comprehending and appreciating the value of spiritual diversity.

Additionally, Baer (2019) discusses the relationship between mindfulness and psychological well-being, showing how mindfulness questionnaires assess present-moment awareness and a nonjudgmental stance. This finding is of great importance because it calls attention to the role of self-awareness in spiritually informed practices and suggests mindfulness as the fundamental element in developing a deeper relationship with oneself and others (Baer, 2019). The processes of learning self- and interpersonal growth outlined by London et al. (2022) emphasize the crucial role of self-awareness in our behavioral patterns influencing our dreams and goals. Behavioral interventions that encourage the development of self-awareness through reflection, feedback, and practice are critical (London et al., 2022). The mentioned way of thinking and the principles of cultural humility adopt an ongoing learning process where social workers kindly perform self-reflection to enrich their self-understanding and appreciation of spiritual diversity.

Gardner (2020) brings up the idea of integrating critical reflection in the curriculum of spiritual care training by stressing the importance of social context knowledge in spiritual care to unite the learner and the outer changes. Through such a lens, there is an opportunity to build more socially conscious organizations by promoting an understanding of spiritual diversity that reaches beyond the personal level to embrace societal concerns. Following, let us purge into the discussion of the contextually sensitive practices and potential strategies.

SPIRITUALLY SENSITIVE PRACTICES AND NEW STRATEGIES

Methods enhance students' learning through interactions, including small-group, online, blended learning with nature, and other spiritually informed practices. Spiritually sensitive practices (Canda et al., 2020) are helpful tools to enhance non-traditional learning and teaching methods. How could a classroom be transformed into an environment of growth and freedom? What empowers people to make changes in their lives? What leads them to deserve consequences and creates a culture of transparency that can conquer society's fragmentation and complexities? These questions need to be tackled while developing contextually sensitive practices and strategies.

Non-traditional Methods of Teaching in Social Work Classroom Settings

Integrating nontraditional teaching models in social work education is a revolutionary step towards more experiential learning (Oxhandler, 2017). This transition is especially crucial regarding spiritual diversities taught in the classroom (Oxhandler, 2017). This approach should be both contextually appropriate and innovative. E-learning is highlighted as a fundamental factor of new teaching models that downgrade the idea of traditional teacher-directed learning to take the place of active learning and collaborative problem-solving (Tularam et al., 2018). This is built on the foundations of constructionism and social constructivism principles, which provide space for collaborative exploration and shared investigation (Tularam et al., 2018). Along with this, simulation-based education is very much transformative. Thus, it utilizes modern technology to form visually lifelike scenarios where students can polish their practical skills in a risk-free atmosphere (Dodds et al., 2018). This approach bridges the theoretical and practical spectra, providing well-rounded social work students with the essential problem-solving skills in real-life situations they will meet in their careers.

Potential Real-Life Examples

The experiential learning within social work education, shown by the favorable reactions of social work students, simulation, role-play, and other learning-by-doing activities, are powerful tools for honing, analyzing, and improving one's skills (Magill et al., 2022). Practical participation is fundamental in enhancing the clarity of social work approaches and methods. For example, students may be encouraged to demonstrate their skills if they are allowed to initiate a spiritual resource center based on their observations and philosophies.

To alleviate the constraints of social work, contemplative practices were integrated into classes to engage students in self-care. Meditation and mindfulness methodologies, for example, improve student health and their abilities to deal with the emotional and psychological challenges of being a social worker. Innovation in teaching strategy goes on to create social innovation skill development through experimental motivation methods and practicum, where students are involved in the inspiration, ideation, and implementation process (Cavalcante et al., 2019). Using this method, students can solve society's problems innovatively by experimenting with ideas and drawing practical strategies for social improvement. For example, students may be asked to come up with new ideas to have a framework for creating a spiritual wellness wheel in their school or campus based on their spiritual skills, strengths, and other values. Another practical area to connect this discussion to their everydayness is that they can be directed to share their spiritual narratives and potentially uplifting stories on diverse platforms.

The combination of different non-conventional approaches, such as flipped classrooms, gamification, case studies, self-learning, and social media, shines a multidimensional picture of the integration of these approaches. Beyond improving technological and professional competence, these approaches also sustain and promote personal abilities and attributes that allow for flexibility and different learning challenges. Such a diversity of teaching techniques is of the utmost importance for the development of education that is flexible, stimulating, and suitable for the requirements of social work education. For example, the instructor could provide a scenario (case study) for the students to respond to, allowing them to respond organically.

Transformational Pedagogical Models

Transformative educational models highlight the factors of experiential learning and critical thinking to establish deep learning (Roberts et al., 2018). The Social Work Week effort demonstrates this by involving students in macro practice social work by group projects (Roberts et al., 2018). Strategies such as this demonstrate the centrality of reflection and critical discussion in transforming the learning paradigm (Roberts et al., 2018). Damianakis et al. (2020) illustrated an inclusive nature of transformative learning to the extent that Master of Social Work students demonstrated tangible personal and professional growth. This integrative way of learning is a gradual process of an individual's mental and emotional development (Damianakis et al., 2020). Archier-Kuhn et al. (2020) point out the crucial role of practicalities in theory applications as they regard the student-supervisor relationship and reflection as effective, transformative learning elements.

Morley and Stenhouse (2020) bring to light the connection of reflective pedagogies with mental health education, which may lead to social justice. Calderwood and Rizzo (2022) propose trust, respect, and engagement as the building blocks of professional identity. Duhaney et al. (2022) suggest that social workers must use critical race pedagogy to dismantle systemic oppression. In their work, Gentle-Genitty et al. (2018) provide the S.A.L.T. model to enhance critical engagement in theory teaching. Cappiali (2023) is based on emancipatory-transformative pedagogy that equips oppressed people with cognitive, physical, and emotional abilities for better communities.

PROMOTION OF SPIRITUAL DIVERSITY PRACTICES

Spiritual diversity practices are unique spiritual experiences and expressions of each person appreciative of various spiritual and religious traditions and tribes. For the social work classrooms in the American context to become a ground for transformational learning, spiritual diversity practices should be promoted (Roberson et al., 2021). CSWE, the Council on Social Work Education, clarifies that faith and spirituality dimensions should be taken as the core identity features that social workers must incorporate ethically in their practices (Roberson et al., 2021). This integration assists in exposing the prejudices and the mindsets of the social workers, which, in turn, helps them make critical decisions at work and effectively benefits them in dealing with faith and spirituality. Moreover, NASW defines recognizing religion/spirituality as one of the most critical aspects of diversity competence (Parada, 2022). Submerging into clients' religious or spiritual beliefs enables identifying behavioral drivers and power sources; however, most professionals consider incorporating them into their practice problematic (Parada, 2022). This implies that ethics education and ethics-based decision-making models are to be prioritized (Parada, 2022).

Integrating spiritual diversity can improve mental health services, and social work being secular limits this inclusion, placing a burden on interventions (Cole, 2020). Cole (2020) provides a system for incorporating spirituality in education by

Toward a Transformational Learning

applying the person-in-environment model. As Adedoyin et al. (2021) put forward, instructional innovation is the most important for effective integration, requiring coherent definition and theological consideration.

Building Transformational Competencies

Educators may cultivate transformational competencies in students by incorporating non-traditional pedagogical practices and creating a teaching context that allows for expressing each student's uniqueness and integrating them into the teaching context. Through storytelling, educators can encourage students to discuss their experiences that are grounded in spiritual manifestations. Promoting eco-spirituality is another non-traditional strategy that educators can bring into the classrooms with the focus that all living things in the entire planetary ecosystem should be respected for their values, worldviews, and traits to achieve harmony with other species and the planet. Given our interdependence with the planet's ecology, eco-spirituality, and eco-centered activities may be conducted inside and outside classroom settings.

Useful Pedagogical Practices

Using spiritual life maps (Hodge, 2015) may be an engaging technique for students to narrate their spiritual stories, highlighting their challenges and learnings historically and contextually. For example, ask students to compose a paper discussing their life's spiritual path thus far. This essay may be a personal account of their "spiritual journey," as seen from a historical standpoint, covering the period from childhood to the present. Life Map determines their spiritual inner talents and describes how they fit into their personality. Ask students to explain how they could use their spiritual power as a tool in their social work practice.

Another pedagogical practice area can be using guest speakers. Here, inviting social work professionals who evaluate clients through spiritual intervention (Hodge, 2011; Canda et al., 2020) to share their experiences with students can facilitate the development of transformational competencies. Relatedly, students could be given an assignment that asks them to interview a social worker with transformational competencies and reflect on the process and the knowledge gained. Students may ask about the procedure, client interactions, the intervention model, and any tools they use. In addition, let the students capture some potential difficulties practitioners faced when assessing their clients and what strategies they used to overcome those unpredictable challenges.

Another non-traditional pedagogical practice is allowing students to evaluate a spiritually sensitive intervention, citing the rationale behind its selection, summarizing its findings, and offering a strategy based on their knowledge of social work practice. Motivating students to role-play in the classroom based on their learning and having a brief discussion afterward would be helpful. Educators' deliberate efforts and competence in transgressing the norms are crucial to an empowering process while addressing social work education and human service inadequacies that limit the development of transformative spiritual competencies for effective social work practice.

Creating a natural and critical learning environment is essential in a world that has myriad mental health issues and challenges. Personal, intellectual, and moral development are essential to a natural and critical learning environment. Raising questions on current topics, questions on the unique purpose of life, and the ancient Greek philosophical question of 'who am I' is part of the Socratic pedagogy (Bain, 2004), where people attempt to find answers to their questions, providing the context for self-discovery and engagement of the discovered self in transformational ways that advance social justice.

Recommendations

The following are some of the **recommendations** that the author wants to propose:

- Promote the social work learning context as a transformational space that embraces and encourages the synergistic link between spirit, soul, and body.
- Normalize and embrace spirituality as a critical dimension of wholeness for an intuitive inquiry.
- Emphasis on the understanding that developing spiritual competencies enhances social work effectiveness that advances social justice.
- Normalize the understanding that spirituality is intertwined with the mundane activities of life. Therefore, based on the core values of integrity and competence, the development of spiritual competencies enables the social worker to practice ethically in ways that honor contextual and cultural sensitivity.
- Encourage an intense desire to welcome students, faculty, and non-teaching staff with dignity and respect, regardless of race, creed, region, caste, or color, that embraces the practice of cultural humility within and outside of the classroom settings.

CONCLUSION

Cultural Humility is often understood as a lifelong desire to learn from others and other cultures by developing cooperative relationships that counterbalance power with due respect for others and being open-minded to new cultural information (Mosher et al., 2017). CH is not a static characteristic but a dynamic relationship of various elements, evolving through theoretical interpretations and empirical findings (Coppola & Taylor, 2022). Developing cultural humility as a *spiritually informed practice* can facilitate discourse and create practice guidelines, policies, and knowledge bases in the academic community.

This chapter looked at how social work educators and future professionals can turn toward an intuitive inquiry using the respective spiritual diversity practices to help people reconnect with their most authentic selves. Further, it explored the significance of transformative learning approaches, holistic experiences, cultural humility, and inclusive assessment strategies. Students, teachers, and their surroundings experience long-lasting changes because transformational learning embraces a genuine spirit of integrating diverse practices and questions people's beliefs, attitudes, and presumptions. Increasing spiritual diversity in social work is possible through professional discourse, drawing alternative spiritual perspectives from diverse religious traditions and systems. A full-fledged social science aims to gather empirical data primarily through research practice and policy. However, it involves a wide range of information derived from the transformational experiences of individuals, groups, and communities. Transformational learning is a method that provides keys to capturing new paths and mechanisms for learning and engagement that encourage trust, respect, engagement, care, and humility.

REFERENCES

Abe, J. (2020). Beyond cultural competence, toward social transformation: Liberation psychologies and the practice of cultural humility. *Journal of Social Work Education*, 56(4), 1–12. 10.1080/10437797.2019.1661911

Archer-Kuhn, B., Samson, P., Damianakis, T., Barrett, B., Matin, S., & Ahern, C. (2020). Transformative learning in field education: Students bridging the theory/practice gap. *British Journal of Social Work*. 10.1093/bjsw/bcaa082

Awkard, T. (2017). The power of reflective action to build teacher efficacy. *Phi Delta Kappan*, 98(6), 53–57. 10.1177/0031721717696479

Baer, R. (2019). Assessment of mindfulness by self-report. *Current Opinion in Psychology*, 28, 42–48. 10.1016/j.copsyc.2018.10.01530423507

Bain, K. (2004). *What the Best College Teachers Do*. Harvard University Press.

Baldacchino, D. (2015). Spiritual care education of health care professionals. *Religions*, 6(2), 594–613. 10.3390/rel6020594

Bellamkond, R. S., Sunanda, M., & Rangola, S. (2023). Review and synthesis of a decade of research on transformational teaching and student engagement. *MIER Journal of Educational Studies, Trends and Practices*, 442–459. 10.52634/mier/2023/v13/i2/2521

Brady, V., Timmins, F., Caldeira, S., Naughton, M. T., McCarthy, A., & Pesut, B. (2021). Supporting diversity in person-centered care: The role of healthcare chaplains. *Nursing Ethics*, 28(6), 935–950. 10.1177/096973302098174633522415

Calderwood, K. A., & Rizzo, L. N. (2022). Co-Creating a transformative earning environment through the student-supervisor relationship: Results of a social work field placement duo-ethnography. *Journal of Transformative Education*. Advance online publication. 10.1177/15413446221079590

Canda, E. R., & Furman, L. D. (2020). *Spiritual Diversity in Social Work Practice*. Oxford University Press.

Cappiali, T. M. (2023). A paradigm shift for a more inclusive, equal, and just academia? Toward a transformative emancipatory pedagogy. *Education Sciences*, 13(9), 876. Advance online publication. 10.3390/educsci13090876

Cole, H. L. (2020). Intersecting social work practice, education, and spirituality: A conceptual model. *Social Thought*, 1–24. 10.1080/15426432.2020.1831420

Damianakis, T., Barrett, B., Archer-Kuhn, B., Samson, P. L., Matin, S., & Ahern, C. (2019). Transformative learning in graduate education: Master of Social Work Students' experiences of personal and professional learning. *Studies in Higher Education*, 1–19. 10.1080/03075079.2019.1650735

Dodds, C., Heslop, P., & Meredith, C. (2018). Using simulation-based education to help social work students prepare for practice. *Social Work Education*, 37(5), 597–602. 10.1080/02615479.2018.1433158

Duhaney, P., Lorenzetti, L., Kusari, K., & Han, E. (2022). Advancing critical race pedagogical approaches in social work education. *Journal of Ethnic & Cultural Diversity in Social Work*, 31(3-5), 1–11. 10.1080/15313204.2022.2070898

El-Lahib, Y., Wehbi, S., Zakharova, G., Perreault-Laird, J., & Khan, M. (2020). Tearing down the "box": Students' perspectives on activating arts-informed methods in social work classrooms. *Social Work Education*, 1–12. 10.1080/02615479.2020.1851360

Hodge, D. R. (2011). Using Spiritual Interventions in Practice: Developing Some Guidelines from Evidence-based Practice. *Social Work*, 56(2), 149–158. 10.1093/sw/56.2.14921553578

Hodge, D. R. (2015). *Spiritual Assessment in Social Work and Mental Health Practice*. Columbia University. 10.7312/hodg16396

Hodge, D. R. (2016). Spiritual Competence: What it is, why it is necessary, and how to develop it. *Journal of Ethnic & Cultural Diversity in Social Work*, 27(2), 124–139. 10.1080/15313204.2016.1228093

Hodge, D. R. (2018). Increasing spiritual diversity in social work discourse: A scientific avenue toward more effective mental health service provision. *Social Work Education*, 38(6), 753–765. 10.1080/02615479.2018.1557630

Isabel, A., Wallengren-Lynch, M., & Archer-Kuhn, B. (2023). Measuring and validating a transformation learning survey through social work education research. *Journal of Transformative Education*, 15413446231222204. Advance online publication. 10.1177/15413446231222204

Kourgiantakis, T., Sewell, K. M., Hu, R., Logan, J., & Bogo, M. (2019). Simulation in social work education: A scoping review. *Research on Social Work Practice*, 30(4), 433–450. 10.1177/1049731519885015

Kramer, M. (2018). Promoting teachers' agency: Reflective practice as transformative disposition. *Reflective Practice*, 19(2), 211–224. 10.1080/14623943.2018.1437405

Kuriakou, G. (2023). Transformative learning in formal schools. *International Journal for Innovation Education and Research*, 11(11), 48–52. 10.31686/ijier.vol11.iss11.4176

Lehtomäki, E., Moate, J., & Posti-Ahokas, H. (2015). Global connectedness in higher education: Student voices on the value of cross-cultural learning dialogue. *Studies in Higher Education*, 41(11), 2011–2027. 10.1080/03075079.2015.1007943

Limb, G. E., Hodge, D. R., Ward, K., Ferrell, A., & Alboroto, R. (2018). Developing cultural competence with LDS clients: Utilizing spiritual genograms in social work practice. *Journal of Religion & Spirituality in Social Work*, 37(2), 166–181. 10.1080/15426432.2018.1448033

London, M., Sessa, V. I., & Shelley, L. A. (2022). Developing self-awareness: Learning processes for self- and interpersonal growth. *Annual Review of Organizational Psychology and Organizational Behavior*, 10(1), 261–288. 10.1146/annurev-orgpsych-120920-044531

Magill, M., Mastroleo, N. R., Kuerbis, A., Sacco, P., Thombs-Cain, G. E., Wagner, E. F., & Velasquez, M. M. (2022). Practice makes perfect: MSW students reflect on skill-based teaching methods in clinical social work education. *Journal of Social Work Education*, 1–15. 10.1080/10437797.2022.210360538155868

Morley, C., & Stenhouse, K. (2020). Educating for critical social work practice in mental health. *Social Work Education*, 40(1), 1–15. 10.1080/02615479.2020.1774535

Morton, T. (2017). Reconceptualizing and describing teachers' knowledge of language for content and language integrated learning (CLIL). *International Journal of Bilingual Education and Bilingualism*, 21(3), 275–286. 10.1080/13670050.2017.1383352

Otaye-Ebede, L., Shaffakat, S., & Foster, S. (2019). A multilevel model examining the relationships between workplace spirituality, ethical climate, and outcomes: A social cognitive theory perspective. *Journal of Business Ethics*, 166(3), 611–626. 10.1007/s10551-019-04133-8

Oxhandler, H. K. (2017). Social work field instructors' integration of religion and spirituality in clinical practice. *Journal of Social Work Education*, 53(3), 449–465. 10.1080/10437797.2016.1269706

Rissanen, I., Kuusisto, E., & Kuusisto, A. (2016). Developing teachers' intercultural sensitivity: Case study on a pilot course in Finnish teacher education. *Teaching and Teacher Education*, 59, 446–456. 10.1016/j.tate.2016.07.018

Roberts, A. R., Sellers, S. L., Franks, K., & Nelson, T. S. (2018). Teaching Note—Social Work Week: Harnessing the Potential of Group Practice to Achieve Transformational Learning. *Journal of Social Work Education*, 54(3), 561–567. 10.1080/10437797.2018.1434431

Ronfeldt, M., Farmer, S. O., McQueen, K., & Grissom, J. A. (2015). Teacher collaboration in instructional teams and student achievement. *American Educational Research Journal*, 52(3), 475–514. 10.3102/0002831215585562

Rosen, D., McCall, J., & Goodkind, S. (2017). Teaching critical self-reflection through the lens of cultural humility: An assignment in a social work diversity course. *Social Work Education*, 36(3), 289–298. 10.1080/02615479.2017.1287260

Rosen, D., McCall, J., & Goodkind, S. (2017). Teaching critical self-reflection through the lens of cultural humility: An assignment in a social work diversity course. *Social Work Education*, 36(3), 289–298. 10.1080/02615479.2017.1287260

Sanchez, N., Norka, A., Corbin, M., & Peters, C. (2019). Use of experiential learning, reflective writing, and metacognition to develop cultural humility among undergraduate students. *Journal of Social Work Education*, 55(1), 75–88. 10.1080/10437797.2018.1498418

Sharma, M. (2017). *Radical Transformational Leadership*. North Atlantic Books.

Sloane, H., & Petra, M. (2019). Modeling cultural humility: Listening to students' stories of religious identity. *Journal of Social Work Education*, 57(1), 1–12. 10.1080/10437797.2019.1662863

Stevens, B. A. (2018). Life tasks: Excellence in spiritual care through self-awareness. *Health and Social Care Chaplaincy*, 6(2), 177–185. 10.1558/hscc.33754

Tervalon, M., & Murray-Garcia, J. (1998). Cultural humility versus cultural competence: A critical distinction in defining physician training outcomes in multicultural education. *Journal of Health Care for the Poor and Underserved*, 9(2), 117–125. 10.1353/hpu.2010.023310073197

Tomaney, J., Blackman, M., Natarajan, L., Panayotopoulos-Tsiros, D., Sutcliffe-Braithwaite, F., & Taylor, M. (2023). Social infrastructure and 'left-behind places'. *Regional Studies*, 1–14.

Tularam, G. A. (2018). Traditional vs non-traditional teaching and learning strategies - the case of E-learning. *International Journal for Mathematics Teaching and Learning*, 19(1), 129–158. 10.4256/ijmtl.v19i1.21

Van Schalkwyk, S. C., Hafler, J., Brewer, T. F., Maley, M. A., Margolis, C., McNamee, L., Meyer, I., Peluso, M. J., Schmutz, A. M., Spak, J. M., & Davies, D. (2019). Transformative learning as pedagogy for the health professions: A scoping review. *Medical Education*, 53(6), 547–558. 10.1111/medu.1380430761602

Yun, K., Kim, S., & Awasu, C. R. (2019). Stress and impact of spirituality as a mediator of coping methods among social work college students. *Journal of Human Behavior in the Social Environment*, 29(1), 125–136. 10.1080/10911359.2018.1491918

Zgierska, A. E., Burzinski, C. A., Cox, J., Kloke, J., Stegner, A., Cook, D. B., Singles, J., Mirgain, S., Coe, C. L., & Bačkonja, M. (2016). Mindfulness meditation and cognitive behavioral therapy intervention reduces pain severity and sensitivity in opioid-treated chronic low back pain: Pilot findings from a randomized controlled trial. *Pain Medicine*, 17(10), 1865–1881. 10.1093/pm/pnw00626968850

Zhu, R., Olcoń, K., Pulliam, R. M., & Gilbert, D. J. (2022). Transformative learning and the development of cultural humility in social work students. *Social Work Education*, 1–16. 10.1080/02615479.2022.2056158

KEY TERMS AND DEFINITIONS:

Non-Traditional Teaching Methods: Methods that are used to enhance the learning of the students with the use of interactions including small-group learning, online learning, and blended learning with nature and other spiritually-informed practices.

Spiritual Diversity Practices: Unique spiritual experiences and expressions of each person appreciative of various spiritual and religious traditions and tribes.

Transformational Learning: Is a method that provides keys to capturing new paths and mechanisms for learning and engagement that encourages trust, respect, engagement, care, and humility.

Conclusion

Helen Katherine Mudd
Campbellsville University, USA

Kimberly Nicole Mudd-Fegett
Campbellsville University, USA

In *Transformational Learning in Social Work and Human Services Education*, we, Helen Katherine Mudd and Kimberly Nicole Mudd-Fegett, set out to explore and elucidate the powerful impact of transformational and experiential learning in social work and human services education. As editors, we have endeavored to compile a comprehensive resource that lays the theoretical groundwork for these learning approaches and offers practical guidance for their implementation.

Throughout this volume, we have witnessed a recurring theme: the undeniable efficacy of experiential learning as a conduit for meaningful education. The chapters collectively emphasize that learning, when anchored in real-world experiences, fosters profound reflection, critical thinking, and problem-solving skills. From fieldwork in local communities to international service-learning projects, these immersive experiences are integral to developing competent and compassionate social workers and human service professionals.

Chapter by chapter, our contributors have demonstrated how transformational learning can reshape educational practices and outcomes. Fred Moonga and Sheila Kafula introduced us to the transformative nature of social work education, highlighting its role in empowerment and social justice. Özge Kutlu provided a thorough conceptual analysis of transformational learning theory, underscoring its significance in fostering personal and professional growth among social work students.

Kimberly Mudd-Fegett, in her examination of transformational teaching, illustrated the life-changing impact of learning that extends beyond classroom walls. This theme was echoed in our discussion on transformational leadership, where we explored how educators and leaders can inspire and mentor their students and colleagues to achieve their highest potential.

Lisa Tokpa, Jennifer Lanham, and Elizabeth Ann Moore extended the conversation to the global stage, showing the benefits and challenges of international field education and partnerships with NGOs. These chapters remind us of the importance of cultural humility and the need to decolonize educational practices to create mutually beneficial partnerships.

Ken Nee Chee's introduction of Affectagogy highlighted the critical intersection of emotions and learning, advocating for a holistic approach that nurtures the heart and mind. Lauren Lunsford, Amanda Nelms, and Sally Barton-Arwood's chapters on experiential learning in digital classrooms, as well as Crystal Aschenbrener's service-learning mentoring projects with Native American youth, showcased innovative methods to enhance diversity, equity, and inclusion through experiential education.

Angie Atwood's chapter on nurse educators leading medical mission trips and Pious Malliar Bellian's exploration of integrating spiritual diversity practices in social work classrooms provided poignant examples of how transformational learning can extend into specialized fields, further enriching the educational landscape.

As we conclude this edited volume, we hope the insights and strategies presented will serve as a valuable resource for educators and administrators. By adopting and integrating these transformational and experiential learning models, social work and human services education can be significantly enhanced, ultimately leading to more effective and empathetic practitioners.

The journey through this book reaffirms our conviction that transformational learning is not merely a pedagogical approach but a profound educational philosophy that has the potential to shape the future of social work and human services. We encourage educators to embrace these concepts with thoughtful planning and intentionality, creating learning environments that are informative and transformative.

In closing, we extend our heartfelt gratitude to all contributors for their invaluable insights and dedication to advancing social work education. It is through their collective wisdom and experience that this book comes to life, offering a beacon of guidance and inspiration for current and future educators. Let us strive for educational practices that empower, inspire, and transform.

Appendix

THE TRANSFORMATIONAL LEARNING TOOLKIT

This book is aimed at educators who wish to enhance their grasp of transformational learning. Experiential learning, a proven and influential approach to transformational learning, is based on the undeniable fact that people learn best through hands-on, immersive experiences. Experiential learning can seamlessly integrate into any subject area, creating a powerful educational experience.

A transformational learning experience does not happen by chance; it requires careful planning and intention. This Appendix provides activities, templates, and resources for transformational learning that can be readily incorporated into any course. The logistical frameworks necessary for successful experiential learning, complete with pre-planning logistics, classroom resources, and evaluation tools essential for designing effective experiential learning events and transformational learning activities are also included. All materials in this Appendix are provided for the readers' use. The materials may be adjusted to align with the user's needs. The authors request that appropriate credit be given when materials are used.

EXPERIENTIAL LEARNING KEY ASSIGNMENT DIRECTIONS AND GRADING RUBRIC

Directions: Experiential Learning Key Assignment in Graduate Social Work Experiential Learning Course

SWK630 Experiential Learning Key Assignment

This assignment assesses your performance in the following Social Work Competencies: A1.1, A1.2, A1.4, A1.5, A2.1, A2.2, A3.1, A3.2, A3.3, A3.4, A4.1, A4.2, A4.3, A4.4, A6.1, A6.2, A6.3, & A6.4. The assignment is worth 90 points.

The Experiential Learning Key Assignment is a crucial part of your learning journey. It's designed to provide you with the opportunity to demonstrate the integration of skills and knowledge gained through reflection upon course content, assignments, and the completion of the experiential learning experience. As you work on this assignment, remember that your reflections should not be limited to just the 10 hours of face-to-face engagement. Significant experiences and learnings that occur across the timeframe of this course are equally important and should be considered as you prepare your answers to each prompt.

Guidelines for Experiential Learning Experience:

- Minimum of 10 Hours in face-to-face interaction with identified people group
- During the face-to-face interaction, the student speaks to agency personnel about

social, economic, and environmental injustices that perpetuate trauma in their identified people group

- Experience must be completed with a people group that the student can support as being oppressed or as with one currently experiencing human rights violations (student will utilize scholarly, professional, and statistical resources to support their selection)
- Experience must be completed with a people group different from the student in a significant manner
- Experience cannot be completed during the field practicum hours or mirror what student is doing at their practicum

The assignment should be 10-15 pages long, follow APA formatting, and use a minimum of 10 sources to support your work.

STEP 1: DESCRIBE AN EXPERIENTIAL LEARNING RELATED EXPERIENCE

Provide an overview of your experience. The reflection should be described objectively and in some detail. Select key pieces of the experience to help focus the reflection, noting significant or reflection-worthy experiences. It is understood that significant learning can occur at any point in the experience, including travel and/or free time. Reflections in this paper may reference and include reflections of interactions with your people group that occurred during the timeframe of this course, regardless of whether they occurred during your identified dedicated 10-hour commitment.

Appendix

Engage With Clients and Colleagues Conveying a Strength-Based Demeanor and Attitude (A1.1)

The student describes an experience that clearly identifies a strength-based demeanor and attitude. This is an overview of the experiential learning experience (who, what, when, where, and why) and should be limited to one page.

Collect and Organize Data and Apply Critical Thinking to Interpret Information From Individuals, Families, Groups, Organizations, Communities, and Constituencies (A4.2)

Student, within the framework of their experiential learning experience, applies critical thinking to analyze their goals by addressing each of the provided prompts:

a) What were my goals for this experience (identified earlier in the course)?
b) What specific steps in this experiential learning experience did I take to attain these goals?
c) What obstacles (internal and external) hindered me?
d) What factors made me more effective?
e) What evidence from experience(s) supports goals being met, partially met, or not?

Deconstruct Situations (Culture, Social, Political, Economic, etc.) Where Human Rights Are Being Violated (A3.2)

Student, within the framework of their experiential learning experience, answers each of the following questions:

a) Identify your selected people group where human rights are being violated
b) Provide evidence to support this group as being oppressed or currently having human rights violated (requires scholarly resources)
c) Provide evidence from your experience to support this group being oppressed or currently having human rights violated, culture, social, political, economic, etc. (first-hand experience--what you witnessed or were told about during your experience)

Appendix

STEP 2: EXAMINATION OF EXPERIENCE FROM PERSONAL, ACADEMIC AND CIVIC ENGAGEMENT PERSPECTIVES

Examine Experience from a Personal Perspective

Engage in Self-Reflection And Self-Care Practices, Including Reflective Trauma Responsive Supervision to Prevent and Address Secondary Trauma in Self and Organization. (A1.5)

Student discusses within the framework of their experiential learning experience.

a) emotional reactions to experience (positively and/or negatively)?
b) how emotional reactions were handled?
c) what self-care was utilized?
d) debriefing exercised with Professor, Colleague, Mentor, Agency Worker, or other significant individual throughout the experience (this is a general discussion, not the exposure of personal trauma)
e) Student included in the appendix a copy of their self-care plan

Apply Self-Awareness to Manage the Influence of Personal Biases and Values in Working With Diverse Individuals, Families, Groups, Organizations, Communities, and Constituencies. (A2.2)

The student applies critical thinking to answer each of the following questions:

a) the most important features of **student's personal culture**
b) how their values have been molded and shaped by their culture;
c) the connection between their values and the institutions that have molded and shaped who they are: their family, their religion, their school, their peers, and so on; (personal culture)
d) the important features of the **culture of their identified population**;
e) how their **identified population's** values have been molded by culture
f) regarding the complex, multi-dimensional, and nuanced nature of culture, the student describes insights gained through experiential learning

Appendix

Utilize Self-Reflective and Intrapersonal Skills to Effectively Engage Diverse Individuals, Families, Groups, Organizations, Communities, and Constituencies (A6.3)

a) Why did I, or did I not, experience difficulty working/interacting with my identified people group? (this might also include encounters with diverse individuals' student experiences while accomplishing the tasks of this class)
b) What might I do differently next time to minimize such difficulties?
c) How have past experiences influenced how I acted or responded to this situation?
d) Am I comfortable with the influence past experiences have on me?
e) What assumptions or expectations did I bring to the situation (including my assumptions about other persons involved), and how did they affect my actions?
f) To what extent did they prove true? If they did not prove true, why was there a discrepancy
g) Did this situation reveal my own attitudes or biases toward other people, toward the organization, etc.? Do I need to make changes? If so, briefly describe

Evaluate How Personal Values and Biases Impact Research-Informed Practice and Practice-Informed Research (A4.3)

Student discusses within the framework of their experiential learning experience

a) assumptions of homogeneity; a perception that it is easier to 'make a difference' in an international/different community rather than a local setting; and the desire to 'give back' may indicate a lack of awareness of power relations and the potential for reinforcing oppression;
b) their cultural expectations and achievement of learning goals for their intercultural experience;
c) fears or concerns and what strategies they used to manage these; how assumptions underpinning motivations, fears, and expectations impacted the learning experience
d) values and biases identified and or witnessed during experiential learning experience (these do not have to be the student's personal biases however, please do not identify other individuals by proper names)

Appendix

Examine Experience From an Academic Perspective

Compare How Social, Economic, Cultural, and Political Frameworks Can Oppress and Violate Human Rights (A3.3)

Discuss how social, economic, cultural, and political frameworks oppress and violate the human rights of your chosen people group. Support your discussion with at least 3 references.

Advocate for Strategies to Improve Practice-Informed Research and Research Informed Practice in Trauma Care (A4.4)

a) Identify a relevant social work academic concept/theory that would be important when advocating for your identified people group. Explain the concept, theory, etc., clearly and concisely so that someone unfamiliar with the material can understand it.
b) How did the student's work on this assignment/class enhance knowledge of the specific reading, theory, or concept?
c) Identify two social work actions that would be important when advocating for research informed practice with your identified people group

Demonstrate Culturally Centered Practice That Recognizes the Impact of Diversity Factors, to Include Trauma Experiences and Responses at the Micro, Mezzo, and Macro Levels (A2.1)

Student discusses within the framework of their experiential learning experience

a) how culturally centered diversity exists between, among, and within groups in relation to their experiential learning experience. (provide an example from experience)
b) how the use of trauma-focused care within interactions at all levels of practice is important
c) how they will apply this learning more broadly in their social work practice

Appendix

Examine Experience from a Civic Perspective

Demonstrate Effective and Diplomatic Skills In Advocacy (A3.1)

a) The Student describes a situation involving advocacy with their people group (it does not have to involve the student personally).
b) What was the student or others trying to accomplish?
c) What roles did the person/group/organization involved in the situation play and why? What alternative roles could each have played?
d) Did students/other individuals act unilaterally or collaboratively? and why? Should students/they have worked with others differently?
e) In taking the actions, was the focus on symptoms of problems or causes of problems?
f) Was the focus (symptom or cause) appropriate to the situation? Explain

Recognize and seek to redress human rights and social, economic, and environmental injustices resulting from or perpetuating trauma. (A3.4)

a) The student summarizes what they learned when they spoke to agency personnel about social, economic, and environmental injustices that perpetuate trauma in their identified people group
b) Student identified and discussed one redress to a specific human right, social, economic, or environmental injustice perpetuating trauma in their people group (support your redress with classroom resources and/or other scholarly resources)

STEP 3: Articulate Learning

Implement Appropriate Engagement Strategies for Individuals, Families, Groups, Organizations, and Communities Within a Particular Theoretical Model (A6.2)

a) Identify a theoretical model from the list below
   1. Crisis and task-centered practice

2. Cognitive-behavioral practice
3. Systems, complexity and chaos
4. Social construction practice: strengths and solutions
5. Social construction practice: narrative practice
6. Humanistic practice, existentialism and spirituality
7. Social justice, advocacy and empowerment
8. Feminist practice

b) Within the framework of your experiential learning for this course, describe an engagement strategy you have utilized with individuals, families, groups, organizations, or communities that exemplifies your chosen theoretical model

c) What social work skills would you like to develop to improve engagement strategies within your chosen theoretical model? Describe the plan for improving identified skills

Establish a Relationally Based Process Encouraging Individuals, Families, Groups, Organizations, and Communities to Participate Equally in Establishing Expected Outcomes (A6.1)

a) Student describes how they adopted a learning process that encouraged colleagues, professors, agency personnel, and recipients of the agency's services to be equal participants in the student's learning process (provide specific examples for clarity)

b) Student describes how their chosen agency of service utilized or did not utilize, a relational-based process that encouraged individuals, families, groups, organizations, and communities to be equal participants in the establishment of expected outcomes (provide specific examples for clarity)

Integrating Trauma-Informed Principles of Engagement With Practices at the Micro, Mezzo, and Macro Levels That Are Responsive to Those Underrepresented and Oppressed in Society (A6.4)

a) Student describes how trauma-informed principles of engagement can be integrated at the micro, mezzo, and macro levels that are responsive to those underrepresented and oppressed in society (give examples of your chosen people group)

Appendix

b) Student describes how their chosen agency of service utilized, or did not utilize, trauma-informed principles of engagement at the micro, mezzo and macro levels that are responsive to those underrepresented and oppressed in society (give examples)

Summary of DEAL Model and Student's Articulated Learning

Appraise, Evaluate, and Propose Various Methods of Program Evaluation (A4.1)

The student used evidence-based guidelines to evaluate the DEAL Model for Critical Reflection (Describe, Examine, and Articulate Learning) and identified its strengths and challenges.

Demonstrate Applying Social Work Ethics and Values to Evaluate Social Intervention (A1.4)

a) Students will integrate information from a minimum of Social Work Core Values, Principles, and/or Ethical Standards **to evaluate their Articulated Learning** (Include NASW Code of Ethics citation(s) including Standard and Sub-standard)
b) Each value/ethic is clearly supported and integrated within the evaluation processes, goal attainment, and experience reflection.
c) Students will clearly and succinctly summarize significant gains in skills, values, and knowledge that occurred during this course.

Appendix

Table 1. Dimensions 5 through 3

Competency & Dimension	5	4.5	4	3.5	3
A1.1 Engage with clients and colleagues conveying a strength-based demeanor and attitude. (Step 1)	The student described an experiential learning-related experience that clearly identified a strength-based demeanor and attitude (see Step 1 in directions). Description objectively and in detail described: What they did. What others did. Who was there? What actions did the student and others take? What was communicated?	Greater than 4 but not quite 5	The student described an experiential learning-related experience that identified a strength-based demeanor and attitude (see Step 1 in directions). Description objectively described: What they did. What others did. Who was there? What actions did the student and others take? What was communicated? Additional detail or increased objectively was needed to fully meet the requirements of Step 1	Greater than 3 but not quite 4	The student described an experiential learning-related experience that did not fully include a strength-based demeanor and attitude (see Step 1 in directions). The description did not fully describe What they did. What others did. Who was there? What actions did the student and others take? What was communicated? Additional detail and increased objectively were needed to fully meet the requirements of Step 1
A1.2 Demonstrate professional and ethical social work conduct in all levels of practice. (K, V, S, C/A) (Entire paper)	There are no more than 3 APA, grammatical, spelling, first person, structure, or word choice errors! No heading errors and appropriate subheading identification and formatting usage. Ten or more resources were cited within the text AND referenced per the APA Manual. Paraphrasing was used and appropriately cited/referenced with no more than 3 direct quotes.	Greater than 4 but not quite 5	There is few APA, grammatical, spelling, first person, structure, or word choice errors! Eight or more resources were cited within the text AND referenced per the APA Manual. Appropriate subheading identification and formatting usage were used. Paraphrasing was used and appropriately cited/referenced with no more than 3 direct quotes.	Greater than 3 but not quite 4	The paper has an average of 2 errors in APA, grammatical, first person, structure, spelling, or word choice errors per page throughout the document! The experience and reference support are difficult to interpret, and evidence with citations is often missing. Assumptions and generalizations are numerous (3 or more). Citations are used, and they closely adhere to the APA Manual but lack perfection. Paraphrasing was used with citation/referencing. Direct quotes are used occasionally. Only 6 references were used in the paper.
A1.4 Demonstrate the ability to apply social work ethics and values to the evaluation of social intervention. (Step 3)	Social work values and ethics are applied to evaluation processes and exceptionally well written. More than four ethics/values are reflected within the process. Each value/ethic is strongly supported and integrated strongly within the evaluation process, goal attainment, and program effectiveness.	Greater than 4 but not quite 5	The student clearly integrated information from more than three social work values and ethics to evaluation processes. Each value/ethic is clearly supported and integrated clearly within the evaluation processes, goal attainment and reflection of the experience.	Greater than 3 but not quite 4	More than two ethics and values are reflected within the process, but are minimally applied to evaluation processes. Each value/ethic is not clearly supported within the evaluation processes, goal attainment, and is not integrated clearly within the evaluation processes, goal attainment and reflection of the experience. .

continued on following page

Appendix

Table 1. Continued

Competency & Dimension	5	4.5	4	3.5	3
A1.5 Engage in self-reflection and self-care practices including reflective trauma responsive supervision to prevent and address secondary trauma in self and organization. (Step 2)	Student thoroughly discusses within the framework of their experiential learning experience a) Emotional reactions of experience (positively and/or negatively)? b) How did they handle emotional reactions? c) Confirmation that the student completed the Secondary Trauma and Self-Care Packet. d) debriefing with Professor, Colleague, Mentor, Agency Worker, or other significant individual throughout the experience. The student included in the appendix a copy of their self-care plan from the Secondary Trauma Self-Care Packet	Greater than 4 but not quite 5	Student discusses within the framework of their experiential learning experience a-d; however, the discussion is vague, or the self-care plan is missing a) Emotional reactions of experience (positively and/or negatively)? b) How did they handle emotional reactions? c) Confirmation that the student completed the Secondary Trauma and Self-Care Packet. d) debriefing with Professor, Colleague, Mentor, Agency Worker, or other significant individual throughout the experience. The student included in the appendix a copy of their self-care plan from the Secondary Trauma Self-Care Packet	Greater than 3 but not quite 4	Student discusses within the framework of their experiential learning experience a-d; however, the discussion is vague, missing one element, and the self-care plan is missing a) Emotional reactions of experience (positively and/or negatively)? b) How did they handle emotional reactions? c) Confirmation that the student completed the Secondary Trauma and Self-Care Packet. d) debriefing with Professor, Colleague, Mentor, Agency Worker, or other significant individual throughout the experience. The student included in the appendix a copy of their self-care plan from the Secondary Trauma Self-Care Packet
A2.1 Demonstrate culturally centered practice that recognizes the impact of diversity factors, to include trauma experiences and responses at the micro, mezzo and macro levels (Step 3)	Student demonstrated an excellent understanding of the culturally centered diversity that exists between, among, and within groups in relation to the experiential learning experience. Student demonstrated mastery at understanding cultural influence and using trauma-focused care within interactions at all levels of practice. Student did an excellent job explaining how they will extend their learning in this area beyond experiential learning experience to their social work practice	Greater than 4 but not quite 5	Student demonstrated a good understanding of the culturally centered diversity that exists between, among, and within groups in relation to the experiential learning experience. Student demonstrated beginning mastery at an understanding of cultural influence and using trauma-focused care within interactions at all levels of practice. Student did a good job explaining how they will extend their learning in this area beyond experiential learning experience to their social work practice	Greater than 3 but not quite 4	Student demonstrated some understanding of the culturally centered diversity that exists between, among, and within groups in relation to experiential learning experience. Student demonstrated a beginning level of an understanding of cultural influence and using trauma-focused care within interactions at all levels of practice. Student needed to provide more detail in explaining how they will extend their learning in this area beyond experiential learning experience to their social work practice
A2.2 Apply self-awareness to manage the influence of personal biases and values in working with diverse individuals, families, groups, organizations, communities and constituencies. (Step 2)	The student demonstrates excellent self-awareness by thoroughly describing: a) the most important features of their culture; b) how their values have been molded and shaped by their culture; c) the important features of the culture of their identified population; d) the connection between their values and the institutions that have molded and shaped them, e) how their identified population's values have been molded by culture and f) the complex, multi-dimensional and nuanced nature of culture, the student describes insights gained through experiential learning	Greater than 4 but not quite 5	The student demonstrates good self-awareness by thoroughly describing five of the six critical elements of this behavior. One critical element is lacking in detail or missing from the description	Greater than 3 but not quite 4	The student demonstrates good self-awareness by thoroughly describing four of the six critical elements of this behavior. Two critical elements are lacking in detail or missing from the description

continued on following page

Appendix

Table 1. Continued

Competency & Dimension	5	4.5	4	3.5	3
A3.1 Demonstrate effective and diplomatic skills in advocacy. (K, V, S & C/A)	The student did an excellent job of a) describing a situation involving advocacy, b) what was trying to be accomplished, c) roles each person/group/organization played, d) whether individuals worked unilaterally or collaboratively, and e) focusing on actions.	Greater than 4 but not quite 5	The student did a good job of a) describing a situation involving advocacy, b) what was trying to be accomplished, c) roles each person/group/organization played, d) whether individuals worked unilaterally or collaboratively, and e) focusing on actions. One area was a bit unclear.	Greater than 3 but not quite 4	The student did a fair job of a) describing a situation involving advocacy, b) what was trying to be accomplished, c) roles each person/group/organization played, d) whether individuals worked unilaterally or collaboratively, and e) focusing on actions. One area was missing and, or two areas were unclear and vague
A3.2 Deconstruct situations (culture, social, political, economic, etc.) where human rights are being violated. (Step 1)	The student did an excellent job a) identifying people groups where human rights are being violated, b) providing scholarly evidence to support the group as being oppressed or currently having human rights violated, c) providing first-hand evidence from experience to support this group being oppressed or currently having human rights violated, culture, social, political, economic.		The student did a good job a) identifying people group where human rights are being violated, b) providing scholarly evidence to support the group as being oppressed or currently having human rights violated, c) providing first-hand evidence from experience to support this group being oppressed or currently having human rights violated, culture, social, political, economic. One area was a bit unclear.		The student did a good job a) identifying people groups where human rights are being violated, b) providing scholarly evidence to support group as being oppressed or currently having human rights violated, c) providing first-hand evidence from experience to support this group being oppressed or currently having human rights violated, culture, social, political, economic. One area was a bit unclear, or scholarly resources did not fully support group as being oppressed
A3.3 Compare how social, economic, cultural, and political frameworks can oppress and violate human rights.	The student did an excellent job utilizing the materials presented in Modules 1, 5, and 6 to discuss how social, economic, cultural, and political frameworks oppress and violate the human rights of your chosen people group. The discussion was supported by a minimum of 3 references from resources in Module 1, 5, or 6.	Greater than 4 but not quite 5	The student did a good job utilizing materials presented in Modules 1, 5 & 6, discussing how social, economic, cultural, and political frameworks oppress and violate the human rights of your chosen people group. The discussion was supported with a minimum of 2 references from resources in Module 1, 5, or 6 or student's discussion was weak in cultural, social, economic or political	Greater than 3 but not quite 4	Student's discussion, utilizing materials presented in Modules 1, 5 & 6 on social, economic, cultural, and political frameworks oppressing and violating the human rights of the student's chosen people group, was vague in more than one area. The discussion was supported with a minimum of 2 references from resources in Module 1, 5, or 6 or the student's discussion was weak in cultural, social, economic or political
A3.4 Recognize and seek to redress human rights, social, economic and environmental injustices resulting from or perpetuating trauma.	The student did an excellent job a) summarizing conversation with agency personnel, b) identifying one redress to a specific human right, social, economic, or environmental injustice perpetuating trauma in their people group and c) providing scholarly support for their selected redress	Greater than 4 but not quite 5	The student did an above-average job of a) summarizing conversations with agency personnel, b) identifying one redress to a specific human right, social, economic, or environmental injustice perpetuating trauma in their people group, and c) providing scholarly support for their selected redress. However, one area of answer needed more clarity	Greater than 3 but not quite 4	Student's job of a) summarizing conversation with agency personnel, b) identifying one redress to a specific human right, social, economic, or environmental injustice perpetuating trauma in their people group and c) providing scholarly support for their selected redress was deficient in detail in more than one area and/or lacking in scholarly resources.

continued on following page

Appendix

Table 1. Continued

Competency & Dimension	5	4.5	4	3.5	3
A4.1 Appraise, evaluate, and propose various methods of program evaluation	The student did an excellent job using evidence-based guidelines to evaluate the DEAL Model for Critical Reflection. Students' understanding of the Model was clearly reflected in their evaluation. Strengths and Challenges of model were identified.	Greater than 4 but not quite 5	The student did a good job evaluating the DEAL Model for Critical Reflection. The students' understanding of the Model was reflected in their evaluation; however, evidence-based support needed to be stronger. The model's strengths and Challenges were identified.	Greater than 3 but not quite 4	The student's evaluation of the DEAL Model for Critical Reflection showed promise in some areas but needed additional detail for the Student's understanding of the Model to be conveyed to the professor. Evidence-based support was provided but was not fully congruent with the student's comments. Strengths and Challenges of model were identified.
A.4.2 Collect and organize data, and apply critical thinking to interpret information from individuals, families, groups, organizations, communities, and constituencies. (Step 1)	Student demonstrates excellent ability to collect and organize data and apply critical thinking to interpret data by thoroughly describing a) Module 2 goals, b) specific conclusions to reach based on their learnings/research, c) specific steps in this experiential learning experience took to attain goals, d) obstacles (internal and external), e) factors contributing to effectiveness, and f) evidence to support goals being met, partially met, or not met	Greater than 4 but not quite 5	Student demonstrates good ability to collect and organize data and apply critical thinking to interpret data by describing a) Module 2 goals, b) specific conclusions to reach based on their learnings/research, c) specific steps in this experiential learning experience took to attain goals, d) obstacles (internal and external), e) factors contributing to effectiveness, and f) evidence to support goals being met, partially met, or not met. <u>One part of the description was unclear.</u>	Greater than 3 but not quite 4	Student demonstrates ability to collect and organize data and apply critical thinking to interpret data by describing a) Module 2 goals, b) specific conclusions to reach based on their learnings/research, c) specific steps in this experiential learning experience took to attain goals, d) obstacles (internal and external), e) factors contributing to effectiveness, and f) evidence to support goals being met, partially, met, or not met. <u>Two parts of the description were unclear or missing</u>
A4.3 Evaluate how personal values and biases impact research-informed practice and practice-informed research (Step 1)	Student does an excellent job within the framework of their experiential learning experience discussing a) assumptions of homogeneity; a perception that it is easier to 'make a difference' in an international/different community rather than a local setting; and the desire to 'give back' may indicate a lack of awareness of power relations and the potential for reinforcing oppression; b) motivations for undertaking an intercultural experience, including their own motivations c) their expectations and achievement of learning goals for their intercultural experience; d) fears or concerns and what strategies they used to manage these; and e) how assumptions underpinning motivations, fears and expectations impacted the learning experience	Greater than 4 but not quite 5	Student does a good job within the framework of their experiential learning experience discussing a) assumptions of homogeneity; a perception that it is easier to 'make a difference' in an international/different community rather than a local setting; and the desire to 'give back' may indicate a lack of awareness of power relations and the potential for reinforcing oppression; b) motivations for undertaking an intercultural experience, including their own motivations c) their expectations and achievement of learning goals for their intercultural experience; d) fears or concerns and what strategies they used to manage these; and e) how assumptions underpinning motivations, fears and expectations impacted the learning experience. <u>One or two areas were a bit unclear.</u>	Greater than 3 but not quite 4	Student does an adequate job discussing within the framework of their experiential learning experience a) assumptions of homogeneity; a perception that it is easier to 'make a difference' in an international/different community rather than a local setting; and the desire to 'give back' may indicate a lack of awareness of power relations and the potential for reinforcing oppression; b) motivations for undertaking an intercultural experience, including their own motivations c) their expectations and achievement of learning goals for their intercultural experience; d) fears or concerns and what strategies they used to manage these; and e) how assumptions underpinning motivations, fears and expectations impacted the learning experience. <u>Two or three areas were unclear and/or lacking in detail</u>

continued on following page

Appendix

Table 1. Continued

Competency & Dimension	5	4.5	4	3.5	3
A4.4 Advocate for strategies to improve practice-informed research and research informed practice in trauma care	Student does an excellent job a) identifying a relevant social work academic concept/theory that would be important when advocating for your identified people group? Explain the concept, theory, etc. clearly and concisely so that someone unfamiliar with the material could understand it, b) discussing how work on this assignment/class enhanced knowledge of the specific reading, theory, or concept? c) Identifying two social work actions that would be important when advocating for research informed practice with your identified people group	Greater than 4 but not quite 5	Student does a good job a) identifying a relevant social work academic concept/theory that would be important when advocating for your identified people group? Explain the concept, theory, etc. clearly and concisely so that someone unfamiliar with the material could understand it, b) discussing how work on this assignment/class enhanced knowledge of the specific reading, theory, or concept? c) Identifying two social work actions that would be important when advocating for research informed practice with your identified people group. One of the three key areas was limited in discussion and/or unclear	Greater than 3 but not quite 4	Student a) identifying a relevant social work academic concept/theory that would be important when advocating for your identified people group? b) discusses how work on this assignment/class enhanced knowledge of the specific reading, theory, or concept? and/or c) identifying two social work actions that would be important when advocating for research informed practice with your identified people group. However, One of three key areas was limited in discussion and/or unclear and the concept, theory, etc. was not clearly explained and/or the two actions steps were not congruent with the concept/theory presented.
A6.1 Establish a relationally based process that encourages individuals, families, groups, organizations, and communities to be equal participants in the establishment of expected outcomes.	Student did an excellent job a) describing how they adopted a learning process that encouraged colleagues, professors, agency personnel, and recipients of agency's services to be equal participants in the student's learning process and b) describing how their chosen agency of service utilized, or did not utilize, a relational based process that encouraged individuals, families, groups, organizations, and communities to be equal participants in the establishment of expected outcomes	Greater than 4 but not quite 5	Student did a good job a) describing how they adopted a learning process that encouraged colleagues, professors, agency personnel, and recipients of agency's services to be equal participants in the student's learning process and b) describing how their chosen agency of service utilized, or did not utilize, a relational based process that encouraged individuals, families, groups, organizations, and communities to be equal participants in the establishment of expected outcomes. One of the descriptions needed additional detail for clarity.	Greater than 3 but not quite 4	Student's descriptions for this behavior showed promise in a) describing how they adopted a learning process that encouraged colleagues, professors, agency personnel, and recipients of agency's services to be equal participants in the student's learning process and b) describing how their chosen agency of service utilized, or did not utilize, a relational based process that encouraged individuals, families, groups, organizations, and communities to be equal participants in the establishment of expected outcomes. Both of the descriptions needed additional detail for clarity.
6.2 Implement appropriate engagement strategies to engage individuals, families, groups, organizations, and communities within a particular theoretical model.	The student did an excellent job a) selecting a theoretical model, b) describing an engagement strategy they utilized that exemplified their chosen theory, and c) identifying social work skills for further development to improve engagement strategies within their chosen model	Greater than 4 but not quite 5	The student did a good job a) selecting a theoretical model, b) describing an engagement strategy they utilized that exemplified their chosen theory, and c) identifying social work skills for further development to improve engagement. One of the descriptions needed additional detail for clarity.	Greater than 3 but not quite 4	Student's descriptions of this behavior showed promise in a) selecting a theoretical model, b) describing an engagement strategy they utilized that exemplified their chosen theory, and c) identifying social work skills for further development to improve engagement. However, description of engagement and their plan for improving skills needed additional detail for clarity

continued on following page

Appendix

Table 1. Continued

Competency & Dimension	5	4.5	4	3.5	3
6.3 Utilize self-reflective and intrapersonal skills to effectively engage diverse individuals, families, groups, organizations, communities, and constituencies.	The student does an excellent job utilizing self-reflective and intrapersonal skills to effectively engage diverse individuals within the framework of their experiential learning experience. The student examines intrapersonal skills by asking, a) why did I, or did I not, experience difficulty working/interacting with other people? b) What might I do differently next time to minimize such difficulties? c) How have past experiences influenced how I acted or responded to this situation? d) Am I comfortable with the influence the past has on me? e) What assumptions or expectations did I bring to the situation (including my assumptions about other persons involved), and how did they affect my actions? f) To what extent did they prove true? If they did not prove true, why was there a discrepancy g) Did this situation reveal my own attitudes or biases toward other people, toward the organization, etc.? Do I need to make changes? If so, briefly describe.	Greater than 4 but not quite 5	Student does a good job within the framework of their experiential learning experience utilizing self-reflective and intrapersonal skills to effectively engage diverse individuals. Student examines intrapersonal skills by asking, why did I, or did I not, experience difficulty working/interacting with other people? What might I do differently next time to minimize such difficulties? How have past experiences influenced the manner in which I acted or responded to this situation? Am I comfortable with the influence the past has on me? What assumptions or expectations did I bring to the situation (including my assumptions about other persons involved) and how did they affect my actions? To what extent did they prove true? If they did not prove true, why was there a discrepancy Did this situation reveal my attitudes or biases toward other people, the organization, etc.? Do I need to make changes? One of the identified prompts was missing or unclear or needed changes were not identified	Greater than 3 but not quite 4	Student does a fair job within the framework of their experiential learning experience utilizing self-reflective and intrapersonal skills to effectively engage diverse individuals. Student examines intrapersonal skills by asking, why did I, or did I not, experience difficulty working/interacting with other people? What might I do differently next time to minimize such difficulties? How have past experiences influenced the manner in which I acted or responded to this situation? Am I comfortable with the influence the past has on me? What assumptions or expectations did I bring to the situation (including my assumptions about other persons involved) and how did they affect my actions? To what extent did they prove true? If they did not prove true, why was there a discrepancy Did this situation reveal my attitudes or biases toward other people, the organization, etc.? Do I need to make changes? Two or Three of the identified prompts were missing or unclear and/or needed changes were not identified
6.4 Integrating trauma-informed principles of engagement with practices at the micro, mezzo and macro levels that are responsive to those underrepresented and oppressed in society	The student did an excellent job a) describing how trauma-informed principles of engagement can be integrated at the micro, mezzo and macro levels that are responsive to those underrepresented and oppressed in society and b) describing how their chosen agency of service utilized or did not utilize, trauma-informed principles of engagement at the micro, mezzo and macro levels that are responsive to those underrepresented and oppressed in society (give examples).	Greater than 4 but not quite 5	The student did a good job a) describing how trauma-informed principles of engagement can be integrated at the micro, mezzo, and macro levels that are responsive to those underrepresented and oppressed in society and b) describing how their chosen agency of service utilized or did not utilize, trauma-informed principles of engagement at the micro, mezzo and macro levels that are responsive to those underrepresented and oppressed in society (give examples). The descriptions and/or the examples needed more clarity	Greater than 3 but not quite 4	Student descriptions of the following prompts were promising a) describing how trauma-informed principles of engagement can be integrated at the micro, mezzo, and macro levels that are responsive to those underrepresented and oppressed in society and b) describing how their chosen agency of service utilized or did not utilize, trauma-informed principles of engagement at the micro, mezzo and macro levels that are responsive to those underrepresented and oppressed in society (give examples). However, the descriptions and/or the examples were incongruent trauma-informed principles

Developed by Helen Mudd, Ph.D., CSW, Co-Author of Chapter 4

Appendix

Table 2. Dimensions 2.5 through 0.5

Competency & Dimension	2.5	2	1.5	1	.5
A1.1 Engage with clients and colleagues conveying a strength-based demeanor and attitude. (Step 1)	Greater than 2 but not quite 3	The student's description of the experiential learning-related experience did not convey a strength-based demeanor and attitude (see Step 1 in directions). The description did not fully describe What they did. What others did. Who was there? What actions did the student and others take? What was communicated? The description was inadequate to provide the reader with a full understanding of the experience	Greater than 1 but not quite 2	Student's description of the experiential learning-related experience did not convey a strength-based demeanor and attitude (see Step 1 in directions). The description only vaguely described some of What they did. What others did. Who was there? What actions did the student and others take? What was communicated? The description was inadequate to provide the reader with an understanding of the experience	Less than 1
A1.2 Demonstrate professional and ethical social work conduct in all levels of practice. (K, V, S, C/A) (Entire paper)	Greater than 2 but not quite 3	Major APA violations in the cover page, header/subheadings, page numbers, font, and/or spacing. General instructions were not followed, and/or one subsection is missing from the paper. Style and flow are choppy or disconnected. Headings or subheadings are misidentified and do not facilitate the organization of the assignment. The reference page is missing or contains 5 or more errors	Greater than 1 but not quite 2	Numerous APA, spelling and/or grammatical errors. It is difficult to follow the logic of ideas in the section/s due to sentence structure and word choice. Outside resources may not have been used to substantiate need, but rather a great deal of personal assumption. Direct quotes were used throughout, with evidence indicating some cut and paste. Length guidelines were ignored, and the document is very brief or much beyond the limit (25% or more pages). Subheadings were not used.	Less than 1
A1.4 Demonstrate the ability to apply social work ethics and values to the evaluation of social intervention. (Step 3)	Greater than 2 but not quite 3	Basic information of social work values and/or ethics are applied to evaluation processes and are poorly written. The processes were unclear in various areas of the evaluation, goal attainment, and program effectiveness.	Greater than 1 but not quite 2	Basic information of social work values and/or ethics are poorly written. Application ethics to evaluation of experience was confusing or vague in its application to the experience	Less than 1

continued on following page

Appendix

Table 2. Continued

Competency & Dimension	2.5	2	1.5	1	.5
A1.5 Engage in self-reflection and self-care practices including reflective trauma responsive supervision to prevent and address secondary trauma in self and organization. (Step 2)	Greater than 2 but not quite 3	Student discusses within the framework of their experiential learning experience only a part of a-d; discussion is vague and/or self-care plan is missing a) Emotional reactions of experience (positively and/or negatively)? b) How did they handle emotional reactions? c) Confirmation that the student completed the Secondary Trauma and Self-Care Packet. d) debriefing with Professor, Colleague, Mentor, Agency Worker, or other significant individual throughout the experience. The student included in the appendix a copy of their self-care plan from the Secondary Trauma Self-Care Packet	Greater than 1 but not quite 2	Student's discussion within the framework of their experiential learning experience of a-d is inadequate or missing. The self-care plan is missing or inadequate. a) Emotional reactions to experience (positively and/or negatively)? b) How did they handle emotional reactions? c) Confirmation that the student completed the Secondary Trauma and Self-Care Packet. d) debriefing with Professor, Colleague, Mentor, Agency Worker, or other significant individual throughout the experience. The student included in the appendix a copy of their self-care plan from the Secondary Trauma Self-Care Packet	Less than 1
A2.1 Demonstrate culturally centered practice that recognizes the impact of diversity factors, to include trauma experiences and responses at the micro, mezzo and macro levels (Step 3)	Greater than 2 but not quite 3	Student demonstrated a very limited understanding of the culturally centered diversity that exists between, among, and within groups in relation to the experiential learning experience. Student demonstrated only a partial understanding of cultural influence and using trauma-focused care within interactions at all levels of practice. The student needed to provide failed to provide detail in explaining how they will extend their learning in this area beyond experiential learning experience to their social work practice	Greater than 1 but not quite 2	Students demonstrated understanding was deficient in all areas of their response to this behavior prompt	Less than 1

continued on following page

Appendix

Table 2. Continued

Competency & Dimension	2.5	2	1.5	1	.5
A2.2 Apply self-awareness to manage the influence of personal biases and values in working with diverse individuals, families, groups, organizations, communities and constituencies. (Step 2)	Greater than 2 but not quite 3	The student demonstrates some self-awareness by thoroughly describing three of the six critical elements of this behavior. Three critical elements are lacking in detail or missing from the description	Greater than 1 but not quite 2	The student demonstrates limited self-awareness by describing only two of the six critical elements of this behavior. Four critical elements are lacking in detail or missing from the description	Less than 1
A3.1 Demonstrate effective and diplomatic skills in advocacy. (K, V, S & C/A)	Greater than 2 but not quite 3	Students did a limited job of addressing the following prompts: a) describing a situation involving advocacy, b) what was trying to be accomplished, c) roles each person/group/organization played, d) whether individuals worked unilaterally or collaboratively, and e) focus of actions. <u>Two or Three areas were missing and, unclear and vague</u>	Greater than 1 but not quite 2	The student did not adequately demonstrate advocacy skills. The discussion was vague, missing, or inadequate in all areas	Less than 1
A3.2 Deconstruct situations (culture, social, political, economic, etc.) where human rights are being violated. (Step 1)		The student did only a fair job of a) identifying people groups where human rights are being violated, b) providing scholarly evidence to support group as being oppressed or currently having human rights violated, c) providing first-hand evidence from experience to support this group being oppressed or currently having human rights violated, culture, social, political, economic. <u>Generally, discussion was vague, and scholarly resources did not fully support group as being oppressed</u>		The student did not adequately demonstrate ability to deconstruct a situation where human rights are being violate. Discussion was limited or missing in all areas	

continued on following page

Appendix

Table 2. Continued

Competency & Dimension	2.5	2	1.5	1	.5
A3.3 Compare how social, economic, cultural, and political frameworks can oppress and violate human rights.	Greater than 2 but not quite 3	Student's discussion, utilizing materials presented in Modules 1, 5 & 6 on social, economic, cultural, and political frameworks oppressing and violating the human rights of the student's chosen people group, was vague in most areas. The discussion was supported with only one reference from resources in Module 1, 5, or 6 or the student's discussion was weak in cultural, social, economic and political areas	Greater than 1 but not quite 2	Students did not adequately compare economic, cultural, political, and social frameworks' oppression of people. Discussion was not well supported and comments were vague and incongruent with class materials	Less than 1
A3.4 Recognize and seek to redress human rights, social, economic and environmental injustices resulting from or perpetuating trauma.	Greater than 2 but not quite 3	The student did a fair job of a) summarizing conversation with agency personnel, b) identifying one redress to a specific human right, social, economic, or environmental injustice perpetuating trauma in their people group and c) providing scholarly support for their selected redress. All areas were deficient in detail and lacking in scholarly resources	Greater than 1 but not quite 2	The student did not adequately demonstrate skills in completing the tasks of this behavior. Discussion was vague, missing, or inadequate in all areas	Less than 1
A4.1 Appraise, evaluate, and propose various methods of program evaluation	Greater than 2 but not quite 3	The student did a fair job of evaluating the DEAL Model for Critical Reflection. Students' understanding of the Model was not clearly reflected in their evaluation. Evidence-based support was missing or inadequate. Strengths and/or Challenges of the model were not clearly identified.	Greater than 1 but not quite 2	The student did not adequately demonstrate skills in completing the tasks of this behavior. The discussion was vague, missing, or inadequate in all areas	Less than 1

continued on following page

Appendix

Table 2. Continued

Competency & Dimension	2.5	2	1.5	1	.5
A.4.2 Collect and organize data, and apply critical thinking to interpret information from individuals, families, groups, organizations, communities, and constituencies. (Step 1)	Greater than 2 but not quite 3	Student demonstrates limited ability to collect and organize data and apply critical thinking to interpret data by describing a) Module 2 goals, b) specific conclusions to reach based on their learnings/research, c) specific steps in this experiential learning experience took to attain goals, d) obstacles (internal and external), e) factors contributing to effectiveness, and f) evidence to support goals being met, partially met, or not met. <u>Three parts of the description were unclear or missing</u>	Greater than 1 but not quite 2	Student fails to adequately demonstrate ability to collect and organize data and apply critical thinking to interpret data. All parts of description were unclear, incomplete or missing	Less than 1
A4.3 Evaluate how personal values and biases impact research-informed practice and practice-informed research (Step 1)	Greater than 2 but not quite 3	Student did not adequately discuss within the framework of their experiential learning experience a) assumptions of homogeneity; a perception that it is easier to 'make a difference' in an international/different community rather than a local setting; and the desire to 'give back' may indicate a lack of awareness of power relations and the potential for reinforcing oppression; b) motivations for undertaking an intercultural experience, including their own motivations c) their expectations and achievement of learning goals for their intercultural experience; d) fears or concerns and what strategies they used to manage these; and e) how assumptions underpinning motivations, fears and expectations impacted the learning experience. <u>More than three areas of discussion were missing or poorly described</u>	Greater than 1 but not quite 2	Student did not demonstrate ability to discuss identified areas of this behavior. All areas were lacking in detail and clarity.	Less than 1

continued on following page

Appendix

Table 2. Continued

Competency & Dimension	2.5	2	1.5	1	.5
A4.4 Advocate for strategies to improve practice-informed research and research informed practice in trauma care	Greater than 2 but not quite 3	Student does not adequately address the following prompts a) identifying two relevant social work academic concepts/theories that would be important when advocating for your identified people group? b) discussing how work on this assignment/class enhanced knowledge of the specific reading, theory, or concept? c) Identifying two social work actions that would be important when advocating for research informed practice with your identified people group. <u>Two of three key areas were limited in discussion and/ or unclear and the</u> concept, theory, etc. was not clearly explained/or missing and the two actions steps were not congruent with the concept/ theory presented or missing.	Greater than 1 but not quite 2	Student did not demonstrate ability to discuss identified areas of this behavior. All areas were lacking in detail and clarity.	Less than 1
A6.1 Establish a relationally based process that encourages individuals, families, groups, organizations, and communities to be equal participants in the establishment of expected outcomes.	Greater than 2 but not quite 3	Student did a fair in a) describing how they adopted a learning process that encouraged colleagues, professors, agency personnel, and recipients of agency's services to be equal participants in the student's learning process and b) describing how their chosen agency of service utilized, or did not utilize, a relational based process that encouraged individuals, families, groups, organizations, and communities to be equal participants in the establishment of expected outcomes. <u>The descriptions provided contained statements that are not congruent with a relational process that encourages full participation by all in outcomes. The descriptions were lacking in detail or missing.</u>	Greater than 1 but not quite 2	Student did not demonstrate ability to discuss identified areas of this behavior. All areas were lacking in detail and clarity.	Less than 1

continued on following page

Appendix

Table 2. Continued

Competency & Dimension	2.5	2	1.5	1	.5
6.2 Implement appropriate engagement strategies to engage individuals, families, groups, organizations, and communities within a particular theoretical model.	Greater than 2 but not quite 3	The student did a fair job in a) selecting a theoretical model, b) describing an engagement strategy they utilized that exemplified their chosen theory, and c) identifying social work skills for further development to improve engagement. <u>Descriptions of engagement and their plan for improving skills needed additional detail for clarity and contained statements that were incongruent with the theory selected</u>	Greater than 1 but not quite 2	The student did not demonstrate the ability to discuss identified areas of this behavior. All areas were lacking in detail and clarity	Less than 1
6.3 Utilize self-reflective and intrapersonal skills to effectively engage diverse individuals, families, groups, organizations, communities, and constituencies.	Greater than 2 but not quite 3	Student demonstrates limited ability in utilizing self-reflective and intrapersonal skills to effectively engage diverse individuals. Student examines intrapersonal skills by asking, why did I, or did I not, experience difficulty working/interacting with other people? What might I do differently next time to minimize such difficulties? How have past experiences influenced the manner in which I acted or responded to this situation? Am I comfortable with the influence the past has on me? What assumptions or expectations did I bring to the situation (including my assumptions about other persons involved) and how did they affect my actions? To what extent did they prove true? If they did not prove true, why was there a discrepancy Did this situation reveal my own attitudes or biases toward other people, toward the organization, etc.? Do I need to make changes? <u>Three or more areas of the identified prompts were missing or unclear and/or needed changes were not identified</u>	Greater than 1 but not quite 2	Student did not demonstrate adequate ability to discuss identified areas of this behavior. All areas were lacking in detail and clarity.	Less than 1

continued on following page

Appendix

Table 2. Continued

Competency & Dimension	2.5	2	1.5	1	.5
6.4 Integrating trauma-informed principles of engagement with practices at the micro, mezzo and macro levels that are responsive to those underrepresented and oppressed in society	Greater than 2 but not quite 3	Student did a fair job a) describing a) describing how trauma-informed principles of engagement can be integrated at the micro, mezzo, and macro levels that are responsive to those underrepresented and oppressed in society and b) describing how their chosen agency of service utilized or did not utilize, trauma-informed principles of engagement at the micro, mezzo and macro levels that are responsive to those underrepresented and oppressed in society (give examples). The descriptions and examples were vague and/or incongruent trauma-informed	Greater than 1 but not quite 2	The student did not demonstrate adequate ability to discuss identified areas of this behavior. All areas were lacking in detail and clarity.	Less than 1

Developed by Helen Mudd, Ph.D., CSW, Co-Author of Chapter 4

COURSE ACTIVITIES FOR TRANSFORMATIONAL TEACHING

Designing Transformative Spiritual Assessments

I. Compose a paper in which you discuss your life's spiritual path thus far. This essay is a personal analysis of your "spiritual journey" from childhood to the present, seen from a historical viewpoint. The first day of class will see the distribution of a class handout. You will be required to create a life map of your life cycle based on your spiritual development from childhood to the present. This will be based on a Life map intervention. You must describe how your inner spiritual strengths have shaped your personality and helped you with a transformational learning experience. Explain how you could use your spiritual strengths as a tool in your social work practice.

II. Have a conversation with a social worker who evaluates clients using spiritual interventions. Kindly inquire about the procedure, client interactions, intervention model, and tools used. Also, inquire about assessment difficulties due to complex situations. Write a report outlining what you learned. Make sure to incorporate a few of the best practices you noticed the social work practitioner(s) using uniquely.

III. Use your social work practice abilities to write a document that evaluates a spiritually sensitive intervention. Explain why you chose it, identify your findings, and offer a strategy. Identify a client system (individual, group, or community) from your fieldwork practicum
   A. Conduct an assessment.
   B. Design a spiritually sensitive intervention.
   C. Explain the reasons for choosing that intervention.
   D. Identify your learnings from this exercise and provide a plan for using them in a case-based approach (for example, promoting ethical, culturally competent, and spiritually sensitive social work practice skills).
IV. Compose a paper outlining how you will use the knowledge, abilities, and values you have acquired during the course in your future work. Write in a notebook summarizing the values, abilities, and facts you have learned from this course. Also, respond to the following questions:
   A. Will you be interested in learning more about a client's spiritual or religious background in your future social work practice?
   B. Provide more justification for your response.
   C. Describe how the knowledge you gained in the Spirituality and Social Work course has influenced your spiritual development.
   D. Make a spiritual inventory of yourself and share your opinions or beliefs

Developed by: Pious Malliar Bellian, MSW, Author of Chapter 11

TRANSFORMATIONAL LEARNING SELF-CARE ACTIVITY

Each week of the course, students are led through various self-care activities that address one component of their self-care plan (spiritual, emotional, physical, mental, and professional) using articles, YouTube videos, and step-by-step instructions. Professors can choose activities appropriate to their course and area of focus. After the activity, students are asked to provide a brief reflection on the activity. After the course, students are asked to complete a self-care vision board composed of all the self-care activities they found useful in the case, answer the questions below, and explain how they plan to maintain their self-care in the future.

Below are examples for each component of the self-care plan

Appendix

Week 1: Physical

Complete one of the following breathing exercises as this week's exercise

Dr. Weil explains how to do his 4-7-8 breathing technique. Matcha.com (2:21)- Video Link Dr. Weil explains his 4-7-8 breathing technique. Relaxing Breathing Exercise (youtube.com)

4-7-8 Breathing Technique (1:33)- Video Link 4-7-8 Breathing Technique (youtube.com)

Week 2: Emotional

Complete one of the following exercises as this week's emotional exercise

The Importance of Self-Care- Video Link The Importance of Self-Care (youtube.com)

Coping Skills and Self-Care for Mental Health- Video Link Video Ad (youtube.com)

Week 3: Spiritual

Complete one of the following exercises as this week's spiritual exercise

National Wellness Week: Focus on Spiritual Wellness! (1.29)- Video LinkNarrated - National Wellness Week: Focus on Spiritual Wellness! (youtube.com)

Week 4: Mental

Complete one of the following exercises as this week's mental exercise

The 5-4-3-2-1 Method: A Grounding Exercise to Manage Anxiety 4:23- Video Link Zip Bags - Jed - Plastic Around the Planet - Intro JED_082322_M - Backend JED_082322_YT (youtube.com)

Find your Focus with Mini Mediation (1:00)- Video Link Find Your Focus with this Mini Meditation (youtube.com)

Let's re-focus! 2 Minute Re-Centering Mindfulness Meditation for De-stressing (2:03) Mindful Breaks- Video Link 2 Minute Re-Centering Mindfulness Meditation for De-stressing (youtube.com)

Week 5: Professional

Strategies for Working with Traumatized Individuals- Video Link Self Care Strategies in Trauma Work (youtube.com)

Purpose: Evaluate your self-care and wellness practices briefly, evaluate their effectiveness, and modify them for sustainability.

Look back at your self-care plans and check-ins and reflect on:

a. What was working or not working?
b. How do you know when your plan is and is not working? What does that look and feel like? What do others say during these times?
c. How did you adapt your wellness when things were not working?
d. What is your wellness sustainability plan to manage secondary/vicarious trauma? Be specific and use SMART goals.
e. How might maintaining self-care help identify/manage bias and prevent secondary/vicarious trauma?

Competencies Addressed:

1.1 Make ethical decisions by applying the standards of the NASW Code of Ethics, relevant laws and regulations, models for ethical decision-making, ethical conduct of research, and additional codes of ethics as appropriate to context

Students will engage in ongoing self-care practices to ensure they maintain their well-being in the best interest of themselves and the individuals they serve. Maintaining secondary trauma and compassion fatigue is an ethical responsibility that must be practiced.

1.2 use reflection and self-regulation to manage personal values and maintain professionalism in practice situations.

Students will maintain personal values and professionalism, including maintaining appropriate boundaries, a work/home life balance, and good mental, physical, and spiritual well-being.

1.3 demonstrate professional demeanor in behavior, appearance; and oral, written, and electronic communication.

Students will maintain professionalism in all aspects of appearance by ensuring self-care and remaining in the best mental, physical, and spiritual state to meet the needs of themselves and the individuals they serve.

2.1 apply and communicate an understanding of the importance of diversity and difference in shaping life experiences in practice at the micro, mezzo, and macro levels.

Appendix

Students will acknowledge and address any life experiences, particularly those of a traumatic nature, that may impact their ability to address the needs of those they serve in a professional, unbiased manner.

Developed by Kimberly N. Mudd, DSW, MSSW, Author Chapter 3 and Co-Author Chapter 4

SERVICE LEARNING--FEED ME FRIDAY

Social Work students, faculty, and administrators partner with Green River Ministries for Feed Me Friday twice a year to provide one hundred meals for individuals in the local area. Faculty and students prepare the menu and food and package each meal individually. Upon arriving at the agency, faculty and students serve the prepared meals while greeting and engaging with the individuals. This activity provides students with an opportunity to engage in a community service that meets the immediate, firsthand needs of individuals within the local community. This activity focuses on Competencies Addressed:

2.1 Apply and communicate understanding of the importance of diversity and difference in shaping life experiences in practice at the micro, mezzo, and macro levels.

Students will engage in meeting the needs of individuals while recognizing these needs from a multi-level perspective of social work practice (service learning project).

2.3 Apply self-awareness and self-regulation to manage the influence of personal biases and values in working with diverse clients and constituencies.

Students will recognize the influence of personal and biases while interacting and working directly with individual in a service setting. Students will be aware of diversity and its impact to practice (service learning project).

3.1 Apply their understanding of social, economic, and environmental justice to advocate for human rights at the individual and system levels.

Students will acknowledge the needs for improvement services, social justice, and policy change for individuals on how service levels. Students will critical analyze how the enhancement of such services would directly impact social work practice (service learning project).

6.1 Apply knowledge of human behavior and the social environment, person-in-environment, and other multidisciplinary theoretical frameworks to engage with clients and constituencies.

Students will apply knowledge of human behavior, and theoretical perspectives to critical apply to engagement with individuals in practice (service learning project).

Developed by Kimberly N. Mudd, DSW, MSSW, Author Chapter 3 and Co-Author Chapter 4

Appendix

BEADS OF PRIVILEGE TRANSFORMATIONAL LEARNING ACTIVITY

For this activity students will be making a bracelet to represent the different identities that they have privilege in. To begin, the beads are all sorted into different dishes and placed around the room, where they are matched to a question sheet. For example, the blue beads would symbolize religious privilege, and students would take a bead for every religious statement where they felt they had experienced privilege. This activity should remain silent while the participants walk around gathering beads. Students are given a bracelet and asked to collect beads (the professor provides an assortment of different colored beads) to represent the different areas of privilege they identify within their lives. After collecting the beads, students are asked to think critically about each area of privilege and prioritize the beads on their bracelet from the most significant to the least. The purpose of the exercise is not to diminish the importance of any privilege but to help the student identify the ones that hold greater significance in their lives. The professor then leads a discussion on the importance of this exercise personally, as well as to their future social work practice. Students are asked to wear their bracelets and share with others the importance of recognizing the privilege we all have in our lives.

Moderations: Remember that these questions (both the privilege statements and the facilitation questions) could change depending on different groups or different facilitation styles. Also note that physical and mental ability can be separated into two categories.

Materials needed:

a) String or band for bracelets
b) Colored beads (enough colors to designate every category a different color)
c) List of questions (works well if you post on board)
d) Facilitation Guide

Processing Questions:

a) What were your initial feelings and thoughts about this activity?
b) Were there any questions that you didn't understand or that came as a surprise to you?
c) What are some of the identities that you think about the most? The least?
d) How often do you think about privilege?
e) Is it hard to be able to physically see it?
f) Were there any missing identifies that you noticed?

Appendix

This exercise is designed to focus on the listed identified competencies:

1.2 Use reflection and self-regulation to manage personal values and maintain professionalism in practice situations.

In this activity, students will use self-reflection to identify areas of privilege, identifying impacting values, experiences, and influences while maintaining professionalism and ethical standards.

1.3 Demonstrate professional demeanor in behavior, appearance, and oral, written, and electronic communication.

The student will maintain professionalism and ethical standards by critically analyzing the influence of privilege and hearing the impact privilege has on their peers. This activity may invoke feelings of bias, incidents of discrimination, and possible trauma.

2.3 Apply self-awareness and self-regulations to manage the influence of personal biases and values in working with diverse clients and constituencies.

Students will be self-aware while assessing the influence of biases, culture, and personal experiences. Students will maintain professionalism and refrain from personal judgment while engaging in open dialogue with others.

Beads represent the following areas of identity:
Class Privilege with various questions
Religious Privilege with various questions
Education Privilege with various questions
Socio-Economic Privilege with various questions
Class Privilege with various questions
Ability Privilege with various questions
Race Privilege with various questions
Language Privilege with various questions
Age Privilege with various questions
Random Privilege—add any type of privilege with questions appropriate to your group

Developed by Kimberly N. Mudd, DSW, MSSW, Author Chapter 3 and Co-Author Chapter 4

Appendix

EXPERIENTIAL LEARNING PLANNING GUIDE

Mapping of Competencies Across Activities

Table 3. Service Learning Trip Planning Guide

Trip:	Dates:
Location:	Lodging:
Faculty Name(s):	On-Site Guides Name(s):
Faculty Contact:	On-Site Guide Contact:
Student Names/Contact Information	Student Names/Contact Information
Competency 1 – Demonstrate Ethical and Professional Behavior	
Competency 2 – Advance Human Rights and Social, Economic, and Environmental Justice	
Competency 3 –Engage Anti-Racism, Diversity, Equity, and Inclusion (ADEI) in Practice	
Competency 4 – Engage in Practice-Informed Research and Research-Informed Practice	
Competency 5 – Engage in Policy Practice	
Competency 6-Engage with Individuals, Families, Groups, Organizations, and Communities	
Competency 7-Assess Individuals, Families, Groups, Organizations, and Communities	
Competency 8-Intervene with Individuals, Families, Groups, Organizations, and Communities	
Competency 9-Evaluate Practice with Individuals, Families, Groups, Organizations, and Communities	

Trip at a Glance

Note: For each day, enter the city, location, and or agencies to be visited. The logistics and details will be entered on the planning chart

Day 1:
Day 2:
Day 3:
Day 4:
Day 5:

Competency 1: Demonstrate Ethical and Professional Behavior

Social workers understand the value base of the profession and its ethical standards, as well as relevant policies, laws, and regulations that may affect practice with individuals, families, groups, organizations, and communities. Social workers understand that ethics are informed by principles of human rights and apply them toward realizing social, racial, economic, and environmental justice in their practice.

Appendix

Social workers understand frameworks of ethical decision-making and apply principles of critical thinking to those frameworks in practice, research, and policy arenas. Social workers recognize and manage personal values and the distinction between personal and professional values. Social workers understand how their evolving worldview, personal experiences, and affective reactions influence their professional judgment and behavior. Social workers take measures to care for themselves professionally and personally, understanding that self-care is paramount for competent and ethical social work practice. Social workers use rights-based, anti-racist, and anti-oppressive lenses to understand and critique the profession's history, mission, roles, and responsibilities and recognize historical and current contexts of oppression in shaping institutions and social work. Social workers understand the role of other professionals when engaged in interprofessional practice. Social workers recognize the importance of lifelong learning and are committed to continually updating their skills to ensure relevant and effective practice. Social workers understand digital technology and the ethical use of technology in social work practice.

Table 4.

Practice Behavior	Task/Activity	Dates	Logistics	Comments
1.1 Make ethical decisions by applying the standards of the NASW Code of Ethics, relevant laws and regulations, models for ethical decision-making, ethical conduct of research, and additional codes of ethics as appropriate to context	*Note: for each behavior experience, insert a task/activity. Be Specific. Delete the behaviors that you will not be addressing.*	*Note: for each behavior, insert dates/times)*	*Note: for each behavior, insert logistics)*	*Note: for each behavior, insert comments on completion or changes to be made for future)*
1.2 demonstrate professional behavior, appearance; and oral, written, and electronic communication;				
1.3 Use technology ethically and appropriately to facilitate practice outcomes				
1.4 Use supervision and consultation to guide professional judgment and behavior				

Appendix

Competency 2: Advance Human Rights and Social, Racial, Economic, and Environmental Justice

Social workers understand that every person regardless of position in society has fundamental human rights. Social workers are knowledgeable about the global intersecting and ongoing injustices throughout history that result in oppression and racism, including social work's role and response. Social workers critically evaluate the distribution of power and privilege in society to promote social, racial, economic, and environmental justice by reducing inequities and ensuring dignity and respect for all. Social workers advocate for and engage in strategies to eliminate oppressive structural barriers to ensure that social resources, rights, and responsibilities are distributed equitably and that civil, political, economic, social, and cultural human rights are protected.

Table 5.

Practice Behavior	Task/Activity	Dates	Logistics	Comments
2.1 advocate for human rights at the individual, family, group, organizational, and community system and the **MICRO** level				
2.2 advocate for human rights at the individual, family, group, organizational, and community system levels; and **MEZZO** level				
2.3 advocate for human rights at the individual, family, group, organizational, and community system levels; and **MACRO** level				
2.4 engage in practices that advance human rights to promote social, racial, economic, and environmental justice. **MICRO** level				
2.5 engage in practices that advance human rights to promote social, racial, economic, and environmental justice. **MEZZO** level				

Appendix

Competency 3: Engage Anti-Racism, Diversity, Equity, and Inclusion (ADEI) in Practice

Social workers understand how racism and oppression shape human experiences and how these two constructs influence practice at the individual, family, group, organizational, and community levels and in policy and research. Social workers understand the pervasive impact of White supremacy and privilege and use their knowledge, awareness, and skills to engage in anti-racist practice. Social workers understand how diversity and intersectionality shape human experiences and identity development and affect equity and inclusion. The dimensions of diversity are understood as the intersectionality of factors including but not limited to age, caste, class, color, culture, disability and ability, ethnicity, gender, gender identity and expression, generational status, immigration status, legal status, marital status, political ideology, race, nationality, religion and spirituality, sex, sexual orientation, and tribal sovereign status. Social workers understand that this intersectionality means that a person's life experiences may include oppression, poverty, marginalization, and alienation as well as privilege and power. Social workers understand the societal and historical roots of social and racial injustices and the forms and mechanisms of oppression and discrimination. Social workers understand cultural humility and recognize the extent to which a culture's structures and values, including social, economic, political, racial, technological, and cultural exclusions, may create privilege and power resulting in systemic oppression.

Table 6.

Practice Behavior	Task/Activity	Dates	Logistics	Comments
3.1 demonstrate anti-racist and anti-oppressive social work practice at the individual, family, group, organizational, community, research, and policy levels; and				
3.2 demonstrate cultural humility by applying critical reflection, self-awareness, and self-regulation to manage the influence of bias, power, privilege, and values in working with clients and constituencies, acknowledging them as experts of their own lived experiences.				

Appendix

Competency 4: Engage in Practice-Informed Research and Research-Informed Practice

Social workers use ethical, culturally informed, anti-racist, and anti-oppressive approaches in conducting research and building knowledge. Social workers use research to inform their practice decision making and articulate how their practice experience informs research and evaluation decisions. Social workers critically evaluate and critique current, empirically sound research to inform decisions pertaining to practice, policy, and programs. Social workers understand the inherent bias in research and evaluate design, analysis, and interpretation using an anti-racist and anti-oppressive perspective. Social workers know how to access, critique, and synthesize the current literature to develop appropriate research questions and hypotheses. Social workers demonstrate knowledge and skills regarding qualitative and quantitative research methods and analysis, and they interpret data derived from these methods. Social workers demonstrate knowledge about methods to assess reliability and validity in social work research. Social workers can articulate and share research findings in ways that are usable to a variety of clients and constituencies. Social workers understand the value of evidence derived from interprofessional and diverse research methods, approaches, and sources.

Table 7.

Practice Behavior	Task/Activity	Dates	Logistics	Comments
4.1 apply research findings to inform and improve practice, policy, and programs; and				
4.2 Identify inherent biases for use in quantitative research methods to advance the purposes of social work.				
4.3 Identify inherent biases for use in qualitative research methods to advance the purposes of social work.				

Appendix

Competency 5: Engage in Policy Practice

Social workers identify social policy at the local, state, federal, and global level that affects well-being, human rights and justice, service delivery, and access to social services. Social workers recognize the historical, social, racial, cultural, economic, organizational, environmental, and global influences that affect social policy. Social workers understand and critique the history and current structures of social policies and services and the role of policy in service delivery through rights-based, anti-oppressive, and anti-racist lenses. Social workers influence policy formulation, analysis, implementation, and evaluation within their practice settings with individuals, families, groups, organizations, and communities. Social workers actively engage in and advocate for anti-racist and anti-oppressive policy practice to effect change in those settings.

Table 8.

Practice Behavior	Task/Activity	Dates	Logistics	Comments
5.1 use social justice, anti-racist, and anti-oppressive lenses to assess how social welfare policies affect the delivery of and access to social services and				
5.2 apply critical thinking to analyze, formulate, and advocate for policies that advance human rights and social, racial, economic, and environmental justice				

Competency 6: Engage with Individuals, Families, Groups, Organizations & Communities

Social workers understand that engagement is an ongoing component of the dynamic and interactive process of social work practice with and on behalf of individuals, families, groups, organizations, and communities. Social workers value the importance of human relationships. Social workers understand theories of human behavior and person-in-environment and critically evaluate and apply this knowledge to facilitate engagement with clients and constituencies, including individuals, families, groups, organizations, and communities. Social workers are self-reflective and understand how bias, power, and privilege as well as their personal values and personal experiences, may affect their ability to engage effectively with diverse clients and constituencies. Social workers use the principles of interprofessional collaboration to facilitate engagement with clients, constituencies, and other professionals as appropriate.

Table 9.

Practice Behavior	Task/Activity	Dates	Logistics	Comments
6.1 Apply knowledge of human behavior and person-in-environment, as well as interprofessional conceptual frameworks, to engage with clients and constituencies and				
6.2 Use empathy, reflection, and interpersonal skills to engage in culturally responsive practice with clients and constituencies				

Appendix

Competency 7: Assess Individuals, Families, Groups, Organizations & Communities

Social workers understand that assessment is an ongoing component of the dynamic and interactive process of social work practice. Social workers understand theories of human behavior and person-in-environment, as well as interprofessional conceptual frameworks, and they critically evaluate and apply this knowledge in culturally responsive assessment with clients and constituencies, including individuals, families, groups, organizations, and communities. Assessment involves a collaborative process of defining presenting challenges and identifying strengths with individuals, families, groups, organizations, and communities to develop a mutually agreed-upon plan. Social workers recognize the implications of the larger practice context in the assessment process and use interprofessional collaboration in this process. Social workers are self-reflective and understand how bias, power, privilege, and their personal values and experiences may affect their assessment and decision-making.

Table 10.

Practice Behavior	**Task/Activity**	**Dates**	**Logistics**	**Comments**
7.1 apply theories of human behavior and person-in-environment, as well as other culturally responsive and interprofessional conceptual frameworks, when assessing clients and constituencies; and				
7.2 demonstrate respect for client self-determination during the assessment process by collaborating with clients and constituencies in developing a mutually agreed-upon plan				

Appendix

Competency 8 – Intervene with Individuals, Families, Groups, Organizations & Communities

Social workers understand that intervention is an ongoing component of the dynamic and interactive process of social work practice. Social workers understand theories of human behavior, person-in-environment, and other interprofessional conceptual frameworks, and they critically evaluate and apply this knowledge in selecting culturally responsive interventions with clients and constituencies, including individuals, families, groups, organizations, and communities. Social workers understand methods of identifying, analyzing, and implementing evidence-informed interventions and participate in interprofessional collaboration to achieve client and constituency goals. Social workers facilitate effective transitions and endings.

Table 11.

Practice Behavior	Task/Activity	Dates	Logistics	Practice Behavior
8.1 engage with clients and constituencies to critically choose and implement culturally responsive, evidence-informed interventions to achieve client and constituency goals; and				
8.2 incorporate culturally responsive methods to negotiate, mediate, and advocate with and on behalf of clients and constituencies.				

Appendix

Competency 9 – Evaluate Practice with Individuals, Families, Groups, Organizations & Communities

Social workers understand that evaluation is an ongoing component of the dynamic and interactive process of social work practice with and on behalf of diverse individuals, families, groups, organizations, and communities. Social workers evaluate processes and outcomes to increase practice, policy, and service delivery effectiveness. Social workers apply anti-racist and anti-oppressive perspectives in evaluating outcomes. Social workers understand theories of human behavior and person-in-environment, as well as interprofessional conceptual frameworks, and critically evaluate and apply this knowledge in evaluating outcomes. Social workers use qualitative and quantitative methods for evaluating outcomes and practice effectiveness.

Table 12.

Practice Behavior	Task/Activity	Dates	Logistics	Comments
9.1 Select culturally responsive methods for evaluation of outcomes and				
9.2 critically analyze outcomes and apply evaluation findings to improve practice effectiveness with individuals, families, groups, organizations, and communities				

Developed by Dr. Helen Mudd, Ph.D., CSW, Co-Author of Chapter 4.

Appendix

SERVICE LEARNING PRE-POST SURVEYS AND DIRECTIONS FOR WRITTEN ASSIGNMENT

Figure 1.

Today & Beyond Program
Service Learning Mentorship Partnership Intervention
Service Learning Project - PRE-Survey
Fall 2021

Section 1:
Social Problems. Describe a social problem related to this service-learning course, identify its causes, and explain what should be done to try to solve this problem:

Explain what you think the difference is between volunteerism and service learning:

Appendix

Figure 2.

Define what you think "culture" and "spirituality" means:

Describe your current awareness of the population involved in the service learning project: (also rate on a scale of 1 to 10 with 1 being most unaware to 10 being very or most aware).

(most unaware)　　　　　　　　　　　　　(most aware)
　　　　1　2　3　4　5　6　7　8　9　10

Comments:

Describe how you expect your awareness of this same population after the service learning project: (also give a project rate on a scale of 1 to 10 with 1 being most unaware to 10 being very aware).

(most unaware)　　　　　　　　　　　　　(most aware)
　　　　1　2　3　4　5　6　7　8　9　10

Comments:

Figure 3.

Section 2: Please check how strongly you agree or disagree with the following statement at this point in time.	Strongly Disagree	Disagree	Neutral	Agree	Strongly Agree
	1	2	3	4	5
Being involved in a program to improve my community is important.					
It is important to work toward equal opportunity (e.g. social, political, vocational) for all people					
It is not necessary to volunteer my time to help people in need.					
I think that people should find time to contribute to their community.					
I feel that I can have a positive impact on local social problems					
We need to work towards changing social systems					
Volunteer work is a temporary solution					
Social issues have very complex causes.					
Solutions will take more time and money.					
It is important to work with people from other cultures.					
I am aware of some of my own biases and prejudices.					

Health Issues					
Neighborhood					
Local Issues					
Environmental Issues					
Education					
Literacy					
School Issues					
Sexism					

Appendix

Figure 4.

Section 5: About You:

Student ID# _____

Name: (optional) _____

Age: _____

Today's Date _____

Class Standing: (Check Only One)

Freshman _____ Sophomore _____ Junior _____ Senior _____ Post Graduate _____

Male _____ Female _____ Other _____

White/Caucasian _____ Asian/Pacific Islander _____ Black/African American _____

American Indian/Alaskan Native _____ Latino/Hispanic _____

Multiracial _____ Other (specify) _____

Figure 5.

Today & Beyond Program
Mentorship Partnership Intervention
Service Learning Project - POST-Survey
Fall 2021

Section 1:
Social Problems. Describe a social problem related to this service-learning course, identify its causes, and explain what should be done to try to solve this problem:

Did participating in this service learning program advance your knowledge about social problems related to this population?   Yes _____ No _____
Comments:

Appendix

Figure 6.

Explain what you think the difference is between volunteerism and service learning:

Did participating in the service learning program advance your knowledge about the difference between volunteerism and service learning?   Yes _____ No _____
Comments:

Figure 7.

Define what you think "culture" and "spirituality" means:

Did participating in this service learning program advance your knowledge about the meaning of "culture" and "spirituality" to this population?   Yes _____ No _____
Comments:

Appendix

Figure 8.

Now that you have completed the service learning program, describe your current awareness of the population in the service learning project (on a scale of 1 to 10, with 1 being most unaware and 10 being very or most aware)

(most unaware)　　　　　　　　　　　　(most aware)
1　2　3　4　5　6　7　8　9　10

Comments:

To the best of your recollection, what did you define as your awareness of this population in the PRE-survey. Please describe if and why your awareness differed from what your pre-survey...what caused the change in awareness (positive or negative)? (estimate what your pre-survey rating was on a scale of 1 to 10 with 1 being most unaware 10 being very or most aware)

(most unaware)　　　　　　　　　　　　(most aware)
1　2　3　4　5　6　7　8　9　10

Comments:

Figure 9.

Section 2: Please check how strongly you agree or disagree with the following statement at this point in time.	Strongly Disagree	Disagree	Neutral	Agree	Strongly Agree
	1	2	3	4	5
Being involved in a program to improve my community is important.					
It is important to work toward equal opportunity (e.g. social, political, vocational) for all people					
It is not necessary to volunteer my time to help people in need.					
I think that people should find time to contribute to their community.					
I feel that I can have a positive impact on local social problems					
We need to work towards changing social systems					
Volunteer work is a temporary solution					
Social issues have very complex causes.					
Solutions will take more time and money.					
It is important to work with people from other cultures.					
I am aware of some of my own biases and prejudices.					

	Not an Issue				
Health Issues	NOT AN ISSUE---------O				
Neighborhood	NOT AN ISSUE---------O				
Local Issues	NOT AN ISSUE---------O				
Environmental Issues	NOT AN ISSUE---------O				
Education	NOT AN ISSUE---------O				
Literacy	NOT AN ISSUE---------O				
School issues	NOT AN ISSUE---------O				
Sexism	NOT AN ISSUE---------O				

Appendix

Figure 10.

Section 5: About You:

Student ID# _____

Name: (optional)_____

Age: _____

Today's Date _____

Class Standing: (Check Only One)

Freshman _____ Sophomore _____ Junior _____ Senior _____ Post Graduate _____

Male _____ Female _____ Other _____

White/Caucasian _____ Asian/Pacific Islander _____ Black/African American _____

American Indian/Alaskan Native _____ Latino/Hispanic _____

Multiracial _____ Other (specify) _____

Figure 11.

Final Comprehensive Paper
SW 325/GEC 331: Native American Service & Research Paper

Paper Format:
- Narrative; professionally written
- Double space, title paper, headings of the required sections, reference page (if needed)
- 10 pages

Questions/Sections:
- Critically reflect on the impact of this course/project on your personal, educational, AND professional future (address all three).
- Critically apply three (3) concepts/terms/theories you have learned from this course and/or previous courses to this field-based learning experience.
- Critically reflect on the impact of the undergraduate research portion of the course/project on your educational and professional future.
- Critically reflect on how useful the undergraduate research portion of the course/project has been and/or will be in helping you learn, implement, and reflect on this mentorship intervention project.
- Critically explain how you think the Native American youth were impacted by the Today & Beyond Program: An Educationally-based Mentorship Project.
- Should this Native American Service & Research Course with the Today & Beyond Program continue? Why or Why not?
- Why should future college students apply or not apply for this course/project? What advice or recommendations do you have for them as future mentors?
- Would you like to stay involved with this program? Why? If yes, in what ways?

Developed by Aschenbrener, DSW, MSW, APSW, Author of Chapter 9

Appendix

COMMUNITY AGENCIES AND STUDENTS BENEFIT FROM SERVICE LEARNING

Universities have a range of resources, such as students, faculty, classrooms, technology, and research expertise, that can be made accessible to the community through partnerships with non-profit organizations or local communities. Service Learning is an important part of the social work learning experience, encouraging students to reflect, think critically, and solve problems. When universities work with agencies and/or communities it is a win-win situation. Students are provided the opportunity to practice and hone their social work skills. Agencies and/or communities receive much-needed labor and expertise. Here are some points to remember.

- Flexibility is a must
- Work can be long and tiring
- Logistics are important—schedule and free time
- Communication is important
- Good Fit
- Expect Challenges

The level of involvement can range from one-time efforts to establishing ongoing partnerships

Level of Involvement	Examples	Requirements for Success
One Time Effort	Thanksgiving Dinner Distribution of Shoes at local elementary school St. Patrick's Day Dance for Exceptional Children Refugees International Day of Service	Effective transfer of information Ethical completion of assigned duties Students have the opportunity to practice social work skills An agency or community has assistance in completing a time-limited effort
Time Limited Effort	Feed-Me Friday Community Mapping	Negotiation and mutual agreement on goals, processes, and products Agency or Community receives time-limited service. This could occur at periodic times on an annual or semi-annual basis
Ongoing Partnership	Buckner International—Long-term commitment to build capacity Disaster Relief Multiple time-limited phases and components	Negotiation and mutual agreement on goals, processes, and products Shared Resources Mutual capacity Enhancement Resolution of Conflicts Benefits to Both Parties (service, field placements, research, etc)

Compilation of References

Abe, J. (2020). Beyond cultural competence, toward social transformation: Liberation psychologies and the practice of cultural humility. *Journal of Social Work Education*, 56(4), 1–12. 10.1080/10437797.2019.1661911

Adams, R. (2003). *Social Work and Empowerment*. Palgrave Macmillan.

Akçay, C. (2012). Dönüşümsel Öğrenme Modeli ve Yetişkin Eğitiminde Dönüşüm. *Milli Eğitim Dergisi*, 5-19.

Akpınar, B. (2010). Transformatif Öğrenme Kuramı: Dönüşerek ve Değişerek Öğrenme. *Anadolu Üniversitesi Sosyal Bilimler Dergisi*, 185-198.

Alessa, G. (2021). The dimensions of transformational leadership and its organizational effects in public universities in Saudi Arabia: A systematic review. *Frontiers in Psychology*, 12.34867578

Alfitri, A., & Hambali, H. (2013). Integration of national character education and social conflict resolution through traditional culture: A case study in South Sumatra Indonesia. *Asian Social Science*, 9(12), 1250135. 10.5539/ass.v9n12p125

Ali, W., Drolet, J., Khatiwada, K., Chilanga, E., & Musah, M. N. (2022). The shifting landscape of international practicum in social work education. *International Journal of Social Work*, 9(1), 15–39. 10.5296/ijsw.v9i1.19129

Allport, G. W. 1. (1954). *The nature of prejudice*. Cambridge,Mass., Addison-Wesley Pub. Co.

American Association of Colleges and Universities (2023). *High-impact practices*. AACU.

Amtmann, J. (2004). Perceived effects of a correctional health education service-learning program. *Journal of Correctional Education*, 55(4), 335–348.

Anderson, A. A. (2005). *The community builder's approach to theory of change: A practical guide to theory development*. Aspen Institute.

Androff, D. (2016). *Practicing rights: Human rights-based approaches to social work practice*. Routledge.

Angelou, M. (1928, April 4).

Compilation of References

Archer-Kuhn, B., Samson, P., Damianakis, T., & Barrett, B., MAtin, S., & Ahern, C. (2020). Transformative Learning in Field Education: Students Bridging the Theory/Practice Gap. *British Journal of Social Work*, 2419–2438.

Archer-Kuhn, B., Samson, P., Damianakis, T., Barrett, B., Matin, S., & Ahern, C. (2021). Transformative learning in field education: Students bridging the theory/practice gap. *British Journal of Social Work*, 51(7), 2419–2438. 10.1093/bjsw/bcaa082

Arnold, K. A. (2017). Transformational leadership and employee psychological well-being: A review and directions for future research. *Journal of Occupational Health Psychology*, 22(3), 381–393. 10.1037/ocp000006228150998

Auer-Frege, I. (2010). *Wege zur Gewalt Freiheit: Methoden der internationalen zivilen Konfliktbearbeitung*. Büttner Verlag.

Awkard, T. (2017). The power of reflective action to build teacher efficacy. *Phi Delta Kappan*, 98(6), 53–57. 10.1177/0031721717696479

Baer, R. (2019). Assessment of mindfulness by self-report. *Current Opinion in Psychology*, 28, 42–48. 10.1016/j.copsyc.2018.10.01530423507

Bain, K. (2004). *What the Best College Teachers Do*. Harvard University Press.

Bakri, H. (2015). Conflict resolution toward local wisdom approach of pela gandong in Ambom City. *The Politics: Jurnal Magistar Ilmu Politik Universitae Hasanuddin*, 18, 51–59.

Baldacchino, D. (2015). Spiritual care education of health care professionals. *Religions*, 6(2), 594–613. 10.3390/rel6020594

Bandura, A. (2012). On the functional properties of perceived self-efficacy revisited. *Journal of Management*, 38(1), 9–44. 10.1177/0149206311410606

Bandyopadhyay, R., & Patil, V. (2017). 'The white woman's burden' - the racialized, gendered politics of volunteer tourism. *Tourism Geographies*, 19(4), 644–657. 10.1080/14616688.2017.1298150

Banks, G., McCauley, K., Gardner, W., & Gular, C. (2016). A meta-analytic review of authentic and transformational leadership: A test for redundancy. *The Leadership Quarterly*, 27(4), 634–652. 10.1016/j.leaqua.2016.02.006

Barbar, A. (2023). *Challenges for ethical humanitarian health responses in contemporary conflict*. Research Gate.

Barsky, A. E. (2019). *Ethics and values in social work: an integrated approach for a comprehensive curriculum* (2nd ed). Oxford University Press.

Bartlett, F. (1958). *Thinking: An Experimental and Social Study*. Basic Books.

Bass, B. M. (1999). Two decades of research and development in transformational leadership. *European Journal of Work and Organizational Psychology*, 8(1), 9–32. 10.1080/135943299398410

Bass, B. M., & Avolio, B. J. (1993). Transformational leadership and organizational culture. *Public Administration Quarterly*, 17(1), 112–121. https://www.jstor.org/stable/40862298

Bass, B. M., & Riggio, R. E. (2006). *Transformational leadership*. Psychology Press. 10.4324/9781410617095

Bass, B. M., & Steidlmeier, P. (1999). Ethics, character, and authentic transformational leadership behavior. *The Leadership Quarterly*, 10(2), 181–217. 10.1016/S1048-9843(99)00016-8

Baumgardner, L. (2019). *Fostering transformative learning in educational settings*. Adult Literacy Education. 10.35847/LBaumgartner.1.1.69

Bednall, T. C., & Rafferty, E., A., Shipton, H., Sanders, K., & J. Jackson, C. (. (2018). Innovative behavior: How much transformational leadership do you need? *British Journal of Management*, 29(4), 796–816. 10.1111/1467-8551.12275

Bekelman, D. B., Dy, S. M., Becker, D. M., Wittstein, I. S., Hendricks, D. E., Yamashita, T. E., & Gottlieb, S. H. (2007). Spiritual well-being and depression in patients with heart failure. *Journal of General Internal Medicine*, 22(4), 470–477. 10.1007/s11606-006-0044-917372795

Bellamkond, R. S., Sunanda, M., & Rangola, S. (2023). Review and synthesis of a decade of research on transformational teaching and student engagement. *MIER Journal of Educational Studies, Trends and Practices*, 442–459. 10.52634/mier/2023/v13/i2/2521

Belliveau, M. (2019). "I need to learn from you": Reflections on cultural humility through study abroad. *Reflections: Narratives of Professional Helping, 25*(1), 70-81.

Bell, K. (2012). Towards a post-conventional philosophical base for social work. *British Journal of Social Work*, 42(3), 408–423. 10.1093/bjsw/bcr073

Bell, K., & Anscombe, A. W. (2013). International field experience in social work: Outcomes of a short-term study abroad programme to India. *Social Work Education*, 32(8), 1032–1047. 10.1080/02615479.2012.730143

Bennett, B. (2019). LGBTQI Aboriginal communities in Australia. *Social Work Education: The InternationalJournal, 38*(5), 604-617. doi:10.1080/02615479.2019.158887210.1080/02615479.2019.1588872

Bennett, G. (2001). Promoting Service Learning Via Online Instruction. *Higher Education, 20*.

Bennis, W. G., & Nanus, B. (2007). *Leaders: The strategies for taking charge*. Harper Publishers.

Berdan, S. N., Goodman, A. E., & Taylor, M. (2013). Preparing for the 21st century: The global imperative. *International Educator*, 22(6), 12–17.

Berger, P., & Luckman, T. (1967). The Social Construction of Reality: A Treatise in the Sociaology of Knowledge. Harmonsworth, Penguin Books.

Berkowicz, J., & Myers, A. (2015). Compassion in the classroom: A "real strength" for education. *Education Week*.

Compilation of References

Betancourt, J. R., Green, A. R., Carrillo, J. E., & Ananeh-Firempong, O. (2003). *Travelers' health*. CDC. https://wwwnc.cdc.gov/travel/

Bibus, A. A., & Koh, B. D. (2021). Intercultural humility in social work education. *Journal of Social Work Education*, 57(1), 16–27. 10.1080/10437797.2019.1661925

Bivens, F., Moriarty, K., & Taylor, P. (2009). Transformative Education and Its Potential for Changing The Lives of Children in Disempowering Contexts. *IDS Bulletin*, 40(1), 97–108. 10.1111/j.1759-5436.2009.00014.x

Blackwell, C. W. (2008). Meeting the objectives of community-based nursing education. In A. Dailey-Hebert, E. Donnelli-Sallee, & L. DiPadovaStocks (Eds.), *Service-eLearning: Educating for citizenship* (pp. 87-94). Charlotte, NC: Information Age Publishing.

Blackwell, C. W. (2008). Meeting the objectives of community-based nursing education. In A.Dailey-Hebert, E. Donnelli-Sallee, & L. DiPadovaStocks (Eds.), *Service-eLearning: Educating for citizenship* (pp. 87-94). Charlotte, NC: Information Age Publishing.

BMZ. (2013). *Entwicklung fur Frieden und Sicherheit: Entwicklungpolitisches Engagement im Kontext von Konflikt, Fragilität und Gewalt*. BMZ—Strategiepapier.

Bogo, M., & Paterson, J. (2005). Promoting self-awareness in beginning social work students. *Social Work Education*, 24(4), 409–423.

Bolger, B., Rowland, G., Reuning-Hummel, C., & Codner, S. (2011). Opportunities for and Barriers to Powerful and Transformative Learning Experiences in Online Learning Environments. *Educational Technology*, 36–41.

Borden, A. W. (2007). The impact of service-learning on ethnocentrism in an intercultural communication course. *Journal of Experiential Education*, 30(2), 171–183. 10.1177/105382590703000206

Boyatzis, R. (2006). An overview of intentional change for a complexity perspective. *Journal of Management Development*, 25(7), 607–623. 10.1108/02621710610678445

Brady, V., Timmins, F., Caldeira, S., Naughton, M. T., McCarthy, A., & Pesut, B. (2021). Supporting diversity in person-centered care: The role of healthcare chaplains. *Nursing Ethics*, 28(6), 935–950. 10.1177/096973302098174633522415

Brannelly, L., & Novelli, M. (2012). The role of non-governmental organisations in education for peacebuilding: A case study of Northern Ireland. *Compare: A Journal of Comparative Education*, 42(1), 53–76.

Brock, S. (2010). Measuring the importance of precursor steps to transformative learning. *Adult Education Quarterly*, 60(2), 122–142. 10.1177/0741713609333084

Broom, C. (2015). Empowering students: Pedagogy that benefits educators and learners. *Citizenship, Social. Economics & Education*, 14(2), 79–86.

Buchanan, M. C., Correia, M. G., & Bleicher, R. E. (2010). Increasing preservice teachers' intercultural awareness through service-learning. *The International Journal of Research on Service-Learning in Teacher Education*, 1(1), 1–19.

Burns, J. (1978). *Leadership*. Harper.

Burton, E. (2003). Distance learning and service-learning in the accelerated format. *New Directions for Adult and Continuing Education*, 2003(97), 63–72. 10.1002/ace.89

Butin, D. W. (2007). Justice-Learning: Service-learning as justice-oriented education. *Equity & Excellence in Education*, 40(2), 177–183. 10.1080/10665680701246492

Buttigieg, S. C., Daher, P., Cassar, V., & Guillaume, Y. (2023). Under the shadow of looming change: Linking employees' appraisals of organizational change as a job demand and transformational leadership to engagement and burnout. *Work and Stress*, 37(2), 148–170. 10.1080/02678373.2022.2120560

Cabrita, C., & Duarte, A. (2023). Passionately demanding: Work's passion's role in the relationship between work demands and affective well-being at work. *Frontiers in Psychology*, 14.

Calderwood, K. A., & Rizzo, L. N. (2022). Co-Creating a transformative earning environment through the student-supervisor relationship: Results of a social work field placement duo-ethnography. *Journal of Transformative Education*. Advance online publication. 10.1177/15413446221079590

Canda, E. R., & Furman, L. D. (2020). *Spiritual Diversity in Social Work Practice*. Oxford University Press.

Cappiali, T. M. (2023). A paradigm shift for a more inclusive, equal, and just academia? Toward a transformative emancipatory pedagogy. *Education Sciences*, 13(9), 876. Advance online publication. 10.3390/educsci13090876

Caron, R. (2020). Anti-imperialist Practice and Field Placements. "Researcher/educator/practitioner" Model for International Social Work Practice. *Journal of Teaching in Social Work*, 40(1), 71–85. 10.1080/08841233.2019.1694619

Caza, A., Caza, B. B., & Posner, B. Z. (2021). Transformational Leadership across Cultures: Follower Perception and Satisfaction. *Administrative Sciences*, 11(1), 32. 10.3390/admsci11010032

Cekaite and, A., & Goodwin, M. H. (2023). Human Touch. *A New Companion to Linguistic Anthropology*, 391-409.

Center, L. (2022, January 09). *TLC Transformational Education*. TLC. https://tlcacademies.com/tlc-transformational-education/

Červený, M., Kratochvílová, I., Hellerová, V., & Tóthová, V. (2022). Methods of increasing cultural competence in nurses working in clinical practice: A scoping review of literature 2011-2021. *Frontiers in Psychology*, 13, 936181. 10.3389/fpsyg.2022.93618136092120

Compilation of References

Chaitali, S. (2022). *Using Emotional Learning Analytics to Improve Students' Engagement in Online Learning.* ASCILITE Publications. 10.14742/apubs.2022.129

Choudhary, A. I., Akhtar, S. A., & Zaheer, A. (2013). Impact of transformational and servant leadership on organizational performance: A comparative analysis. *Journal of Business Ethics*, 116(2), 433–440. 10.1007/s10551-012-1470-8

Christholm, L. A. (2000). *Charting and hero's journey.* International Partnership for Service Learning.

Chung, Y.-C., Carter, E. W., & Sisco, L. G.Yun-Ching. (2012, December). Chung., Erik, W., Carter., Lynn, G., Sisco. (2012). A Systematic Review of Interventions to Increase Peer Interactions for Students with Complex Communication Challenges. *Research and Practice for Persons with Severe Disabilities : the Journal of TASH*, 37(4), 271–287. Advance online publication. 10.2511/027494813805327304

Church, C., & Rogers, M. M. (2006). *Designing for results: Integrating monitoring and evaluation in conflict transformation programs.* Search for Common Ground.

Çimen, O., & Yılmaz, M. (2014). Dönüşümsel Öğrenme Kuramına Dayalı Çevre Eğitiminin Biyoloji Öğretmen Adaylarının Çevre Sorunlarına Yönelik Algılarına Etkisi . *Bartın Üniversitesi Eğitim Fakültesi Dergisi*, 339-359.

Clark, M., & Wilson, A. (1991). Context and Rationality in Mezirow's Theory of Transformational Learning. *Adult Education Quarterly*, 41(2), 75–91. 10.1177/0001848191041002002

Cleak, H., Anand, J., & Das, C. (2016). Asking the critical questions: An evaluation of social work students' experiences in an international placement. *British Journal of Social Work*, 46(1), 389–408. 10.1093/bjsw/bcu126

Cole, T. (2012, March 21). The white-savior industrial complex. *The Atlantic.* https://www.theatlantic.com/international/archive/2012/03/the-white-savior-industrial-complex/254843/

Cole, H. L. (2020). Intersecting social work practice, education, and spirituality: A conceptual model. *Social Thought*, 1–24. 10.1080/15426432.2020.1831420

Collard, S., & Law, M. (1989). The Limits of Perspective Transformation: A Critique of Mezirow's Theory. *Adult Education Quarterly*, 39(2), 99–107. 10.1177/0001848189039002004

Confraria, H., Godinho, M. M., & Wang, L. (2017). Determinants of citation impact: A comparative analysis of the global south versus the global north. *Research Policy*, 46(1), 265–279. 10.1016/j.respol.2016.11.004

Conner, J., & Erickson, J. (2017). When does service-learning work? Contact theory and service-learning courses in higher education. *Michigan Journal of Community Service Learning*, 23(2), 53–65. 10.3998/mjcsloa.3239521.0023.204

Corcoran, K. E. (2013). Divine exchanges: Applying social exchange theory to religious behavior. *Rationality and Society*, 25(2), 335–369. 10.1177/1043463113492306

Council on Social Work Education. (2022). *2022 educational policy and accreditation standards*. CSWE.

Council on Social Work Education. (2022). *Educational policy and accreditation standards*. CSWE. https://www.cswe.org/getmedia/bb5d8afe-7680-42dc-a332-a6e6103f4998/2022-EPAS.pdf

Courtney, B., Merriam, S., & Reeves, P. (1998). The Centrality of Meaningmaking in Transformational Learning: How HIV-Positive Adults Make Sense of Their Lives. *Adult Education Quarterly*, 48(2), 65–84. 10.1177/074171369804800203

Cranton, P. (1994). *Understanding and Promoting Transformative Learning: A Guide for Educators of Adults*. Jossey-Bass.

Cranton, P. (1996). *Professional Development as Transformative Learning: New Perspectives for Teachers of Adults*. Jossey-Bass.

Cranton, P. (2002). *Teaching for Transformation. New Directions for Adult and Continuing Education: No. 93. Contemporary Viewpoints on Teaching Adults Effectively*. Jossey-Bass.

Cranton, P. (2006). Fostering Authentic Relationships in The Transformative Classroom. *New Directions for Adult and Continuing Education*, 2006(109), 5–13. 10.1002/ace.203

Crump, J. A., Sugarman, J., & Barry, M. A. (2020). Ethical considerations for short-term experiences by trainees in global health. *Journal of the American Medical Association*, 324(7), 737–738. 10.1001/jama.300.12.145618812538

Cunningham, P. (1992). From Freire to Feminism: The North American Experience with Critical Pedagogy. *Adult Education Quarterly*, 42(3), 180–191. 10.1177/074171369204200306

Curle, A. (1994). New challenges for citizen peacemaking. *Medicine and War*, 10(2), 96–105. 10.1080/07488009408409148

D'ambrosio, M. (2020). Educating emotions: The pedagogical approach of emotional action. *Education Sciences & Society - Open Access*, 11(1). 10.3280/ess1-2020oa9292

Daly, E., & Sarkin, J. (2007). *Reconciliation in divided societies: Finding common ground*. University of Pennsylvania Press. 10.9783/9780812206388

Damianakis, T., Barrett, B., Archer-Kuhn, B., Samson, P. L., Matin, S., & Ahern, C. (2020). Transformative learning in graduate education: Masters of social work students' experiences of personal and professional learning. *Studies in Higher Education*, 45(9), 2011–2029. 10.1080/03075079.2019.1650735

David, B. (2022, August 29). Colm, McGuinness., Aiden, Carthy. (2022). Do educators value the promotion of students' wellbeing? Quantifying educators' attitudes toward wellbeing promotion. *PLoS One*, 17(8), e0273522. Advance online publication. 10.1371/journal.pone.0273522

De Vivo, K. (2022). A new research base for rigorous base project-based learning. *Connecting Education Research, Policy, and Practice* .

Compilation of References

Dean, N. (2021, Sep 04). On a medical mission: Granville's Healing Art Missions helps Haiti through unrest, and earthquakes. *The Advocate*. https://www.proquest.com/newspapers/on-medical-mission/docview/2568860421/se-2

Deardorff, D. K., Hunter, L. E., & Wallace, M. J. (2014). The impact of study abroad on college students' intercultural competence. *Frontiers: The Interdisciplinary Journal of Study Abroad*, 24, 239–251.

Delgado, L., & Mulder, L. (2017). Eliminating racism, decolonizing education and building an inclusive society: The role of universities in the Kingdom of the Netherlands. *Race Equality Teaching*, 34(2), 15–20. 10.18546/RET.34.2.04

Denborough, D. (2014). Michael White and adventures downunder. *Australian and New Zealand Journal of Family Therapy*, 35(1), 110–120. 10.1002/anzf.1049

Deng, C., Gulseren, D., Isola, C., Grocutt, K., & Turner, N. (2023). Transformational leadership effectiveness: An evidence-based primer. *Human Resource Development International*, 26(5), 627–641. 10.1080/13678868.2022.2135938

Dessel, A., Bolen, R., & Shepardson, C. (2012). Hopes for intergroup dialogue: Affirmation and allies. *Journal of Social Work Education*, 48(2), 361–367. 10.5175/JSWE.2012.201100091

Dirkx, J. (2006). Engaging emotions in adult learning: A Jungian Perspective on Emotion And Transformative Learning. *New Directions for Adult and Continuing Education*, 2006(109), 15–26. 10.1002/ace.204

Dirkx, J. M. (1998). Transformative learning theory in the practice of adult education: An overview. *PAACE Journal of Lifelong Learning*, 7, 1–14.

Dodds, C., Heslop, P., & Meredith, C. (2018). Using simulation-based education to help social work students prepare for practice. *Social Work Education*, 37(5), 597–602. 10.1080/02615479.2018.1433158

Dolan, P., & Connolly, J. (2017). Cultural and creative activities as a means of social inclusion and community cohesion: A case study of Ireland. *International Journal of Cultural Policy*, 23(5), 567–581.

Domakin, A. (2019). Experiential learning: Transforming theory into practice. *Social Work Education*, 38(2), 141–154.

Donaldson, L. P., & Daughtery, L. (2011). Introducing asset-based models of social justice into service learning: A social work approach. *Journal of Community Practice*, 19(1), 80–99. 10.1080/10705422.2011.550262

Dortonne, N. (2016). *The dangers of poverty porn*. CNN. https://www.cnn.com/2016/12/08/health/poverty-porn-danger-feat/index.html

Drolet, J. L., and Nicholas, D. B. (2023). Welcome to the first issue of Transformative Social Work: A special issue on the impacts of the COVID-19 pandemic. *Transformative Social Work, 1*(1).

Duarte, A., Ribeiro, N., Sernedo, A., & Gornes, D. (2021). Individual performance: Affective commitment and individual creativity's sequential mediation. *Frontiers in Psychology*, 12(06), 675749. 10.3389/fpsyg.2021.675749

Duhaney, P., Lorenzetti, L., Kusari, K., & Han, E. (2022). Advancing critical race pedagogical approaches in social work education. *Journal of Ethnic & Cultural Diversity in Social Work*, 31(3-5), 1–11. 10.1080/15313204.2022.2070898

Dundonald International Ice Bowl. (2023, August 24). *The HEROS programme glides back to Dundonald International Ice Bowl*. DIIB.

Dunlap, A., & Mapp, S. C. (2017). Effectively preparing students for international field placements through a pre-departure class. *Social Work Education*, 36(8), 893–904. 10.1080/02615479.2017.1360858

Durlak, J. A., Weissberg, R. P., Dymnicki, A. B., Taylor, R. D., & Schellinger, K. B. (2011). The impact of enhancing students' social and emotional learning: A meta-analysis of school-based universal interventions. *Child Development*, 82(1), 405–432. 10.1111/j.1467-8624.2010.01564.x21291449

Eisenberg, J., Post, C., & DiTomaso, N. (2019). Team dispersion and performance: The role of team communication and transformational leadership. *Small Group Research*, 50(3), 348–380. 10.1177/1046496419827376

Elder, G. (1999). *Children of the Great Depression: Social change in life experience*. University of Chicago press.

El-Lahib, Y., Wehbi, S., Zakharova, G., Perreault-Laird, J., & Khan, M. (2020). Tearing down the "box": Students' perspectives on activating arts-informed methods in social work classrooms. *Social Work Education*, 1–12. 10.1080/02615479.2020.1851360

Engelbrecht, A., Van Aswegen, A., & Theron, C. (2005). The effect of ethical values on transformational leadership and ethical climate in organizations. *South African Journal of Business Management*, 36(2), 9–26. 10.4102/sajbm.v36i2.624

Enkhtur, A., & Yamamoto, B. A. (2017). Transformative Learning Theory and its Application in Higher. *PAACE Journal of Lifelong Learning*, 7, 1–14.

Erasmus, V. (2001). Community mobilization as a tool for peacebuilding. In Reychler, L., & Paffenholz, T. (Eds.), *Peacebuilding: A field guide* (pp. 246–257).

Erden, Ş., & Yıldız, A. (2020). Dönüştürücü Öğrenme Kuramı: Kavramlar, Kökenler ve Eleştiriler. *Yetişkin Eğitimi Dergisi*, 97-118.

Escobar, A. (1995). *Encountering development: The making and unmaking of the third world*. Princeton University Press.

Eyler, J., & Giles, D. E. (1999). *Where's the learning in service-learning?* Jossey- Bass.

Compilation of References

Fanning, R. M., & Gaba, D. M. (2017). The role of debriefing in simulation-based learning. *Simulation in healthcare. Simulation in Healthcare*, 2(2), 115–125. Retrieved January 12, 2024, from. 10.1097/SIH.0b013e318031553919088616

Farley, A., Feaster, D., Schapmire, T., D'Ambrosio, J., Bruce, L., Oak, S., & Sar, B. (2009). The challenges of implementing evidence based practice: ethical considerations in practice, education, policy, and research. *Social Work and Society International Online Journal*, 7(2) .

Farooq, M. S., & Asim, I. (2018). Nurturing inclusive education through cooperative learning as pedagogical approach at primary school level. *PJE*, 35(3). 10.30971/pje.v35i3.780

Feize, L., & Faver, C. (2018). Teaching self-awareness: Social work educator's endeavors and struggles. *Social Work Education*, 38(2), 159–176. 10.1080/02615479.2018.1523383

Fernsler, T. (2015). Transformational leadership. *Nonprofit World*, 33(1), 17–17.

Ferranto, M. L. G. (2015). A qualitative study of baccalaureate nursing students following an eight-day international cultural experience in Tanzania: Cultural humility as an outcome. *Procedia: Social and Behavioral Sciences*, 174, 91–102. 10.1016/j.sbspro.2015.01.631

Figuccio, M. (2020). Examining the efficacy of e-service learning. *Secondary Teacher Education,* (5).

Fisher-Borne, M., Cain, J. M., & Martin, S. L. (2015). From mastery to accountability: Cultural humility as an alternative to cultural competence. *Social Work Education*, 34(2), 165–181. 10.1080/02615479.2014.977244

Fisher, C. M., & Grettenberger, S. E. (2015). Community-based participatory study abroad: A proposed model for social work education. *Journal of Social Work Education*, 51(3), 566–582. 10.1080/10437797.2015.1046342

Fleming, J. (2018). Transformative learning in social work education: A review of the literature. *Social Work Education*, 37(6), 688–702.

Fleming, T. (2022). Mezirow's theory of transformative learning and Freire's pedagogy: Theories in dialogue. *Adult Education Critical Issues*, 2(2), 7–19. 10.12681/haea.32302

Ford, J., & Harding, N. (2017). The impossibility of the "true self" of authentic leadership. *Sage Journals*, 7(4).

Foronda, C., Baptiste, D. L., Reinholdt, M. M., & Ousman, K. (2016). Cultural humility: A concept analysis. *Journal of Transcultural Nursing*, 27(3), 210–217. 10.1177/1043659615592 67726122618

Fox, G. R. (2012). Race, power, and polemic: Whiteness in the anthropology of Africa. *Totem: The University of Western Ontario Journal of Anthropology*, 20(1).

Frenk, J., Chen, L., Bhutta, Z. A., Cohen, J., Crisp, N., Evans, T., Fineberg, H., Garcia, P., Ke, Y., Kelley, P., Kistnasamy, B., Meleis, A., Naylor, D., Pablos-Mendez, A., Reddy, S., Scrimshaw, S., Sepulveda, J., Serwadda, D., & Zurayk, H. (2010). Health professionals for a new century: Transforming education to strengthen health systems in an interdependent world. *Lancet*, 376(9756), 1923–1958. 10.1016/S0140-6736(10)61854-521112623

Friedendienst, Z. (2014). *Grundlagen, Akteure und Verfahren des ZFD*. https://www.ziviler-friedensdienst.org/sites/default/files/media/file/2022/zfd-ziviler-friedensdienst-zfd-kompakt-2264_23.pdf

Fuglei, M. (2021). *Transformational teaching: A learning revolution*. Medium.

Fullerton, J. (2010). *Transformative Learning in College Students: A Mixed Methods Study*. University of Nebrask.

Gabel, S. G., & Yang, N. (2022). Transnational advocacy at the United Nations for social workers. *Journal of Human Rights and Social Work*, 7(4), 417–427. 10.1007/s41134-022-00216-135971383

Galtung, J. (1996). Peace by peaceful means: Peace and conflict, development, and civilization. *Sage (Atlanta, Ga.)*. Advance online publication. 10.4135/9781446221631

Gargan, E. A. (1993, January 14). Refugees Fleeing Tajikistan Strife. *New York Times*.

General Assembly of the International Association of Social Workers & International Federation of Social Workers. (2018). Global Social Work Statement of Ethical Principles. General Assembly of the International Association of Social Workers & International Federation of Social Workers.

Geray, C. (2002). *Halk Eğitimi*. İmaj Yayınevi.

Giorgi, S., Lockwood, C., & Glynn, M. A. (2015). The many faces of culture: Making sense of 30 years of research on culture in organization studies. *The Academy of Management Annals*, 9(1), 1–54. 10.5465/19416520.2015.1007645

Goleman, D. (1995). *Emotional Intelligence: Why It Can Matter More Than IQ*. Bantam Books.

Gottlieb, M. (2020). The case for a cultural humility framework in social work practice. *Journal of Ethnic & Cultural Diversity in Social Work*, 9(1), 1–19. 10.1080/15313204.2020.1753615

Goudge, P. (2003). *The whiteness of power: Racism in third world development and aid*. Lawrence & Wishart.

Gravett, S. (2004). Action Research and Transformative Learning in Teaching Development. *Educational Action Research*, 12(2), 259–272. 10.1080/09650790400200248

Gray, M., & Coates, J. (2018). Changing gears: Shifting to an environmental perspective in social work education. In *Environmental Justice* (pp. 48–58). Routledge.

Gray, M., & Lombard, A. (2008). The post-1994 transformation of social work in South Africa. *International Journal of Social Welfare*, 17(2), 132–145. 10.1111/j.1468-2397.2007.00545.x

Compilation of References

Green, D. (2016, October 19). Academics and NGOs can work together in partnership but must do so earlier and with genuine knowledge exchange. *Impact of Social Sciences*.

Greenfield, E. A., Davis, R. T., & Fedor, J. P. (2012). The effect of international social work education: Study abroad versus on-campus courses. *Journal of Social Work Education*, 48(4), 739–761. 10.5175/JSWE.2012.201100147

Greenleaf, R. (1970). *The Servant as Leader*. Center for Applied Studies.

Güçlü, N. (2000). Öğretmen davranışları. *Millî Eğitim Dergisi*, 21-23.

Gunawan, G. (2020). The influence of transformational leadership, school culture, and work motivation on school effectiveness in junior high school in Medan. *Budapest International Research and Critics Institute Humanities and Social Sciences*, 3(1), 625–634. 10.33258/birci.v3i1.824

Guth, L. J., & Asner-Self, K. K. (2017). International group work research: Guidelines in cultural contexts. *Journal for Specialists in Group Work*, 42(1), 33–53. 10.1080/01933922.2016.1264519

Guzzardo, M., Khosia, N., Adams, A., Bussmann, J., Engekman, A., Ingnaham, N., & Taylor, S. (2021). The ones that make a difference: Perspective on student- faculty relationships. *Innovative Higher Education*, 46(1), 41–58. 10.1007/s10755-020-09522-w33012971

Halbert, L. A. (1923). *What is Professional Social Work*. Kansas City. *Survey (London, England)*.

Hamilton, L., Tokpa, L., McCain, H., & Donovan, S. (2021). #WhiteSaviorComplex: Confidentiality, human dignity, social media, and social work study abroad. *Journal of Social Work Education*, 59(4), 1–11. 10.1080/10437797.2021.1997685

Hamlin, M. (2015). *Technology in Transformative Learning Environments*. IGI Global. 10.4018/978-1-4666-8571-0.ch004

Hariharan, K., & Anand, V. (2023). Transformational leadership and learning flows. *The Learning Organization*, 30(3), 309–325. 10.1108/TLO-09-2021-0115

Hartoyo, H., & Fahmi, T. (2018). Towards a new village development paradigm in Lampung province, Indonesia. *Journal of Legal, Ethical and Regulatory Issues, 21*.

Hay, I. (2006). Transformational leadership: Characteristics and criticisms. *E-Journal of Organizational Learning and Leadership*, 5(2). http://www.weleadinlearning.org/ejournal.htm

Hay, K., Lowe, S., Barnes, G., Dentener, A., Doyle, R., Hinii, G., & Morris, H. (2018). 'Times that by 100': Student learning from international practicum. *International Social Work*, 61(6), 1187–1197. 10.1177/0020872817702707

Healy, L. M., & Thomas, R. L. (2020). *International social work: Professional action in an interdependent world*. Oxford University Press.

Heather, F. (2023, May 28). Jane, W., Davidson., Amanda, Krause. (2023). Examining the empathic voice teacher. *Research Studies in Music Education*, 1321103X2311720. 10.1177/1321103X231172065

Hodge, D. R. (2011). Using Spiritual Interventions in Practice: Developing Some Guidelines from Evidence-based Practice. *Social Work*, 56(2), 149–158. 10.1093/sw/56.2.14921553578

Hodge, D. R. (2015). *Spiritual Assessment in Social Work and Mental Health Practice*. Columbia University. 10.7312/hodg16396

Hodge, D. R. (2016). Spiritual Competence: What it is, why it is necessary, and how to develop it. *Journal of Ethnic & Cultural Diversity in Social Work*, 27(2), 124–139. 10.1080/15313204.2016.1228093

Hodge, D. R. (2018). Increasing spiritual diversity in social work discourse: A scientific avenue toward more effective mental health service provision. *Social Work Education*, 38(6), 753–765. 10.1080/02615479.2018.1557630

Hodge, D., & Kasule, K. (2022). Addressing the global inequality in social work research: Challenges, opportunities, and key insights and strategies in Sub-Saharan Africa. *Social Work Research*, 46(1), 84–92. 10.1093/swr/svab020

Hogg, B. (2024, February 22). *10 Characteristics of Transformational Leaders*. Billhogg. https://www.billhogg.ca/10-characteristics-of-transformational-leaders/

Hoggan, C., Malkki, K., & Finnegan, F. (2017). Developing the Theory of Perspective Transformation: Continuity, Intersubjectivity, and Emancipatory Praxis. *Adult Education Quarterly*, 67(1), 48–64. 10.1177/0741713616674076

Holsapple, M. (2012). Service-learning and student diversity outcomes: Existing evidence and directions for future research. *Michigan Journal of Community Service Learning*, 5–18.

Homans, G. (1974). *Social behavior: Its elementary forms* (2nd ed.). Harcourt Brace Jovanovich.

Homonoff, E. (2008). The heart of social work: Best practitioners rise to challenges in field instruction. *The Clinical Supervisor*, 27(2), 135–169. 10.1080/07325220802490828

Hook, J. N., Davis, D. E., Owen, J., Worthington, E. L., & Utsey, S. O. (2013). Cultural humility: Measuring openness to culturally diverse clients. *Journal of Counseling Psychology*, 60(3), 353–366. 10.1037/a003259523647387

House, R. J., Hanges, P. J., Javidan, M., Dorfman, P. W., & Gupta, V. (Eds.). (2004). *Culture, leadership, and organizations: The GLOBE study of 62 Societies*. Sage Publications.

Hughes, C., Welsh, M., Mayer, A., Bolay, J., & Southard, K. (2009). An innovative university-based mentoring program: Affecting college students' attitudes and engagement. *Michigan Journal of Community Service Learning*, 16(1), 69–78.

Hutchings, T. (2016). *Teachings as a high-risk profession*. Protecting the Professional- Professional Ethics in the Classroom.

Illeris, K. (2004). Transformative Learning in the Perspective of a Comprehensive Learning Theory. *Journal of Transformative Education*, 2(2), 79–89. 10.1177/1541344603262315

Compilation of References

Illeris, K. (2014). Transformative learning and identity. *Journal of Transformative Education*, 12(2), 148–163. 10.1177/1541344614548423

International Federation of Social Workers (IFSW), (2014). *Global Definition of social work*. Global Definition of Social Work – International Federation of Social Workers (ifsw.org).

International Federation of Social WorkersInternational Association of SchoolInternational Council on Social Wel. (2012). The global agenda for social work and social development: Commitment to action. *Journal of Social Work Education*, 48(4), 837–843. 10.1080/10437797.2012.10662225

Iram, A.Nasreen, A. (2021). Effect of teachers' emotional intelligence on student' involvement and task orientation in classroom learning environment at secondary school level. *Pakistan Journal of Educational Research*, 4(4). 10.52337/pjer.v4i4.353

Isaacson, M. (2014). Clarifying concepts: Cultural humility or competency. *Journal of Professional Nursing*, 30(3), 251–258. 10.1016/j.profnurs.2013.09.01124939335

Isabel, A., Wallengren-Lynch, M., & Archer-Kuhn, B. (2023). Measuring and validating a transformation learning survey through social work education research. *Journal of Transformative Education*, 15413446231222204. Advance online publication. 10.1177/15413446231222204

Jianhui, Yu. (2020). *Changqin, Huang., Xizhe, Wang., Yaxin, Tu.* Exploring the Relationships Among Interaction, Emotional Engagement and Learning Persistence in Online Learning Environments., 10.1109/ISET49818.2020.00070

Johnson Bailey, J., & Alfred, M. (2006). Transformational Teaching and the Practices of Black Women Educators. *New Directions for Adult and Continuing Education*, 2006(109), 49–58. 10.1002/ace.207

Jonassen, D. H. (1994). Thinking Technology: Toward a Constructivist Design Model. *Educational Technology*, 34(4), 34–37. https://www.learntechlib.org/p/171050/

Jonassen, D., Howland, J., Moore, J., & Marra, R. (2003). *Learning to Solve Problems With Technology*. Merrill Prentice.

Jönsson, J. H., & Flem, A. L. (2018). International field training in social work education: Beyond colonial divides. *Social Work Education*, 37(7), 895–908. 10.1080/02615479.2018.1461823

Joshua, K. (2020). *Classroom Culture: Stories of Empathy and Belonging*. IGI Global. 10.4018/978-1-7998-2971-3.ch011

Kaban, M., & Sitepu, S. (2017). The efforts of inheritance dispute resolution for customary land on Indigenous peoples in Karo North Sumatra, Indonesia. *International Journal of Private Law*, 8(3/4), 281–298. 10.1504/IJPL.2017.087364

Kanyangale, P., & Mwaura, N. K. (2019). Social work students' engagement with non-governmental organizations in conflict-affected communities: A case study of Malawi. *International Social Work*, 62(6), 1587–1601.

Kareem, J., Patrick, H., Prabakaran, N. B. V., Tantia, V., Kumar, P., & Mukherjee, U. (2023). Transformational educational leaders inspire school educators' commitment. *Frontiers in Education*, 8. 10.3389/feduc.2023.1171513

Kasonde, N., Hambulo, F., Haambokoma, N., & Tomaida, M. (2013). The Contribution of Behaviourism Theory to Education. *Journal: Zambia Journal of Education*, 4(1), 58–74.

Keen, C., & Woods, R. (2016). Creating activating events for transformative learning in a prison classroom. *Journal of Transformative Education*, 14(1), 15–33. 10.1177/1541344615602342

Ken, G. (2007, July). Solvegi, Shmulsky. (2007). Meeting the Needs of Students with Complex Psychological and Educational Profiles. *College Teaching*, 55(3), 134–136. 10.3200/CTCH.55.3.134-136

Khoury-Kassabri, M., & Benbenishty, R. (2018). Social work education in conflict and post-conflict countries: An exploratory study among Palestinian and Israeli students. *British Journal of Social Work*, 48(1), 1–19.

Killian, J. (2004). Pedagogical experimentation: Combining traditional, distance, and service learning techniques. *Journal of Public Affairs Education*, 10(3), 209–224. 10.1080/15236803.2004.12001360

Kimberly, A. (2023). Promoting cultural competence in nursing: Strategies for providing inclusive patient care. *Opinion Journal of Advanced Practices in Nursing, 8*(6). https://www.hilarispublisher.com/open-access/promoting-cultural-competence-in-nursing-strategies-for-providing-inclusive-patient-care.pdf

Kim-Daniel, V. (2023). Students' experiences of peer feedback practices as related to awareness raising of learning goals, self-monitoring, self-efficacy, anxiety, and enjoyment in teaching EFL and mathematics. *Scandinavian Journal of Educational Research*, 1–15. 10.1080/00313831.2023.2192772

Kincheloe, J. L., Steinberg, & Shirley, R. (2008). Indigenous knowledges in education: Complexities, dangers, and profound benefits. In N. K. Denzin, Y. S. Lincoln, & L. Tuhiwai Smith (Eds.), *Handbook of critical and indigenous methodologies* (1st ed., pp. 135–156). Thousand Oaks, CA: Sage.

King James Bible. (2017). King James Bible Online (Original work published 1769).

King, K. (2011). Teaching in An Age of Transformation: Understanding Unique Instructional Technology Choices Which Transformative Learning Affords. *Educational Technology*, 4–10.

Kirst-Ashman, K., & Hull, G. (2015). *Generalist practice with organizations and communities* (6th ed.). Cengage.

Kjersti, L. (2023). *107 Emotion in language education and pedagogy*. DEG. 10.1515/9783110795486-043

Compilation of References

Koç Akran, S., & Epçaçan, E. (2018). Dönüşümsel Öğrenme Modelinin 6. Sınıf Fen Bilimleri Dersinde Öğrencilerin Eleştirel Düşünme Eğilimlerine ve Bilişötesi Farkındalıklarına Etkisi. *Necatibey Eğitim Fakültesi Elektronik Fen ve Matematik Eğitimi Dergisi*, 538-571.

Kolb, A. Y., & Kolb, D. A. (2011). Experiential learning theory: A dynamic, holistic approach to management learning, education and development. *The SAGE handbook of management learning, education and development, 7*(2), 42-68.

Kolb, A., & Kolb, D. (2017). Experiential learning theory as a guide for experiential educators in higher education. *Experiential Learning & Teaching in Higher Education*, *1*(1).

Kolb, D. A. (1984). *Experiential learning: Experience as the source of learning and development*. Prentice-Hall.

Kolb, D. A., Boyatzis, R. E., & Mainemelis, C. (2014). Experiential learning theory: Previous research and new directions. In *Perspectives on thinking, learning, and cognitive styles* (pp. 227–247). Routledge. 10.4324/9781410605986-9

Konstantinos, B., & Stavros, S. (2022). Working with Students on Establishing a Student-Oriented Classroom Culture: A Teaching Initiative Designed to Build an Inclusive and Highly Engaging Learning Environment in Online and Face to Face Environments. In *Higher Education* (pp. 73–82). CRC Press. 10.1201/9781003021230-6

Kourgiantakis, T., Sewell, K. M., Hu, R., Logan, J., & Bogo, M. (2019). Simulation in social work education: A scoping review. *Research on Social Work Practice*, 30(4), 433–450. 10.1177/1049731519885015

Kouzes, J. M., & Posner, B. Z. (2017). *The leadership challenge* (3rd ed.). Jossey-Bass.

Kovan, J., & Dirkx, J. (2003). Being Called Awake: The Role of Transformative Learning in the Lives of Environmental Activists. *Adult Education Quarterly*, 53(2), 99–118. 10.1177/0741713602238906

Kramer, M. (2018). Promoting teachers' agency: Reflective practice as transformative disposition. *Reflective Practice*, 19(2), 211–224. 10.1080/14623943.2018.1437405

Kuriakou, G. (2023). Transformative learning in formal schools. *International Journal for Innovation Education and Research*, 11(11), 48–52. 10.31686/ijier.vol11.iss11.4176

Lager, P., Mathieson, S., Rodgers, M., & Cox, S. (2010). *Guidebook for International Field Placements and Student Exchanges Planning, Implementation, and Sustainability*. CSWE Press.

Lai, A. (2011). Transformational-transactional leadership theory. *2011 AHS Capstone Projects*. Digital Commons. http://digitalcommons.olin. edu/ahs_capstone_2011/17

Lai, F.-Y., Tang, H.-C., & Lin, C.-C. (2020). Transformational leadership and job performance: The mediating role of work engagement. *SAGE Open*, 10(1). 10.1177/2158244019899085

Lam, Y. J. (2002). Defining the effects of transformational leadership on organizational learning: A cross-cultural comparison. *School Leadership & Management*, 22(4), 439–452. 10.1080/1363243022000053448

Lancefield, D., & Rangen, C. (2021). *4 Actions Transformational Leaders Take*. Business Management.

Langof, J., & Guldenberg, S. (2019). Servant leadership: A systematic literature review- toward a model of antecedents and outcomes. *Sage Journals*, 34, 4.

Law, K. Y., & Lee, K. M. (2016). Importing Western values versus indigenization: Social work practice with ethnic minorities in Hong Kong. *International Social Work*, 59(1), 60–72. 10.1177/0020872813500804

Lazar, J., & Preece, J. (1999) Implementing Service Learning in an Online Communities Course. *14th Annual Conference*. International Academy of Information Management.

Lazar, J., & Preece, J. (1999) Implementing Service Learning in an Online Communities Course. International Academy of Information Management.

Lederach, J. (1997). *Building peace: Sustainable reconciliation in divided societies*. United States Institute of Peace Press.

Lederach, J. P. (2015). Measuring impact in peacebuilding: Looking beyond the sum of the parts. *Journal of Peacebuilding & Development*, 10(1), 14–27. 10.1177/1542316614555755

Lee, M. Y., & Greene, G. J. (2004). A teaching framework for transformative multicultural social work education. *Journal of Ethnic & Cultural Diversity in Social Work*, 12(3), 1–28. 10.1300/J051v12n03_01

Lehtomäki, E., Moate, J., & Posti-Ahokas, H. (2015). Global connectedness in higher education: Student voices on the value of cross-cultural learning dialogue. *Studies in Higher Education*, 41(11), 2011–2027. 10.1080/03075079.2015.1007943

Lightman, D. (2004). *Power optimism: Enjoy the life you have...create the success you want*. Power Optimism.

Limb, G. E., Hodge, D. R., Ward, K., Ferrell, A., & Alboroto, R. (2018). Developing cultural competence with LDS clients: Utilizing spiritual genograms in social work practice. *Journal of Religion & Spirituality in Social Work*, 37(2), 166–181. 10.1080/15426432.2018.1448033

LImniou, M., Sedghi, N., Kumari, D., & Drousiotis, E. (2022). Student engagement, learning engagements and the Covid-19 pandemic: A comparsion between psychology and engineering undergraduate students in the UK. *Education Sciences*, 12(10).

Lindberg, C. (2022). *Transformational Leadership vs. Servant Leadership*. Webinar Recording: https://www.leadershipahoy.com/transformational-vs-servant-leadership

Compilation of References

Liu, J., & Zhang, Y. (2018). Exploring the partnership strategies between social work education and non-governmental organizations: A systematic literature review. *Social Sciences*, 7(8), 131. 10.3390/socsci7080131

Loftsdóttir, K. (2002). Never forgetting? Gender and racial-ethnic identity during fieldwork. *Social Anthropology*, 10(3), 303–317. 10.1111/j.1469-8676.2002.tb00061.x

London, M., Sessa, V. I., & Shelley, L. A. (2022). Developing self-awareness: Learning processes for self- and interpersonal growth. *Annual Review of Organizational Psychology and Organizational Behavior*, 10(1), 261–288. 10.1146/annurev-orgpsych-120920-044531

Lorenzetti, L., Dhungel, R., Lorenzetti, D., Oschepkova, T., & Haile, L. (2017, June). A transformative approach to social work education. In *Proceedings of the 3rd International Conference on Higher Education Advances* (pp. 801-809). Editorial Universitat Politècnica de València. 10.4995/HEAD17.2017.5422

Lorraine, D. (2019). *Developing Employable, Emotionally Intelligent, and Resilient Graduate Citizens of the Future*. Springer. 10.1007/978-3-030-26342-3_6

Lough, B. J., & Toms, C. (2017). Global service-learning in institutions of higher education: Concerns from a community of practice. *Globalisation, Societies and Education*. 10.1080/14767724.2017.1356705

Lough, B. (2009). Principles of effective practice in international social work field placements. *Journal of Social Work Education*, 45(3), 467–479. 10.5175/JSWE.2009.200800083

Lough, B., & Carter-Black, J. (2015). Confronting the white elephant: International volunteering and racial (dis)advantage. *Progress in Development Studies*, 15(3), 207–220. 10.1177/1464993415578983

Loya, M., & Peters, K. (2019). Critical literacy: Engaging students to enhance cultural humility in study abroad. Reflections. *Narratives of Professional Helping*, 25(1), 82–94.

Luciano, D. (2020). An immersion experience in China: Cultivating cultural humility among social work students. *Journal of Ethnographic and Qualitative Research*, 14(3), 199–215.

Luisa-Marie. (2021). *Hartmann., Stanislaw, Schukajlow*. Interest and Emotions While Solving Real-World Problems Inside and Outside the Classroom., 10.1007/978-3-030-66996-6_13

MacGinty, R., & Richmond, O. (2013). The local turn in peacebuilding: A critical agenda for peace. *Third World Quarterly*, 34(4), 763–783. 10.1080/01436597.2013.800750

Maciej, G. (2022). *Assessing Young Children's Emotional Well-Being: Enacting a Strength-Based Approach in Early Childhood Education*. 10.1007/978-981-19-5959-2_9

Magill, M., Mastroleo, N. R., Kuerbis, A., Sacco, P., Thombs-Cain, G. E., Wagner, E. F., & Velasquez, M. M. (2022). Practice makes perfect: MSW students reflect on skill-based teaching methods in clinical social work education. *Journal of Social Work Education*, 1–15. 10.1080/10437797.2022.210360538155868

Mapp, S., & Rice, K. (2019). Conducting rights-based short-term study abroad experiences. *Social Work Education*, 38(4), 427–438. 10.1080/02615479.2018.1560403

Markula, A., & Aksela, M. (2022). The key charateristics of project-based learning: How teachers implement projects in K-12 science education. *Disciplinary and Interdiscplinary Science Education Research*, 4(2).

Martin, M. E. (2015). *Advocacy for social justice: A global perspective*. Pearson.

Mathiesen, S., & Lager, P. (2007). A model for developing international student exchanges. *Social Work Education*, 26(3), 280–291. 10.1080/02615470601049867

Matthew, A. (2018, February). Scult., Ahmad, R., Hariri. (2018). A brief introduction to the neurogenetics of cognition-emotion interactions. *Current Opinion in Behavioral Sciences*, 19, 50–54. 10.1016/j.cobeha.2017.09.014

Matthew, R. (2023, October 13). The relations between students' belongingness, self-efficacy, and response to active learning in science, math, and engineering classes. *International Journal of Science Education*, 45(15), 1241–1261. 10.1080/09500693.2023.2196643

Matthews, G. (2020). Developing emotionally intelligent teachers: A panacea for quality teacher education. *International Journal on Integrated Education*, 3(6), 92–98. 10.31149/ijie.v3i10.676

Mayer, J. D., & Salovey, P. (1997). What is emotional intelligence? In Salovey, P., & Sluyter, D. J. (Eds.), *Emotional development and emotional intelligence: Educational implications* (pp. 3–31). Basic Books.

McCadden, T. (2020). Book Review: Transformational Learning in Community Colleges: Charting a Course for Academic Success by Hoggan, C. D., & Browning, B. *Adult Learning*, 136–137.

McEvoy-Levy, S. (2001). Youth as social and political agents: Issues in post-settlement peace building. *Kroc Institute Occasional Paper, 21*(OP:2), 1-36.

McGuire, D. (2020). *Adult Learning Theories*. SAGE Encyclopedia of Higher Education.

McWhinney, W., & Markos, L. (2003). Transformative Education Across The Threshold. *Journal of Transformative Education*, 1(1), 16–37. 10.1177/1541344603252098

Mehul, S. Vikas, Agarwal., Latika, Gupta. (2020). Human touch in digital education-a solution. *Clinical Rheumatology*. 10.1007/s10067-020-05448-y

Mencl, J., Wefald, A., & Ittersum, K. (2018). Transformational leader attributes: Interpersonal skills, engagement, and well-being. *Leadership and Organization Development Journal*, 37(5), 635–657. 10.1108/LODJ-09-2014-0178

Mendenhall, M. E., Reiche, S. B., Bird, A., & Osland, J. S. (2012). Defining the 'global' in global leadership. *Journal of World Business*, 47(4), 493–503. 10.1016/j.jwb.2012.01.003

Metraux, A. (2019). Voodoo in Haiti. In *Voodoo in Haiti* (pp. 1-25). Routledge (Original work published 1959).

Compilation of References

Meyers, S. (2008). Using Transformative Pedagogy When Teaching Online. *College Teaching*, 56(4), 219–224. 10.3200/CTCH.56.4.219-224

Mezirow, J. (1985). A critical theory of self-directed learning. *New directions for continuing education*, 17-30.

Mezirow, J. (1978). Perspective transformation. *Adult Education*, 28(2), 100–110. 10.1177/074171367802800202

Mezirow, J. (1991). *Transformative Dimensions of Adult Learning*. Jossey-Bass.

Mezirow, J. (1994). Understanding transformation theory. *Adult Education Quarterly*, 44(4), 222–232. 10.1177/074171369404400403

Mezirow, J. (1996). *Faced Visions and Fresh Commitments: Adult Education's Social Goals*. National Louis University.

Mezirow, J. (1997). *Transformative learning: Theory to Practice. P. Cranton içinde, Transformative Learning in Action: Insights from Practice*. Jossey-Bass.

Mezirow, J. (2000). *Learning tothinklike an adult: transformation theory: core concepts. J. Mezirow, & Associates içinde, Learning as transformation: Critical perspectives on a theory in progress*. Jossey-Bass.

Mezirow, J. (2003). Transformative Learning as Discourse. *Journal of Transformative Education*, 1(1), 58–63. 10.1177/1541344603252172

Mezirow, J., & Marsick, V. (1978). *Education for Perspective Transformation: Women's Re-entry Programs in Community Collages*. Columbia University.

Mezirow, J., & Taylor, E. (2009). *Transformative Learning in Practice: Insights from Community, Workplace, and Higher Education*. Jossey-Bass.

Midgley, J. (1995). *Social Development: The developmental perspective in social welfare*. Sage publications.

Mihaela, M. (2022, April 11). Emotional and Social Engagement in the English Language Classroom for Higher Education Students in the COVID-19 Online Context. *Sustainability (Basel)*, 14(8), 4527. 10.3390/su14084527

Minahan, A. (1981). Purpose and objectives of social work revisited [Introduction to Special Issue]. *Social Work*, 26, 5–6.

Moncrieffe, J. (2009). Intergenerational transmissions and race inequalities: Why the subjective and relational matter. *IDS Bulletin*, 40(1), 87–96. 10.1111/j.1759-5436.2009.00013.x

Moonga, F. (2018). Social protection and social work practice in Zambia. In Gray, M. (Ed.), *The Handbook of Social Work and Social Development in Africa* (pp. 72–83).

Morley, C., & Stenhouse, K. (2020). Educating for critical social work practice in mental health. *Social Work Education*, 40(1), 1–15. 10.1080/02615479.2020.1774535

Morton, T. (2017). Reconceptualizing and describing teachers' knowledge of language for content and language integrated learning (CLIL). *International Journal of Bilingual Education and Bilingualism*, 21(3), 275–286. 10.1080/13670050.2017.1383352

Mosley, P. (2005). Redesigning web design. *Academic Exchange Quarterly*.

Moudatsou, M., Stavropoulou, A., Philalithis, A., & Koukouli, S. (2020). The Role of Empathy in Health and Social Care Professionals. *Healthcare (Basel)*, 8(1), 26. 10.3390/healthcare801002632019104

Muniroh, A. (2021). Empathy Education Based Classroom Through Emotional Engagement during the Pandemic. *EDUTEC: Journal of Education And Technology*, 4(4), 644–650. 10.29062/edu.v4i4.226

Murdach, A. D. (2008). Negotiating with antisocial clients. *Social Work*, 53(2), 179–182. 10.1093/sw/53.2.17918595451

Mystakidis, S. (2021). Deep meaningful learning. *Encyclopedia*, 1(3), 988–997. 10.3390/encyclopedia1030075

Nadan, Y. (2017). Rethinking 'cultural competence' in international social work. *International Social Work*, 60(1), 74–83. 10.1177/0020872814539986

Nanda, S., & Warms, R. L. (1998). *Cultural anthropology* (6th ed.). Wadsworth.

National Association of Social Workers. (2021). *Code of Ethics*. NASW. https://www.socialworkers.org/About/Ethics/Code-of-Ethics/Code-of-Ethics-English

National Association of Social Workers. (2021). *Code of ethics*. National Association of Social Workers. https://www.socialworkers.org/About/Ethics/Code-of-Ethics/Code-of-Ethics-English

National Association of Social Workers. (2021). *NASW Code of Ethics*. NASW. https//www.socialworkers.org/About/Ethics/Code-of-Ethics/Code-of-Ethics-English

Neimeyer, R., Herrero, O., & Botella, L. (2006). Chaos to Coherence: Psychotherapy Integration of Traumatic Loss. *Journal of Constructivist Psychology*, 19(2), 127–148. 10.1080/10720530500508738

New International Version. (2023). Biblica.

Newman, M. (1994). Response to Understanding Transformation Theory. *Adult Education Quarterly*, 44(4), 236–242. 10.1177/074171369404400405

Ngai, G., Lau, K.-H., & Kwan, K.-P. (2024). A Large-Scale Study of Students' E-Service-Learning Experiences and Outcomes During the Pandemic. *Journal of Experiential Education*, 47(1), 29–52. 10.1177/10538259231171852

Compilation of References

Nguyen, T., & Tu, A. N. (2022). Developing Emotional Intelligence for Education Innovation in Schools. *VNU Journal of Science: Education Research*. 10.25073/2588-1159/vnuer.4659

Northouse, P. (2021). *Leadership: Theory and practice* (9th ed.). Sage Publications, Inc.

Noyoo, N. (2021). *Social Welfare and Social Work in Southern Africa*. African Sun Media. 10.18820/9781928480778

Nushi, M., Momeni, A., & Roshanbin, M. (2022). Characteristics of an effective university professor from students' perspective: Are the qualities changing? *Frontiers in Education*, 7, 842640. 10.3389/feduc.2022.842640

Nuttman-Shwartz, O., & Berger, R. (2012). Field education in international social work: Where we are and where we should go. *International Social Work*, 55(2), 225–243. 10.1177/0020872811414597

O'Doherty, J., McKeown, S., & Gallagher, T. (2019). The impact of a cross-community music project on young people's attitudes to peacebuilding in Northern Ireland. *Music Education Research*, 21(4), 375–389.

O'Grady, K., & Mannion, G. (2018). Crosscare's peacebuilding initiatives in Dublin: A case study in community-based approaches to conflict transformation. *Journal of Peacebuilding & Development*, 13(2), 32–47.

Ode, Y. (2023). Educator and Student Interaction in a Classroom Learning Atmosphere. AURELIA: *Jurnal Penelitian dan Pengabdian Masyarakat Indonesia*. 10.57235/aurelia.v2i1.309

Okçabol, R. (2006). *Halk eğitimi (Yetişkin eğitimi)*. Ütopya Yayınevi.

Oliver, M. (2018). *Beyond CLIL: Fostering Student and Teacher Engagement for Personal Growth and Deeper Learning*. Springer. 10.1007/978-3-319-75438-3_16

Onosu, O. (2021). The impact of study abroad on the self-identity of social work students. *Journal of International Social Work*, 64(1), 67–82.

Ortega, R., & Faller, K. C. (2011). Training child welfare workers from an intersectional cultural humility perspective: A paradigm shift. *Child Welfare*, 90(5), 27–49.22533053

Otaye-Ebede, L., Shaffakat, S., & Foster, S. (2019). A multilevel model examining the relationships between workplace spirituality, ethical climate, and outcomes: A social cognitive theory perspective. *Journal of Business Ethics*, 166(3), 611–626. 10.1007/s10551-019-04133-8

Ouma, B., & Dimaras, H. (2013). Views from the global south: Exploring how student volunteers from the global north can achieve sustainable impact in global health. *Globalization and Health*, 9(1), 1–6. 10.1186/1744-8603-9-3223889908

Oxhandler, H. K. (2017). Social work field instructors' integration of religion and spirituality in clinical practice. *Journal of Social Work Education*, 53(3), 449–465. 10.1080/10437797.2016.1269706

Oyeniyi, A. (2017). Conflict resolution in the Extractives: A consideration of traditional conflict resolution paradigms in post-colonial Africa. *Williamette Journal of International Law and Dispute Resolution*, 25(1), 56–77.

Paffenholz, T. (2015). Beyond the normative: Can women's inclusion really make for better peace processes? *International Affairs*, 91(3), 537–554.

Paffenholz, T. (2015). Unpacking the local turn in peacebuilding: A critical assessment towards an agenda for future research. *Third World Quarterly*, 36(5), 857–874. 10.1080/01436597.2015.1029908

Parker, D. (2007). *Planning for inquiry; Its not an oxymoron*. Center for Inquiry-Based Learning.

Parker, J., Crabtree, S. A., Azman, A., Carlo, D. P., & Cutler, C. (2015). Problematising international placements as a site of intercultural learning. *European Journal of Social Work*, 18(3), 383–396. 10.1080/13691457.2014.925849

Pease, B. (2010). *Undoing privilege: Unearned advantage in a divided world*. Zed Books. 10.5040/9781350223738

Phillips, J., Ajrouch, K., & Hillcoat-Nalletamby, S. (2010). *Key concepts in social Gerontology*. Sage publications. 10.4135/9781446251058

Pietrykowski, B. (1998). Modern and Postmodern Tensions in Adult Education Theory: A Response to Jack Mezirow. *Adult Education Quarterly*, 49(1), 67–70. 10.1177/074171369804900108

Plann, S. (2002). Latinos and literacy: An upper-division Spanish course with service-learning. *Hispania*, 85(2), 330–338. 10.2307/4141094

Polak, A., Pavel, J., & Bajramlić, E. (2015). Approaches, methods and techniques used for developing emotional competency in the classroom. *Studia Edukacyjne*, 34, 325–344. 10.14746/se.2015.34.20

Pon, G. (2009). Cultural competency as new racism: An ontology of forgetting. *Journal of Progressive Human Services*, 20(1), 59–71. 10.1080/10428230902871173

Pounder, J. S., & Coleman, M. (2002). Women – Better leaders than men? In general and educational management it still "all depends.". *Leadership and Organization Development Journal*, 23(3), 122–133. 10.1108/01437730210424066

Puchalski, C. M. (2023). Integrating spirituality into patient care: An essential element of person-centered care. *Polish Archives of Internal Medicine*, 123(9), 491–497. 10.20452/pamw.189324084250

Purcia, E., Ygrubay, R. A., & Marbibi, A. M. (2023). Emotions as Language Learning Enhancers of Grade 11 Students. *American Journal of Multidisciplinary Research and Innovation*, 2(3), 9–14. 10.54536/ajmri.v2i3.1543

Compilation of References

Ravulo, J. (2018). Australian students going to the Pacific Islands: International social work placements and learning across Oceania. *Aotearoa New Zealand Social Work*, 30(4), 56–69. 10.11157/anzswj-vol30iss4id613

Razack, N. (2009). Decolonizing the pedagogy and practice of international social work. *International Social Work*, 52(1), 9–21. 10.1177/0020872808097748

Razack, N. (2012). International Social Work. In Gray, M., Midgley, J., & Webb, S. (Eds.), *The Sage handbook of social work* (pp. 707–722). Sage. 10.4135/9781446247648.n46

Reisinger, Y. (2013). Transformation and Transformational Learning Theory. *Transformational tourism: Tourist perspectives*, 17-26.

Rissanen, I., Kuusisto, E., & Kuusisto, A. (2016). Developing teachers' intercultural sensitivity: Case study on a pilot course in Finnish teacher education. *Teaching and Teacher Education*, 59, 446–456. 10.1016/j.tate.2016.07.018

Roberts, A. R., Sellers, S. L., Franks, K., & Nelson, T. S. (2018). Teaching Note—Social Work Week: Harnessing the Potential of Group Practice to Achieve Transformational Learning. *Journal of Social Work Education*, 54(3), 561–567. 10.1080/10437797.2018.1434431

Rodenborg, N., & Boisen, L. A. (2013). Aversive racism and intergroup contact theories: Cultural competence in a segregated world. *Journal of Social Work Education*, 49(4), 564–579. 10.1080/10437797.2013.812463

Rodenborg, N., & Bosch, L. (2009). Intergroup dialog: Introduction. In Gitterman, A., & Salmon, R. (Eds.), *Encyclopedia of social work with groups* (pp. 78–83). Routledge.

Roe, E. P. (2015). *Exploring the influence of international social work practicums on career choices and practice approaches*. [Doctoral (PhD) thesis, Memorial University of Newfoundland]. https://research.library.mun.ca/9735/

Rogers, A. T. (2020). *Human behavior in the social environment: Perspectives on development, the life course, and macro contexts*. Routledge. 10.4324/9781003025382

Rokach, A. (2016). The impact professors have on college students. *International Journal of Studies in Nursing*, 1(1), 9. 10.20849/ijsn.v1i1.80

Romano, A. (2018). Transformative Learning: A Review of the Assessment Tools. *Journal of Transformative Learning*, 53-70.

Ronfeldt, M., Farmer, S. O., McQueen, K., & Grissom, J. A. (2015). Teacher collaboration in instructional teams and student achievement. *American Educational Research Journal*, 52(3), 475–514. 10.3102/0002831215585562

Rosen, D., McCall, J., & Goodkind, S. (2017). Teaching critical self-reflection through the lens of cultural humility: An assignment in a social work diversity course. *Social Work Education*, 36(3), 289–298. 10.1080/02615479.2017.1287260

Ross, C. (2020). *Building a Secure Learning Environment Through Social Connectedness*. Taylor & Francis. 10.4324/9780429027833-8

Şahin, M., Erisen, Y., & Çeliköz, N. (2016). The Transformational Learning of Three Adult Academicians. *Online Submission*, 299-307.

Şahin, İ. (2023). *Dönüşümsel Öğrenme ve Pozitif Psikoloji Kuramı Temelinde Spritüel Turizm Deneyimine Yönelik Ölçek Geliştirme ve Yapısal Modelleme Çalışması*. Akdeniz Üniversitesi Sosyal Bilimler Enstitüsü.

Salam, M., Awang Iskandar, D. N., Ibrahim, D. H. A., & Farooq, M. S. (2019). Service learning in higher education: A systematic literature review. *Asia Pacific Education Review*, 20(4), 573–593. 10.1007/s12564-019-09580-6

Sánchez, G., & Gavin, L. (2016). Youth and peacebuilding: From the margins to the center. *Journal of Peacebuilding & Development*, 11(1), 26–40.

Sanchez, N., Norka, A., Corbin, M., & Peters, C. (2019). Use of experiential learning, reflective writing, and metacognition to develop cultural humility among undergraduate students. *Journal of Social Work Education*, 55(1), 75–88. 10.1080/10437797.2018.1498418

Sands, D., & Tennant, M. (2010). Transformative Learning in the Context of Suicide Bereavement. *Adult Education Quarterly*, 60(2), 99–121. 10.1177/0741713609349932

Saputra, I., Rini, R., & Hariri, H. (2022). Principal's transformational leadership in the education era. *International Journal of Current Science Research and Review*, 5(8). 10.47191/ijcsrr/V5-i8-07

Schirch, L. (2011). *Measuring the impact of peacebuilding: A review of current practice*. USIP. https://www.usip.org/publications/2011/11/measuring-impact-peacebuilding-review-current-practice

Schmidt, M. E. (2021). Embracing e-service learning in the age of COVID and beyond. *Scholarship of Teaching and Learning in Psychology*. 10.1037/stl0000283

Schweinitz, K. (1984). Political Capacity in Developing Societies A. H. Somjee. *Economic Development and Cultural Change*, 33(1), 182–185. 10.1086/451452

Sebates-Wheeler, R., & Devereaux, S. (2009). Transformative Social Protection: The currency of social justice. In Barrientos, A., & Hulme, D. (Eds.), *Social Protection for the Poor and Poorest: Concepts* (pp. 64–84). Policies and Politics.

Şen, E., & Şahin, H. (2017). Dönüşümsel Öğrenme Kuramı: Baskın Paradigmayı Yıkmak. *Tıp Eğitimi Dünyası*, 39-48.

Seon, H. (2022). *The Effects of Emotional Expression Activities Using Picture Books on Young Children's Emotional Intelligence and Empathic Ability*. Korean Association For Learner-Centered Curriculum And Instruction. 10.22251/jlcci.2022.22.18.877

Compilation of References

Sewpaul, V., & Henrickson, M. (2019). The (r)evolution and decolonization of social work ethics: The global social work statement of ethical principles. *International Social Work*, 62(6), 1469–1481. 10.1177/0020872819846238

Sharma, M. (2017). *Radical Transformational Leadership*. North Atlantic Books.

Shishov, S., Popey-Ool, S., Abylkasymova, A., Kalnei, V., & Ryakhimova, E. (2022). Transformational learning of teachers. *Revista on line de Política e Gestão Educacional*, 1-10.

Silva, C. R. D., Veiga, F., Pinto, É. S., & Ferreira, I. (2020). Retention in school: Could student's affective engagement play an essential role in its prevention? *Millenium*, 14(2), 59–68.

Singgih, E. (2016). Suffering as grounds for religious tolerance: An attempt to broaden Panikkar's insight on religious pluralism. *Exchange*, 45(2), 111–129. 10.1163/1572543X-12341396

Slavich, G. (2005). Tranformational teaching. *Excellence in Teaching*, 5.

Slavich, G., & Zimbardo, P. (2012). Transformational teaching: Theoretical underpinnings, basic principles, and core methods. *Educational Psychology Review*, 24(4), 569–608. 10.1007/s10648-012-9199-623162369

Sleegers, P. (2019). Understanding school-NGO partnerships. *Journal of Educational Administration*, 57(4), 322–328. 10.1108/JEA-03-2019-0053

Sloane, H., & Petra, M. (2019). Modeling cultural humility: Listening to students' stories of religious identity. *Journal of Social Work Education*, 57(1), 1–12. 10.1080/10437797.2019.1662863

Smale, G., Tuson, G., & Statham, D. (2000). *Social work and social problems*. Macmillan Press. 10.5040/9781350392618

Sosa, L. V., & Lesniewski, J. (2020). De-colonizing study abroad: Social workers confronting racism, sexism and poverty in Guatemala. 40(2), 1-18. *Social Work Education*. 10.1080/02615479.2020.1770719

Sossou, M. A., & Dubus, N. (2013). International social work field placement or volunteer tourism? Developing an asset-based justice-learning field experience. *Journal of Learning Design*, 6(1), 10–19. 10.5204/jld.v6i1.113

Southworth, J. (2022). Bridging critical thinking and transformative learning: The role of perspective-taking. *Theory and Research in Education*, 20(1), 44–63. 10.1177/14778785221090853

Spector, B. (2013). Lee Iacocca and the origins of transformational leadership. *Leadership*, 10(3), 361–379. 10.1177/1742715013514881

Stevens, B. A. (2018). Life tasks: Excellence in spiritual care through self-awareness. *Health and Social Care Chaplaincy*, 6(2), 177–185. 10.1558/hscc.33754

Storti, C. (2001). *The Art of Crossing Cultures* (2nd ed.). Intercultural Press.

Streden, P. (1997). A.H. Somjee Development Theory: Critique and Explorations. *Economic Development and Cultural Change*, 41(1), 207–211. 10.1086/452004

Streeter, J. R. (2022). Humanizing the curriculum: Exploring the use of drama pedagogy in faculty development. In *The Routledge Companion to Drama in Education* (pp. 357–363). Routledge. 10.4324/9781003000914-38

Stuart, M. (2023). Inclusive Education for Students With Diverse Learning Needs in Mainstream Schools. *International perspectives on inclusive education*. Emerald. 10.1108/S1479-363620230000020009

Stuckey, H., Taylor, E., & Cranton, P. (2013). Developing A Survey of Transformative Learning Outcomes and Processes Based on Theoretical Principles. *Journal of Transformative Education*, 11(4), 211–228. 10.1177/1541344614540335

Suifan, T. S., Abdallah, A. B., & Al Janini, M. (2018). The impact of transformational leadership on employees' creativity. *Management Research Review*, 41(1), 113–132. 10.1108/MRR-02-2017-0032

Tascón, S. M., & Ife, J. (Eds.). (2019). *Disrupting Whiteness in social work*. Routledge. 10.4324/9780429284182

Taylor, E. (1998). *The theory and practice of transformative learning: A critical review. Information Series 374*. ERIC Clearinghouse on Adult, Career, and Vocational Education.

Taylor, E. (2008). Transformative Learning Theory. *New Directions for Adult and Continuing Education*, 2008(119), 5–15. 10.1002/ace.301

Tennant, M. (1993). Perspective Transformation and Adult Development. *Adult Education Quarterly*, 44(1), 34–42. 10.1177/0741713693044001003

Terence, . (2022, June). School connection through engagement associated with grade scores and emotions of adolescents: Four factors to build engagement in schools. *Social Psychology of Education*, 25(2-3), 675–696. 10.1007/s11218-022-09697-4

Tervalon, M., & Murray-García, J. (1998). *Cultural humility versus cultural competence: A critical distinction in defining physician training outcomes in multicultural education.*

Tervalon, M., & Murray-García, J. (1998). Cultural humility versus cultural competence: A critical distinction in defining physician training outcomes in multicultural education. *Journal of Health Care for the Poor and Underserved*, 9(2), 117–125. 10.1353/hpu.2010.023310073197

Thampi, K. (2017). Social work education crossing the borders: A field education programme for international internship. *Social Work Education*, 36(6), 609–622. 10.1080/02615479.2017.1291606

Thanh, N., & Quang, N. (2022). Transformational, transactional, laissez-faire leadership styles and employee engagement Evidence from Vietnam's public sector. *SAGE Open*, 12(2), 2022. 10.1177/21582440221094606

Compilation of References

The General Assembly of the World Medical Association. (2015). *Ethical principles of health care in the times of armed conflict and other emergencies*. WMA. https://www.wma.net/wp-content/uploads/2016/11/4245_002_Ethical_principles_web.pdf

Therese, F. (2023). Reflecting on Students' Reflections: Exploring Students' Experiences in Order to Enhance Course Delivery. *The Qualitative Report*. 10.46743/2160-3715/2023.5868

Thomas, I. (2009). Critical Thinking, Transformative Learning, Sustainable Education, And Problem-Based Learning in Universities. *Journal of Transformative Education*, 7(3), 245–264. 10.1177/1541344610385753

Tichy, N., & Ulrich, D. (1984). The leadership challenge: A call for transformational leader. *Sloan Management Review*, 26(1).

Tomaney, J., Blackman, M., Natarajan, L., Panayotopoulos-Tsiros, D., Sutcliffe-Braithwaite, F., & Taylor, M. (2023). Social infrastructure and 'left-behind places'. *Regional Studies*, 1–14.

Tomaszewski, L., Zarestky, J., & Gonzalez, E. (2020). Planning qualitative research: Design and decision making for new researchers. *International Journal of Qualitative Methods*, 19. 10.1177/1609406920967174

Torres, I., Statti, A., & Torres, K. M. (2022). Emotion and online learning. In *Online Distance Learning Course Design and Multimedia in E-Learning* (pp. 81–113). IGI Global. 10.4018/978-1-7998-9706-4.ch004

Trevithick, P. (2005). *Social work skills*. Open University Press.

Triana, M. D. C., Richard, O. C., & Yucel, I. (2017). Status incongruence and supervisor gender as moderators of the transformational leadership to subordinate affective organizational commitment relationship. *Personnel Psychology*, 70(2), 429–467. 10.1111/peps.12154

Truell, R. (2021). The role of social workers in conflict situations. *International Review of the Red Cross*, 103(912), 277–2911.

Tularam, G. A. (2018). Traditional vs non-traditional teaching and learning strategies - the case of E-learning. *International Journal for Mathematics Teaching and Learning*, 19(1), 129–158. 10.4256/ijmtl.v19i1.21

Tusting, K., & Barton, D. (2011). *Öğrenme Kuramları ve Yetişkin Öğrenme Modelleri Üzerine Kısa Bir İnceleme*. Dipnot Yayınları.

Twikirize, J., & Spitzer, H. (2019). Indigious and innovative social work practice in Africa: Evidence from East Africa, In Twikirize and Spitzer (Eds), *Social work practice in Africa: Indiginous and Innovative approaches*. Fountain Publishers

U.S. Department of State. (n.d.). *International travel*. US DoS. https://travel.state.gov/content/travel/en/international-travel.html

Ungar, M., & Hadfield, K. (2019). The differential impact of environment and resilience on youth outcomes. *Canadian Journal of Behavioural Science, 51*(2), 135-146.

Urdang, E. (2010). Awareness of self- A critical tool. *Social Work Education*, 5.

Uzun, C., & Uygun, K. (2022). The effect of simulation-based experiential learning applications on problem solving skills in social studies education. *International Journal (Toronto, Ont.).*

Van Schalkwyk, S. C., Hafler, J., Brewer, T. F., Maley, M. A., Margolis, C., McNamee, L., Meyer, I., Peluso, M. J., Schmutz, A. M., Spak, J. M., & Davies, D. (2019). Transformative learning as pedagogy for the health professions: A scoping review. *Medical Education*, 53(6), 547–558. 10.1111/medu.1380430761602

Venkatesh, S., & Fischer, C. E. (2019). Cognitive factors associated with emotional intelligence. *International Psychogeriatrics*, 31(9), 1229–1231. 10.1017/S1041610219000091734658311

Vera, D., & Crossan, M. (2004). Strategic leadership and organizational learning. *Academy of Management Review*, 29(2), 222–240. 10.2307/20159030

Vinh, N., Hien, L., & Do, Q. (2022). The relationship between transformation leadership, job satisfaction, and employee motivation in the tourism industry. *Administrative Sciences*, 12(4), 161. 10.3390/admsci12040161

Waldner, L. S., Widener, M. C., & McGorry, S. Y. (2012). E-service learning: The evolution of service-learning to engage a growing online student population. *Journal of Higher Education Outreach & Engagement*, 16(2), 123–150.

Walter, D., & Laven, D. (Eds.). (2017). *Heritage and Peacebuilding*. The Boyell Press. 10.1515/9781782049951

Wearing, S. (2001). *Volunteer tourism: Experiences that make a difference.* Oxon: CABI. Wiebe, M. (2012). Shifting sites of practice, field education in Canada. *Social Work Education, 31*(5), 681-682. https://doi.org/10.1079/9780851995335.0000

Weick, A., Rapp, C., Sullivan, W. P., & Kisthardt, W. (1989). A strengths perspective for social work practice. *Social Work*, 34(4), 350–354. 10.1093/sw/34.4.350

Weiss-Gal, I. (2008). The Person-in-Environment Approach: Professional Ideology and Practice of Workers in Israel. *Social Work*, 53(1), 65–75. 10.1093/sw/53.1.6518610822

Welsh, J., Wise, P., & Sepúlveda, J. (2023). Preface. *Daedalus*, 152(2), 6–12. 10.1162/daed_e_01988

Western Governor University. (2021). *Retrieved from Defining Transactional Leadership*. EGU. https://www.egu.edu/transactional-leadership2103.html

Wheatley, K. (2018). Inquiry-based learning: Effects on student engagement. *Student Scholarship*, 417.

White, S., & Nitkin, M. (2014). Cceating a transformational learning experience: Immersing students in an intensive interdisciplinary learning environment. *Teaching and Learning*, 8(2).

Compilation of References

Whiteman, M. (2018). *Ethics in Life and Vocation*. Milne.

Widyaningsih, R., & Kuntarto, B. (2019). Local Wisdom approach to develop counter radicalization strategy. In Proceedings of 1st International Conference on Life and Applied Sciences for Sustainable Rural Development. *IOP Conference Series. Earth and Environmental Science*, 255(1), 20–49.

Wilson, J. M., Goodman, P. S., & Cronin, M. A. (2007). Group learning. *Academy of Management Review*, 32(4), 1041–1059. 10.5465/amr.2007.26585724

Winslade, J., & Monk, G. (2008). *Practicing narrative mediation: Loosening the grip of conflict*. Jossey-Bass.

Wise, P. H., Shiel, A., Southard, N., Bendavid, E., Welsh, J., Stedman, S., Fazal, T., Felbab-Brown, V., Polatty, D., Waldman, R. J., Spiegel, P. B., Blanchet, K., Dayoub, R., Zakayo, A., Barry, M., Martinez Garcia, D., Pagano, H., Black, R., Gaffey, M. F., & Bhutta, Z. A. (2021). The political and security dimensions of the humanitarian health response to violent conflict. *Lancet*, 397(10273), 511–521. 10.1016/S0140-6736(21)00130-633503458

Wrenn, J., & Wrenn, B. (2009). Enhancing Learning by Integrating Theory and Practice. *International Journal on Teaching and Learning in Higher Education*, 21(2).

Xenikou, A. (2017). Transformational leadership, transactional contingent reward, and organizational identification: The mediating effect of perceived innovation and goal culture orientations. *Frontiers in Psychology*, 8, 8. 10.3389/fpsyg.2017.0175429093688

Xie, L. (2020). The impact of servant leadership and transformational leadership on learning organization: A comparative analysis. [Servant and transformational leadership and learning]. *Leadership and Organization Development Journal*, 41(2), 220–236. 10.1108/LODJ-04-2019-0148

Y., Reva. (2022). Humanization of pedagogical communication is effective harmonious influence on student personality development educational process. *Osvìtnìj vimìr*. 10.31812/educdim.5708

Yang, Y., & Wang, J. Z. (2017). From structure to behavior in basolateral amygdala-hippocampus circuits. *Frontiers in Neural Circuits*, 11, 86. 10.3389/fncir.2017.0008629163066

YIn, J. (2019). Connecting theory and practice in teacher education: English-as-a-foreign-language pre-service teachers' perceptions of practicum experience. *Innovación Educativa (México, D.F.)*, 1(4).

Yuner, B. (2020). Transformational teaching in higher education: The relationship between the transformational teaching of academic staff and students' self-efficacy for learning. *Educational Policy Analysis and Strategic Research*, 15(4).

Yunfei, S. (2022). The Connection Between Empathy and Equity in Higher Education. 10.4018/978-1-7998-9746-0.ch001

Yun, K., Kim, S., & Awasu, C. R. (2019). Stress and impact of spirituality as a mediator of coping methods among social work college students. *Journal of Human Behavior in the Social Environment*, 29(1), 125–136. 10.1080/10911359.2018.1491918

Zarate, M. E. (2007). Understanding Latino Parental Involvement in Education: Perceptions, Expectations, and Recommendations. Los Angeles, California. The Tomás Rivera Policy Institute. University of Southern California.

Zarate, M. E. (2007). Understanding Latino Parental Involvement in Education: Perceptions, Expectations, and Recommendations. The Tomás Rivera Policy Institute. University of Southern California.

Zgierska, A. E., Burzinski, C. A., Cox, J., Kloke, J., Stegner, A., Cook, D. B., Singles, J., Mirgain, S., Coe, C. L., & Bačkonja, M. (2016). Mindfulness meditation and cognitive behavioral therapy intervention reduces pain severity and sensitivity in opioid-treated chronic low back pain: Pilot findings from a randomized controlled trial. *Pain Medicine*, 17(10), 1865–1881. 10.1093/pm/pnw00626968850

Zhang, I. (2022). The impact of emotional arousal on amygdala activity, memory consolidation, and long-term potentiation in the hippocampus. *Journal of Student Research*, 11(2). 10.47611/jsr.v11i2.1614

Zhao, N., Fan, D., & Chen, Y. (2021). Understanding the Impact of Transformational Leadership on Project Success: A Meta-Analysis Perspective. *Computational Intelligence and Neuroscience*, 2021, 1–12. 10.1155/2021/751779134707652

Zhao, Y., Lei, J., Yan, B., Lai, C., & Tan, H. S. (2005). What makes the difference? A practical analysis of research on the effectiveness of distance education. *Teachers College Record*, 107(8), 1836–1884. 10.1177/016146810510700812

Zhu, R., Olcoń, K., Pulliam, R. M., & Gilbert, D. J. (2023). Transformative learning and the development of cultural humility in social work students. *Social Work Education*, 42(5), 694–709. 10.1080/02615479.2022.2056158

Related References

To continue our tradition of advancing academic research, we have compiled a list of recommended IGI Global readings. These references will provide additional information and guidance to further enrich your knowledge and assist you with your own research and future publications.

Aburezeq, I. M., & Dweikat, F. F. (2017). Cloud Applications in Language Teaching: Examining Pre-Service Teachers' Expertise, Perceptions and Integration. *International Journal of Distance Education Technologies*, 15(4), 39–60. 10.4018/IJDET.2017100103

Acharjya, B., & Das, S. (2022). Adoption of E-Learning During the COVID-19 Pandemic: The Moderating Role of Age and Gender. *International Journal of Web-Based Learning and Teaching Technologies*, 17(2), 1–14. https://doi.org/10.4018/IJWLTT.20220301.oa4

Adams, J. L., & Thomas, S. K. (2022). Non-Linear Curriculum Experiences for Student Learning and Work Design: What Is the Maximum Potential of a Chat Bot? In Ramlall, S., Cross, T., & Love, M. (Eds.), *Handbook of Research on Future of Work and Education: Implications for Curriculum Delivery and Work Design* (pp. 299–306). IGI Global. https://doi.org/10.4018/978-1-7998-8275-6.ch018

Adera, B. (2017). Supporting Language and Literacy Development for English Language Learners. In Keengwe, J. (Ed.), *Handbook of Research on Promoting Cross-Cultural Competence and Social Justice in Teacher Education* (pp. 339–354). Hershey, PA: IGI Global. 10.4018/978-1-5225-0897-7.ch018

Ahamer, G. (2017). Quality Assurance for a Developmental "Global Studies" (GS) Curriculum. In I. Management Association (Ed.), *Educational Leadership and Administration: Concepts, Methodologies, Tools, and Applications* (pp. 438-477). Hershey, PA: IGI Global. https://doi.org/10.4018/978-1-5225-1624-8.ch023

Ahamer, G. (2017). Quality Assurance for a Developmental "Global Studies" (GS) Curriculum. In I. Management Association (Ed.), *Educational Leadership and Administration: Concepts, Methodologies, Tools, and Applications* (pp. 438-477). Hershey, PA: IGI Global. https://doi.org/10.4018/978-1-5225-1624-8.ch023

Akayoğlu, S., & Seferoğlu, G. (2019). An Analysis of Negotiation of Meaning Functions of Advanced EFL Learners in Second Life: Negotiation of Meaning in Second Life. In Kruk, M. (Ed.), *Assessing the Effectiveness of Virtual Technologies in Foreign and Second Language Instruction* (pp. 61–85). IGI Global. https://doi.org/10.4018/978-1-5225-7286-2.ch003

Akella, N. R. (2022). Unravelling the Web of Qualitative Dissertation Writing!: A Student Reflects. In Zimmerman, A. (Ed.), *Methodological Innovations in Research and Academic Writing* (pp. 260–282). IGI Global. https://doi.org/10.4018/978-1-7998-8283-1.ch014

Alegre de la Rosa, O. M., & Angulo, L. M. (2017). Social Inclusion and Intercultural Values in a School of Education. In Mukerji, S., & Tripathi, P. (Eds.), *Handbook of Research on Administration, Policy, and Leadership in Higher Education* (pp. 518–531). Hershey, PA: IGI Global. 10.4018/978-1-5225-0672-0.ch020

Alexander, C. (2019). Using Gamification Strategies to Cultivate and Measure Professional Educator Dispositions. *International Journal of Game-Based Learning*, 9(1), 15–29. https://doi.org/10.4018/IJGBL.2019010102

Anderson, K. M. (2017). Preparing Teachers in the Age of Equity and Inclusion. In I. Management Association (Ed.), *Medical Education and Ethics: Concepts, Methodologies, Tools, and Applications* (pp. 1532-1554). Hershey, PA: IGI Global. 10.4018/978-1-5225-0978-3.ch069

Awdziej, M. (2017). Case Study as a Teaching Method in Marketing. In Latusek, D. (Ed.), *Case Studies as a Teaching Tool in Management Education* (pp. 244–263). Hershey, PA: IGI Global. 10.4018/978-1-5225-0770-3.ch013

Bakos, J. (2019). Sociolinguistic Factors Influencing English Language Learning. In Erdogan, N., & Wei, M. (Eds.), *Applied Linguistics for Teachers of Culturally and Linguistically Diverse Learners* (pp. 403–424). IGI Global. https://doi.org/10.4018/978-1-5225-8467-4.ch017

Banas, J. R., & York, C. S. (2017). Pre-Service Teachers' Motivation to Use Technology and the Impact of Authentic Learning Exercises. In Tomei, L. (Ed.), *Exploring the New Era of Technology-Infused Education* (pp. 121–140). Hershey, PA: IGI Global. 10.4018/978-1-5225-1709-2.ch008

Barton, T. P. (2021). Empowering Educator Allyship by Exploring Racial Trauma and the Disengagement of Black Students. In Reneau, C., & Villarreal, M. (Eds.), *Handbook of Research on Leading Higher Education Transformation With Social Justice, Equity, and Inclusion* (pp. 186–197). IGI Global. https://doi.org/10.4018/978-1-7998-7152-1.ch013

Benhima, M. (2021). Moroccan English Department Student Attitudes Towards the Use of Distance Education During COVID-19: Moulay Ismail University as a Case Study. *International Journal of Information and Communication Technology Education*, 17(3), 105–122. https://doi.org/10.4018/IJICTE.20210701.oa7

Beycioglu, K., & Wildy, H. (2017). Principal Preparation: The Case of Novice Principals in Turkey. In I. Management Association (Ed.), *Educational Leadership and Administration: Concepts, Methodologies, Tools, and Applications* (pp. 1152-1169). Hershey, PA: IGI Global. https://doi.org/10.4018/978-1-5225-1624-8.ch054

Bharwani, S., & Musunuri, D. (2018). Reflection as a Process From Theory to Practice. In M. Khosrow-Pour, D.B.A. (Ed.), *Encyclopedia of Information Science and Technology, Fourth Edition* (pp. 1529-1539). Hershey, PA: IGI Global. 10.4018/978-1-5225-2255-3.ch132

Bhushan, A., Garza, K. B., Perumal, O., Das, S. K., Feola, D. J., Farrell, D., & Birnbaum, A. (2022). Lessons Learned From the COVID-19 Pandemic and the Implications for Pharmaceutical Graduate Education and Research. In Ford, C., & Garza, K. (Eds.), *Handbook of Research on Updating and Innovating Health Professions Education: Post-Pandemic Perspectives* (pp. 324–345). IGI Global. https://doi.org/10.4018/978-1-7998-7623-6.ch014

Bintz, W., Ciecierski, L. M., & Royan, E. (2021). Using Picture Books With Instructional Strategies to Address New Challenges and Teach Literacy Skills in a Digital World. In Haas, L., & Tussey, J. (Eds.), *Connecting Disciplinary Literacy and Digital Storytelling in K-12 Education* (pp. 38–58). IGI Global. https://doi.org/10.4018/978-1-7998-5770-9.ch003

Bohjanen, S. L., Cameron-Standerford, A., & Meidl, T. D. (2018). Capacity Building Pedagogy for Diverse Learners. In Keengwe, J. (Ed.), *Handbook of Research on Pedagogical Models for Next-Generation Teaching and Learning* (pp. 195–212). Hershey, PA: IGI Global. 10.4018/978-1-5225-3873-8.ch011

Brewer, J. C. (2018). Measuring Text Readability Using Reading Level. In M. Khosrow-Pour, D.B.A. (Ed.), *Encyclopedia of Information Science and Technology, Fourth Edition* (pp. 1499-1507). Hershey, PA: IGI Global. 10.4018/978-1-5225-2255-3.ch129

Brookbanks, B. C. (2022). Student Perspectives on Business Education in the USA: Current Attitudes and Necessary Changes in an Age of Disruption. In Zhuplev, A., & Koepp, R. (Eds.), *Global Trends, Dynamics, and Imperatives for Strategic Development in Business Education in an Age of Disruption* (pp. 214–231). IGI Global. 10.4018/978-1-7998-7548-2.ch011

Brown, L. V., Dari, T., & Spencer, N. (2019). Addressing the Impact of Trauma in High Poverty Elementary Schools: An Ecological Model for School Counseling. In Daniels, K., & Billingsley, K. (Eds.), *Creating Caring and Supportive Educational Environments for Meaningful Learning* (pp. 135–153). IGI Global. https://doi.org/10.4018/978-1-5225-5748-7.ch008

Brown, S. L. (2017). A Case Study of Strategic Leadership and Research in Practice: Principal Preparation Programs that Work – An Educational Administration Perspective of Best Practices for Master's Degree Programs for Principal Preparation. In Wang, V. (Ed.), *Encyclopedia of Strategic Leadership and Management* (pp. 1226–1244). Hershey, PA: IGI Global. 10.4018/978-1-5225-1049-9.ch086

Brzozowski, M., & Ferster, I. (2017). Educational Management Leadership: High School Principal's Management Style and Parental Involvement in School Management in Israel. In Potocan, V., Ünğan, M., & Nedelko, Z. (Eds.), *Handbook of Research on Managerial Solutions in Non-Profit Organizations* (pp. 55–74). Hershey, PA: IGI Global. 10.4018/978-1-5225-0731-4.ch003

Cahapay, M. B. (2020). Delphi Technique in the Development of Emerging Contents in High School Science Curriculum. *International Journal of Curriculum Development and Learning Measurement*, 1(2), 1–9. https://doi.org/10.4018/IJCDLM.2020070101

Camacho, L. F., & Leon Guerrero, A. E. (2022). Indigenous Student Experience in Higher Education: Implementation of Culturally Sensitive Support. In Pangelinan, P., & McVey, T. (Eds.), *Learning and Reconciliation Through Indigenous Education in Oceania* (pp. 254–266). IGI Global. https://doi.org/10.4018/978-1-7998-7736-3.ch016

Cannaday, J. (2017). The Masking Effect: Hidden Gifts and Disabilities of 2e Students. In Dickenson, P., Keough, P., & Courduff, J. (Eds.), *Preparing Pre-Service Teachers for the Inclusive Classroom* (pp. 220–231). Hershey, PA: IGI Global. 10.4018/978-1-5225-1753-5.ch011

Cederquist, S., Fishman, B., & Teasley, S. D. (2022). What's Missing From the College Transcript?: How Employers Make Sense of Student Skills. In Huang, Y. (Ed.), *Handbook of Research on Credential Innovations for Inclusive Pathways to Professions* (pp. 234–253). IGI Global. https://doi.org/10.4018/978-1-7998-3820-3.ch012

Cockrell, P., & Gibson, T. (2019). The Untold Stories of Black and Brown Student Experiences in Historically White Fraternities and Sororities. In Hoffman-Miller, P., James, M., & Hermond, D. (Eds.), *African American Suburbanization and the Consequential Loss of Identity* (pp. 153–171). IGI Global. https://doi.org/10.4018/978-1-5225-7835-2.ch009

Cohen, M. (2022). Leveraging Content Creation to Boost Student Engagement. In Driscoll, T.III, (Ed.), *Designing Effective Distance and Blended Learning Environments in K-12* (pp. 223–239). IGI Global. https://doi.org/10.4018/978-1-7998-6829-3.ch013

Contreras, E. C., & Contreras, I. I. (2018). Development of Communication Skills through Auditory Training Software in Special Education. In M. Khosrow-Pour, D.B.A. (Ed.), *Encyclopedia of Information Science and Technology, Fourth Edition* (pp. 2431-2441). Hershey, PA: IGI Global. 10.4018/978-1-5225-2255-3.ch212

Cooke, L., Schugar, J., Schugar, H., Penny, C., & Bruning, H. (2020). Can Everyone Code?: Preparing Teachers to Teach Computer Languages as a Literacy. In Mitchell, J., & Vaughn, E. (Eds.), *Participatory Literacy Practices for P-12 Classrooms in the Digital Age* (pp. 163–183). IGI Global. https://doi.org/10.4018/978-1-7998-0000-2.ch009

Cooley, D., & Whitten, E. (2017). Special Education Leadership and the Implementation of Response to Intervention. In Topor, F. (Ed.), *Handbook of Research on Individualism and Identity in the Globalized Digital Age* (pp. 265–286). Hershey, PA: IGI Global. 10.4018/978-1-5225-0522-8.ch012

Cosner, S., Tozer, S., & Zavitkovsky, P. (2017). Enacting a Cycle of Inquiry Capstone Research Project in Doctoral-Level Leadership Preparation. In I. Management Association (Ed.), *Educational Leadership and Administration: Concepts, Methodologies, Tools, and Applications* (pp. 1460-1481). Hershey, PA: IGI Global. 10.4018/978-1-5225-1624-8.ch067

Crawford, C. M. (2018). Instructional Real World Community Engagement. In M. Khosrow-Pour, D.B.A. (Ed.), *Encyclopedia of Information Science and Technology, Fourth Edition* (pp. 1474-1486). Hershey, PA: IGI Global. 10.4018/978-1-5225-2255-3.ch127

Crosby-Cooper, T., & Pacis, D. (2017). Implementing Effective Student Support Teams. In Dickenson, P., Keough, P., & Courduff, J. (Eds.), *Preparing Pre-Service Teachers for the Inclusive Classroom* (pp. 248–262). Hershey, PA: IGI Global. 10.4018/978-1-5225-1753-5.ch013

Curran, C. M., & Hawbaker, B. W. (2017). Cultivating Communities of Inclusive Practice: Professional Development for Educators – Research and Practice. In Curran, C., & Petersen, A. (Eds.), *Handbook of Research on Classroom Diversity and Inclusive Education Practice* (pp. 120–153). Hershey, PA: IGI Global. 10.4018/978-1-5225-2520-2.ch006

Dass, S., & Dabbagh, N. (2018). Faculty Adoption of 3D Avatar-Based Virtual World Learning Environments: An Exploratory Case Study. In I. Management Association (Ed.), *Technology Adoption and Social Issues: Concepts, Methodologies, Tools, and Applications* (pp. 1000-1033). Hershey, PA: IGI Global. https://doi.org/10.4018/978-1-5225-5201-7.ch045

Davison, A. M., & Scholl, K. G. (2017). Inclusive Recreation as Part of the IEP Process. In Curran, C., & Petersen, A. (Eds.), *Handbook of Research on Classroom Diversity and Inclusive Education Practice* (pp. 311–330). Hershey, PA: IGI Global. 10.4018/978-1-5225-2520-2.ch013

DeCoito, I. (2018). Addressing Digital Competencies, Curriculum Development, and Instructional Design in Science Teacher Education. In M. Khosrow-Pour, D.B.A. (Ed.), *Encyclopedia of Information Science and Technology, Fourth Edition* (pp. 1420-1431). Hershey, PA: IGI Global. https://doi.org/10.4018/978-1-5225-2255-3.ch122

DeCoito, I., & Richardson, T. (2017). Beyond Angry Birds™: Using Web-Based Tools to Engage Learners and Promote Inquiry in STEM Learning. In Levin, I., & Tsybulsky, D. (Eds.), *Digital Tools and Solutions for Inquiry-Based STEM Learning* (pp. 166–196). Hershey, PA: IGI Global. 10.4018/978-1-5225-2525-7.ch007

Delmas, P. M. (2017). Research-Based Leadership for Next-Generation Leaders. In Styron, R.Jr, & Styron, J. (Eds.), *Comprehensive Problem-Solving and Skill Development for Next-Generation Leaders* (pp. 1–39). Hershey, PA: IGI Global. 10.4018/978-1-5225-1968-3.ch001

Demiray, U., & Ekren, G. (2018). Administrative-Related Evaluation for Distance Education Institutions in Turkey. In Buyuk, K., Kocdar, S., & Bozkurt, A. (Eds.), *Administrative Leadership in Open and Distance Learning Programs* (pp. 263–288). Hershey, PA: IGI Global. 10.4018/978-1-5225-2645-2.ch011

Dickenson, P. (2017). What do we Know and Where Can We Grow?: Teachers Preparation for the Inclusive Classroom. In Dickenson, P., Keough, P., & Courduff, J. (Eds.), *Preparing Pre-Service Teachers for the Inclusive Classroom* (pp. 1–22). Hershey, PA: IGI Global. 10.4018/978-1-5225-1753-5.ch001

Ding, Q., & Zhu, H. (2021). Flipping the Classroom in STEM Education. In Keengwe, J. (Ed.), *Handbook of Research on Innovations in Non-Traditional Educational Practices* (pp. 155–173). IGI Global. https://doi.org/10.4018/978-1-7998-4360-3.ch008

Dixon, T., & Christison, M. (2021). Teaching English Grammar in a Hybrid Academic ESL Course: A Mixed Methods Study. In Kelch, K., Byun, P., Safavi, S., & Cervantes, S. (Eds.), *CALL Theory Applications for Online TESOL Education* (pp. 229–251). IGI Global. https://doi.org/10.4018/978-1-7998-6609-1.ch010

Donne, V., & Hansen, M. (2017). Teachers' Use of Assistive Technologies in Education. In Tomei, L. (Ed.), *Exploring the New Era of Technology-Infused Education* (pp. 86–101). Hershey, PA: IGI Global. 10.4018/978-1-5225-1709-2.ch006

Donne, V., & Hansen, M. A. (2018). Business and Technology Educators: Practices for Inclusion. In I. Management Association (Ed.), *Business Education and Ethics: Concepts, Methodologies, Tools, and Applications* (pp. 471-484). Hershey, PA: IGI Global. https://doi.org/10.4018/978-1-5225-3153-1.ch026

Dos Santos, L. M. (2022). Completing Student-Teaching Internships Online: Instructional Changes During the COVID-19 Pandemic. In Alaali, M. (Ed.), *Assessing University Governance and Policies in Relation to the COVID-19 Pandemic* (pp. 106–127). IGI Global. https://doi.org/10.4018/978-1-7998-8279-4.ch007

Dreon, O., Shettel, J., & Bower, K. M. (2017). Preparing Next Generation Elementary Teachers for the Tools of Tomorrow. In Grassetti, M., & Brookby, S. (Eds.), *Advancing Next-Generation Teacher Education through Digital Tools and Applications* (pp. 143–159). Hershey, PA: IGI Global. 10.4018/978-1-5225-0965-3.ch008

Durak, H. Y., & Güyer, T. (2018). Design and Development of an Instructional Program for Teaching Programming Processes to Gifted Students Using Scratch. In Cannaday, J. (Ed.), *Curriculum Development for Gifted Education Programs* (pp. 61–99). Hershey, PA: IGI Global. 10.4018/978-1-5225-3041-1.ch004

Egorkina, E., Ivanov, M., & Valyavskiy, A. Y. (2018). Students' Research Competence Formation of the Quality of Open and Distance Learning. In Mkrttchian, V., & Belyanina, L. (Eds.), *Handbook of Research on Students' Research Competence in Modern Educational Contexts* (pp. 364–384). Hershey, PA: IGI Global. 10.4018/978-1-5225-3485-3.ch019

Ekren, G., Karataş, S., & Demiray, U. (2017). Understanding of Leadership in Distance Education Management. In I. Management Association (Ed.), *Educational Leadership and Administration: Concepts, Methodologies, Tools, and Applications* (pp. 34-50). Hershey, PA: IGI Global. https://doi.org/10.4018/978-1-5225-1624-8.ch003

Elmore, W. M., Young, J. K., Harris, S., & Mason, D. (2017). The Relationship between Individual Student Attributes and Online Course Completion. In Shelton, K., & Pedersen, K. (Eds.), *Handbook of Research on Building, Growing, and Sustaining Quality E-Learning Programs* (pp. 151–173). Hershey, PA: IGI Global. 10.4018/978-1-5225-0877-9.ch008

Ercegovac, I. R., Alfirević, N., & Koludrović, M. (2017). School Principals' Communication and Co-Operation Assessment: The Croatian Experience. In I. Management Association (Ed.), *Educational Leadership and Administration: Concepts, Methodologies, Tools, and Applications* (pp. 1568-1589). Hershey, PA: IGI Global. https://doi.org/10.4018/978-1-5225-1624-8.ch072

Everhart, D., & Seymour, D. M. (2017). Challenges and Opportunities in the Currency of Higher Education. In Rasmussen, K., Northrup, P., & Colson, R. (Eds.), *Handbook of Research on Competency-Based Education in University Settings* (pp. 41–65). Hershey, PA: IGI Global. 10.4018/978-1-5225-0932-5.ch003

Farmer, L. S. (2017). Managing Portable Technologies for Special Education. In Wang, V. (Ed.), *Encyclopedia of Strategic Leadership and Management* (pp. 977–987). Hershey, PA: IGI Global. 10.4018/978-1-5225-1049-9.ch068

Farmer, L. S. (2018). Optimizing OERs for Optimal ICT Literacy in Higher Education. In Keengwe, J. (Ed.), *Handbook of Research on Mobile Technology, Constructivism, and Meaningful Learning* (pp. 366–390). Hershey, PA: IGI Global. 10.4018/978-1-5225-3949-0.ch020

Ferguson, B. T. (2019). Supporting Affective Development of Children With Disabilities Through Moral Dilemmas. In Ikuta, S. (Ed.), *Handmade Teaching Materials for Students With Disabilities* (pp. 253–275). IGI Global. 10.4018/978-1-5225-6240-5.ch011

Fındık, L. Y. (2017). Self-Assessment of Principals Based on Leadership in Complexity. In I. Management Association (Ed.), *Educational Leadership and Administration: Concepts, Methodologies, Tools, and Applications* (pp. 978-991). Hershey, PA: IGI Global. https://doi.org/10.4018/978-1-5225-1624-8.ch047

Flor, A. G., & Gonzalez-Flor, B. (2018). Dysfunctional Digital Demeanors: Tales From (and Policy Implications of) eLearning's Dark Side. In I. Management Association (Ed.), The Dark Web: Breakthroughs in Research and Practice (pp. 37-50). Hershey, PA: IGI Global. https://doi.org/10.4018/978-1-5225-3163-0.ch003

Floyd, K. K., & Shambaugh, N. (2017). Instructional Design for Simulations in Special Education Virtual Learning Spaces. In Kidd, T., & Morris, L.Jr., (Eds.), *Handbook of Research on Instructional Systems and Educational Technology* (pp. 202–215). Hershey, PA: IGI Global. 10.4018/978-1-5225-2399-4.ch018

Freeland, S. F. (2020). Community Schools: Improving Academic Achievement Through Meaningful Engagement. In Kronick, R. (Ed.), *Emerging Perspectives on Community Schools and the Engaged University* (pp. 132–144). IGI Global. https://doi.org/10.4018/978-1-7998-0280-8.ch008

Ghanbarzadeh, R., & Ghapanchi, A. H. (2019). Applied Areas of Three Dimensional Virtual Worlds in Learning and Teaching: A Review of Higher Education. In I. Management Association (Ed.), *Virtual Reality in Education: Breakthroughs in Research and Practice* (pp. 172-192). IGI Global. https://doi.org/10.4018/978-1-5225-8179-6.ch008

Giovannini, J. M. (2017). Technology Integration in Preservice Teacher Education Programs: Research-based Recommendations. In Grassetti, M., & Brookby, S. (Eds.), *Advancing Next-Generation Teacher Education through Digital Tools and Applications* (pp. 82–102). Hershey, PA: IGI Global. 10.4018/978-1-5225-0965-3.ch005

Good, S., & Clarke, V. B. (2017). An Integral Analysis of One Urban School System's Efforts to Support Student-Centered Teaching. In Keengwe, J., & Onchwari, G. (Eds.), *Handbook of Research on Learner-Centered Pedagogy in Teacher Education and Professional Development* (pp. 45–68). Hershey, PA: IGI Global. 10.4018/978-1-5225-0892-2.ch003

Guetzoian, E. (2022). Gamification Strategies for Higher Education Student Worker Training. In Lane, C. (Ed.), *Handbook of Research on Acquiring 21st Century Literacy Skills Through Game-Based Learning* (pp. 164–179). IGI Global. https://doi.org/10.4018/978-1-7998-7271-9.ch009

Hamidi, F., Owuor, P. M., Hynie, M., Baljko, M., & McGrath, S. (2017). Potentials of Digital Assistive Technology and Special Education in Kenya. In Ayo, C., & Mbarika, V. (Eds.), *Sustainable ICT Adoption and Integration for Socio-Economic Development* (pp. 125–151). Hershey, PA: IGI Global. 10.4018/978-1-5225-2565-3.ch006

Hamim, T., Benabbou, F., & Sael, N. (2022). Student Profile Modeling Using Boosting Algorithms. *International Journal of Web-Based Learning and Teaching Technologies*, 17(5), 1–13. https://doi.org/10.4018/IJWLTT.20220901.oa4

Henderson, L. K. (2017). Meltdown at Fukushima: Global Catastrophic Events, Visual Literacy, and Art Education. In Shin, R. (Ed.), *Convergence of Contemporary Art, Visual Culture, and Global Civic Engagement* (pp. 80–99). Hershey, PA: IGI Global. 10.4018/978-1-5225-1665-1.ch005

Hudgins, T., & Holland, J. L. (2018). Digital Badges: Tracking Knowledge Acquisition Within an Innovation Framework. In I. Management Association (Ed.), *Wearable Technologies: Concepts, Methodologies, Tools, and Applications* (pp. 1118-1132). Hershey, PA: IGI Global. https://doi.org/10.4018/978-1-5225-5484-4.ch051

Hwang, R., Lin, H., Sun, J. C., & Wu, J. (2019). Improving Learning Achievement in Science Education for Elementary School Students via Blended Learning. *International Journal of Online Pedagogy and Course Design*, 9(2), 44–62. https://doi.org/10.4018/IJOPCD.2019040104

Jančec, L., & Vodopivec, J. L. (2019). The Implicit Pedagogy and the Hidden Curriculum in Postmodern Education. In Vodopivec, J., Jančec, L., & Štemberger, T. (Eds.), *Implicit Pedagogy for Optimized Learning in Contemporary Education* (pp. 41–59). IGI Global. https://doi.org/10.4018/978-1-5225-5799-9.ch003

Janus, M., & Siddiqua, A. (2018). Challenges for Children With Special Health Needs at the Time of Transition to School. In I. Management Association (Ed.), *Autism Spectrum Disorders: Breakthroughs in Research and Practice* (pp. 339-371). Hershey, PA: IGI Global. 10.4018/978-1-5225-3827-1.ch018

Jesus, R. A. (2018). Screencasts and Learning Styles. In M. Khosrow-Pour, D.B.A. (Ed.), *Encyclopedia of Information Science and Technology, Fourth Edition* (pp. 1548-1558). Hershey, PA: IGI Global. 10.4018/978-1-5225-2255-3.ch134

John, G., Francis, N., & Santhakumar, A. B. (2022). Student Engagement: Past, Present, and Future. In Ramlall, S., Cross, T., & Love, M. (Eds.), *Handbook of Research on Future of Work and Education: Implications for Curriculum Delivery and Work Design* (pp. 329–341). IGI Global. https://doi.org/10.4018/978-1-7998-8275-6.ch020

Karpinski, A. C., D'Agostino, J. V., Williams, A. K., Highland, S. A., & Mellott, J. A. (2018). The Relationship Between Online Formative Assessment and State Test Scores Using Multilevel Modeling. In M. Khosrow-Pour, D.B.A. (Ed.), *Encyclopedia of Information Science and Technology, Fourth Edition* (pp. 5183-5192). Hershey, PA: IGI Global. 10.4018/978-1-5225-2255-3.ch450

Kats, Y. (2017). Educational Leadership and Integrated Support for Students with Autism Spectrum Disorders. In I. Management Association (Ed.), *Educational Leadership and Administration: Concepts, Methodologies, Tools, and Applications* (pp. 101-114). Hershey, PA: IGI Global. https://doi.org/10.4018/978-1-5225-1624-8.ch007

Kaya, G., & Altun, A. (2018). Educational Ontology Development. In M. Khosrow-Pour, D.B.A. (Ed.), *Encyclopedia of Information Science and Technology, Fourth Edition* (pp. 1441-1450). Hershey, PA: IGI Global. 10.4018/978-1-5225-2255-3.ch124

Keough, P. D., & Pacis, D. (2017). Best Practices Implementing Special Education Curriculum and Common Core State Standards using UDL. In Dickenson, P., Keough, P., & Courduff, J. (Eds.), *Preparing Pre-Service Teachers for the Inclusive Classroom* (pp. 107–123). Hershey, PA: IGI Global. 10.4018/978-1-5225-1753-5.ch006

Kilburn, M., Henckell, M., & Starrett, D. (2018). Factors Contributing to the Effectiveness of Online Students and Instructors. In M. Khosrow-Pour, D.B.A. (Ed.), *Encyclopedia of Information Science and Technology, Fourth Edition* (pp. 1451-1462). Hershey, PA: IGI Global. 10.4018/978-1-5225-2255-3.ch125

Koban Koç, D. (2021). Gender and Language: A Sociolinguistic Analysis of Second Language Writing. In Hancı-Azizoglu, E., & Kavaklı, N. (Eds.), *Futuristic and Linguistic Perspectives on Teaching Writing to Second Language Students* (pp. 161–177). IGI Global. https://doi.org/10.4018/978-1-7998-6508-7.ch010

Konecny, L. T. (2017). Hybrid, Online, and Flipped Classrooms in Health Science: Enhanced Learning Environments. In I. Management Association (Ed.), *Flipped Instruction: Breakthroughs in Research and Practice* (pp. 355-370). Hershey, PA: IGI Global. https://doi.org/10.4018/978-1-5225-1803-7.ch020

Kupietz, K. D. (2021). Gaming and Simulation in Public Education: Teaching Others to Help Themselves and Their Neighbors. In Drumhiller, N., Wilkin, T., & Srba, K. (Eds.), *Simulation and Game-Based Learning in Emergency and Disaster Management* (pp. 41–62). IGI Global. https://doi.org/10.4018/978-1-7998-4087-9.ch003

Kwee, C. T. (2022). Assessing the International Student Enrolment Strategies in Australian Universities: A Case Study During the COVID-19 Pandemic. In Alaali, M. (Ed.), *Assessing University Governance and Policies in Relation to the COVID-19 Pandemic* (pp. 162–188). IGI Global. https://doi.org/10.4018/978-1-7998-8279-4.ch010

Lauricella, S., & McArthur, F. A. (2022). Taking a Student-Centred Approach to Alternative Digital Credentials: Multiple Pathways Toward the Acquisition of Microcredentials. In Piedra, D. (Ed.), *Innovations in the Design and Application of Alternative Digital Credentials* (pp. 57–69). IGI Global. https://doi.org/10.4018/978-1-7998-7697-7.ch003

Llamas, M. F. (2019). Intercultural Awareness in Teaching English for Early Childhood: A Film-Based Approach. In Domínguez Romero, E., Bobkina, J., & Stefanova, S. (Eds.), *Teaching Literature and Language Through Multimodal Texts* (pp. 54–68). IGI Global. https://doi.org/10.4018/978-1-5225-5796-8.ch004

Lokhtina, I., & Kkese, E. T. (2022). Reflecting and Adapting to an Academic Workplace Before and After the Lockdown in Greek-Speaking Cyprus: Opportunities and Challenges. In Zhuplev, A., & Koepp, R. (Eds.), *Global Trends, Dynamics, and Imperatives for Strategic Development in Business Education in an Age of Disruption* (pp. 126–148). IGI Global. https://doi.org/10.4018/978-1-7998-7548-2.ch007

Lovell, K. L. (2017). Development and Evaluation of Neuroscience Computer-Based Modules for Medical Students: Instructional Design Principles and Effectiveness. In Stefaniak, J. (Ed.), *Advancing Medical Education Through Strategic Instructional Design* (pp. 262–276). Hershey, PA: IGI Global. 10.4018/978-1-5225-2098-6.ch013

Maher, D. (2019). The Use of Course Management Systems in Pre-Service Teacher Education. In Keengwe, J. (Ed.), *Handbook of Research on Blended Learning Pedagogies and Professional Development in Higher Education* (pp. 196–213). IGI Global. https://doi.org/10.4018/978-1-5225-5557-5.ch011

Makewa, L. N. (2019). Teacher Technology Competence Base. In Makewa, L., Ngussa, B., & Kuboja, J. (Eds.), *Technology-Supported Teaching and Research Methods for Educators* (pp. 247–267). IGI Global. https://doi.org/10.4018/978-1-5225-5915-3.ch014

Mallett, C. A. (2022). School Resource (Police) Officers in Schools: Impact on Campus Safety, Student Discipline, and Learning. In Crews, G. (Ed.), *Impact of School Shootings on Classroom Culture, Curriculum, and Learning* (pp. 53–70). IGI Global. https://doi.org/10.4018/978-1-7998-5200-1.ch004

Marinho, J. E., Freitas, I. R., Leão, I. B., Pacheco, L. O., Gonçalves, M. P., Castro, M. J., Silva, P. D., & Moreira, R. J. (2022). Project-Based Learning Application in Higher Education: Student Experiences and Perspectives. In Alves, A., & van Hattum-Janssen, N. (Eds.), *Training Engineering Students for Modern Technological Advancement* (pp. 146–164). IGI Global. https://doi.org/10.4018/978-1-7998-8816-1.ch007

McCleskey, J. A., & Melton, R. M. (2022). Rolling With the Flow: Online Faculty and Student Presence in a Post-COVID-19 World. In Ramlall, S., Cross, T., & Love, M. (Eds.), *Handbook of Research on Future of Work and Education: Implications for Curriculum Delivery and Work Design* (pp. 307–328). IGI Global. https://doi.org/10.4018/978-1-7998-8275-6.ch019

McCormack, V. F., Stauffer, M., Fishley, K., Hohenbrink, J., Mascazine, J. R., & Zigler, T. (2018). Designing a Dual Licensure Path for Middle Childhood and Special Education Teacher Candidates. In Polly, D., Putman, M., Petty, T., & Good, A. (Eds.), *Innovative Practices in Teacher Preparation and Graduate-Level Teacher Education Programs* (pp. 21–36). Hershey, PA: IGI Global. 10.4018/978-1-5225-3068-8.ch002

McDaniel, R. (2017). Strategic Leadership in Instructional Design: Applying the Principles of Instructional Design through the Lens of Strategic Leadership to Distance Education. In Wang, V. (Ed.), *Encyclopedia of Strategic Leadership and Management* (pp. 1570–1584). Hershey, PA: IGI Global. 10.4018/978-1-5225-1049-9.ch109

McKinney, R. E., Halli-Tierney, A. D., Gold, A. E., Allen, R. S., & Carroll, D. G. (2022). Interprofessional Education: Using Standardized Cases in Face-to-Face and Remote Learning Settings. In Ford, C., & Garza, K. (Eds.), *Handbook of Research on Updating and Innovating Health Professions Education: Post-Pandemic Perspectives* (pp. 24–42). IGI Global. https://doi.org/10.4018/978-1-7998-7623-6.ch002

Meintjes, H. H. (2021). Learner Views of a Facebook Page as a Supportive Digital Pedagogical Tool at a Public South African School in a Grade 12 Business Studies Class. *International Journal of Smart Education and Urban Society*, 12(2), 32–45. https://doi.org/10.4018/IJSEUS.2021040104

Melero-García, F. (2022). Training Bilingual Interpreters in Healthcare Settings: Student Perceptions of Online Learning. In LeLoup, J., & Swanson, P. (Eds.), *Handbook of Research on Effective Online Language Teaching in a Disruptive Environment* (pp. 288–310). IGI Global. https://doi.org/10.4018/978-1-7998-7720-2.ch015

Meletiadou, E. (2022). The Use of Peer Assessment as an Inclusive Learning Strategy in Higher Education Institutions: Enhancing Student Writing Skills and Motivation. In Meletiadou, E. (Ed.), *Handbook of Research on Policies and Practices for Assessing Inclusive Teaching and Learning* (pp. 1–26). IGI Global. https://doi.org/10.4018/978-1-7998-8579-5.ch001

Memon, R. N., Ahmad, R., & Salim, S. S. (2018). Critical Issues in Requirements Engineering Education. In I. Management Association (Ed.), *Computer Systems and Software Engineering: Concepts, Methodologies, Tools, and Applications* (pp. 1953-1976). Hershey, PA: IGI Global. 10.4018/978-1-5225-3923-0.ch081

Mendenhall, R. (2017). Western Governors University: CBE Innovator and National Model. In Rasmussen, K., Northrup, P., & Colson, R. (Eds.), *Handbook of Research on Competency-Based Education in University Settings* (pp. 379–400). Hershey, PA: IGI Global. 10.4018/978-1-5225-0932-5.ch019

Mense, E. G., Griggs, D. M., & Shanks, J. N. (2018). School Leaders in a Time of Accountability and Data Use: Preparing Our Future School Leaders in Leadership Preparation Programs. In Mense, E., & Crain-Dorough, M. (Eds.), *Data Leadership for K-12 Schools in a Time of Accountability* (pp. 235–259). Hershey, PA: IGI Global. 10.4018/978-1-5225-3188-3.ch012

Mense, E. G., Griggs, D. M., & Shanks, J. N. (2018). School Leaders in a Time of Accountability and Data Use: Preparing Our Future School Leaders in Leadership Preparation Programs. In Mense, E., & Crain-Dorough, M. (Eds.), *Data Leadership for K-12 Schools in a Time of Accountability* (pp. 235–259). Hershey, PA: IGI Global. 10.4018/978-1-5225-3188-3.ch012

Mestry, R., & Naicker, S. R. (2017). Exploring Distributive Leadership in South African Public Primary Schools in the Soweto Region. In I. Management Association (Ed.), *Educational Leadership and Administration: Concepts, Methodologies, Tools, and Applications* (pp. 1041-1064). Hershey, PA: IGI Global. 10.4018/978-1-5225-1624-8.ch050

Monaghan, C. H., & Boboc, M. (2017). (Re)Defining Leadership in Higher Education in the U.S. In Wang, V. (Ed.), *Encyclopedia of Strategic Leadership and Management* (pp. 567–579). Hershey, PA: IGI Global. 10.4018/978-1-5225-1049-9.ch040

Morall, M. B. (2021). Reimagining Mobile Phones: Multiple Literacies and Digital Media Compositions. In C. Moran (Eds.), *Affordances and Constraints of Mobile Phone Use in English Language Arts Classrooms* (pp. 41-53). IGI Global. https://doi.org/10.4018/978-1-7998-5805-8.ch003

Mthethwa, V. (2022). Student Governance and the Academic Minefield During COVID-19 Lockdown in South Africa. In Alaali, M. (Ed.), *Assessing University Governance and Policies in Relation to the COVID-19 Pandemic* (pp. 255–276). IGI Global. https://doi.org/10.4018/978-1-7998-8279-4.ch015

Muthee, J. M., & Murungi, C. G. (2018). Relationship Among Intelligence, Achievement Motivation, Type of School, and Academic Performance of Kenyan Urban Primary School Pupils. In M. Khosrow-Pour, D.B.A. (Ed.), *Encyclopedia of Information Science and Technology, Fourth Edition* (pp. 1540-1547). Hershey, PA: IGI Global. https://doi.org/10.4018/978-1-5225-2255-3.ch133

Naranjo, J. (2018). Meeting the Need for Inclusive Educators Online: Teacher Education in Inclusive Special Education and Dual-Certification. In Polly, D., Putman, M., Petty, T., & Good, A. (Eds.), *Innovative Practices in Teacher Preparation and Graduate-Level Teacher Education Programs* (pp. 106–122). Hershey, PA: IGI Global. 10.4018/978-1-5225-3068-8.ch007

Nkabinde, Z. P. (2017). Multiculturalism in Special Education: Perspectives of Minority Children in Urban Schools. In Keengwe, J. (Ed.), *Handbook of Research on Promoting Cross-Cultural Competence and Social Justice in Teacher Education* (pp. 382–397). Hershey, PA: IGI Global. 10.4018/978-1-5225-0897-7.ch020

Nkabinde, Z. P. (2018). Online Instruction: Is the Quality the Same as Face-to-Face Instruction? In Keengwe, J. (Ed.), *Handbook of Research on Digital Content, Mobile Learning, and Technology Integration Models in Teacher Education* (pp. 300–314). Hershey, PA: IGI Global. 10.4018/978-1-5225-2953-8.ch016

Nugroho, A., & Albusaidi, S. S. (2022). Internationalization of Higher Education: The Methodological Critiques on the Research Related to Study Overseas and International Experience. In Magd, H., & Kunjumuhammed, S. (Eds.), *Global Perspectives on Quality Assurance and Accreditation in Higher Education Institutions* (pp. 75–89). IGI Global. https://doi.org/10.4018/978-1-7998-8085-1.ch005

Nulty, Z., & West, S. G. (2022). Student Engagement and Supporting Students With Accommodations. In Bull, P., & Patterson, G. (Eds.), *Redefining Teacher Education and Teacher Preparation Programs in the Post-COVID-19 Era* (pp. 99–116). IGI Global. https://doi.org/10.4018/978-1-7998-8298-5.ch006

O'Connor, J. R.Jr, & Jackson, K. N. (2017). The Use of iPad® Devices and "Apps" for ASD Students in Special Education and Speech Therapy. In Kats, Y. (Ed.), *Supporting the Education of Children with Autism Spectrum Disorders* (pp. 267–283). Hershey, PA: IGI Global. 10.4018/978-1-5225-0816-8.ch014

Okolie, U. C., & Yasin, A. M. (2017). TVET in Developing Nations and Human Development. In Okolie, U., & Yasin, A. (Eds.), *Technical Education and Vocational Training in Developing Nations* (pp. 1–25). Hershey, PA: IGI Global. 10.4018/978-1-5225-1811-2.ch001

Pack, A., & Barrett, A. (2021). A Review of Virtual Reality and English for Academic Purposes: Understanding Where to Start. *International Journal of Computer-Assisted Language Learning and Teaching*, 11(1), 72–80. https://doi.org/10.4018/IJCALLT.2021010105

Pashollari, E. (2019). Building Sustainability Through Environmental Education: Education for Sustainable Development. In L. Wilson, & C. Stevenson (Eds.), *Building Sustainability Through Environmental Education* (pp. 72-88). IGI Global. https://doi.org/10.4018/978-1-5225-7727-0.ch004

Paulson, E. N. (2017). Adapting and Advocating for an Online EdD Program in Changing Times and "Sacred" Cultures. In I. Management Association (Ed.), *Educational Leadership and Administration: Concepts, Methodologies, Tools, and Applications* (pp. 1849-1876). Hershey, PA: IGI Global. https://doi.org/10.4018/978-1-5225-1624-8.ch085

Petersen, A. J., Elser, C. F., Al Nassir, M. N., Stakey, J., & Everson, K. (2017). The Year of Teaching Inclusively: Building an Elementary Classroom for All Students. In Curran, C., & Petersen, A. (Eds.), *Handbook of Research on Classroom Diversity and Inclusive Education Practice* (pp. 332–348). Hershey, PA: IGI Global. 10.4018/978-1-5225-2520-2.ch014

Pfannenstiel, K. H., & Sanders, J. (2017). Characteristics and Instructional Strategies for Students With Mathematical Difficulties: In the Inclusive Classroom. In Curran, C., & Petersen, A. (Eds.), *Handbook of Research on Classroom Diversity and Inclusive Education Practice* (pp. 250–281). Hershey, PA: IGI Global. 10.4018/978-1-5225-2520-2.ch011

Phan, A. N. (2022). Quality Assurance of Higher Education From the Glonacal Agency Heuristic: An Example From Vietnam. In Magd, H., & Kunjumuhammed, S. (Eds.), *Global Perspectives on Quality Assurance and Accreditation in Higher Education Institutions* (pp. 136–155). IGI Global. https://doi.org/10.4018/978-1-7998-8085-1.ch008

Preast, J. L., Bowman, N., & Rose, C. A. (2017). Creating Inclusive Classroom Communities Through Social and Emotional Learning to Reduce Social Marginalization Among Students. In Curran, C., & Petersen, A. (Eds.), *Handbook of Research on Classroom Diversity and Inclusive Education Practice* (pp. 183–200). Hershey, PA: IGI Global. 10.4018/978-1-5225-2520-2.ch008

Randolph, K. M., & Brady, M. P. (2018). Evolution of Covert Coaching as an Evidence-Based Practice in Professional Development and Preparation of Teachers. In Bryan, V., Musgrove, A., & Powers, J. (Eds.), *Handbook of Research on Human Development in the Digital Age* (pp. 281–299). Hershey, PA: IGI Global. 10.4018/978-1-5225-2838-8.ch013

Rell, A. B., Puig, R. A., Roll, F., Valles, V., Espinoza, M., & Duque, A. L. (2017). Addressing Cultural Diversity and Global Competence: The Dual Language Framework. In Leavitt, L., Wisdom, S., & Leavitt, K. (Eds.), *Cultural Awareness and Competency Development in Higher Education* (pp. 111–131). Hershey, PA: IGI Global. 10.4018/978-1-5225-2145-7.ch007

Richards, M., & Guzman, I. R. (2020). Academic Assessment of Critical Thinking in Distance Education Information Technology Programs. In I. Management Association (Ed.), *Learning and Performance Assessment: Concepts, Methodologies, Tools, and Applications* (pp. 1-19). IGI Global. https://doi.org/10.4018/978-1-7998-0420-8.ch001

Riel, J., Lawless, K. A., & Brown, S. W. (2017). Defining and Designing Responsive Online Professional Development (ROPD): A Framework to Support Curriculum Implementation. In Kidd, T., & Morris, L.Jr., (Eds.), *Handbook of Research on Instructional Systems and Educational Technology* (pp. 104–115). Hershey, PA: IGI Global. 10.4018/978-1-5225-2399-4.ch010

Roberts, C. (2017). Advancing Women Leaders in Academe: Creating a Culture of Inclusion. In Mukerji, S., & Tripathi, P. (Eds.), *Handbook of Research on Administration, Policy, and Leadership in Higher Education* (pp. 256–273). Hershey, PA: IGI Global. 10.4018/978-1-5225-0672-0.ch012

Rodgers, W. J., Kennedy, M. J., Alves, K. D., & Romig, J. E. (2017). A Multimedia Tool for Teacher Education and Professional Development. In Martin, C., & Polly, D. (Eds.), *Handbook of Research on Teacher Education and Professional Development* (pp. 285–296). Hershey, PA: IGI Global. 10.4018/978-1-5225-1067-3.ch015

Romanowski, M. H. (2017). Qatar's Educational Reform: Critical Issues Facing Principals. In I. Management Association (Ed.), *Educational Leadership and Administration: Concepts, Methodologies, Tools, and Applications* (pp. 1758-1773). Hershey, PA: IGI Global. https://doi.org/10.4018/978-1-5225-1624-8.ch080

Ruffin, T. R., Hawkins, D. P., & Lee, D. I. (2018). Increasing Student Engagement and Participation Through Course Methodology. In M. Khosrow-Pour, D.B.A. (Ed.), *Encyclopedia of Information Science and Technology, Fourth Edition* (pp. 1463-1473). Hershey, PA: IGI Global. 10.4018/978-1-5225-2255-3.ch126

Sabina, L. L., Curry, K. A., Harris, E. L., Krumm, B. L., & Vencill, V. (2017). Assessing the Performance of a Cohort-Based Model Using Domestic and International Practices. In I. Management Association (Ed.), *Educational Leadership and Administration: Concepts, Methodologies, Tools, and Applications*(pp. 913-929). Hershey, PA: IGI Global. https://doi.org/10.4018/978-1-5225-1624-8.ch044

Samkian, A., Pascarella, J., & Slayton, J. (2022). Towards an Anti-Racist, Culturally Responsive, and LGBTQ+ Inclusive Education: Developing Critically-Conscious Educational Leaders. In Cain-Sanschagrin, E., Filback, R., & Crawford, J. (Eds.), *Cases on Academic Program Redesign for Greater Racial and Social Justice* (pp. 150–175). IGI Global. https://doi.org/10.4018/978-1-7998-8463-7.ch007

Santamaría, A. P., Webber, M., & Santamaría, L. J. (2017). Effective School Leadership for Māori Achievement: Building Capacity through Indigenous, National, and International Cross-Cultural Collaboration. In I. Management Association (Ed.), *Educational Leadership and Administration: Concepts, Methodologies, Tools, and Applications* (pp. 1547-1567). Hershey, PA: IGI Global. https://doi.org/10.4018/978-1-5225-1624-8.ch071

Santamaría, L. J. (2017). Culturally Responsive Educational Leadership in Cross-Cultural International Contexts. In I. Management Association (Ed.), *Educational Leadership and Administration: Concepts, Methodologies, Tools, and Applications* (pp. 1380-1400). Hershey, PA: IGI Global. https://doi.org/10.4018/978-1-5225-1624-8.ch064

Segredo, M. R., Cistone, P. J., & Reio, T. G. (2017). Relationships Between Emotional Intelligence, Leadership Style, and School Culture. *International Journal of Adult Vocational Education and Technology*, 8(3), 25–43. 10.4018/IJAVET.2017070103

Shalev, N. (2017). Empathy and Leadership From the Organizational Perspective. In Nedelko, Z., & Brzozowski, M. (Eds.), *Exploring the Influence of Personal Values and Cultures in the Workplace* (pp. 348–363). Hershey, PA: IGI Global. 10.4018/978-1-5225-2480-9.ch018

Siamak, M., Fathi, S., & Isfandyari-Moghaddam, A. (2018). Assessment and Measurement of Education Programs of Information Literacy. In Bhardwaj, R. (Ed.), *Digitizing the Modern Library and the Transition From Print to Electronic* (pp. 164–192). Hershey, PA: IGI Global. 10.4018/978-1-5225-2119-8.ch007

Siu, K. W., & García, G. J. (2017). Disruptive Technologies and Education: Is There Any Disruption After All? In I. Management Association (Ed.), *Educational Leadership and Administration: Concepts, Methodologies, Tools, and Applications* (pp. 757-778). Hershey, PA: IGI Global. https://doi.org/10.4018/978-1-5225-1624-8.ch037

Slagter van Tryon, P. J. (2017). The Nurse Educator's Role in Designing Instruction and Instructional Strategies for Academic and Clinical Settings. In Stefaniak, J. (Ed.), *Advancing Medical Education Through Strategic Instructional Design* (pp. 133–149). Hershey, PA: IGI Global. 10.4018/978-1-5225-2098-6.ch006

Slattery, C. A. (2018). Literacy Intervention and the Differentiated Plan of Instruction. In *Developing Effective Literacy Intervention Strategies: Emerging Research and Opportunities* (pp. 41–62). Hershey, PA: IGI Global. 10.4018/978-1-5225-5007-5.ch003

Smith, A. R. (2017). Ensuring Quality: The Faculty Role in Online Higher Education. In Shelton, K., & Pedersen, K. (Eds.), *Handbook of Research on Building, Growing, and Sustaining Quality E-Learning Programs* (pp. 210–231). Hershey, PA: IGI Global. 10.4018/978-1-5225-0877-9.ch011

Souders, T. M. (2017). Understanding Your Learner: Conducting a Learner Analysis. In Stefaniak, J. (Ed.), *Advancing Medical Education Through Strategic Instructional Design* (pp. 1–29). Hershey, PA: IGI Global. 10.4018/978-1-5225-2098-6.ch001

Spring, K. J., Graham, C. R., & Ikahihifo, T. B. (2018). Learner Engagement in Blended Learning. In M. Khosrow-Pour, D.B.A. (Ed.), *Encyclopedia of Information Science and Technology, Fourth Edition* (pp. 1487-1498). Hershey, PA: IGI Global. 10.4018/978-1-5225-2255-3.ch128

Storey, V. A., Anthony, A. K., & Wahid, P. (2017). Gender-Based Leadership Barriers: Advancement of Female Faculty to Leadership Positions in Higher Education. In Wang, V. (Ed.), *Encyclopedia of Strategic Leadership and Management* (pp. 244–258). Hershey, PA: IGI Global. 10.4018/978-1-5225-1049-9.ch018

Stottlemyer, D. (2018). Develop a Teaching Model Plan for a Differentiated Learning Approach. In *Differentiated Instructional Design for Multicultural Environments: Emerging Research and Opportunities* (pp. 106–130). Hershey, PA: IGI Global. 10.4018/978-1-5225-5106-5.ch005

Stottlemyer, D. (2018). Developing a Multicultural Environment. In *Differentiated Instructional Design for Multicultural Environments: Emerging Research and Opportunities* (pp. 1–27). Hershey, PA: IGI Global. 10.4018/978-1-5225-5106-5.ch001

Swagerty, T. (2022). Digital Access to Culturally Relevant Curricula: The Impact on the Native and Indigenous Student. In Reeves, E., & McIntyre, C. (Eds.), *Multidisciplinary Perspectives on Diversity and Equity in a Virtual World* (pp. 99–113). IGI Global. https://doi.org/10.4018/978-1-7998-8028-8.ch006

Swami, B. N., Gobona, T., & Tsimako, J. J. (2017). Academic Leadership: A Case Study of the University of Botswana. In Baporikar, N. (Ed.), *Innovation and Shifting Perspectives in Management Education* (pp. 1–32). Hershey, PA: IGI Global. 10.4018/978-1-5225-1019-2.ch001

Swanson, K. W., & Collins, G. (2018). Designing Engaging Instruction for the Adult Learners. In M. Khosrow-Pour, D.B.A. (Ed.), *Encyclopedia of Information Science and Technology, Fourth Edition* (pp. 1432-1440). Hershey, PA: IGI Global. 10.4018/978-1-5225-2255-3.ch123

Swartz, B. A., Lynch, J. M., & Lynch, S. D. (2018). Embedding Elementary Teacher Education Coursework in Local Classrooms: Examples in Mathematics and Special Education. In Polly, D., Putman, M., Petty, T., & Good, A. (Eds.), *Innovative Practices in Teacher Preparation and Graduate-Level Teacher Education Programs* (pp. 262–292). Hershey, PA: IGI Global. 10.4018/978-1-5225-3068-8.ch015

Taliadorou, N., & Pashiardis, P. (2017). Emotional Intelligence and Political Skill Really Matter in Educational Leadership. In I. Management Association (Ed.), *Educational Leadership and Administration: Concepts, Methodologies, Tools, and Applications* (pp. 1274-1303). Hershey, PA: IGI Global. https://doi.org/10.4018/978-1-5225-1624-8.ch060

Tandoh, K. A., & Ebe-Arthur, J. E. (2018). Effective Educational Leadership in the Digital Age: An Examination of Professional Qualities and Best Practices. In Keengwe, J. (Ed.), *Handbook of Research on Digital Content, Mobile Learning, and Technology Integration Models in Teacher Education* (pp. 244–265). Hershey, PA: IGI Global. 10.4018/978-1-5225-2953-8.ch013

Tobin, M. T. (2018). Multimodal Literacy. In M. Khosrow-Pour, D.B.A. (Ed.), *Encyclopedia of Information Science and Technology, Fourth Edition* (pp. 1508-1516). Hershey, PA: IGI Global. 10.4018/978-1-5225-2255-3.ch130

Torres, K. M., Arrastia-Chisholm, M. C., & Tackett, S. (2019). A Phenomenological Study of Pre-Service Teachers' Perceptions of Completing ESOL Field Placements. *International Journal of Teacher Education and Professional Development*, 2(2), 85–101. https://doi.org/10.4018/IJTEPD.2019070106

Torres, M. C., Salamanca, Y. N., Cely, J. P., & Aguilar, J. L. (2020). All We Need is a Boost! Using Multimodal Tools and the Translanguaging Strategy: Strengthening Speaking in the EFL Classroom. *International Journal of Computer-Assisted Language Learning and Teaching*, 10(3), 28–47. 10.4018/IJCALLT.2020070103

Torres, M. L., & Ramos, V. J. (2018). Music Therapy: A Pedagogical Alternative for ASD and ID Students in Regular Classrooms. In Epler, P. (Ed.), *Instructional Strategies in General Education and Putting the Individuals With Disabilities Act (IDEA) Into Practice* (pp. 222-244). Hershey, PA: IGI Global. 10.4018/978-1-5225-3111-1.ch008

Toulassi, B. (2017). Educational Administration and Leadership in Francophone Africa: 5 Dynamics to Change Education. In Mukerji, S., & Tripathi, P. (Eds.), *Handbook of Research on Administration, Policy, and Leadership in Higher Education* (pp. 20–45). Hershey, PA: IGI Global. 10.4018/978-1-5225-0672-0.ch002

Umair, S., & Sharif, M. M. (2018). Predicting Students Grades Using Artificial Neural Networks and Support Vector Machine. In M. Khosrow-Pour, D.B.A. (Ed.), *Encyclopedia of Information Science and Technology, Fourth Edition* (pp. 5169-5182). Hershey, PA: IGI Global. 10.4018/978-1-5225-2255-3.ch449

Vettraino, L., Castello, V., Guspini, M., & Guglielman, E. (2018). Self-Awareness and Motivation Contrasting ESL and NEET Using the SAVE System. In M. Khosrow-Pour, D.B.A. (Ed.), *Encyclopedia of Information Science and Technology, Fourth Edition* (pp. 1559-1568). Hershey, PA: IGI Global. 10.4018/978-1-5225-2255-3.ch135

Wiemelt, J. (2017). Critical Bilingual Leadership for Emergent Bilingual Students. In I. Management Association (Ed.), *Educational Leadership and Administration: Concepts, Methodologies, Tools, and Applications* (pp. 1606-1631). Hershey, PA: IGI Global. 10.4018/978-1-5225-1624-8.ch074

Wolf, F., Seyfarth, F. C., & Pflaum, E. (2018). Scalable Capacity-Building for Geographically Dispersed Learners: Designing the MOOC "Sustainable Energy in Small Island Developing States (SIDS)". In Pandey, U., & Indrakanti, V. (Eds.), *Open and Distance Learning Initiatives for Sustainable Development* (pp. 58–83). Hershey, PA: IGI Global. 10.4018/978-1-5225-2621-6.ch003

Woodley, X. M., Mucundanyi, G., & Lockard, M. (2017). Designing Counter-Narratives: Constructing Culturally Responsive Curriculum Online. *International Journal of Online Pedagogy and Course Design*, 7(1), 43–56. 10.4018/IJOPCD.2017010104

Yell, M. L., & Christle, C. A. (2017). The Foundation of Inclusion in Federal Legislation and Litigation. In Curran, C., & Petersen, A. (Eds.), *Handbook of Research on Classroom Diversity and Inclusive Education Practice* (pp. 27–52). Hershey, PA: IGI Global. 10.4018/978-1-5225-2520-2.ch002

Zinner, L. (2019). Fostering Academic Citizenship With a Shared Leadership Approach. In Zhu, C., & Zayim-Kurtay, M. (Eds.), *University Governance and Academic Leadership in the EU and China* (pp. 99–117). IGI Global. https://doi.org/10.4018/978-1-5225-7441-5.ch007

About the Contributors

Crystal Aschenbrener is currently teaching remotely for a large online graduate-level social work program at a private university. Previously, she has served in many leadership roles at an array of universities during her 15 years in higher education. She has worked on accreditation processes with the national social work education and licensure procedures with state social work departments. She has developed, taught, and mentored a holistic array of social work courses, which includes having the ability to teach, role model, assess, and evaluate on current best practices. Aschenbrener's primary goal with teaching is to ensure students are able to partner with individuals to communities, by providing client-centered, culturally-respectful, evidenced-based, and strength-focused practices. Because of a partnership Dr. Aschenbrener has developed with the Native American population, she created a nationally-known mentoring intervention, the Today & Beyond Program. She has repeatedly collaborated with this population via doctoral dissertation, conference presentations, scholarly articles, and national boards. The Today & Beyond Program is where college students serve as the mentors and the youth of a tribal school are the mentees. Her research studies both the college mentors' and the youth mentees' experiences. With teaching, service, research, and administration roles, Dr. Aschenbrener is compassionate of the students' and youths' needs and empowering of their strengths while delivering real world opportunities. This philosophy was and is demonstrated in her interactions with students, faculty, staff, and administration as well as youth, tribal schools, and tribal communities, including being purposeful in curriculum, program development, and initiatives.

Angie G. Atwood, PhD, RN, serves full time as an Assistant Professor at the School of Nursing at Campbellsville University. With extensive experience in both traditional and online teaching, Dr. Atwood has taught across the nursing curriculum and also serves full-times an adjunct faculty member at Union College. Her expertise lies in nursing education, particularly in preparing students for the NCLEX-RN examination. Dr. Atwood is recognized among her peers as a leader and faculty success mentor. She obtained her Associate Degree in Nursing (ADN), Bachelor of Science in Nursing (BSN), and Master of Science in Nursing (MSN) degrees from Western Kentucky University. She later earned her Doctor of Philosophy (PhD) from Capella University. Dr. Atwood's clinical nursing career began in 1999, and her passion for nursing education emerged in 2004. Beyond her academic pursuits, she is deeply committed to servant leadership, particularly in the context of foreign medical missions. Over the past decade, Dr. Atwood has led nursing students on numerous mission trips, including ten to Port-au-Prince, Haiti, and one to Tanzania, Africa. Driven by her dedication to preparing future nurses and fostering servant leadership, Dr. Atwood aims to provide students with transformative learning experiences. She endeavors to instill in them the values of Christian servant leadership, empowering them to serve others with compassion and excellence in the nursing profession.

About the Contributors

Sally Barton-Arwood joined the Belmont community in 2006. She holds a Bachelor's degree in Psychology from the University of Tennessee and Master's and Doctoral degrees in Special Education from Vanderbilt University. Prior to coming to Belmont, Sally worked for over 20 years in K-12 private and public schools as a special education teacher, and as a school administrator. Sally teaches a range of courses in the College of Education related to special education, classroom management, and disability studies. Teaching and special education are Dr. B.'s passions, and in her courses, she shares those passions while ensuring that her students are learning best practices to meet the needs of all leaners in K-12 schools. Sally was the recipient of a 2016 Harold Love Outstanding Community Service Award presented by the Tennessee Higher Education Commission.

Chee Ken Nee is a distinguished educator with over 12 years of experience in high school teaching and a Ph.D. in Educational Technology. Having served at a top-tier secondary school, he previosuly holds the position of Assistant Director at the Educational Technology and Resources Division, Ministry of Education, Malaysia, providing him with valuable insights into educational challenges. Currently a senior lecturer at Universiti Pendidikan Sultan Idris, he is a registered professional Technologist and senior IEEE member. Dr. Chee's impactful contributions include 15 high-quality journal papers indexed in ISI and Scopus, focusing on mobile learning, educational technology, and computer-based learning, investigating their effects on student learning outcomes. With a passion for innovative teaching methods, particularly in the face of the pandemic, he has achieved an H-index in Google Scholar of 9 with 482 citations in six years. Dr. Chee's accolades include the Global Teacher Award (2020). Beyond research, he actively participates as a reviewer for ISI and Scopus indexed journals and serves as a jury member for prestigious innovation competitions worldwide, including in the United Kingdom. His international influence extends to speaking engagements in several countries which included United States of America, and as keynote speaker in India, Tunisia, Austria and Thailand and so forth, further solidifying his reputation as a thought leader in educational technology. Notably, he was recognized as a finalist in the 'educator setting a trend' category at the Edtech Award 2023 and as a finalist for 'Enhancing Teaching and Learning Quality' at the esteemed 2023 Gartner Eye on Innovation Award for Education, underscoring his innovative contributions to the field.

Özge Kutlu graduated from Social Work and Social Policy Master's Program in 2022. She is a doctoral student in the Social Work program at Hacettepe University. Kutlu, who worked as a Social Worker at Burdur Provincial Health Directorate between 2019-2023, has been working as a lecturer in Burdur Mehmet Akif Ersoy University Elderly Care program since February 2023. She works on the provision of rights-based social work practices for the elderly and their families.

Jennifer Lanham has a Bachelor's degree in Psychology and Family Studies and a Master's in Social Work from the University of Kentucky. She completed her Ph.D. at the University of Denver. Dr. Lanham has been a psychotherapist in the mental health and substance use disorder field for over 29 years and is currently a full-time Professor at Campbellsville University. Dr. Lanham's research interests lie in global engagement, mental health, rural women, and collaborative learning. She is currently involved in various collaborative research projects focused on transformational learning, integrating artificial intelligence (AI) and collaborative learning, and interprofessional development. Dr. Lanham has led several cohorts of students abroad studying peacebuilding initiatives and sectarian conflict in Ireland. She is currently advancing her knowledge as a postgraduate student in the esteemed Program in Social Policy and Practice at Trinity College Dublin.

Lauren Lunsford is a Professor in the Department of Education. Dr. Lunsford joined the Belmont faculty in 2006 and she has served Belmont University in a number of roles. Her work has centered on preparing teachers to meet the needs of all of their students, particularly in the areas of literacy and technology. She currently teaches in their newly launched Special Education program specifically teaching literacy courses and collaboration courses for teacher candidates. Dr. Lunsford publishes and presents widely on the areas of literacy, teacher collaboration, and technology in the classroom.

About the Contributors

Pious Malliar Bellian is a Ph.D. Candidate and an Adjunct Faculty at Indiana University School of Social Work, Indianapolis. His research interests include spirituality, spiritual healing, and holistic wellness. He holds a master's degree in social work from IGNOU (India) and a Bachelor of Theology and Philosophy from St. Peter's Pontifical Institute. He is also an ordained minister in the Roman Catholic Church. He has disseminated research findings through scholarly conferences and presentations on various social work topics, innovative research designs, and collaborations. He offers a unique position as a priest and a social work instructor with his multicultural lived experiences in India, Canada, and the USA, which adds value to the insightful learning process of the scholarly world. Over the last ten years, he has communicated his findings through scholarly conferences and presentations on numerous social work subjects and innovative research designs.

Fred Moonga is a Lecturer and Head of the Department of Sociology and Social work at the University of Eswatini. Previously, he was Lecturer and Head of Department at Mulungushi in Zambia. He has also worked in various international NGOs. He holds a PhD in Social work from Stellenbosch University, South Africa; MSc University of Southampton, UK; MSc, Gothenburg University, Sweden; BSW, University of Zambia. His research interests are in social gerontology, social protection, child welfare, ecological social work and comparative social policy.

E. Moore is an Assistant Professor for Carver School of Social Work. Her areas of focus and research are transformational learning experiences for students, Forensic Social Work and Substance Use Disorder. To enhance her academic work with students and colleagues, she has a private practice working with a range of clinical issues with clients.

Amanda Nelms is an Assistant Professor of Education at Belmont University. Dr. Nelms has served as a classroom teacher, instructional coach, and English Language Development Coordinator for Metro Nashville Public Schools. She has worked with instructional leaders on national and international projects to provide equitable opportunities for multilingual learners. Dr. Nelms has presented at state, national, and international conferences on topics such as effective communication to support Els (English learners) across districts and states, revising teacher preparation programs to include an emphasis on advocacy for multilingual students, providing EL services in blended learning environments, and the impact of students' attitudes and beliefs about multilingual students on the college experiences.

Lisa Tokpa is the Director of Field Education at the Uganda Studies Program (USP) at Uganda Christian University, guiding the program's community engagement efforts through internships in the social work, global health, and interdisciplinary emphases. This position builds upon her decade as the USP Social Work Coordinator and Faculty developing the social work curriculum, cultivating mutually beneficial partnerships within the community and with North American social work programs, teaching the in-country BSW seminar and supervising social work field placements. Lisa obtained her Master of Social Work from the Brown School at Washington University in St. Louis and then worked for 12 years in child welfare programs in the U.S., Liberia, and Kenya. Now based in Colorado, she utilizes her experience in both domestic and international social work practice to build bridges in higher education towards shared learning, symbiotic partnerships, and decolonized social work education.

Index

A

Affectagogy 141, 142, 143, 144, 145, 146, 147, 148, 149, 150, 151, 152, 157

C

Campbellsville University 42, 63, 116, 169, 180
Clinical Training 180
Collaboration 31, 71, 72, 96, 99, 103, 104, 105, 116, 117, 125, 126, 127, 128, 131, 134, 148, 184, 188, 189, 195, 197, 211
Criticality 2, 14, 16
critical reflection 23, 24, 28, 31, 32, 40, 46, 86, 89, 122, 132, 134, 201
Crosscare 127, 128, 138
cross-cultural learning 85, 86, 210
Cultural Humility 84, 86, 87, 88, 89, 91, 92, 94, 96, 97, 98, 100, 101, 102, 106, 108, 111, 112, 113, 114, 115, 124, 125, 128, 129, 131, 132, 135, 136, 138, 139, 184, 187, 191, 193, 194, 198, 199, 200, 201, 206, 207, 208, 211, 212

D

decolonization 88, 114, 133
digital classroom 158, 162, 166, 173, 176
diversity 16, 18, 28, 49, 50, 85, 86, 91, 93, 94, 99, 102, 112, 122, 123, 124, 127, 128, 129, 131, 133, 146, 158, 159, 160, 161, 162, 164, 167, 170, 171, 172, 173, 175, 178, 184, 186, 193, 194, 195, 196, 197, 199, 200, 201, 202, 203, 204, 207, 208, 209, 211, 212

E

Education 1, 2, 3, 4, 6, 8, 9, 10, 11, 14, 16, 17, 18, 19, 20, 21, 30, 31, 32, 33, 34, 35, 36, 37, 38, 39, 40, 42, 43, 45, 54, 60, 61, 62, 79, 81, 82, 84, 85, 86, 87, 88, 89, 96, 98, 99, 100, 102, 109, 110, 111, 112, 113, 114, 115, 117, 124, 127, 129, 131, 135, 136, 137, 138, 139, 140, 141, 142, 143, 146, 147, 148, 149, 150, 151, 152, 153, 154, 155, 156, 158, 159, 160, 162, 166, 167, 168, 170, 171, 173, 176, 178, 179, 181, 182, 184, 186, 188, 190, 192, 194, 195, 196, 197, 200, 202, 203, 204, 206, 208, 209, 210, 211, 212
Emotional learning 143, 150, 153, 157
Empathy 21, 28, 34, 35, 51, 54, 72, 73, 117, 123, 125, 141, 142, 144, 146, 147, 148, 149, 150, 154, 155, 156, 157, 184, 188, 191, 200
Empowerment 1, 2, 3, 6, 8, 9, 10, 11, 12, 13, 14, 15, 16, 17, 51, 58, 69, 71, 72, 96, 129, 130, 131, 148
environment 5, 6, 7, 8, 11, 14, 15, 19, 24, 26, 27, 28, 30, 31, 32, 33, 34, 43, 44, 50, 52, 57, 58, 62, 64, 65, 66, 67, 71, 72, 118, 120, 121, 123, 134, 139, 142, 144, 146, 147, 148, 153, 154, 155, 157, 158, 159, 170, 183, 186, 193, 194, 195, 197, 199, 200, 202, 205, 206, 208, 212
equity 16, 65, 85, 91, 94, 110, 156, 158, 159, 170
Ethical Leadership 70
Experiential learning 1, 3, 4, 10, 11, 16, 18, 43, 44, 61, 86, 136, 158, 159, 160, 161, 162, 165, 166, 168, 170, 171, 172, 173, 175, 177, 179, 183, 190, 192, 194, 195, 202, 203, 211
Experimental Learning 44, 47, 48, 50

H

Human-Touch Learning 141, 142, 144, 157

I

IFSW 2, 15, 18, 103
inclusion 68, 85, 91, 94, 100, 129, 136, 138, 158, 159, 160, 161, 170, 171, 172, 200, 204

L

Life-Long Learning 42, 43, 64, 86, 97, 100, 180, 181
local expertise 94, 100, 104

M

mentoring 31, 32, 63, 64, 72, 73, 167, 169, 178
Missions 92, 180, 181, 182, 184, 185, 186, 188, 190, 191
Mission Work 180, 181, 182
mixed methods 37
mutually beneficial partnerships 84, 89, 98, 104, 106

N

NASW 73, 75, 82, 86, 89, 91, 94, 97, 107, 133, 138, 204
NASW Code of Ethics 73, 75, 82, 89, 107, 133
Native American youth 169
Non-traditional teaching methods 193, 194, 212
Northern Ireland 123, 126, 127, 128, 135, 138
Nursing 61, 111, 112, 136, 167, 178, 181, 184, 191, 208

O

Outside the Classroom Walls 42, 43, 44, 53

P

Passion 42, 47, 51, 52, 55, 56, 58, 60, 71, 72, 75, 117, 123
pedagogy 10, 14, 17, 37, 38, 60, 102, 114, 141, 145, 154, 156, 160, 163, 164, 171, 174, 193, 194, 195, 197, 204, 206, 208, 212
policy 3, 60, 62, 85, 93, 106, 107, 110, 111, 124, 135, 136, 168, 179, 207
practicums 98, 99, 107, 114

R

Revitalization 65, 125

S

Service 2, 3, 11, 12, 13, 14, 15, 16, 43, 44, 47, 48, 50, 53, 62, 67, 68, 70, 71, 73, 74, 91, 110, 111, 113, 121, 133, 158, 159, 160, 161, 162, 163, 164, 165, 166, 167, 168, 169, 170, 171, 172, 173, 174, 175, 176, 178, 179, 181, 182, 183, 184, 185, 190, 206, 209
Service-learning 43, 50, 110, 113, 158, 159, 160, 161, 162, 163, 164, 165, 166, 167, 168, 169, 170, 171, 172, 173, 174, 175, 178, 179
Social justice 1, 2, 4, 8, 10, 13, 15, 16, 19, 20, 21, 32, 33, 35, 50, 70, 91, 98, 101, 111, 129, 133, 138, 200, 204, 206
Social Work 1, 2, 3, 4, 5, 6, 7, 8, 10, 11, 12, 13, 14, 15, 16, 17, 18, 19, 20, 21, 31, 32, 33, 34, 35, 36, 47, 49, 50, 53, 55, 56, 58, 60, 61, 62, 70, 73, 75, 76, 79, 84, 85, 86, 87, 88, 89, 90, 91, 94, 95, 96, 97, 98, 99, 100, 101, 102, 103, 104, 105, 106, 107, 108, 109, 110, 111, 112, 113, 114, 115, 116, 117, 118, 119, 122, 123, 124, 125, 126, 127, 128, 129, 130, 131, 132, 133, 135, 136, 137, 138, 193, 194, 195, 196, 197, 198, 199, 200, 201, 202, 203, 204, 205, 206, 207, 208, 209, 210, 211, 212
Social work education 1, 2, 4, 10, 14, 16, 17, 18, 20, 21, 31, 32, 33, 34, 35, 60, 62, 85, 89, 99, 102, 110, 111, 112, 113, 114, 115, 124, 135, 136, 137, 194, 195, 196, 197, 200, 202, 203, 204, 206, 208, 209, 210, 211, 212
Social Work ethics 87, 108, 114
Spiritual diversity practices 193, 194, 195, 196, 197, 199, 204, 207, 212
Spiritually-informed practice 193
study abroad 85, 86, 87, 89, 93, 94, 95, 98, 102, 106, 108, 110, 111, 112, 113, 115, 117, 122, 124, 135, 136, 138, 159

323

T

Teaching 12, 18, 28, 31, 32, 37, 38, 40, 42, 43, 44, 45, 47, 50, 51, 52, 53, 54, 55, 57, 60, 61, 62, 75, 82, 98, 102, 109, 110, 111, 141, 142, 143, 145, 146, 149, 154, 159, 168, 170, 179, 193, 194, 195, 196, 197, 202, 203, 204, 205, 206, 208, 210, 211, 212

Transformational Leadership 3, 51, 60, 63, 64, 65, 66, 67, 68, 69, 70, 71, 72, 73, 74, 75, 76, 77, 79, 80, 81, 82, 83, 211

Transformational learning 3, 20, 21, 22, 23, 24, 25, 27, 28, 29, 30, 31, 32, 33, 34, 35, 36, 38, 39, 40, 41, 44, 47, 49, 52, 62, 74, 84, 89, 116, 122, 193, 194, 196, 197, 199, 204, 207, 211, 212

Transformational learning theory 20, 21, 22, 25, 28, 30, 31, 34, 35, 39, 196

Transformational Teaching 31, 37, 42, 43, 44, 45, 47, 51, 52, 53, 54, 57, 60, 61, 62, 75, 82, 197, 208

Transformational theory of teaching 194, 196, 197

Transformative learning 2, 3, 4, 5, 7, 8, 9, 11, 17, 18, 36, 37, 38, 39, 40, 45, 60, 61, 79, 85, 108, 115, 116, 117, 122, 123, 126, 136, 190, 193, 194, 196, 197, 200, 204, 207, 208, 209, 210, 212

Transformative Teaching 197

U

Uganda Studies Program 84, 86, 87, 88, 96, 97

Ukraine 126, 127

undergraduate students 61, 169, 194, 211

Publishing Tomorrow's Research Today

Uncover Current Insights and Future Trends in Education
with IGI Global's Cutting-Edge Recommended Books

Print Only, E-Book Only, or Print + E-Book.
Order direct through IGI Global's Online Bookstore at **www.igi-global.com** or through your preferred provider.

Artificial Intelligence Applications Using ChatGPT in Education: Case Studies and Practices
ISBN: 9781668493007
© 2023; 234 pp.
List Price: US$ **215**

Generative AI in Teaching and Learning
ISBN: 9798369300749
© 2024; 383 pp.
List Price: US$ **230**

Dynamic Curriculum Development and Design Strategies for Effective Online Learning in Higher Education
ISBN: 9781668486467
© 2023; 471 pp.
List Price: US$ **215**

Illuminating and Advancing the Path for Mathematical Writing Research
ISBN: 9781668465387
© 2024; 389 pp.
List Price: US$ **215**

Cases on Economics Education and Tools for Educators
ISBN: 9781668475836
© 2024; 359 pp.
List Price: US$ **215**

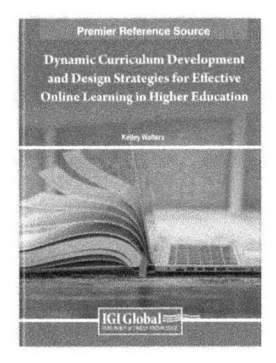

Emerging Trends and Historical Perspectives Surrounding Digital Transformation in Education: Achieving Open and Blended Learning Environments
ISBN: 9781668444238
© 2023; 334 pp.
List Price: US$ **240**

Do you want to stay current on the latest research trends, product announcements, news, and special offers?
Join IGI Global's mailing list to receive customized recommendations, exclusive discounts, and more.
Sign up at: www.igi-global.com/newsletters.

Scan the QR Code here to view more related titles in Education.

www.igi-global.com | Sign up at www.igi-global.com/newsletters | facebook.com/igiglobal | twitter.com/igiglobal | linkedin.com/igiglobal

Ensure Quality Research is Introduced to the Academic Community

Become a Reviewer for IGI Global Authored Book Projects

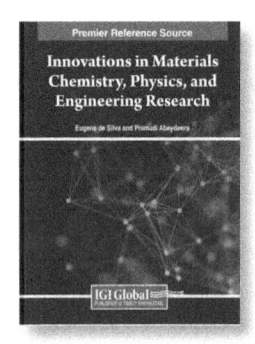

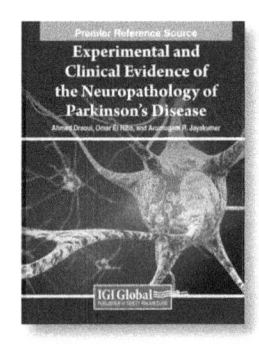

The overall success of an authored book project is dependent on quality and timely manuscript evaluations.

Applications and Inquiries may be sent to:
development@igi-global.com

Applicants must have a doctorate (or equivalent degree) as well as publishing, research, and reviewing experience. Authored Book Evaluators are appointed for one-year terms and are expected to complete at least three evaluations per term. Upon successful completion of this term, evaluators can be considered for an additional term.

If you have a colleague that may be interested in this opportunity, we encourage you to share this information with them.

IGI Global's Open Access Journal Program

Publishing Tomorrow's Research Today

Including Nearly 200 Peer-Reviewed, Gold (Full) Open Access Journals across IGI Global's Three Academic Subject Areas: Business & Management; Scientific, Technical, and Medical (STM); and Education

Consider Submitting Your Manuscript to One of These Nearly 200 Open Access Journals for to Increase Their Discoverability & Citation Impact

Web of Science Impact Factor	Journal
6.5	Journal of Organizational and End User Computing
4.7	Journal of Global Information Management
3.2	International Journal on Semantic Web and Information Systems
2.6	Journal of Database Management

Choosing IGI Global's Open Access Journal Program Can Greatly Increase the Reach of Your Research

Higher Usage
Open access papers are 2-3 times more likely to be read than non-open access papers.

Higher Download Rates
Open access papers benefit from 89% higher download rates than non-open access papers.

Higher Citation Rates
Open access papers are 47% more likely to be cited than non-open access papers.

Submitting an article to a journal offers an invaluable opportunity for you to share your work with the broader academic community, fostering knowledge dissemination and constructive feedback.

Submit an Article and Browse the IGI Global Call for Papers Pages

We can work with you to find the journal most well-suited for your next research manuscript. For open access publishing support, contact: journaleditor@igi-global.com

Are You Ready to Publish Your Research?

IGI Global
Publishing Tomorrow's Research Today

IGI Global offers book authorship and editorship opportunities across three major subject areas, including Business, STM, and Education.

Benefits of Publishing with IGI Global:

- Free one-on-one editorial and promotional support.
- Expedited publishing timelines that can take your book from start to finish in less than one (1) year.
- Choose from a variety of formats, including Edited and Authored References, Handbooks of Research, Encyclopedias, and Research Insights.
- Utilize IGI Global's eEditorial Discovery® submission system in support of conducting the submission and double-blind peer review process.
- IGI Global maintains a strict adherence to ethical practices due in part to our full membership with the Committee on Publication Ethics (COPE).
- Indexing potential in prestigious indices such as Scopus®, Web of Science™, PsycINFO®, and ERIC – Education Resources Information Center.
- Ability to connect your ORCID iD to your IGI Global publications.
- Earn honorariums and royalties on your full book publications as well as complimentary content and exclusive discounts.

Join Your Colleagues from Prestigious Institutions, Including:

Australian National University
Massachusetts Institute of Technology
Johns Hopkins University
Tsinghua University
Harvard University
Columbia University in the City of New York

Learn More at: www.igi-global.com/publish
or by Contacting the Acquisitions Department at: acquisition@igi-global.com

Milton Keynes UK
Ingram Content Group UK Ltd.
UKHW011953080824
446595UK00005B/138